D0933228

ZAGAT

Chicago
Restaurants
2012/13

Including
Milwaukee

LOCAL EDITORS
Alice Van Housen with Jennifer Olvera,
and Ann Christenson
STAFF EDITOR
Emily Rothschild

Published and distributed by
Zagat Survey, LLC
76 Ninth Avenue
New York, NY 10011
T: 212.977.6000
E: chicago@zagat.com
www.zagat.com

ACKNOWLEDGMENTS

We thank Hilary Sims (editor), Julie Alvin, Erin Behan, Christa Bourg, Simon Butler, Katharine Critchlow, Karen Hudes, Michele Laudig, Mike Lima, Craig Nelson, Jamie Selzer, Simon Spelling, Victoria Spencer, William Travis and Thomas Van Housen, as well as the following members of our staff: Caitlin Miehl (editor), Brian Albert, Sean Beachell, Maryanne Bertollo, Danielle Borovoy, Reni Chin, Larry Cohn, Nicole Diaz, Kelly Dobkin, Jeff Freier, Alison Gainor, Matthew Hamm, Justin Hartung, Marc Henson, Ryutaro Ishikane, Cynthia Kilian, Natalie Lebert, Mike Liao, Vivian Ma, James Mulcahy, Polina Paley, Amanda Spurlock, Chris Walsh, Jacqueline Wasilczyk, Sharon Yates, Anna Zappia and Kyle Zolner.

The reviews in this guide are based on public opinion surveys. The ratings reflect the average scores given by the survey participants who voted on each establishment. The text is based on quotes from, or paraphrasings of, the surveyors' comments. Phone numbers, addresses and other factual data were correct to the best of our knowledge when published in this guide.

Our guides are printed using environmentally preferable inks containing 20%, by weight, renewable resources on papers sourced from well-managed forests. Deluxe editions are covered with Skivertex Recover® Double containing a minimum of 30% post-consumer waste fiber.

© 2012 Zagat Survey, LLC
ISBN-13: 978-1-60478-454-1
ISBN-10: 1-60478-454-7
Printed in the
United States of America

Contents

Ratings & Symbols

Zagat Top Spot	Name	Symbols	Cuisine	Zagat Ratings			
				FOOD	DECOR	SERVICE	COST

Area, Address & Contact	🆉 **Tim & Nina's** ◗ *Pizza*	▽ 23	9	13	$15

Hyde Park | 456 E. Chicago Ave. (Division St.) | 312-555-3867 | www.zagat.com

Review, surveyor comments in quotes

Hordes of "unkempt" U of C students have gone nuclear over this "low-budget" cafeteria-style "24/7 dive", which "single-handedly" started the "deep-dish sushi pizza craze" that's "sweeping the Windy City like a lake-effect tsunami"; try the "to-die-for" eel-pepperoni-wasabi-mozzarella or Osaka-Napolitano pies – but be patient, since "the service here blows hot and cold – mostly cold."

Ratings

Food, Decor & **Service** are rated on a 30-point scale.

0 – 10	poor to fair
11 – 15	fair to good
16 – 20	good to very good
21 – 25	very good to excellent
26 – 30	extraordinary to perfection
▽	low response	less reliable

Cost

The price of dinner with a drink and tip; lunch is usually 25% to 30% less. For unrated **newcomers** or **write-ins,** the price range is as follows:

I	$25 and below	E	$41 to $65
M	$26 to $40	VE	$66 or above

Symbols

🆉	highest ratings, popularity and importance
◗	serves after 11 PM
🅂 🅼	closed on Sunday or Monday
🚫	no credit cards accepted

Maps

Index maps show the restaurants with the highest Food ratings in those areas.

About This Survey

Here are the results of our **2012/13 Chicago Restaurants Survey,** covering 1,367 eateries in the Chicago area and Milwaukee. Like all our guides, this one is based on input from avid local diners – 6,211 all told. Our editors have synopsized this feedback, including representative comments (in quotation marks within each review). To read full surveyor comments – and share your own opinions – visit **zagat.com,** where you will also find the latest restaurant news, special events, deals, reservations, menus, photos and lots more, **all for free.**

ABOUT ZAGAT: In 1979, we started asking friends to rate and review restaurants purely for fun. The term "user-generated content" had yet to be coined. That hobby grew into Zagat Survey; 33 years later, we have over 375,000 surveyors and cover airlines, bars, dining, fast food, entertaining, golf, hotels, movies, music, resorts, shopping, spas, theater and tourist attractions in over 100 countries. Along the way, we evolved from being a print publisher to a digital content provider, e.g. **zagat.com** and Zagat mobile apps (for Android, iPad, iPhone, BlackBerry, Windows Phone 7 and Palm webOS). We also produce marketing tools for a wide range of blue-chip corporate clients. And you can find us on Google+ and just about any other social media network.

UNDERLYING PREMISES: Three simple ideas underlie our ratings and reviews. First, we believe that the collective opinions of large numbers of consumers are more accurate than those of any single person. (Consider that our surveyors bring some 967,000 annual meals' worth of experience to this survey, visiting restaurants regularly year-round, anonymously – and on their own dime.) Second, food quality is only part of the equation when choosing a restaurant, thus we ask our surveyors to rate food, decor and service separately and then estimate the cost of a meal. Third, since people need reliable information in an easy-to-digest format, we strive to be concise and we offer our content on every platform – print, online and mobile. Our Top Ratings lists (pages 7–16) and indexes (starting on page 198) are also designed to help you quickly choose the best place for any occasion, be it for business or pleasure. Milwaukee's Top Ratings and indexes start on pages 255 and 276, respectively.

THANKS: We're grateful to our local Chicago editors, Alice Van Housen and Jennifer Olvera, both freelance writers and editors; and Ann Christenson, the dining critic for *Milwaukee Magazine.* We also sincerely thank the thousands of people who participated in this survey – this guide is really "theirs."

JOIN IN: To improve our guides, we solicit your comments – positive or negative; it's vital that we hear your opinions. Just contact us at **nina-tim@zagat.com.** We also invite you to join our surveys at **zagat.com.** Do so and you'll receive a choice of rewards in exchange.

New York, NY
June 20, 2012

Nina and Tim

Nina and Tim Zagat

What's New

From burger joints to hip, happening 'in' spots, restaurants opened at a breakneck pace over the past year, which may help explain why surveyors reported eating out an average of 3.0 meals per week, up from 2.8 in the last survey (and the first rise post-recession). What's more, the city's overall dining scene rose a notch in surveyors' estimation, earning a 25 (on a 30-point scale) for culinary creativity and a 21 for hospitality – both up a point from the past two surveys – and holding steady at 26 for choice/diversity.

ENTREES OUT: Small plates are making big waves, showing up at new wine bars **Telegraph** (Logan Square) and **Vera** (West Loop), as well as at Nuevo Latino **Libertad** (Skokie) and a trio of new hot spots from Windy City notables: Ryan Poli's **Tavernita** (River North), Matthias Merges' **Yusho** (Avondale) and the DMK team's **Ada St.** (Bucktown). Milwaukee got into the small-plates action too, with newcomers such as **Braise** and **Industri** in Walker's Point.

CHECKING BACK IN: It was all about makeovers at many hotel dining rooms. The former **Seasons** in the Gold Coast's Four Seasons morphed into **Allium** with Kevin Hickey at the helm, **Aja** in River North's Dana Hotel became **Argent** with Jackie Shen (ex **Chicago Cut**) in the kitchen and the new Public Hotel got a glitzy boost via Jean-Georges Vongerichten's incarnation of **The Pump Room.** **NoMI** in the Park Hyatt became the more relaxed **NoMI Kitchen,** while **Perennial** got a renovation and menu remake courtesy of Paul Virant, emerging as **Perennial Virant** in the new Hotel Lincoln.

BIG BUH-BYES: Some surprising closings rocked the culinary world, including the shuttering of longtime favorites **Bistro 110, Sushi Wabi** and **Crofton on Wells** (the latter rumored to be reconcepting). Fine-dining **Carlos'** downscaled to **Nieto's** in Highland Park and game-changing **Charlie Trotter's** saddened many with the news that it's closing its doors in mid-August, while suburban destination **Le Titi de Paris** will reportedly be bidding adieu in June.

WHAT'S ON TAP: A formidable roster of chefs have projects in the pipeline. Stephanie Izard's **Little Goat** diner, Curtis Duffy's **Grace,** Graham Elliott Bowles' funky **G.E.B. Bistro** and Bill Kim's **Belly Q** Asian barbecue are all set for a Randolph Street debut. Impending River North action includes **The Boarding House** from former LEYE wine wizard Alpana Singh; Euro steakhouse **Bavette's** from Brendan Sodikoff; Tony Priolo's **Piccolo Sogno Due;** Prohibition-inspired **The Tortoise Club;** a Melman clan resurrection of **Bub City** with a tiki bar in the basement; and a French newcomer from **Naha's** Nahabedians. Also in the works are French brasserie **Maison** from the **Custom House Tavern** crew and farm-to-table-focused **The Trenchermen** from Sheerin brothers Mike and Patrick.

Chicago, IL
Milwaukee, WI
June 20, 2012

Alice Van Housen
Ann Christenson

Chicago Most Popular

This list is plotted on the map at the back of this book.

1. Alinea | *Amer.*
2. Frontera Grill | *Mexican*
3. Girl & The Goat | *Amer.*
4. Gibsons | *Steak*
5. Charlie Trotter's | *Amer.*
6. Joe's Sea/Steak | *Seafood/Steak*
7. Topolobampo | *Mexican*
8. Lou Malnati's | *Pizza*
9. Next | *Eclectic*
10. Blackbird | *Amer.*
11. Tru | *French*
12. Avec | *Med.*
13. Wildfire | *Steak*
14. Spiaggia | *Italian*
15. Shaw's Crab | *Seafood*
16. Purple Pig | *Med.*
17. Gene & Georgetti | *Steak*
18. Capital Grille | *Steak*
19. Morton's Steak | *Steak*
20. Publican | *Amer.*
21. Les Nomades | *French*
22. Everest | *French*
23. Hot Doug's | *Hot Dogs*
24. Xoco | *Mexican*
25. Francesca's | *Italian*
26. MK | *Amer.*
27. Hugo's Frog/Fish | *Seafood*
28. Smoque BBQ | *BBQ*
29. Piccolo Sogno | *Italian*
30. Naha | *Amer.*
31. Giordano's | *Pizza*
32. Chicago Cut Steak | *Steak*
33. Bob Chinn's Crab | *Seafood*
34. Coco Pazzo | *Italian*
35. Maggiano's | *Italian*
36. Al's Beef | *Sandwiches*
37. Portillo's Hot Dogs* | *Hot Dogs*
38. Takashi | *Amer./French*
39. Lawry's Prime Rib | *Amer./Steak*
40. Longman & Eagle* | *Amer.*
41. L2O* | *Seafood*
42. Quartino | *Italian*
43. Mercat a la Planxa | *Spanish*
44. North Pond | *Amer.*
45. Ruth's Chris | *Steak*
46. Le Colonial | *Vietnamese*
47. Big Star | *Mexican*
48. Bistro Campagne* | *French*
49. Chicago Chop* | *Steak*
50. Heaven on Seven | *Cajun/Creole*
51. Vie* | *Amer*
52. Cooper's Hawk | *Amer.*
53. GT Fish & Oyster* | *Seafood*
54. Mon Ami Gabi* | *French*

Many of the above restaurants are among the Chicago area's most expensive, but if popularity were calibrated to price, a number of other restaurants would surely join their ranks. To illustrate this, we have included two lists comprising 80 Best Buys on page 16.

* Indicates a tie with restaurant above

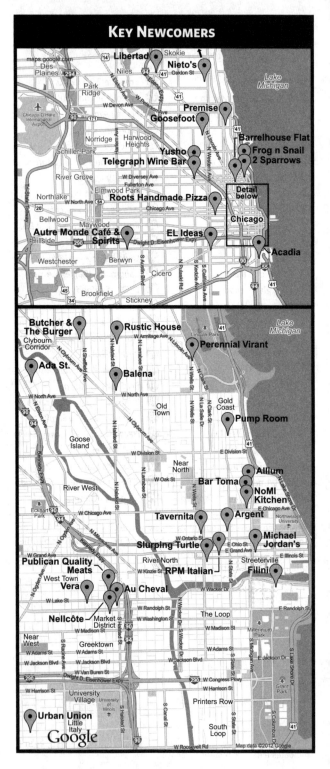

KEY NEWCOMERS

maps.google.com

Libertad · Skokie
Nieto's
Premise
Goosefoot
Barrelhouse Flat
Frog n Snail
2 Sparrows
Yusho
Telegraph Wine Bar
Roots Handmade Pizza
Detail below
Chicago
Autre Monde Café & Spirits
EL Ideas
Acadia

Butcher & The Burger
Rustic House
Perennial Virant
Ada St.
Balena
Pump Room
Allium
Bar Toma
NoMI Kitchen
Tavernita
Argent
Slurping Turtle
Michael Jordan's
Publican Quality Meats
RPM Italian
Filini
Vera
Au Cheval
Nellcôte
Urban Union

Google

Map data ©2012 Google

Vote at zagat.com

Key Newcomers

Our editors' picks among this year's arrivals. See full list at p. 239.

Acadia | *Amer./Seafood* | High-end seasonal cuisine in the South Loop

Ada St. | *Amer./Med.* | Ultrachic Bucktown entry from the DMK duo

Allium | *Amer.* | Gold Coast hotel remake starring sustainable plates

Argent | *Amer.* | Chicago World's Fair–themed fare in River North

Au Cheval | *Amer.* | Über-hip Brendan Sodikoff diner in the West Loop

Autre Monde | *Med.* | Hyperlocal eats via Spiaggia vets in Berwyn

Balena | *Italian* | Hot Lincoln Park collab from Bristol and Boka players

Barrelhouse Flat | *Amer.* | Hip, cocktail-focused Lincoln Park hangout

Bar Toma | *Italian/Pizza* | Shiny Gold Coast arrival from Tony Mantuano

Butcher & The Burger | *Burgers* | New-school patties in Lincoln Park

EL Ideas | *Amer.* | Inventive multicourse fare in a tiny Pilsen locale

Filini | *Italian* | Authentic cooking in a contemporary Loop setting

Frog n Snail | *Amer./French* | More affordable Sprout counterpart in Lakeview

Goosefoot | *Amer.* | Upscale Lincoln Square BYO via a Les Nomades vet

Libertad | *Nuevo Latino* | Happening Skokie hideaway with flavorful offerings

Michael Jordan's Steak House | *Steak* | Classic cuisine in Streeterville

Nellcôte | *Amer.* | Posh West Loop add from an Old Town Social chef

Nieto's | *Amer.* | Informal Carlos do-over in Highland Park

NoMI Kitchen | *Amer.* | Relaxed yet still elegant Gold Coast remake

Perennial Virant | *Amer.* | Lincoln Park redo with Paul Virant

Premise | *Amer.* | Inspired Andersonville eats via a Graham Elliot vet

Publican Quality Meats | *Amer./Sandwiches* | Kahan's latest in the West Loop

Pump Room | *Amer.* | Glitzy Gold Coast revamp from Jean-Georges

Roots Handmade Pizza | *Amer./Pizza* | 'Quad Cities'-style pies in West Town

RPM Italian | *Italian* | Melman-backed River Norther with scene appeal

Rustic House | *Amer.* | Artisanal and rotisserie offerings in Lincoln Park

Slurping Turtle | *Japanese/Noodles* | Casual River North sib to Takashi

Tavernita | *Spanish* | River North hot spot from the Mercadito team

Telegraph Wine Bar | *Amer.* | Cozy Logan Square drinking and dining

2 Sparrows | *Amer.* | Daytime Lincoln Park 'in' spot from Trotter's vets

Urban Union | *Amer.* | Small plates in a rustic-chic Little Italy setting

Vera | *Spanish* | West Loop wine bar with share plates and global vinos

Yusho | *Japanese* | Elevated street food from a Trotter's alum in Avondale

Top Food

CHICAGO

29 Alinea | *Amer.*	Girl & The Goat | *Amer.*
Katsu | *Japanese*	Frontera Grill | *Mexican*
Next | *Eclectic*	Joe's Sea/Steak | *Sea./Steak*
28 Riccardo Trattoria | *Italian*	Lula Cafe | *Eclectic*
Les Nomades | *French*	Arun's | *Thai*
Takashi | *Amer./French*	Everest | *French*
Avec | *Med.*	Blackbird | *Amer.*
Green Zebra | *Vegetarian*	Davanti Enoteca | *Italian*
MK | *Amer.*	Aviary | *Eclectic*
Schwa | *Amer.*	Moto | *Eclectic*
Topolobampo | *Mexican*	Shanghai Terrace | *Chinese*
Sprout | *Amer.*	Ria | *Amer.*
Fontano's Subs | *Sandwiches*	Great Lake | *Pizza*
Tru | *French*	Sai Café | *Japanese*
Ruxbin | *Eclectic*	Nightwood | *Amer.*
Charlie Trotter's | *Amer.*	Naha | *Amer.*
27 Mixteco Grill | *Mexican*	Kuma's Corner | *Burgers*
Bonsoirée | *Amer./French*	Henni | *Amer.*
Arami | *Japanese*	Mirai Sushi | *Japanese*
Longman & Eagle | *Amer.*	TAC Quick | *Thai*

SUBURBS

29 Vie | *Amer.*	Adelle's | *Amer.*
28 Courtright's | *Amer.*	Tallgrass | *French*
Fontano's Subs | *Sandwiches*	Edzo's Burger Shop | *Burgers*
27 Le Titi/Paris | *French*	Wholly Frijoles | *Mexican*
Michael | *French*	**26** Morton's Steak | *Steak*

BY CUISINE

AMERICAN (NEW)
29 Alinea
Vie
28 Takashi
Courtright's
MK

AMERICAN (TRAD.)
26 West Town Tavern
Lawry's Prime Rib
25 Keefer's
Table Fifty-two
Glenn's Diner/Seafood
24 Hot Chocolate

BARBECUE
26 Smoque BBQ
24 Uncle Bub's

22 Lillie's Q
Twin Anchors
Hecky's

BURGERS
27 Edzo's Burger Shop
Kuma's Corner
23 Burger Bar
21 DMK Burger Bar
20 Counter

CHINESE
27 Shanghai Terrace
25 Sun Wah BBQ
24 Lao Beijing
Phoenix
23 Yu's Mandarin

Excludes places with low votes

DINERS

- 25 Glenn's Diner/Seafood
- 24 Lou Mitchell's
- Manny's
- Original/Walker Pancake
- 23 Chicago Diner

ECLECTIC

- 29 Next
- 28 Ruxbin
- 27 Lula Cafe
- Aviary
- Moto

FRENCH

- 28 Les Nomades
- Takashi
- Tru
- 27 Bonsoirée
- Le Titi/Paris

GASTROPUB

- 27 Longman & Eagle
- 26 Publican
- Gilt Bar
- 25 Bristol
- 24 Hopleaf

GREEK

- 26 Taxim
- 23 Opa! Estiatorio
- 22 Santorini
- Avli
- Roditys

HOT DOGS

- 26 Hot Doug's
- Franks 'N' Dawgs
- 24 Gene & Jude's
- 23 Portillo's Hot Dogs
- 21 Superdawg

INDIAN

- 24 Cumin
- 23 Marigold
- Vermilion
- 22 India House
- Gaylord Indian

ITALIAN

- 28 Riccardo Trattoria
- 27 Davanti Enoteca
- 26 Pelago
- Piccolo Sogno
- Spiaggia

JAPANESE

- 29 Katsu
- 27 Arami
- Sai Café
- Mirai Sushi
- 26 Macku Sushi

MEDITERRANEAN

- 28 Avec
- 26 Purple Pig
- 24 Pita Inn
- 22 Dawali
- Roti Mediterranean

MEXICAN

- 28 Topolobampo
- 27 Mixteco Grill
- Frontera Grill
- Wholly Frijoles
- 26 Xoco

MIDDLE EASTERN

- 25 Turquoise
- 24 Pita Inn
- Noon-O-Kabab
- 23 Sayat Nova
- 22 Dawali

PIZZA

- 27 Great Lake
- 26 Spacca Napoli
- Vito & Nick's
- 25 Home Run Inn Pizza
- Lou Malnati's

SEAFOOD

- 27 Joe's Sea/Steak
- 26 GT Fish & Oyster
- 25 L2O
- Oceanique
- Tin Fish*

SMALL PLATES

- 28 Avec
- Green Zebra
- 27 Girl & The Goat
- Davanti Enoteca
- Aviary

SPANISH/TAPAS

- 26 Mercat a la Planxa
- 25 Mesón Sabika
- 24 Emilio's Tapas
- 23 Tapas Gitana
- Cafe Ba-Ba-Reeba!

STEAKHOUSES

27| Joe's Sea/Steak
26| Mastro's Steak
Chicago Cut Steak
Morton's Steak
Gibsons

THAI

27| Arun's
TAC Quick

25| Thai Pastry
24| Opart Thai
23| Indie Cafe

VEGETARIAN

28| Green Zebra
26| Mana Food Bar
23| Chicago Diner
Karyn's on Green
Native Foods

BY SPECIAL FEATURE

BREAKFAST

27| Lula
25| M Henry/Henrietta
Tre Kronor
24| Lou Mitchell's
Manny's

BRUNCH

27| Frontera Grill
Nightwood
26| North Pond
NoMI Kitchen
Yoshi's Café

BUSINESS DINING

29| Alinea
Next
28| Les Nomades
Takashi
MK

CHILD-FRIENDLY

26| Hot Doug's
Smoque BBQ
Lawry's
Sapori Trattoria
25| Lou Malnati's

HOTEL DINING

27| Shanghai Terrace (Peninsula)
Ria (Waldorf-Astoria)
26| Pelago (Raffaello)
NoMI Kitchen (Park Hyatt)
Perennial Virant (Hotel Lincoln)

LATE DINING

28| Avec
27| Longman/Eagle

Kuma's Corner
26| Purple Pig
Mastro's Steak

LIVE ENTERTAINMENT

25| Mesón Sabika
Sabatino's
Shaw's Crab
24| Lobby
Catch 35

MEET FOR A DRINK

27| Girl & The Goat
Joe's Sea/Steak
26| Perennial Virant
Barrelhouse Flat
Nellcôte

NEWCOMERS (RATED)

26| NoMI Kitchen
Perennial Virant
25| Roka Akor
23| Telegraph Wine Bar
Bistro Voltaire

PEOPLE-WATCHING

28| Avec
27| Longman/Eagle
Girl & The Goat
Joe's Sea/Steak
Blackbird

WINNING WINE LISTS

29| Alinea
Next
28| Les Nomades
Takashi
Avec

BY LOCATION

ANDERSONVILLE/ EDGEWATER

26 Great Lake
Anteprima
25 M Henry/Henrietta
Apart Pizza
Big Jones

BUCKTOWN

28 Takashi
25 Coast Sushi/Southcoast
Bristol
24 Jane's
Hot Chocolate

CHINATOWN

24 Lao Beijing
Phoenix
23 Ba Le Sandwich
22 Three Happiness
21 Joy Yee

GOLD COAST

27 Ria
26 NoMI Kitchen
Spiaggia
Morton's Steak
Gibsons
25 Café Spiaggia

GREEKTOWN

23 Karyn's on Green
22 Santorini
Roditys
Greek Islands
21 Pegasus

LAKEVIEW

27 Mixteco Grill
26 Yoshi's Café
25 HB Home Bistro
Chilam Balam
24 Mia Francesca

LINCOLN PARK

29 Alinea
28 Riccardo Trattoria
Sprout
Charlie Trotter's
27 Sai Café

LINCOLN SQ./UPTOWN

26 Tweet
San Soo Gab San

LITTLE ITALY

25 Dorado
Sun Wah BBQ
LM

LITTLE ITALY

27 Davanti Enoteca
26 Chez Joël
25 Sweet Maple
24 Conte Di Savoia
Tufano's Tap

LOOP

27 Everest
Henri
26 Morton's Steak
25 Trattoria No. 10
24 Lou Mitchell's

OLD TOWN

26 Topo Gigio
25 Salpicón
24 Old Town Social
23 Trattoria Roma
22 Kamehachi

RIVER NORTH

28 Topolobampo
27 Frontera Grill
Joe's Sea/Steak
Shanghai Terrace
Naha

STREETERVILLE

28 Les Nomades
Tru
26 Pelago
Capital Grille
24 Volare

WEST LOOP

29 Next
28 Avec
27 Girl & The Goat
Blackbird
Aviary

WICKER PARK

28 Schwa
27 Mirai Sushi
26 Taxim
Big Star
Mana Food Bar

Top Decor

28 Shanghai Terrace	Next
Alinea	Carnivale
Sixteen	Gilt Bar
Courtright's	Signature Room*
L2O	Vie
Everest	Japonais
North Pond*	Charlie Trotter's
27 Tru	**25** Pelago
Ria	Sunda
NoMI Kitchen	MK
Les Nomades	Karyn's on Green
Henri	Custom House Tavern
Aviary	Tallgrass*
Bedford	Terzo Piano
Pump Room	Capital Grille
RL	Chicago Cut Steak
Spiaggia	Maude's Liquor Bar
26 Roka Akor	Atwood Cafe
Sepia	Café/Architectes
Lobby	Union Sushi + BBQ Bar*

OUTDOORS

Big Star	Piccolo Sogno
Estate Ultra Bar	Shanghai Terrace
NoMI Kitchen	Sixteen
Paris Club	Terzo Piano
Park Grill	Zed 451

ROMANCE

Ada St.	Les Nomades
Geja's	Nellcôte
Gilt Bar	North Pond
Henri	Pump Room
Le Colonial	Telegraph

ROOMS

Aviary	Pump Room
Bedford	RL
Girl & The Goat	Roka Akor
L2O	RPM Italian
Nellcôte	Tavernita

VIEWS

Chicago Cut Steak	North Pond
Cité	Signature Room
Everest	Smith & Wollensky
Fulton's	Spiaggia
NoMI Kitchen	Terzo Piano

Vote at zagat.com

Top Service

29	Next		Michael
	Alinea		Topolobampo
28	Vie		Joe's Sea/Steak
	Les Nomades		Pelago
	Tru		A Tavola
	Courtright's		Lawry's Prime Rib
	Tallgrass		Benny's Chop House
	Charlie Trotter's		North Pond
27	Ria		Quince
	Moto	25	Chicago Cut Steak
	Everest		Sprout
	Arun's		Sepia
26	Aviary		NoMI Kitchen
	Spiaggia		Blackbird
	L2O		Riccardo Trattoria
	Henri		Keefer's
	MK		Shanghai Terrace
	Seasons 52		Green Zebra
	Capital Grille		Boka
	Adelle's		Naha

Best Buys

In order of Bang for the Buck rating.

1. Gene & Jude's
2. Ba Le Sandwich
3. Dimo's Pizza
4. Fontano's Subs
5. Chicago Bagel
6. Conte Di Savoia
7. Superdawg
8. Cafecito
9. Portillo's Hot Dogs
10. Byron's Hot Dog
11. Edzo's Burger Shop
12. Margie's Candies
13. Southern Mac
14. Cozy Noodles & Rice
15. Hot Doug's
16. Sultan's Market
17. Aloha Eats
18. Wow Bao
19. Roti Mediterranean
20. Cemitas Puebla
21. Hannah's Bretzel
22. Bourgeois Pig
23. Potbelly Sandwich
24. Ricobene's
25. Al's Beef
26. Five Guys
27. Birchwood Kitchen
28. Franks 'N' Dawgs
29. Pita Inn
30. Freshii
31. Mr. Beef
32. Pret A Manger
33. Milk & Honey
34. Big & Little's
35. Native Foods
36. Crisp
37. Pockets
38. Apart Pizza
39. Wiener's Circle
40. Gold Coast Dogs

OTHER GOOD VALUES

Akai Hana
Athenian Room
Bacchanalia
Big Bowl
Birrieria Zaragoza
Dave's Italian
Dining Room/Kendall College
Flat Top Grill
Francesca's
Glenn's Diner/Seafood
Greek Islands
Hackney's
Hai Yen
Half Shell
Indie Cafe
Irazu
John's Place
Joy Yee's
Los Nopales
LuLu's Dim Sum
Miller's Pub
Moody's Pub
Nookies
Noon-O-Kabab
Old Jerusalem
Original/Walker Pancake
Parthenon
Pegasus
Penny's Noodle
Phò Xe Tång
Rosal's Italian Kitchen
Rose Angelis
Sabatino's
San Soo Gab San
Silver Seafood
Sun Wah BBQ
TAC Quick
Thai Pastry
Tre Kronor
Wholly Frijoles

CHICAGO
RESTAURANT
DIRECTORY

	FOOD	DECOR	SERVICE	COST

The Abbey ● *Pub Food* — 18 | 17 | 18 | $21

Northwest Side | 3420 W. Grace St. (Elston Ave.) | 773-478-4408 | www.abbeypub.com

An "old standby" since 1973, this Northwest Side "hangout" is "two venues in one" – part "concert area" and part Irish resto-bar offering "finger licking good" pub eats; if a few whisper it "suffers from age", more focus instead on its "great staff", affordable tabs and summer patio.

Abigail's ⊠ⓜ *American* — 25 | 21 | 22 | $40

Highland Park | Ravinia Business District | 493 Roger Williams Ave. (St. Johns Ave.) | 847-780-4862 | www.abigails493.com

"Carefully orchestrated", "imaginative" New American fare, "good wines by the glass, carafe or bottle" and "classic cocktails" lure "ladies who lunch" and "pre or post-Ravinia"-goers to this "quaint" North Shore "gem"; the "cramped" space often gets "too noisy" and limited reservations (accepted only until 6 PM) can mean "long waits", but moderate prices help ensure it's still "deservedly crowded", so some simply suggest you "go early" or "when you can sit outside."

NEW Acadia ⓜ *American/Seafood* — - | - | - | E

South Loop | 1639 S. Wabash Ave. (bet. 16th & 18th Sts.) | 312-360-9500 | www.acadiachicago.com

Ryan McCaskey's South Loop American, a spendy nod to summers spent in Maine, serves ingredient-driven seasonal plates, including many seafood-focused offerings like lobster pot pie and shrimp with cuttlefish noodles; the dramatically lit, airy setting is awash in earthy, neutral hues, and there's an elegant lounge perfect for enjoying modernized classic cocktails.

Acre *American* — 20 | 21 | 20 | $33

Andersonville | 5308 N. Clark St. (bet. Berwyn & Summerdale Aves.) | 773-334-7600 | www.acrerestaurant.com

"Creative", farm-focused American "comfort food" gets a boost from an "extensive beer list", plus wine and house cocktails at this "gentrified" Andersonville gastropub with a "bar side" and fireplace-enhanced "sit-down side"; "professional" service, a "relaxed atmosphere" and moderate prices also work in its favor, so even if it's "not worth a long journey", it's still "nice to have in the neighborhood", and especially "excellent" for brunch; P.S. adjacent Italian small-plates sister Ombra opened post-Survey.

NEW Ada St. *American/Mediterranean* — - | - | - | M

Bucktown | 1664 N. Ada St. (Concord Pl.) | 773-697-7069 | www.adastreetchicago.com

Michael Kornick and David Morton (DMK Burger Bar, Fish Bar) are behind this ultrachic, Bucktown Mediterranean–New American offering up a moderate and compact small plates–focused menu including cheese and charcuterie served alongside craft cocktails and a thoughtful wine list; up front is a cozy lounge in a former elevator shaft, in back a rustic candlelit dining room with custom Scandinavian wood tables, banquettes upholstered in army blankets and a garage door that opens to the seasonal patio.

⁊ Adelle's Ⓜ *American* | 27 | 22 | 26 | $45 |

Wheaton | 535 W. Liberty Dr. (West St.) | 630-784-8015 | www.adelles.com

"Top-notch", "imaginatively prepared" New American fare and "friendly, warm" service prove that this moderate Wheaton "jewel" "hasn't missed a beat" since its relocation; it's "more spacious" and perhaps "less homey", but "the bar area is now quite inviting", and you can still dine on the patio or by the fireplaces; P.S. there's live jazz most Thursdays.

Adobo Grill *Mexican* | 21 | 20 | 21 | $33 |

Old Town | 1610 N. Wells St. (North Ave.) | 312-266-7999 | www.adobogrill.com

"Reliable" for "midscale Mexican", this Old Town "hangout" is favored most for its "amazingly fresh" guac "made at your table" and "don't-miss" margaritas, even if the rest of the "more creative" than typical menu is a "little less memorable"; "great people-watching" and "casual, capable service" help make it "a safe choice", and a "festive and efficient" one "before/after Second City", just be aware the "noise level" may be "more fit for the younger crowd."

Agami *Japanese* | 23 | 21 | 21 | $43 |

Uptown | 4712 N. Broadway (Leland Ave.) | 773-506-1845 | www.agamisushi.com

"Creative" "well-above average sushi creations" are "pricey, but worth it" at this Uptown Japanese where the "large bar turns out delicious cocktails" along with a "great selection of sake and Japanese beers" and the "surreal decor" makes "you feel as though you are eating in an aquarium"; "helpful" service is another plus, leading fans to crown it a "godsend" to the "embattled neighborhood"; P.S. it's "perfect for pre-Riviera concerts or a trip to the Green Mill for jazz."

Ai Sushi Lounge *Japanese* | 22 | 21 | 19 | $43 |

River North | 358 W. Ontario St. (Orleans St.) | 312-335-9888 | www.aichicago.us

"Fresh", "authentic" sushi and sashimi, "creative" rolls and the "opportunity to eat fugu" (blowfish) make this midpriced River North Japanese "worth going"; "service can shift from mediocre to great", but "trendy music, stylish people" and "contemporary loftlike" environs still help it reach "staple" status.

Akai Hana *Japanese* | 20 | 14 | 19 | $29 |

Wilmette | 3223 W. Lake Ave. (Skokie Rd.) | 847-251-0384 | www.akaihanasushi.com

"Cheap and cheerful", this Wilmette Japanese is "consistent" for "reliably fresh" "sushi with minimal fuss" plus "solid tempura and teriyakis"; so while it's "not innovative or startling" and its strip-mall setting is "generic", service that "aims to please" helps compensate and it remains a "popular" "local favorite."

	FOOD	DECOR	SERVICE	COST

NEW Al Dente M *American/Eclectic* — | — | — | M

Northwest Side | 3939 W. Irving Park Rd. (bet. Harding Ave. & Pulaski Rd.) | 773-942-7771 | www.aldentechicago.com

Expect seasonal New American fare with Mexican influences (pork mole verde, adobo-crusted salmon with housemade chorizo) courtesy of well-traveled chef Javier Perez (ex MK, Spiaggia) at this Irving Park BYO; the informal setting features green walls lined with banquettes, a dining bar and pendant lighting.

Alhambra Palace Restaurant *Mideastern* 18 | 24 | 15 | $39

West Loop | 1240 W. Randolph St. (bet. Elizabeth St. & Racine Ave.) | 312-666-9555 | www.alhambrapalacerestaurant.com

"Sumptuous and fanciful decor" enlivened by "entertaining belly dancing shows" has diners declaring it's "all about the ambiance" at this massive, multilevel West Loop Mideastern; the "decent" fare may "lack inspiration", and service is sometimes "slow", but it's still "fun for a special event" or "group outing", especially since prices are moderate.

Z Alinea M *American* 29 | 28 | 29 | $225

Lincoln Park | 1723 N. Halsted St. (bet. North Ave. & Willow St.) | 312-867-0110 | www.alinea-restaurant.com

Grant Achatz is "like a real-life Willy Wonka in his ability to imbue his creations with magic" at this "ultimate" Lincoln Park New American that earns No. 1 Food and Most Popular honors in Chicago thanks to a "spectacularly innovative" multicourse "culinary art show" featuring "playful", "awe-inspiring" "gastronomic delights" presented with "unparalleled attention to detail"; "impeccable" service ensures that meals are "timed perfectly" in the "ultra-modern" surroundings, so while tabs are "sky-high", "if your wallet can take the hit" (and you come with "an open mind and sense of adventure"), "serious foodies" say it "ranks with seeing the wonders of the world."

Allgauer's *American* 21 | 20 | 21 | $39

Lisle | The Hilton | 3003 Corporate West Dr. (Warrenville Rd.) | 630-245-7650 | www.hiltonlislenaperville.com/allgauers

"Nothing fancy", but "reliable" contend patrons of this West 'Burbs' American in the Hilton, an "oasis" for "straightforward", "reasonably priced" fare you can "rely on"; though it may be "getting a bit dated", its "comfortable setting" helps keep it a "relaxed" choice.

NEW Allium *American* — | — | — | E

Gold Coast | Four Seasons Hotel Chicago | 120 E. Delaware Pl., 7th fl. (bet. Michigan Ave. & Rush St.) | 312-799-4900 | www.alliumchicago.com

Taking over for the former Seasons (in the Four Seasons), this more approachable (yet still pricey) Gold Coast dining room offers chef Kevin Hickey's sustainable farm-to-table American cuisine, ranging from snacks and sharing plates to steaks, accompanied by cocktail classics, regional microbrews and many wines by the glass; the gracious, sumptuous setting features rich colors, leather and animal prints, a marble fireplace and mahogany walls.

	FOOD	DECOR	SERVICE	COST

Aloha Eats *Hawaiian* (fka Aloha Grill)

| 19 | 13 | 20 | $11 |

Lincoln Park | 2534 N. Clark St. (Deming Pl.) | 773-935-6828 | www.alohaeats.com

A "small, cozy" counter-serve, this no-frills Lincoln Park Hawaiian does "expats" a solid with "true island cuisine" like what "you'd find on a typical diner menu in Honolulu" (chicken katsu, spam musubi, BBQ); you also get "lots of food for a cheap price", so it's "great for a quick, but filling" meal.

Al's Beef *Sandwiches*

| 23 | 9 | 16 | $11 |

Loop | 28 E. Jackson Blvd. (bet. State St. & Wabash Ave.) | 312-461-9292
Loop | 601 W. Adams St. (Jefferson St.) | 312-559-2333
River North | 169 W. Ontario St. (Wells St.) | 312-943-3222 ◗
Wrigleyville | 3420 N. Clark St. (Sheffield Ave.) | 773-935-2333 ◗
Chinatown | 5441 S. Wentworth Ave. (Garfield Blvd.) | 773-373-4700 ◗
Little Italy/University Village | 1079 W. Taylor St. (Aberdeen St.) | 312-226-4017 🖢🐷
Niles | 5948 W. Touhy Ave. (Lehigh Ave.) | 847-647-1577
Park Ridge | 1036 W. Higgins Rd. (Cumberland Ave.) | 847-825-2345
Chicago Heights | 551 W. 14th St. (Division St.) | 708-748-2333
Tinley Park | 7132 183rd St. (Harlem Ave.) | 708-444-2333
www.alsbeef.com
Additional locations throughout the Chicago area

"You'll want seconds – and a shower" after visiting this "no-frills, no-nonsense" "institution" where "big, juicy" "Italian beef sandwiches" that "drip on your shirt" (or "down your arm") are "ridiculously good" and represent a "major Chicago food group"; the "spicy sausage" and "fresh-cut fries" deserve a try too, so though decor is as "expected" for a fast-food place, those "in the mood for some comfort food" "keep going back"; P.S. insiders suggest a "pilgrimage" to the original on Taylor Street.

American Girl Place Cafe *American*

| 14 | 23 | 22 | $30 |

Streeterville | American Girl Place, Water Tower Place Mall | 835 N. Michigan Ave. (bet. Chestnut & Pearson Sts.) | 312-943-9400 | www.americangirlplace.com

"They certainly know how to treat a five year old" at this "delightful" "must-see" for "little ones" in Streeterville's Water Tower Place where "terrific" details like "matching dinnerware" for the dolls and "hair scrunchie" napkin rings make it "the place to go" when your children "need spoiling"; yes, the American offerings are "nothing great for adults" and it doesn't come cheap, but patient parents who appreciate the "organized dining experience" suggest just "soaking in" the "smiles" of the kids who "love every minute."

NEW Amoremia Cucina Italiana Ⓜ *Italian*

| – | – | – | I |

Old Irving Park | 3824 N. Kedzie Ave. (bet. Byron & Grace Sts.) | 773-293-6628 | www.amoremiachicago.com

Expect multiregional Italian including classics like fried calamari and eggplant parmigiana at this budget-friendly Irving Park BYO; the inviting setting is done up with deep-blue walls, framed mirrors and cozy candlelight.

🆕 Amuse *American*

- | - | - | M

Loop | Swissôtel Chicago | 323 E. Wacker Dr. (bet. Columbus Dr. & Field Blvd.) | 312-565-0565

Dan McGee (he of the Frankfort namesake) mans the stoves at this New American in the Loop's Swissôtel lobby serving moderately priced creative snacks plus a drinks list showcasing craft cocktails and brown booze; the sleek open space is done in neutrals and modern lighting with a granite bar, communal high-tops and lounge groupings.

Andies *Mediterranean/Mideastern*

21 | 18 | 20 | $24

Andersonville | 5253 N. Clark St. (Berwyn Ave.) | 773-784-8616
Lakeview | 1467 W. Montrose Ave. (Greenview Ave.) | 773-348-0654 Ⓜ
www.andiesres.com

All the "simple", "authentic" Middle Eastern and Mediterranean dishes "you want and need", including "many vegetarian choices", are on the "huge menu" at these Andersonville and Lakeview "standbys" where an "unusually eclectic and interesting staff" provides "friendly" if occasionally "spotty service"; while "nothing fancy", they're "low-key" and "affordable", making them "reliable" "meeting places with friends."

Angelina Ristorante *Italian*

24 | 21 | 23 | $33

Lakeview | 3561 N. Broadway (Addison St.) | 773-935-5933 | www.angelinaristorante.com

"A little piece of Italy", this "quaint" Lakeview "delight" lures diners with "reliably solid" Italian dishes featuring a "wide variety of flavors and aromas", plus "reasonably priced wines" and "romantic", "calming" confines; "truly friendly" service and affordable prices further make it good for "first dates, family dinners" or "girls' nights out"; P.S. "Sunday brunch" – with "bottomless" champagne drinks and "spontaneous outbursts of dancing from the flamboyant crowd" – is "legendary."

Anna Maria Pasteria *Italian*

▽ 21 | 18 | 22 | $34

Ravenswood | 4400 N. Clark St. (Montrose Ave.) | 773-506-2662 | www.annamariapasteria.com

"Owned by sisters (one works in the kitchen and the other the dining room)", this "low-key" Ravenswood "gem" serves a "tasty", affordable menu of "homestyle" Italian cooking in "a warm, inviting" setting; "knowledgeable service" and seasonal sidewalk seating are additional pluses.

🆕 Anna's Asian Bistro *Asian*

- | - | - | M

West Loop | 813 W. Lake St. (bet. Green & Halsted Sts.) | 312-344-1090 | www.annasbistro.com

The namesake Anna (former partner in Thalia Spice) and her chef mom are behind this mod West Loop BYO serving an exhaustive menu of sushi and mixed Asian fare (Chinese, Thai, Vietnamese) plus bubble teas, lunch specials and weekend brunch; a Sputnik light

	FOOD	DECOR	SERVICE	COST

fixture and recessed candle alcoves create romantic lighting amid exposed brick, wheel-inspired ceiling screens and black tablecloths.

Ann Sather *American/Swedish*
| | 22 | 16 | 20 | $17 |

Andersonville | 5207 N. Clark St. (Foster Ave.) | 773-271-6677
Lakeview | 909 W. Belmont Ave. (Clark St.) | 773-348-2378

Ann Sather Café *American/Swedish*
Lakeview | 3411 N. Broadway (Roscoe St.) | 773-305-0024
Lakeview | 3416 N. Southport Ave. (Roscoe St.) | 773-404-4475
www.annsather.com

Prepare to "indulge" and "eat too much" at this "iconic breakfast/brunch" chainlet best known for its "large plates of hearty", "waistline-challenging" Swedish-American fare including the "most irresistible" "must-order" "sticky" cinnamon rolls; the "old-fashioned" decor may be "getting a little tired", but prices are "reasonable" and service "efficient", so "when you're craving serious comfort food" it's a "reliable" "Chicago classic."

Anteprima *Italian*
| | 26 | 21 | 24 | $42 |

Andersonville | 5316 N. Clark St. (bet. Berwyn & Summerdale Aves.) | 773-506-9990 | www.anteprimachicago.net

Acolytes "still dream" about the "market-driven" "authentic Italian cuisine" at this "lively" (some say "noisy") "little" Andersonville "storefront" where a "well-chosen" wine list complements the mid-priced menu; "professional, accommodating" service and "cozy" environs complete with a "romantic outdoor patio" further leave regulars rhapsodizing "so sophisticated, so simple, so neighborhood fantastic."

NEW The Anthem ◐ *Pub Food*
| | - | - | - | I |

Ukrainian Village | 1725 W. Division St. (Hermitage Ave.) | 773-697-4804 | www.theanthemchicago.com

Step back in time at this boisterous Ukrainian Village sports bar from the Bangers & Lace team, where the '70s vibe extends from the retro wood-paneled surrounds to the pub eats featuring the likes of hamburger mac 'n' cheese, fish sticks and other nostalgic comfort-food classics (there's also weekend brunch and late-night fare); massive TVs are often tuned to the game, and front windows open in warm weather.

Antico Posto *Italian*
| | 24 | 21 | 23 | $34 |

Oak Brook | Oakbrook Center Mall | 118 Oakbrook Ctr. (Rte. 83) | 630-586-9200 | www.antico-posto.com

"Easy to like", this Oakbrook Center "oasis" is "reliable", delivering "well-prepared", "simple" Italian fare like "tasty brick-oven pizza" and "delicious ravioli" that "change with the seasons"; "good wine deals", "timely", "attentive" service and "value" prices also find favor, and if some say it's a bit "noisy from shopper victory talk", most maintain it's an overall "pleasant" pick.

Apart Pizza Company *Pizza*
| | 25 | 12 | 20 | $15 |

Edgewater | 5624 N. Broadway St. (bet. Bryn Mawr & Hollywood Aves.) | 773-784-1550

(continued)

(continued)

Apart Pizza Company

Ravenswood | 2205 W. Montrose Ave. (Lincoln Ave.) | 773-588-1550
www.apartpizzacompany.com

The "incredible" pizzas are "creative", "flavorful" and topped by "quality" ingredients, but it's the "crisp" yet "chewy" thin crust that devotees agree really does set this Edgewater and Ravenswood duo "apart from the crowd"; service is "accommodating" and tabs "reasonable", but small, "bare-bones" settings with "lackluster" decor and limited seating make them "highly recommended for takeout and delivery."

Aquitaine *American/French*   21 | 18 | 20 | $38

Lincoln Park | 2221 N. Lincoln Ave. (bet. Belden & Webster Aves.) | 773-698-8456 | www.aquitainerestaurant.com

"Well-seasoned", solid French–New American fare (including "to-die-for" duck confit mac 'n' cheese) at "reasonable prices" render this "unexpected" Lincoln Park "bistro in the heart of sports bar row" a "good neighborhood option"; "friendly" service and a "warm, intimate setting" also add appeal, so even if it's "not spectacular" it's still a "charming" choice.

☑ Arami Ⓜ *Japanese*   27 | 23 | 23 | $48

West Town | 1829 W. Chicago Ave. (bet. Wolcott Ave. & Wood St.) | 312-243-1535 | www.aramichicago.com

"Sushi lovers" are among the "converted" at this "hip, urban" West Town storefront delivering "exceptionally fresh, amazingly creative" rolls alongside other "delicious and serious Japanese" offerings like the "not-to-be-missed" ramen; "helpful service" enhances the "relaxing" "spa"-like setting, and if some dub it "Zen for a lot of yen", most counter "premium" "quality is not cheap."

ⓃⒺⓌ Argent ⓈⓂ *American*   - | - | - | M

River North | Dana Hotel & Spa | 660 N. State St. (Erie St.) | 312-202-6050 | www.argentrestaurant.com

Chicago's 1893 World's Fair provides inspiration for this River North American in the Dana Hotel where the menu – a collaboration between Rodelio Aglibot (ex Sunda) and Jackie Shen (ex Chicago Cut) – includes time-traveling nibbles like chipped beef-topped toast, chop suey, elevated cotton candy and more; soaring windows and natural wood set an earthy-elegant tone, while arching black banquettes and a steel staircase leading to a mezzanine raw bar add modern appeal.

Aria *Asian*   24 | 22 | 23 | $59

Loop | Fairmont Chicago Hotel | 200 N. Columbus Dr. (bet. Randolph St. & Wacker Dr.) | 312-444-9494 | www.ariachicago.com

Just "off the beaten path" in the Loop's Fairmont Hotel, this "upscale" sushi specialist "stands on its own" with "consistently delicious", "Asian-inspired" plates set down by "attentive" servers in a "quiet", "pretty space"; despite a few complaints that it's "a little overpriced", many rank it "worth the side trip" from "downtown traffic", especially for a "business lunch."

	FOOD	DECOR	SERVICE	COST

Art of Pizza *Pizza*　　23 | 10 | 17 | $14

Lakeview | 3033 N. Ashland Ave. (Nelson St.) | 773-327-5600 | www.theartofpizzainc.com

"Fresh ingredients", solid sauce and "lots of cheese" add up to "oh-so-good" pies (deep-dish, thin-crust and other styles) at this counter-service" Lakeview pie purveyor that "also sells by the slice so you don't have to wait"; it may be "nothing to look at", but BYO keeps the tabs extra "reasonable" and service is "quick", making it a "darned good" option.

Artopolis ● *Greek/Mediterranean*　　21 | 20 | 17 | $21

Greektown | 306 S. Halsted St. (Jackson Blvd.) | 312-559-9000 | www.artopolischicago.com

A "bright place for a light meal", this "cozy" Greektowner offering both counter and table service bakes up "beautiful breads" and "interesting savory pastries" to go with other "tasty", "affordable" Greek-Mediterranean bites; "too busy for the service to be perfect", it's still "quick" and easy for lunch or an "after-theater/concert snack."

☑ Arun's ⓜ *Thai*　　27 | 23 | 27 | $94

Northwest Side | 4156 N. Kedzie Ave. (bet. Irving Park Rd. & Montrose Ave.) | 773-539-1909 | www.arunsthai.com

For a "Thai food experience that's unmatched in Chicago", fans rave about this "legendary" Northwest Side "jewel" where chef-owner Arun Sampanthavivat crafts "simply wonderful" prix fixe meals featuring dishes "so beautiful you feel guilty putting a fork in them"; while the generally "pleasing" space falls a bit short of the cuisine, the "caring" staff ensures that guests feel "pampered" and "satisfied", even if they need a "high-limit credit card" to cover it all.

Ashkenaz Deli *Deli*　　19 | 8 | 13 | $17

Gold Coast | 12 E. Cedar St. (bet. Lake Shore Dr. & State St.) | 312-944-5006 | www.ashkenazdeli.com

Fressers with a "hankering for corned beef" head to this "kosher-style" Gold Coast deli offering the "usual selection" of eats, including "stacked" sandwiches and "matzo ball soup like your grandma used to make"; the setting is "uncomfortable" and service can be "lacking", so some say "it's best for carryout", especially "when you need that chopped-liver fix."

A Tavola ⓢ *Italian*　　26 | 22 | 26 | $48

Ukrainian Village | 2148 W. Chicago Ave. (bet. Hoyne Ave. & Leavitt St.) | 773-276-7567 | www.atavolachicago.com

The "pillow-soft" gnocchi "trumps any relationship" swear fans of this "intimate", "long-standing" Ukrainian Village "treasure", a "quiet" and "charming world" where "excellent versions of Italian classics" are "high-end without being pretentious", the "regional" wine is "exceptional" and "fair" tabs don't "break the bank"; "fantastic", "knowledgeable" service and a "magical" outdoor courtyard further make it *"molto buono"* for "special occasions."

	FOOD	DECOR	SERVICE	COST

Athena *Greek*
21 | 22 | 21 | $29

Greektown | 212 S. Halsted St. (Adams St.) | 312-655-0000 |
www.athenarestaurantchicago.com

The "killer" patio provides "stellar views of the Chicago skyline" at
this inviting Greektowner where the "classic" Hellenic dishes are
also served in the spacious, fireplace-enhanced dining room; tabs are
modest and service "organized", so even holdouts who feel the food
is "nothing to die for" assure it's "awesome" on a "gorgeous night."

Athenian Room *American/Greek*
22 | 12 | 19 | $19

Lincoln Park | 807 W. Webster Ave. (Halsted St.) | 773-348-5155
Situated "in the heart of Lincoln Park", this long-standing American-
Greek is a "casual" "neighborhood standby" thanks to "basic"
dishes "done right", including "delish" chicken and "incredible"
"juice-soaked fries that are magically still crispy"; "quick", "friendly"
servers contribute to the "laid-back atmosphere", and "large portions" and "low" prices make it an "insane bargain", so the "minimal
decor" doesn't bother most.

Atwood Cafe *American*
22 | 25 | 22 | $40

Loop | Hotel Burnham | 1 W. Washington St. (State St.) | 312-368-1900 |
www.atwoodcafe.com

"Huge floor-to-ceiling windows" and "stylish", "quirky" decor make
this "charming" New American "retreat" in the "elegant" Hotel
Burnham (a "historic landmark") a "beautiful spot to relax in the
Loop" while dining on "innovative" plates set down by "gracious"
servers; though some find it "pricey" for what's on offer, fans say it's
"one of the warmest places to have a meal", and especially "solid"
"before the theater."

NEW Au Cheval ☻ *American*
- | - | - | M

West Loop | 800 W. Randolph St. (Halsted St.) | 312-929-4580 |
www.aucheval.tumblr.com

Brendan Sodikoff (Gilt, Maude's Liquor Bar) brings über-hip, moderately priced 'diner' delights (chopped chicken liver, foie gras and eggs),
craft beers and updated cocktail classics to this no-reservations West
Loop American; the scenester-ready setting features a wood-clad exterior, an open kitchen with counter seating, tufted leather booths and
hot music pumping till 2 AM Monday–Saturday (till 1 AM Sunday).

Aurelio's Pizza *Pizza*
23 | 16 | 20 | $19

Loop | Holiday Inn Chicago Downtown | 506 W. Harrison St. (Canal St.) |
312-994-2000
Addison | Centennial Plaza | 1455 W. Lake St. (Lombard Rd.) |
630-889-9560
Chicago Heights | 1545 Western Ave. (15th St.) | 708-481-5040
Homewood | 18162 Harwood Ave. (183rd St.) | 708-798-8050
South Holland | 601 E. 170th St. (Park Ave.) | 708-333-0310
Palos Heights | 6543 W. 127th St. (Ridgeland Ave.) |
708-389-5170
Tinley Park | 15901 Oak Park Ave. (Rte. 6) | 708-429-4600
Downers Grove | 940 Warren Ave. (Highland Ave.) |
630-810-0078

(continued)

Aurelio's Pizza

Naperville | 931 W. 75th St. (Plainfield-Naperville Rd.) | 630-369-0077
Oak Brook | 100 E. Roosevelt Rd. (Summit Rd.) | 630-829-3200
www.aureliospizza.com
Additional locations throughout the Chicago area

Supporters swear "the best pizza in the Chicagoland area" hails from this affordable "local" chain, where "delicious, crispy, thin" pies ("deep pan" too) have "tangy sauce" and "cheese that melts to the edges"; "efficient", "pleasant" service compensates for sometimes "lackluster" decor, and the "original" Homewood "institution" gains praise when orders are cooked "in the old oven"; P.S. some locations are carryout and delivery only.

NEW Autre Monde Café & Spirits ▣ *Mediterranean*

▽ 25 | 20 | 25 | $39

Berwyn | 6727 W. Roosevelt Rd. (bet. Eulicid & Oak Park Aves.) | 708-775-8122 | www.autremondecafe.net

Chef-owners Dan Pancake and Beth Partridge (both ex Spiaggia) "have hit it right" at this Berwyn Mediterranean, a "sophisticated (but not pretentious) gem" that makes use of ingredients often sourced from their own Cakeridge Farms or on-site greenhouse in "flavorful" small plates and mains, boosted by "interesting" wines and "must"-try cocktails; "friendly" servers elevate the "warm, minimalist" space, so though it's a "little loud" for some, most say it's an overall "charmer."

☑ Avec ● *Mediterranean*

28 | 23 | 24 | $48

West Loop | 615 W. Randolph St. (bet. Desplaines & Jefferson Sts.) | 312-377-2002 | www.avecrestaurant.com

Blackbird's "more playful", less expensive sibling, this adjacent West Loop "small-plates delight" showcases chef Koren Grieveson's "true artistry" and "spot-on" execution, offering "inventive", "dream-worthy" Mediterranean dishes ("don't miss the incredible chorizo-stuffed dates") delivered by a "knowledgeable" staff in "hip", "cozy" environs with a "lively buzz"; the "stranger-phobic" may be wary of "tight" seating at communal tables, but "foodies" don't mind, insisting the "only drawback" is the no-reservations policy, which often results in "long waits."

☑ The Aviary ▣ *Eclectic*

27 | 27 | 26 | $56

West Loop | 955 W. Fulton Mkt. (Morgan St.) | 312-226-0868 | www.theaviary.com

"Incredible feats of mixologists' art" "star" at Grant Achatz's "extremely chic" West Loop "cocktail theater" ("to call it a bar or lounge is an insult") attached to Next, where "intricate", "interactive" drinks via "unique serving vessels" are accompanied by "outstanding", "well-crafted" Eclectic "small bites"; service is "of the highest standard" too, so though "money disappears rather quickly, and getting a reservation isn't easy", imbibers say it's a "must at least once", especially to "catch a glimpse into Alinea-style food at a fraction of the price."

	FOOD	DECOR	SERVICE	COST

Avli Restaurant *Greek*

| 22 | 20 | 22 | $34 |

Winnetka | 566 Chestnut St. (bet. Elm & Spruce Sts.) | 847-446-9300 | www.avli.us

"Authentic and robust" Hellenic cooking is "done with a little extra flair" at this "value" Greek in Winnetka, where "the menu goes way beyond tired standards" in delivering "traditional and contemporary dishes prepared to exacting standards"; "gracious" service, an "extensive" wine list and a "comfortable" "relaxed room (no Greektown hoopla here)" further ensure it's a "go-to on the North Shore."

Bacchanalia ⊘ *Italian*

| 24 | 14 | 22 | $32 |

Southwest Side | 2413 S. Oakley Ave. (bet. 24th & 25th Sts.) | 773-254-6555 | www.bacchanaliainchicago.com

Situated in a little "pocket" of town called Heart of Italy, this "family-owned" "red-saucer" delivers "mounds of pasta" and other "huge" plates just like "nonna" used to make to "crowded tables" of regulars; the muralled decor "hasn't been updated" in years, but the "old-school" staff is "wonderful", and it's a "real bargain" to boot; P.S. "there's valet parking and an ATM inside" (it's cash-only).

Bacino's *Italian*

| 22 | 15 | 18 | $23 |

Lincoln Park | 2204 N. Lincoln Ave. (Webster Ave.) | 773-472-7400
West Loop | 118 S. Clinton St. (Adams St.) | 312-876-1188 Ⓢ
www.bacinos.com

Bella Bacino's *Italian*

Loop | 75 E. Wacker Dr. (Upper Michigan Ave.) | 312-263-2350
La Grange | 36 S. La Grange Rd. (Harris Ave.) | 708-352-8882 Ⓜ
www.bellabacinos.com

"Extra thin crust" pies are offered alongside "pretty darn good stuffed 'zas" so "each team wins" at this "quaint" Italian foursome (the Bellas have fuller trattoria menus, the others are more pizza focused); some maintain they're merely "middle-of-the-road", but those who call them "solid" cite "helpful" service and affordable prices; P.S. the West Looper offers weekday lunch only.

NEW BadHappy
Poutine Shop Ⓢ Ⓜ *Eclectic*

| - | - | - | I |

River North | 939 N. Orleans St. (Oak St.) | 312-890-2165 | www.badhappypoutineshop.com

As its name suggests, expect many cheekily named poutines at this inexpensive River North BYO where housegound burgers, salads and shakes round out the Eclectic menu; the small open kitchen–enhanced space has a handful of tables, and late-night hours (till 2 AM) Fridays and Saturdays plus a Sunday brunch lend further appeal.

The Bagel *Deli*

| 20 | 13 | 19 | $18 |

Lakeview | 3107 N. Broadway (Belmont Ave.) | 773-477-0300
Skokie | Westfield Shoppingtown | 4999 Old Orchard Ctr. (Skokie Blvd.) | 847-677-0100
www.bagelrestaurant.com

"Everything you could want for a quick meal" can be found at this deli duo dispensing "homestyle" Jewish "comfort food" like "delicious corned beef ", "cure-all" soups (with "matzo balls the size of planets") and of course "perfectly satisfying bagels with all the trimmings"; sure, the "dinerlike" settings are "dated", but the "brisk" servers "know how to take care of their customers' whims", and the portions are "big", so "share and share nice."

NEW Baker & Nosh 🗷 M *Bakery/Sandwiches* — | — | — | I

Uptown | 1303 W. Wilson Ave. (Malden St.) | 773-989-7393 | www.bakerandnosh.com

Sandwiches get a lift from the wide variety of housemade breads at this Uptown bakery/cafe also piquing noshers' interest with pizzas, soup and a number of sweet offerings all made on-site; set in a vintage wood-trimmed storefront, it gets a seasonal boost from garden seating, while intimate baking classes provide DIY appeal.

NEW Bakersfield *American* — | — | — | M

Westmont | 330 E Ogden Ave. (bet. Blackhawk Dr. & Richmond Ave.) | 630-568-3615 | www.bakersfieldrestaurant.com

Anchored by a wood-oven grill, this expansive Westmont American – a sib to Standard Market – features an eclectic lineup of house-butchered steaks, sushi and seafood, turned from an open kitchen; its sleek, spacious patio (equipped with a fire pit) encourages lingering over craft cocktails and a well-chosen lineup of wine and beer.

Bakin' & Eggs *American* 21 | 19 | 18 | $17

Lakeview | 3120 N. Lincoln Ave. (bet. Barry & Belmont Aves.) | 773-525-7005 | www.bakinandeggschicago.com

"The flight of bacon trumps all else" (though the eggs are "tasty" too) at this "bustling" Lakeview brunchery complete with an "amazing" counter for coffee and pastries "while you wait for your table"; "pleasant" (if "slow") staffers tend the "eclectic", "shabby-chic" space, so even if a few find it too "hurried" and "not distinguished" enough for the price, most agree it's a "comfortable" place for "families, friends or business meetings"; P.S. closes at 3 PM daily.

NEW Balena *Italian* — | — | — | M

Lincoln Park | 1633 N. Halsted St. (bet. North Ave. & Willow St.) | 312-867-3888 | www.balenachicago.com

Chef Chris Pandel (The Bristol) and the Boka crew are behind this midpriced Lincoln Park Italian where handmade pastas, wood-fired mains and pizzas, and ambitious desserts are accompanied by complex culinary cocktails and an endless wine list; the vaulted, earth-toned space includes a brown leather and steel bar, and private dining rooms upstairs provide an escape from the well-heeled throngs.

Ba Le Sandwich & 23 | 14 | 18 | $9
Bakery *Sandwiches/Vietnamese*

Uptown | 5014 N. Broadway (Rosemont Ave.) | 773-561-4424
NEW Chinatown | 2141 S. Archer Ave. (bet. Princeton & Wentworth Aves.) | 312-528-6967
www.balesandwich.com

"Authentic" banh mi sandwiches "made to order" on "freshly baked", "superbly crackly" French bread "can't be beat for price or quality" at this "modern" Uptown shop that's "downright pleasant" following a move from its old "utilitarian" digs; there are also smoothies, iced coffees and a "refrigerator full of Vietnamese snacks and drinks", and while skittish types warn "some things are a little off-the-charts for non-Asian palates", most call it "terrific" all around; P.S. there's also a new Chinatown branch.

Balsan *European*   24 | 23 | 23 | $52

Gold Coast | The Elysian | 11 E. Walton St. (bet. Rush & State Sts.) | 312-646-1400 | www.balsanrestaurant.com

"Informal" yet "posh", this "elegant but hardly stuffy" Euro cafe in the Gold Coast's "spectacular Elysian Hotel" presents charcuterie, tarte flambé and other "beautifully prepared" plates ("much better than hotel food") in a "lively", "stylish" room inspired by Paris in the '20s; it "can be as laid-back or fancy as you want to make it", and though the bites can get "pricey", the "Sunday supper is a steal."

Bandera *American*   23 | 22 | 22 | $34

Streeterville | 535 N. Michigan Ave., 2nd fl. (bet. Grand Ave. & Ohio St.) | 312-644-3524 | www.hillstone.com

A Southwestern "take on American favorites", including "top-notch rotisserie chicken", "skillet cornbread" and "huge salads", is on offer at this "comfortable" chain link with a "high-profile" Streeterville location "overlooking Michigan Avenue"; "polite" service, live jazz and "dim lighting in the evening" add to the "inviting" ambiance – just be prepared to "fight with the tourists" for a window seat.

Bangers & Lace ◑ *American*   20 | 23 | 18 | $22

Wicker Park | 1670 W. Division St. (Paulina St.) | 773-252-6499 | www.bangersandlacechicago.com

An "interesting menu" of "tasty upscale pub food" with an emphasis on sausages is buoyed by an "outstanding" brew selection that "always changes" at this lodgelike Wicker Park watering hole "run by colorful people who really know their beverages"; despite the potential "beer education", some sudsers find the service "aloof", but otherwise it's a fine "go-to" for "wasting away an afternoon, evening or both."

NEW Banh Mi & Co. *Sandwiches/Vietnamese*   – | – | – | I

Lakeview | 3141 N. Broadway (bet. Belmont Ave. & Briar Pl.) | 773-754-5545 | www.banhmiandco.com

Affordable Vietnamese sandwiches made on house-baked bread (and stuffed with the likes of pork, sardines, tofu and more), plus spring rolls and salads are on offer at this quick-serve Lakeview BYO; industrial ductwork, a tin ceiling and high-top counter seats feature in the tiny space.

Bank Lane Bistro ⊠ *American*   22 | 19 | 21 | $50

Lake Forest | 670 N. Bank Ln., 2nd fl. (bet. Deerpath Rd. & Market Sq.) | 847-234-8802 | www.banklanebistro.com

Customers commend this "neat" little upstairs bistro for its "creative" New American fare served in a "lovely" setting with an open kitchen and a balcony providing "views of the Lake Forest square";

"accommodating" service is another plus, though some doubters dub the food merely "average" and a bit "steep" "for the 'burbs."

NEW Barbari M *Mideastern/Pizza*   – | – | – | I

Ukrainian Village | 2020 W. Chicago Ave. (bet. Damen & Hoyne Aves.) | 773-342-8220 | www.barbarichicago.com

An uncommon mix of Persian and pizza is proffered at this budget-friendly West Town BYO where the house-baked flatbread that inspired the name is served as a side with the likes of pomegranate soup, yogurt dips and organic salads (plus vegetarian options aplenty); the casual storefront with bright-yellow walls is decorated with birds and branches, tin ceiling candle chandeliers and blue booths.

Bar Louie ● *Pub Food*   17 | 16 | 16 | $23

O'Hare Area | Holiday Inn Chicago O'Hare | 5615 N. Cumberland Ave. (Bryn Mawr Ave.) | 773-332-8029 | www.barlouieamerica.com
Hyde Park | 5500 S. Shore Dr. (55th St.) | 773-363-5300 | www.barlouieamerica.com
Printers Row | 47 W. Polk St. (Dearborn St.) | 312-347-0000 | www.barlouieamerica.com
Evanston | 1520 Sherman Ave. (Grove St.) | 847-733-8300 | www.barlouieamerica.com
Skokie | Holiday Inn North Shore | 5300 Touhy Ave. (Niles Center Rd.) | 847-763-3056 | www.barlouieamerica.com
Mt. Prospect | Holiday Inn Mount Prospect | 200 E. Rand Rd. (Kensington Rd.) | 847-394-3456 | www.barlouieamerica.com
Bolingbrook | 619 E. Boughton Rd. (Feather Sound Dr.) | 630-410-7100 | www.restaurants-america.com
Naperville | 22 E. Chicago Ave. (Washington St.) | 630-983-1600 | www.barlouieamerica.com
NEW Oakbrook Terrace | 17 W. 350 22nd St. (Maple Pl.) | 630-478-8040 | www.barlouieamerica.com
Oak Park | 1122 Lake St. (Harlem Ave.) | 708-725-3300 | www.barlouieamerica.com
Additional locations throughout the Chicago area

"Loud" and sometimes "rowdy", this predominantly suburban chain of chowhouses slings "basic", "crowd-pleasing" pub grub backed by "reasonably priced" "drinky drinks" including "lots to choose from on tap"; service gets mixed marks ("friendly" vs. "slow") and it's too "generic" for some, but others, especially "sports lovers" cheering "TVs everywhere", call it the "perfect after-work place to meet and eat."

NEW Barrelhouse Flat ●☒ *American*   – | – | – | M

Lincoln Park | 2624 N. Lincoln Ave. (bet. Seminary & Sheffield Aves.) | 773-857-0421 | www.barrelhouseflat.com

A sprawling cocktail menu including house creations and punches by the pitcher or bowl is offered alongside haute New American bar plates like pig-faced poutine and beignets at this midpriced Lincoln Park hot spot; patrons can choose between the casual, convivial first floor bearing booths, barstools and Edison bulbs, or head upstairs to the intimate lounge with plush seating, vintage-inspired wallpaper and a pool table.

Barrington Country Bistro ⌧ *French* | 25 | 20 | 22 | $50 |

Barrington | Foundry Shopping Ctr. | 718 W. Northwest Hwy. (Hart Rd.) | 847-842-1300 | www.barringtoncountrybistro.com

"Tried-and-true", this "authentic", "first-rate" Barrington "standby" offers "excellent" "bistro cuisine" via "friendly, respectful" servers in a "charming" strip-mall space; it delivers a "real French experience" "without the 'tude" so most overlook tabs that are "high for the area."

NEW Barrio Urban Taqueria *Mexican* | - | - | - | M |

Lakeview | 714 W. Diversey Pkwy. (bet. Burling & Orchard Sts.) | 773-360-8316 | www.barriotaqueria.com

Expect "unusual taco filling choices" (everything from tongue to tilapia), "guacamole made tableside" and other "impressive" Mex favorites at this Lakeview taqueria also offering specialty drinks like "fantastic blood orange margaritas"; "reasonable prices" and casual surroundings decked out with arty red walls complete the picture.

NEW Bar Toma ● *Italian/Pizza* | 17 | 18 | 18 | $38 |

Gold Coast | 110 E. Pearson St. (bet. Michigan Ave. & Rush St.) | 312-266-3110 | www.bartomachicago.com

Opinions are split on this "shiny" new Gold Coast Italian by owner Tony Mantuano (Spiaggia), with some "enjoying an array of cheeses", artisan pizzas and small plates, as well as "terrific hours" for late-night dining and others knocking "uneven", "disappointing" results and "upscale food-court decor"; still, its "wonderful location" makes it appealing "for a break" while shopping, so those who "wanted to love it" "hope they get it together" soon.

Basil Leaf Café *Italian* | 20 | 20 | 20 | $30 |

Lincoln Park | 2465 N. Clark St. (Fullerton Pkwy.) | 773-935-3388 | www.basilleaf.com

A "large selection" of "nicely prepared" pasta dishes is the "strength" of this "low-key" Northern Italian in Lincoln Park with a "cozy" feel for "not-too-noisy" lunches and dinners (especially weeknights); a few fault the "varied" menu as too "random", but the "friendly" "neighborhood" vibe and "reasonable prices" override that for regulars.

⌅ The Bedford ● *American* | 17 | 27 | 17 | $39 |

Wicker Park | 1612 W. Division St. (Ashland Ave.) | 773-235-8800 | www.bedfordchicago.com

"Whole walls sparkle" with "security lock boxes" at this "supercool" Wicker Park New American set in a refurbished bank where diners gather to down ambitious "drink concoctions" and "creative", midpriced eats by Mark Steuer (ex Hot Chocolate, The Gage); while some report mixed service and say the food "fails to live up to expectations", the "outstanding atmosphere" still draws the "'in' crowd."

Bella Notte *Italian* | 24 | 21 | 22 | $36 |

Noble Square | 1374 W. Grand Ave. (Noble St.) | 312-733-5136 | www.bellanottechicago.com

A "favorite of the locals" for "reliable, old-time" Southern Italian, this "family-run" Noble Square "standby" dishes up "terrific homemade

FOOD DECOR SERVICE COST

cavatelli" and other "more than generous" specialties, all at moderate prices; "classic" surroundings and "professional" service also work in its favor, just be advised it can get hectic on UC game nights.

Bella Via *Italian* | 21 | 18 | 22 | $35 |

Highland Park | 1899 Second St. (Elm Pl.) | 847-681-8300 | www.bellaviahp.com

Admirers appreciate the "generous" servings of "traditional" Italian fare and selections from the "large wine cellar" at this Highland Parker where "reasonable prices" and "friendly" service in a "comfortable" setting add "family dining" appeal; a handful complaining of "high noise levels" and "pedestrian" offerings are outnumbered by satisfied regulars who "go over and over again."

Belly Shack Ⓜ *Asian* | 25 | 16 | 19 | $17 |

Humboldt Park | 1912 N. Western Ave. (Homer St.) | 773-252-1414 | www.bellyshack.com

"So inventive and it all works" say foodies who "crave" the "always tasty, never boring" fare at chef-owner Bill Kim's Humboldt Park "hipster" haven, offering a "limited" yet "extraordinary" menu of "solidly executed" Asian dishes with Nuevo Latino accents, capped off with "must"-try soft-serve; "affordable" tabs match the "über-casual" digs and "BYO never hurts either."

Benihana *Japanese/Steak* | 21 | 20 | 23 | $37 |

Wheeling | 150 N. Milwaukee Ave. (bet. Dundee Rd. & Shadow Bend Dr.) | 847-465-6021

Schaumburg | 1200 E. Higgins Rd. (bet. Meacham Rd. & National Pkwy.) | 847-995-8201

Lombard | 747 E. Butterfield Rd. (Technology Dr.) | 630-571-4440 www.benihana.com

The "chefs put on quite a show" at this "consistent" Japanese steakhouse chain, a "great social experience" where "better-than-average" fare is prepared tableside by knife-wielding teppanyaki masters; if tepped-out talliers tag it as "outdated" and "overpriced for what you get", fans say it's "fun with a group" and "the kids love it."

NEW Benjamin Ⓢ Ⓜ *American* | ▽ 16 | 23 | 14 | $62 |

Highland Park | 1849 Second St. (bet. Central Ave. & Elm Pl.) | 847-748-8737 | www.benjaminrestaurant.com

Richly designed, this loungey Highland Park newcomer by chef-owner Benjamin Brittsan "may be a little exotic for the neighborhood", as a few early samplers report "interesting" New American dishes served in a "lovely atmosphere", and others opine it's "just ok" for the high price tag; service also ranges from "friendly" to "arrogant", leading critics to conclude it's bigger on "attitude than delivery."

Benny's Chop House *Steak* | 26 | 24 | 26 | $67 |

River North | 444 N. Wabash Ave. (bet. Hubbard & Illinois Sts.) | 312-626-2444 | www.bennyschophouse.com

Carnivores assure you "can't miss" at this River North chophouse "with flair", where the "melt-in-your-mouth tender" steaks and "sides big enough to share" are ferried by a "helpful, polite" staff that goes "above and beyond" expectations; "marvelous people-watching", a "relaxing atmosphere" and frequent live piano also explain why it's "pricey but perfect for a special occasion."

Bento Box ☒ Asian — | — | — | I

Bucktown | 2246 W. Armitage Ave. (bet. Leavitt St. & Oakley Ave.) | 773-278-3932 | www.artisancateringchicago.com

"If you can get a table, it's well worth it" advise admirers of this "tiny" Bucktown counter-service BYO, an offshoot of a catering company that "wows" with a changing chalkboard menu of "well-cooked" Asian fare full of "nuanced flavors"; food comes in bento boxes for low-cost lunches and dinners, so despite its "generic" looks, it's "worth seeking out."

Berghoff Restaurant/Cafe ☒ German — 20 | 19 | 18 | $29

Loop | 17 W. Adams St. (bet. Dearborn & State Sts.) | 312-427-3170

Berghoff Cafe German

O'Hare Area | O'Hare Int'l Airport | Terminal 1 (I-190) | 773-601-9180
www.theberghoff.com

"Faithfully prepared" German "classics" like "schnitzel and co." "dominate" the midpriced menu at this redone Loop "landmark", a "sentimental favorite" where "honest, generous" eats and drinks take you "back in time" – and lure in plenty of "tourists" too; "charming" and "faithful to the original" in many ways (the house-label microbrew and "best homemade root beer" remain), it's bittersweet for those who "hope the old Berghoffs will magically reappear" and note the "staff clearly isn't from Bavaria anymore"; P.S. the downstairs cafe and airport spin-off are also "reliable" for "hearty sandwiches."

Bien Trucha ☒Ⓜ Mexican ▽ 29 | 21 | 25 | $33

Geneva | 410 W. State St. (bet. 4th & 5th Sts.) | 630-232-2665 | www.bientrucha.com

Enthusiasts "create food memories" at this wallet-friendly Geneva "favorite" tended by "attentive" staffers who deliver "inventive, skillfully prepared" drinks and "authentic" Mexican fare highlighting "perfect levels of spice and acidity"; the "tiny" light-toned space gets "packed" quickly, so "get there before it opens" or you may "wait for hours."

Big & Little's ☒⇄ Seafood 25 | 8 | 18 | $13

River North | 860 N. Orleans St. (bet. Chestnut & Locust Sts.) | 312-943-0000 | www.bigandlittleschicago.com

Traversing "uncharted territory" when it comes to "fast food", this "bang-for-the-buck" River North seafood specialist by former *Hell's Kitchen* contestant Tony D'Alessandro "rocks" for "fresh-dipped" fish 'n' chips and "do-not-miss" mahi tacos, plus "delicious" burgers and "indulgent truffle fries that can make your whole week better"; "there's more seating" following a move to a new, nearby space (not fully reflected in the Decor score), but wait times can still be "tough, especially at lunch."

	FOOD	DECOR	SERVICE	COST

Big Bowl *Asian*

20 | 18 | 20 | $26

River North | 60 E. Ohio St. (Rush St.) | 312-951-1888
Gold Coast | 6 E. Cedar St. (State St.) | 312-640-8888
Lincolnshire | 215 Parkway Dr. (Milwaukee Ave.) | 847-808-8880
Schaumburg | 1950 E. Higgins Rd. (Rte. 53) | 847-517-8881
www.bigbowl.com

A "consistent" option for "quick", "tasty" Asian eats with an "emphasis on more healthy choices", "local ingredients" and "gourmet flourishes", this "create-your-own" stir-fry chain offers a "large menu variety", "homemade drinks" (including "fresh ginger ale") and "right-on" service; though it's too "Americanized" for some, most agree it's a "cheap and cheerful" choice.

NEW The Big Easy by Jimmy Bannos 🗷Ⓜ *Cajun/Creole*

- | - | - | I

Loop | Chase Tower | 10 S. Dearborn St. (Madison St.) | 312-732-6505

The namesake founder of Heaven on Seven and The Purple Pig is the force behind this Loop quick-serve in Chase Tower's Urban Market serving a pared-down classic Cajun-Creole menu (plus a well-edited hot sauce collection); the affordable eats are ordered at a harlequin-painted counter and consumed in an open modern court area.

Big Jones *Southern*

25 | 22 | 22 | $32

Andersonville | 5347 N. Clark St. (bet. Balmoral & Summerdale Aves.) | 773-275-5725 | www.bigjoneschicago.com

"When you miss NOLA" or long for "a night out in Charleston", pop over to this midpriced Andersonville "destination" where fans say you're in for a "genuine, quality Southern food experience" (especially at the "don't-miss brunch") courtesy of a "surprising" menu featuring both "locally sourced" products and ingredients somewhat "unheard of" in Chicago; "helpful" servers, "warm, welcoming" environs and a landscaped outdoor patio also make for a "memorable" experience.

Big Star ❶🖙 *Mexican*

26 | 19 | 18 | $19

Wicker Park | 1531 N. Damen Ave. (Wicker Park Ave.) | 773-235-4039 | www.bigstarchicago.com

"Life-changing" "gourmet tacos and other Mexican street foods", plus "brilliant beers", "strong, fresh margaritas" and an "expansive collection of whiskey", fuel an "über-cool" "hipster" scene (lots of "plaid shirts") at this Wicker Park "hit" by Paul Kahan (Avec, Blackbird); it's "cash-only" but pretty "cheap", and though the "jam-packed" crowd means "insane" waits, most are willing to "fight for a table" on "one of the most happening patios in the city"; P.S. there's an "outside take-out window" too.

Bijan's Bistro ❶ *American*

19 | 18 | 17 | $31

River North | 663 N. State St. (Erie St.) | 312-202-1904 | www.bijansbistrochicago.com

Staying "a step above regular bar fare", with some "French touches" and "comforting" breakfast plates (the "best" steak and eggs), this "pleasant" River North New American is "popular" among pub-"hoppers" of all stripes (even "Kanye and Kardashians"); though a few knock it as a "schizoid mix of bistro and sports bar" and add the menu "needs some updating", its late hours earn it a "gold star for availability" when the "hunger monster calls."

Billy Goat Tavern *Burgers*   16 | 12 | 15 | $14

Loop | 330 S. Wells St. (Van Buren St.) | 312-554-0297 🆑
River North | Merchandise Mart | 222 W. Merchandise Mart Plaza (bet. Orleans & Wells Sts.) | 312-464-1045
River North | 430 N. Lower Michigan Ave. (bet. Hubbard & Illinois Sts.) | 312-222-1525 ◐⊟
Streeterville | Navy Pier | 700 E. Grand Ave. (Lake Shore Dr.) | 312-670-8789
O'Hare Area | O'Hare Field Terminal 1 | Terminal 1 (I-190) | 773-462-9368
West Loop | 1535 W. Madison St. (Ogden Ave.) | 312-733-9132 ⊟
www.billygoattavern.com

Those "longing for good old grease" hit these "classic" Chicago "hamburger joints" to relive the famous *SNL* skit over "cheezborgers" and "no fries, chips" served with the "expected rude service"; many gripe they're "tired" and "overhyped", but concede the "underground" original on Lower Michigan Avenue is an "institution" that's "worth the trip."

Bin 36 *American*   22 | 21 | 22 | $42

River North | 339 N. Dearborn St. (Kinzie St.) | 312-755-9463 | www.bin36.com

An "inspired wine list" (including "flights up the wazoo") is matched with "incredible cheese" and other "well-prepared" New American plates at this "reasonably priced" River North "meeting spot"; "knowledgeable staffers" offering "pairing suggestions" add to a "convivial atmosphere" in the "contemporary, open" space, and diners can buy bottles of their favorites from the adjoining shop; P.S. there's a more casual Wicker Park cafe sib.

Bin Wine Cafe *American*   20 | 18 | 17 | $44

Wicker Park | 1559 N. Milwaukee Ave. (Damen Ave.) | 773-486-2233 | www.binwinecafe.com

You can "grab a nice glass of wine with friends" and make a meal of it with "creative" New American "nibbles and cheese flights" at this rustic brick-walled cafe "in the center" of "happening" Wicker Park; gripers, however, grumble about "hit-or-miss service" and suggest you "save your money for the Bin 36 in River North."

Birchwood Kitchen Ⓜ *Sandwiches*   24 | 20 | 22 | $15

Wicker Park | 2211 W. North Ave. (bet. Bell Ave. & Leavitt St.) | 773-276-2100 | www.birchwoodkitchen.com

"You can always depend on something delicious" at this counter-service Wicker Park BYO where "quality" offerings like "savory" brunch dishes, "terrific" burgers and "creative" sandwiches in "well-thought-out combinations" highlight "top-shelf" local ingredients;

the "cozy" space comes with a "sunny patio" and "welcoming" staffers "remember your name", so it's a "regular stop" for many.

Birrieria Zaragoza 🗷 *Mexican* `_ | _ | _ | I`
Southwest Side | 4852 S. Pulaski Rd. (49th St.) | 773-523-3700
NEW Birrieria Zaragoza II *Mexican*
Melrose Park | 2211 W. Lake St. (Carson Dr.) | 708-344-3400
www.birrieriazaragoza.com

"They do basically one thing and they do it very well" say Southwest Siders of this inexpensive Mexican storefront dishing "perfectly seasoned", "succulent" goat offered in tacos, quesadillas and by itself; "run by the nicest family" it feels just "like being at the Zaragoza home", just be aware it closes at 7; P.S. a Melrose Park sequel opened post–Survey.

Bistro Bordeaux *French* `24 | 21 | 22 | $48`
Evanston | 618 Church St. (Chicago Ave.) | 847-424-1483 | www.lebistrobordeaux.com

For "a slice of the Left Bank" on the North Shore, Francophiles favor this "tiny, charming" "date-night" destination serving a "simple menu of beautifully prepared", "authentic" "bistro faves" accompanied by "lovely wines"; "friendly, convivial" service sans the "Parisian disdain" and "medium" prices help loyalists overlook "close quarters" that can get "noisy."

Bistro Campagne *French* `25 | 23 | 22 | $43`
Lincoln Square | 4518 N. Lincoln Ave. (bet. Sunnyside & Wilson Aves.) | 773-271-6100 | www.bistrocampagne.com

"Consistently solid, traditional French food in an adorable, comfortable setting" sums up this "upscale" Lincoln Square bistro specializing in "authentic" seasonal "country" cooking bolstered by "great Belgian beers" and "an excellent, reasonably priced wine list"; "hospitable" service and "cozy" wood-accented environs complete with an "enchanting" outside garden also help make it a "mainstay."

Bistronomic *French* `23 | 20 | 21 | $49`
Gold Coast | 840 N. Wabash Ave. (bet. Chestnut & Pearson Sts.) | 312-944-8400 | www.bistronomic.net

Chef-owner Martial Noguier (ex Café des Architectes) "continues to surprise and delight" at this "ultrachic", "elbow-to-elbow" Gold Coast New French where "you can eat light or really dine" on "delicious, imaginative" "small, medium and large" plates representing a "modern twist on bistro food" (if you "never order chicken anywhere else, you should here"); generally "accommodating" servers tend the "sophisticated", "minimalist" space, and though it can get "noisy", "surprisingly reasonable prices considering the location" help.

Bistrot Margot *French* `22 | 21 | 21 | $39`
Old Town | 1437 N. Wells St. (bet. North Ave. & Schiller St.) | 312-587-3660 | www.bistrotmargot.com

Offering a bit of "Paris on Wells", this Old Town "mainstay" delivers "simple", "authentic French" fare in a "charming", "classic bistro" setting; "reasonable" prices and "friendly" servers are other pluses, so even if some sniff it's "not spectacular", most agree it's "reliable" for "romance" or "an easy night out" "with family or friends."

Bistrot Zinc *French*   21 | 22 | 22 | $40

Gold Coast | 1131 N. State St. (bet. Cedar & Elm Sts.) | 312-337-1131 | www.bistrotzinc.com

"Wonderfully unintimidating", this "high-energy" Gold Coast boîte featuring front windows that open on a warm day and a "beautiful" zinc bar is "like being in Paris" with its "authentic" French "comfort food" and "true bistro feel"; "friendly, helpful" servers contribute to the "warm, cozy neighborhood vibe", and prices are "modest", so though "nothing exciting", it's "reliable" for a "bit of Rive Gauche in Chicago."

NEW Bistro Voltaire *French*   23 | 23 | 23 | $45

Near North | 226 W. Chicago Ave. (Franklin St.) | 312-265-0911 | www.bistrovoltaire.com

"The food is pure French bistro" at this authentic" Near Norther where "well-prepared" plates highlighting "delicate, refined" flavors are served alongside an "interesting selection of wines" in "cozy, upscale-comfortable" surroundings; "prices are reasonable" and service "friendly", so though "tables are tight" in the "small quarters", fans say it's easy to "feel right at home"; P.S. lunch is offered seasonally.

Bite Cafe ◑ *American*   22 | 13 | 18 | $20

Ukrainian Village | 1039 N. Western Ave. (Cortez St.) | 773-395-2483 | www.bitecafechicago.com

"Solid" and "remarkably affordable", this "funky" Ukranian Village BYO adjacent to nightclub sib Empty Bottle cooks "tasty, mildly inventive" American "comfort food", offering "a selection not found everywhere" including a number of vegetarian choices; the basic, brick-accented space may lag behind, but service is "fast" (if a little "sassy"), so it's still an "enjoyable" "neighborhood joint."

Z Blackbird Ⓢ *American*   27 | 23 | 25 | $69

West Loop | 619 W. Randolph St. (bet. Desplaines & Jefferson Sts.) | 312-715-0708 | www.blackbirdrestaurant.com

"Inspired", "thoughtful" New American plates are "meticulously put together" by chef-owner Paul Kahan and his "passionate and talented" team at this "energetic" West Loop "winner" "fit for foodies"; with a "sleek" "pristine setting" and "sophisticated" service, it "nails the essentials of fine, hip dining", so though prices may attract "expense-account" types and "seating is crowded", fans say it's "not to be missed"; P.S. "don't forget" the "phenomenal" prix fixe lunch.

Z Black Dog Gelato ⊘ *Ice Cream*   26 | 14 | 19 | $7

Ukrainian Village | 859 N. Damen Ave. (W. Iowa St.) | 773-235-3116 | www.blackdogchicago.com

"Wow" is the word at this "friendly little" Ukrainian Village gelateria, where "quality ingredients" make for "incredible" scoops, and "new, inventive" flavors (goat cheese cashew, "to-die-for" salted peanut) "have somehow morphed into local classics"; "decor is sort of empty" and it's cash-only, but who cares when you "always leave wanting more."

Blackie's *American*
20 | 15 | 17 | $22

Loop | 755 S. Clark St. (Polk St.) | 312-786-1161 | www.blackieschicago.com

A "local place to eat and hang out" since 1939, this Loop tavern sates "burger lovers" and others looking for "good, casual" American fare; sure, the decor is "a bit tired", but longtime regulars insist "that only adds to its charm", and with "friendly" enough service and "cheap" tabs it's a "reliable" pick for "grabbing a quick bite" or "getting a drink", especially "if you want to avoid the high priced stuff" nearby.

Blind Faith Café Ⓜ *Vegetarian*
20 | 16 | 20 | $23

Evanston | 525 Dempster St. (bet. Chicago & Hinman Aves.) | 847-328-6875 | www.blindfaithcafe.com

"One of the first meat-free zones" in town, this "down-to-earth" Evanston "institution" is "veggie heaven", serving "imaginative" "no-guilt" dishes so "tasty" you won't be "embarrassed or nervous about taking your non-vegetarian parents"; "accommodating" servers elevate the "simple" "hole-in-the-wall" space, and if detractors deem it "nothing special" and say "portions could be bigger and prices lower", the faithful figure it's "been around for over 30 years, so it must be doing something right."

Blokes & Birds ❷ *British*
18 | 20 | 20 | $30

Lakeview | 3343 N. Clark St. (bet. Roscoe & School Sts.) | 773-472-5252 | www.blokesandbirdschicago.com

"Interesting craft cocktails" and an "extensive beer list" pair with "contemporary English comfort food" at this "upscale" Lakeview pub in a bi-level, wood-accented space featuring two fireplaces and a pool table; "knowledgeable", "friendly" servers contribute to the "casual" vibe, so even if budgeters believe it's "a bit expensive for what it is", most maintain it's "a great addition to the sometimes-too-sporty neighborhood."

Blue Agave Restaurant ❷ *Mexican*
15 | 14 | 16 | $24

Near North | 1 W. Maple St. (State St.) | 312-335-8900 | www.blueagavechicago.com

"Killer" margaritas will "get your night off to a roaring start" at this Near North Mexican also dishing "solid" if "mostly typical" fare in "casual" digs with a "spring break feel"; true, "better options" exist but realists say "let's be honest, you don't go for the food" since it's "better suited for pre-party drinking than it is to quality dining."

The Bluebird ❷ *American*
23 | 23 | 21 | $40

Bucktown | 1749 N. Damen Ave. (Willow St.) | 773-486-2473 | www.bluebirdchicago.com

"Tasty" New American small plates "perfect for sharing" backed by an "endless" beer selection and "interesting" wines bring attention to this "cozy" Bucktown "gem" that's often "singing on the weekends with lively crowds"; moderate prices ease the sting of inconsis-

	FOOD	DECOR	SERVICE	COST

tent service ("helpful" vs. "snooty"), so many ultimately find it a "reliable" choice.

Bluegrass ⓜ *American* | 23 | 18 | 23 | $35 |

Highland Park | 1636 Old Deerfield Rd. (Richfield Ave.) | 847-831-0595 | www.bluegrasshp.com

Southern-influenced American fare is the draw at this midpriced Highland Park "joint" where "inventive" offerings plus "tried-but-true" classics make for a "fine all around menu" "with many winners"; "eager-to-please" staffers and a "warm", wood-accented space are other reasons it "can get crowded."

Bob Chinn's Crab House *Seafood* | 24 | 15 | 19 | $41 |

Wheeling | 393 S. Milwaukee Ave. (Mors Ave.) | 847-520-3633 | www.bobchinns.com

"If you're craving fresh shellfish", this "hectic", "high-energy" Wheeling "landmark" is "the place" say finatics touting the "huge selection" of seafood, including "out-of-this-world" crab, plus "deliciously lethal" garlic rolls and "famous mai tais"; the "huge", "warehouse"-like space is often "packed", and service can be a little too "fast" ("turnover is the name of the game"), but the ambiance is "upbeat" and tabs are "middle of the road", so it remains a "favorite."

Bob San *Japanese* | 23 | 18 | 21 | $39 |

Wicker Park | 1805 W. Division St. (Wood St.) | 773-235-8888 | www.bob-san.com

This spacious Wicker Park Japanese "gets it just right", offering "high-quality" "sushi standards" "without ridiculous prices"; service is solid and the menu is "large enough to suit everyone", so it's "good for groups", and if a few sniff it's "uninspiring", most leave with "no complaints."

Boka *American* | 26 | 24 | 25 | $66 |

Lincoln Park | 1729 N. Halsted St. (Willow St.) | 312-337-6070 | www.bokachicago.com

"Fresh ingredients are cleverly and innovatively combined" at Giuseppe Tentori's "consistently outstanding" (and "pricey") Lincoln Park "foodie destination" where "beautifully plated" New American dishes are paired with "wonderful" mixed drinks and "well-thought-out" wines, all ferried by "knowledgeable", "down-to-earth" servers; a recent renovation (which may not be reflected in the Decor score) gave the "swanky", "urban" setting a more modern feel and added a lounge to the "cozy bar" area, while the "casual and "lovely" candlelit back garden patio remains.

🆕 Bombay Spice Grill & Wine *Indian* ▽ 21 | 22 | 23 | $23 |

River North | 111 W. Illinois St. (enter on Clark St.) | 312-477-7657 | www.bombayspice.com

A "healthy twist" on Indian is the draw of this affordable River North chain link offering "delicious" dishes, including "create-your-own" options, all made with olive oil instead of the more traditional butter/ghee; "helpful" servers and a "beautiful" earth-toned space add further appeal.

	FOOD	DECOR	SERVICE	COST

NEW Bongiorno's Italian
Deli & Pizzeria *Italian/Pizza*

| - | - | - | I |

River North | River Plaza | 405 N. Wabash Ave. (Hubbard St.) | 312-755-1255 | www.bongiornoschicago.com

Antipasti, red and white thin-crust pizzas, fresh pasta and more add up to casual Italian dining at this modern River North deli; done in black and white with high ceilings, it offers counter ordering (food is brought to the tables) and seasonal outdoor seating on the plaza.

Bongo Room *American*

| 24 | 17 | 19 | $19 |

NEW Andersonville | 5022 N. Clark St. (Winnemac Ave.) | 773-728-7900

Wicker Park | 1470 N. Milwaukee Ave. (Honore St.) | 773-489-0690

South Loop | 1152 S. Wabash Ave. (Roosevelt Rd.) | 312-291-0100

www.thebongoroom.com

"Bring your appetite" to this "trendy" South Loop and Wicker Park duo where "gigantic" portions of "inventive", "decadent" American fare like "must-try" pancakes "bigger than your head" and "hearty, savory" egg dishes make it "the bomb.com of breakfast" (lunch is also served during the week); "reasonable prices" and a "laid-back" staff further ensure there's "always a wait", but it's "totally worth it" say fans, so "put the diet aside and indulge"; P.S. an Andersonville outpost opened post–Survey.

☑ Bonsoirée Ⓜ *American/French*

| 27 | 19 | 24 | $91 |

Logan Square | 2728 W. Armitage Ave. (Fairfield Ave.) | 773-486-7511 | www.bon-soiree.com

Chef-owner Shin Thompson's "inventive and slightly irreverent" New American–New French tasting menus are "as accessible as experimental cuisine gets" at his "memorable" Logan Square "foodie heaven" tended by an "energetic and devoted staff"; you may need to "bring a shoehorn to squeeze into the intimate space" and tabs aren't cheap, but many deem prices "reasonable" given the "haute" fare and say "BYO helps keep the cost way down" too.

Boston Blackie's *Burgers*

| 17 | 14 | 17 | $20 |

Loop | 120 S. Riverside Plaza (bet. Adams & Monroe Sts.) | 312-382-0700 Ⓢ

Deerfield | 405 Lake Cook Rd. (Rte. 43) | 847-418-3400

www.bostonblackies.com

"Good old greasy burgers" and other "reliable", if "pedestrian", American pub eats like the "great garbage salad" bring diners to these "friendly", "well-patronized" Deerfield and Loop links of the longtime chain; if critics sniff they're "too expensive for what you get" with "nothing-special", "old-fashioned decor", fans point to "fast, in-and-out service" and swear they "don't disappoint."

Bourgeois Pig *Coffeehouse/Sandwiches*

| 21 | 19 | 16 | $12 |

Lincoln Park | 738 W. Fullerton Ave. (bet. Burling & Halsted Sts.) | 773-883-5282 | www.bpigcafe.com

A "vestige of the old Lincoln Park", this "charming" cafe set inside an old row house "with creaky wooden floors and perfectly worn furniture" offers a "massive menu" of "tasty", "inventive" sandwiches" (many with "clever" "literary names"), "yummy pastries" and a "wide variety of fresh teas"; "lots of cozy nooks" and "cushy couches" further make it "everything a coffee shop should be."

Branch 27 *American* | 20 | 19 | 21 | $33 |

Noble Square | 1371 W. Chicago Ave. (Noble St.) | 312-850-2700 | www.branch27.com

Expect "solidly good" cooking "with just enough creativity to keep it interesting" at this "reasonably priced" Noble Square New American; "excellent brew selections" contribute to the "gastropub vibe" while highly rated service helps make it an overall "pleasant" choice.

NEW Brasserie by LM *French* | - | - | - | M |

South Loop | Essex Inn | 800 S. Michigan Ave. (bet. 8th & 9th Sts.) | 312-431-1788 | www.brasseriebylm.com

Set within the South Loop's Essex Inn, this "trippy-looking Francophile with geometric details, a ductwork ceiling and spacious patio overlooking Grant Park has built-in power-breakfast and after-office cred; meanwhile, familiar, all-day offerings (crêpes, croques, stuffed baguettes and plats) are more affordable than its LM Restaurant affiliation may suggest.

Brazzaz *Brazilian/Steak* | 21 | 20 | 22 | $59 |

River North | 539 N. Dearborn St. (Grand Ave.) | 312-595-9000 | www.brazzaz.com

"Bring your appetite" to this all-you-can-eat River North Brazilian for the "bottomless" "gourmet salad bar" and "never-ending meat parade" delivered by service "with flair"; it's not cheap, but the "warm" wood-accented space has an "overall nice feel", so fans say you might "want to stay forever" – just "let your belt out a few notches" first.

NEW Bread & Wine 🈂🅼 *American/Eclectic* | - | - | - | I |

Old Irving Park | 3732 W. Irving Park Rd. (bet. Hamlin & Ridgeway Aves.) | 773-866-5266 | www.breadandwinechicago.com

At this affordable Eclectic Irving Parker, local ingredients are crafted into small and large plates, including numerous vegetarian options, cheese and charcuterie; white counters, molded chairs and abstract light fixtures stand out in an industrial backdrop of concrete and raw wood, with rough-hewn tables, an open kitchen and a display area featuring gourmet foods, wine and beer.

Bricks *Pizza* | 25 | 15 | 17 | $23 |

Lincoln Park | 1909 N. Lincoln Ave. (Wisconsin St.) | 312-255-0851 www.brickschicago.com

NEW Big Bricks ☻ *BBQ/Pizza*

North Center/St. Ben's | 3830 N. Lincoln Ave. (Berenice Ave.) | 773-525-5022

Don't let the "homely" looking "dark basement" entrance discourage you because when you're "looking for something other than deep dish" this affordable Lincoln Park "pizza gem" delivers with thin-crust pies "featuring a variety of high-quality topping"; other pluses included "a very extensive beer menu", "fully loaded wine

FOOD | DECOR | SERVICE | COST

list" and "relaxing and low-key" atmosphere; P.S. a more barbecue-focused North Center sib opened post-Survey.

Bridge Bar Chicago *American*

| - | - | - | M |

River North | 315 N. LaSalle St. (bet. Kinzie St. & Wacker Dr.) | 312-822-0100 | www.bridgebarchicago.com

Creative American food and even more creative drinks (spotlighting interesting ingredients like candied bacon and jerky-infused vodka) is the concept at this midpriced River North 'cocktail kitchen' above Fulton's on the River; beer is also a focus, though it's outshone by an extensive brown booze selection, which you can sip in the funky, sprawling setting with massive columns and industrial ductwork.

NEW Bridge House Tavern Ⓜ *American*

| ∇ 18 | 21 | 19 | $32 |

River North | 321 N. Clark St. (bet. Kinzie St. & Wacker Dr.) | 312-644-0283 | www.bridgehousetavern.com

A "great place to enjoy the river view", this moderate River North tavern offers "wonderful" "waterside seating", "decent" American pub fare and "friendly" service; the "quaint" amber-hued dining room has "people-watching" appeal, but terrace tables are the bigger draw given the "impressive scenery."

Brio Tuscan Grille *Italian*

| 20 | 21 | 20 | $33 |

Lombard | Shops on Butterfield | 330 Yorktown Ctr. (Butterfield Rd.) | 630-424-1515 | www.brioitalian.com

"You wouldn't mistake it for an authentic local Italian place", but this "relaxed" Lombard chain link in the Shops on Butterfield still "holds its own" with a "wide range" of "decent quality" dishes at "reasonable prices", plus happy-hour specials and "one of the best kids' menus"; service is "accommodating" too, so even if foes find it merely "adequate", most agree it's "never a disappointment."

The Bristol *American*

| 25 | 21 | 23 | $43 |

Bucktown | 2152 N. Damen Ave. (bet. Shakespeare & Webster Aves.) | 773-862-5555 | www.thebristolchicago.com

A "locavore heaven" rave raters of this "buzzy" Bucktown New American where chef-owner Chris Pandel's "thoughtful use of interesting ingredients" results in "consistently creative" "farm-to-table" fare, including "life-changing" raviolo, "freaking awesome" duck-fat fries and "unusual meats" that "make for a fun adventure" in the "rustic" gastropub environs; not everyone's into the "new togetherness" (aka communal tables), but "friendly, knowledgeable" servers add to the "alluring", "peppy" vibe and with moderate prices, many confer it with "must-stop" status, especially since it now takes reservations.

Broadway Cellars *American*

| 24 | 22 | 25 | $30 |

Edgewater | 5900 N. Broadway (Rosedale Ave.) | 773-944-1208 | www.broadwaycellars.net

"One of the best values" around promise patrons of this "friendly" Edgewater New American offering "creative" and "flavorful" cuisine accompanied by design-your-own wine flights; "attentive" servers give the bistro environs a "wonderfully warm" feel so locals say each visit is "like coming home."

	FOOD	DECOR	SERVICE	COST

Browntrout ⓜ *American* `24` `19` `22` `$42`

North Center/St. Ben's | 4111 N. Lincoln Ave. (bet. Belle Plaine & Warner Aves.) | 773-472-4111 | www.browntroutchicago.com

They "use local ingredients creatively" at this "exciting" North Center New American that reels in diners with "surprising, inspiring" small and large plates and "well-chosen" wines via "patient", "knowledge-able" servers; if "decor is a bit low-budget" for some, others find the "casual" space "comfie", and while prices inspire further disagreement ("reasonable" vs. "high"), most say it's "definitely worth the try."

Bruna's Ristorante *Italian* ▽ `24` `14` `22` `$34`

Southwest Side | 2424 S. Oakley Ave. (24th Pl.) | 773-254-5550 | www.brunasristorante.com

Set in a "quiet" Southwest Side locale, this circa-1933 "landmark" ladles "large portions" of "traditional" Italian fare "made the way it should be made"; the "tiny" "old-school" digs are "nothing to look at", but "you're treated like family" and tabs are moderate, so it's "still a great haunt", especially when you need a "comfort-food blanket."

🆕 Brunch *American/Sandwiches* `15` `16` `14` `$18`

River North | 644 N. Orleans St. (Erie St.) | 312-265-1411 | www.brunchit.com

Hearty American breakfast, brunch and lunch fare is served at this big, bustling casual-chic River North BYO specializing in signature skillets, sandwiches and salads; the loftlike setting features rustic wood pillars, oversized drum light fixtures, a diner counter, a separate coffee bar and, most unusually, a working shoe-shine booth.

🆕 Bullhead Cantina ●ⓜ⇤ *Mexican* `-` `-` `-` `I`

Humboldt Park | 1143 N. California Ave. (bet. Division St. & Haddon Ave.) | 773-772-8895 | www.bullheadcantina.com

Tacos get top billing at this casual Humboldt Park cantina where farm-fresh ingredients and handmade corn tortillas elevate the more than a dozen options offered alongside a few fill-ins (burger, salad, quesadilla), plus craft cocktails, brews and brown beverages; the low-lit room is decorated with funky signage and Americana, and would-be diners should bring cash or hit the in-house ATM.

Burger Bar *Burgers* `23` `15` `18` `$22`

Lincoln Park | 1578 N. Clybourn Ave. (bet. Dayton & Halsted Sts.) | 312-255-0055 | burgerbarchicago.com

"It's build-your-own burger time" at this "mix-and-match" Lincoln Park "joint" offering "ridiculously good" patties, "creative toppings" and a "solid selection of draft beer"; some suggest "service could be improved" and say it's too "loud", but others appreciate "an atmosphere condusive to all age groups."

🆕 Burger Joint *Burgers* `-` `-` `-` `I`

River North | 675 N. Franklin St. (bet. Erie & Huron Sts.) | 312-440-8600 | www.burgerjointchicago.com

Not your usual burger joint, this River North quick-serve specializes in burgers, gyros and burgers topped with gyros, plus dogs and a

	FOOD	DECOR	SERVICE	COST

bevy of fry flavors (including renditions made with feta and Merkts cheddar), along with cookies and shakes; the funky setting is done up with rustic woodwork and photo murals of Chicago's skyline and El trains – which seem to come to life when the real thing rumbles by; P.S. night owls can nosh until 5 AM Fridays and Saturdays.

NEW Burger Point *Burgers*

	-	-	-	I

South Loop | 1900 S. State St. (bet. Archer Ave. & Cullerton St.) | 312-842-1900 | www.theburgerpoint.com

At this sun-drenched counter-serve burger entry in the South Loop, house-ground patties get topped with a dizzying number of gourmet garnishes and ordered via iPads; add-ons of fresh-cut sweet potatoes or Slinky-like spuds, seasonally sauced wings and chili further the casual, crowd-pleasing theme.

NEW Butcher & The Burger *Burgers*

	∇ 26	20	21	$15

Lincoln Park | 1021 W. Armitage Ave. (Kenmore Ave.) | 773-697-3735 | www.butcherandtheburger.com

Chef-owner Allen Sternweiler (ex Duchamp, Allen's) "wows" with "ah-mazing" "build-your-own burgers" featuring "awfully good customizing options", from the "unsurpassed rubs and variety of meat" to the "non-soggy" buns, plus "fries to die for" and a "nice selection of sodas" at this retro-looking counter-service BYO in Lincoln Park; thriftsters say it "could benefit from a bit of a lower price point", but converts only "wish it had more seating"; P.S. there are also breakfast burgers, beignets and butcher-shop take-out options.

Butch McGuire's Tavern ● *American*

	20	20	20	$23

Near North | 20 W. Division St. (Dearborn St.) | 312-787-4318 | www.butchmcguires.com

"Don't let the nightlife posture fool you", because though this inexpensive Near North "watering hole" "landmark" (since 1961) turns into a "boisterous" "pickup" scene at night, by day it's a suitable "lunch place for families" with solid American eats ferried by "friendly" servers; loyalists also note its "famous" "holiday display" makes it a "Christmastime tradition."

Butterfly Sushi Bar & Thai Cuisine *Japanese/Thai*

	21	16	19	$27

Noble Square | 1156 W. Grand Ave. (bet. May St. & Racine Ave.) | 312-563-5555
West Loop | 1131 W. Madison St. (bet. Aberdeen St. & Racine Ave.) | 312-997-9988
West Town | 1421 W. Chicago Ave. (bet. Bishop & Noble Sts.) | 312-492-9955
www.butterflysushibar.com

A "broad menu with lots of options", including "inventive" sushi and "satisfying" Thai specialties all "at a decent price", makes this Asian BYO trio a "consistent" "go-to"; grumps, however, knock "non-traditional ingredients" and servers often in a hurry to "usher you out the door", even if they ultimately concede "you won't be wowed, but you also won't be disappointed."

Byron's Hot Dog *Hot Dogs* | 21 | 8 | 16 | $9 |

Ravenswood | 1701 W. Lawrence Ave. (Paulina St.) | 773-271-0900

Byron's Hot Dog Haus *Hot Dogs*

Lakeview | 1017 W. Irving Park Rd. (Sheridan Rd.) | 773-281-7474 | www.byronshd.com

For "Chicago dogs the way they should be", eaters hit up these Lakeview and Ravenswood "huts" where the "friendly enough" "cats behind the counter" "practically put an entire salad" atop the wieners and "worthy" burgers; other offerings from subs and salads to quesadillas round out the inexpensive menu, and since the "decor makes you want to bring the food elsewhere to eat" many opt for takeout.

Café Absinthe Ⓜ *American/French* | ▽ 23 | 19 | 21 | $44 |

Bucktown | 1954 W. North Ave. (Damen Ave.) | 773-278-4488

"Clever and tasty" seasonal American-French fare in an "intimate" setting is the draw of this longtime Bucktown bistro; if some complain the "close" seating is "not conversation-friendly", loyalists point instead to moderate tabs and say "well-meaning" staffers contribute to the overall "good vibe."

Cafe Ba-Ba-Reeba! *Spanish* | 23 | 20 | 20 | $32 |

Lincoln Park | 2024 N. Halsted St. (Armitage Ave.) | 773-935-5000 | www.cafebabareeba.com

A "Chicago classic" that's "been around forever" (or since 1985), this "lively", "always reliable" Lincoln Park Spaniard "never fails to please" with its "vast menu" of "interesting", "authentic" small plates, plus "delish" paella and "the best" sangria, all at "approachable" prices; "snappy" servers work the "cozy" confines, "keeping a steady pace of food coming", so it's still a "great go-to" for "groups of friends or romantic dates"; P.S. the "beautiful" patio is now enclosed thanks to a post-Survey remodel (which may not be reflected in the Decor score).

Cafe Central Ⓜ *French* | 23 | 19 | 23 | $38 |

Highland Park | 455 Central Ave. (bet. Linden & St. Johns Aves.) | 847-266-7878 | www.cafecentral.net

The "classic bistro menu brings comfort" and the "noisy", "busy atmosphere" brings "great people-watching" at this "casual" Highland Park Frenchie putting out "well-prepared", "classic bistro" dishes; despite "tight quarters", "friendly" staffers "make diners feel comfortable", and while it may be "nothing fancy", "reasonable prices" further ensure it comes "recommended."

Cafecito *Coffeehouse/Cuban* | 23 | 11 | 18 | $10 |

Loop | 26 E. Congress Pkwy. (Wasabash Ave.) | 312-922-2233 | www.cafecitochicago.com

"Delicious", "pressed to perfection" Cuban sandwiches star at this "festive" Loop cafe that's a "charming" place to "grab a bite"; "out-of-this-world" coffee, "quick, friendly" service and "easy-on-the-wallet" prices provide other reasons to "go over and over again."

	FOOD	DECOR	SERVICE	COST

Café des Architectes *French*

24 | 25 | 24 | $56

Gold Coast | Sofitel Chicago Water Tower | 20 E. Chestnut St. (Wabash Ave.) | 312-324-4063 | www.cafedesarchitectes.com

"*C'est si bon*" cheer fans of this "chic" Gold Coast getaway "hidden" in the Sofitel Chicago Water Tower where "innovative", "contemporary" French fare (including one of the city's "best breakfasts") and "polished service" make for a "fine-dining" experience; it's not cheap, but many say prices are "reasonable" given its "swanky atmosphere", leaving some to wonder why it's still "somewhat overlooked" by "the cool crowd"; P.S. the Food score may not reflect a recent chef change.

Café Iberico ❶ *Spanish*

22 | 17 | 19 | $30

River North | 737 N. LaSalle Dr. (bet. Chicago Ave. & Superior St.) | 312-573-1510 | www.cafeiberico.com

"Every day is a party" at this "bustling, boisterous" River North "tapas standard", "a favorite for large groups" seeking a "wide selection" of "well-crafted" "authentic" Spanish plates bolstered by "amazing sangria"; sure, the "huge" "community center"-like space "lacks decor", service can be "slow" and a no-reservations policy (except for parties of six or more) often results in "long waits" (especially on weekends), but "affordable" tabs still ensure it's a "must."

Cafe Laguardia *Cuban/Mexican*

22 | 20 | 21 | $28

Bucktown | 2111 W. Armitage Ave. (bet. Hoyne Ave. & Leavitt St.) | 773-862-5996 | www.cafelaguardia.com

Be "transported to Havana" at this "casual", "reasonably priced" Bucktown "break from Chicago" featuring "well-seasoned" "authentic" Cuban-Mexican dishes ferried by "caring" servers who "go that extra mile"; the funky space includes a lounge area "full of charm and character", and live music (Tuesdays and Wednesdays) provides an opportunity to "salsa the night away."

Cafe Lucci *Italian*

25 | 21 | 24 | $38

Glenview | 609 Milwaukee Ave. (Central Rd.) | 847-729-2268 | www.cafelucci.com

"Gourmet" "old-school Italian" cooking highlighting "some interesting combinations" pairs with "a wine list to excite anyone's palate" at this "small" Glenview "gem; "elegant decor", "friendly, efficient" servers and moderate prices further explain why it "draws a big crowd."

Café Selmarie *American*

22 | 16 | 20 | $24

Lincoln Square | 4729 N. Lincoln Ave. (bet. Lawrence & Leland Aves.) | 773-989-5595 | www.cafeselmarie.com

"Go for brunch, stay for lunch" (or dinner) say fans of this "no-fuss, no-attitude" Lincoln Square "fixture" known for "homestyle" American cooking including "out-of-this-world" pastries and "to-die-for" desserts from its "top-notch bakery"; "cozy" confines and solid service make it a "pleasant" choice when you want to "eat with a friend and just be", so if it's "pricey" for the category, most insist it's "worth the splurge"; P.S. "on a nice day", try brunch on the "wonderful" patio.

Café Spiaggia *Italian*
25 | 23 | 24 | $57

Gold Coast | 980 N. Michigan Ave., 2nd fl. (Oak St.) | 312-280-2750 | www.cafespiaggia.com

"More approachable" than its "über high-end" "Mama" next door, this "divine" Gold Coast "must eat" turns out "exquisite pastas" and other "exceptionally executed" Italian dishes, allowing diners to experience "the flavors of Spiaggia" "without the fanciness" ("keep your jeans on and your jacket off"); "personable" staffers tend the "intimate, rustic" space and windows provide "magnificent views of the Magnificent Mile", so though it "ain't cheap", at least you "don't need a loan" to enjoy the "special" "Chicago experience."

Café Touché Ⓜ *French*
24 | 22 | 21 | $39

Edison Park | 6731 N. Northwest Hwy. (Oshkosh Ave.) | 773-775-0909 | www.cafetouche.com

Locals choose this "secret little" Edison Park bistro for "perfect portions" of "excellent French country food" backed by a "good wine list"; the wood and brick-lined space can get "a bit loud" but prices are "reasonable" and service solid, so most say it's an overall "treat", especially when dining outside on the sidewalk.

Cafe 28 *Cuban/Mexican*
25 | 20 | 22 | $32

North Center/St. Ben's | 1800 W. Irving Park Rd. (Ravenswood Ave.) | 773-528-2883 | www.cafe28.org

The Cuban-Mexican dishes "sing" at this "reasonably priced" North Center "favorite" where "large portions" of "delicious" fare, including "incredible honey-jalapeño pork chops", and "mojitos to die for" are set down by "friendly servers" "passionate about the food"; add in a "comfortable bar", casual dining room and "hidden patio", and it's a "neighborhood go-to", especially for the "great weekend brunch."

NEW Caffè Italia *Italian*
- | - | - | M

Elmwood Park | 2625 N. Harlem Ave. (bet. Schubert & Wrightwood Aves.) | 773-889-0455 | www.caffeitalia.com

Elmwood Park's specialty coffee roasters have expanded and remodeled into this cafe offering a midpriced Italian menu of antipasti, salumi, panini, brick-oven red and white pizza, pastas and gelato; it's all washed down with imported beer, wine and spirits in a modern brick storefront with an open kitchen, a bar, plenty of seating and walls papered with bright travel posters.

Caffè Rom *Italian*
24 | 25 | 27 | $10

Loop | Prudential Plaza | 180 N. Stetson Ave. (bet. E. Lake & E. Randolph Sts.) | 312-948-8888 Ⓢ

Loop | The Shoreham | 400 E. South Water St. (bet. E. Randolph St. & Lower Wacker Dr.) | 312-981-7766

Loop | Hyatt Center | 71 S. Wacker Dr. (bet. W. Arcade Pl. & W. Monroe St.) | 312-379-0291 Ⓢ
www.cafferom.com

Fans say you can find "some of the best coffee and espresso drinks in the Loop" at this Italian-style cafe trio also offering "tasty breakfast treats" and more "wholesome" "light" bites like sandwiches and

	FOOD	DECOR	SERVICE	COST

panini; a "welcoming", "European feel" elevates the "bright, modern" surrounds and "exemplary", "engaging" service is the cherry on top, making it a "great alternative to the big chains."

Calo Ristorante ⊘ *Italian* — 22 | 20 | 22 | $26

Andersonville | 5343 N. Clark St. (bet. Bryn Mawr & Foster Aves.) | 773-271-7782 | www.calorestaurant.com

An Andersonville "institution" since 1963, this "old-time" Italian delivers "large quantities" of "quality" fare, including "traditional pastas", all at "reasonable prices"; the "comfortable" room features front windows that open in summer and service is "always great", so loyalists insist it's "consistently good."

Campagnola *Italian* — 24 | 20 | 24 | $44

Evanston | 815 Chicago Ave. (Washington St.) | 847-475-6100 | www.campagnolarestaurant.com

"Casual Italian gets a serious upgrade" at this "consistent" Evanston "gem" where the "authentic" fare features "first-rate, fresh ingredients straightforwardly and thoughtfully prepared"; "pleasant" servers work the "comfortable" rustic environs, which along with "reasonable prices" help make it a "neighborhood go-to."

NEW Cantina Laredo *Mexican* — 17 | 23 | 19 | $32

River North | 508 N. State St. (bet. Grand Ave. & Illinois St.) | 312-955-0014 | www.cantinalaredo.com

Set in a "huge" "modern" space featuring fireplaces, skylights and a floating staircase, this midpriced River North link of a Texas-based chain offers "average to good" Mexican eats that don't quite live up to the "beautiful" setting; still, service is "attentive" and the overall "cool vibe" attracts a "lively" crowd.

Cape Cod *Seafood* — 22 | 23 | 24 | $60

Streeterville | Drake Hotel | 140 E. Walton St. (Michigan Ave.) | 312-787-2200 | www.thedrakehotel.com

"What a trip down memory lane" wax nostalgics of this "venerable" dining room in Streeterville's Drake Hotel, a circa-1933 "oldie but goodie" known for "classic" New England seafood, "lovely cocktails" and "old-school top-notch" service that beckons "back to a time when dining was elegant and people dressed for dinner"; while complainers find it a bit "tired" and "stuffy" and bemoan "expense-account" prices, it remains a "comfortable tradition, like going home" for many.

☒ Capital Grille *Steak* — 26 | 25 | 26 | $65

Streeterville | 633 N. St. Clair St. (Ontario St.) | 312-337-9400
Rosemont | 5340 N. River Rd. (bet. Foster Ave. & Technology Blvd.) | 847-671-8125
Lombard | 87 Yorktown Shopping Ctr. (Highland Ave.) | 630-627-9800
www.thecapitalgrille.com

"Let this be your splurge for red meat" exhort enthusiasts of this "upscale" steakhouse chain, a "carnivore's delight" delivering "quality", "cooked to perfection" chops, "heart-stopping" wines and sides that "aren't just an afterthought"; grouches grumble "been to one, been to them all", but fans point to "refined" service and "clubby" wood-accented surroundings that help it "hold its own" among the competition – just "be prepared to pay" for the "high-end" experience.

NEW Caravan *Mediterranean/Mideastern*   - | - | - | I

Uptown | 4810 N. Broadway (Rosemont Ave.) | 773-271-6022 | www.caravanrestaurantchicago.com

The antithesis of your neighborhood falafel shack, this Uptown arrival offers midpriced Middle Eastern and Med fare; the swanky, opulent setting, done up with chandeliers and disco balls, includes two bars, plush gold-patterned chairs and funky settees, and weekend nights heat up with DJs.

NEW Carlos & Carlos Ⓜ *Italian*   - | - | - | M

Arlington Heights | 27 W. Campbell St. (bet. Dunton & Vail Aves.) | 847-259-2600 | www.carlosandcarlosinc.com

After relocating (again), this Arlington Heights "keeper", a reprise of the onetime Bucktown original, has a "broadened" menu of "inventive" Northern Italian fare at "value" prices that extend to the "aggressively priced" wine list; bistro-style surroundings and an outdoor patio complete the picture.

Carlucci *Italian*   22 | 21 | 23 | $49

Rosemont | Riverway Complex | 6111 N. River Rd. (Higgins Rd.) | 847-518-0990 | www.carluccirosemont.com

The "combination of good food and good service" makes this "bustling", "slightly upscale" Rosemont Italian set in Tuscan-style digs a "safe bet" for "business crowds" and travelers just in from O'Hare; if it seems "overpriced" to some, others say it's an "always consistent" "meeting spot"; P.S. the Downers Grove locale is unaffiliated.

Carlucci *Italian*   20 | 20 | 22 | $43

Downers Grove | 1801 Butterfield Rd. (I-355) | 630-512-0990 | www.carluccirestaurant.com

For "traditional" Italian fare in contemporary white-tablecloth surrounds, diners find this moderate Downers Grove spot a "relaxing" pick; the space is divided up into three separate rooms (one with a fireplace), and "friendly" service provides additional appeal; P.S. it's unaffiliated with the Rosemont locale.

Carmichael's Chicago   20 | 21 | 22 | $48
Steak House *Steak*

West Loop | 1052 W. Monroe St. (bet. Aberdeen & Morgan Sts.) | 312-433-0025 | www.carmichaelsteakhouse.com

"Take your man" to this West Loop chophouse for "steaks and martinis without the attitude" suggest diners who find the staff "friendly" and the location "easy"; the clubby space has an "old-time" feel, and though it's not cheap many say it's "reasonable" for the genre."

Carmine's *Italian*   21 | 20 | 21 | $41

Gold Coast | 1043 N. Rush St. (bet. Bellevue Pl. & Cedar St.) | 312-988-7676 | www.rosebudrestaurants.com

Relive "the glory days of the Rush Street supper club scene" at this "lively" Gold Coaster from the Rosebud team where "mammoth por-

	FOOD	DECOR	SERVICE	COST

tions" of "traditional" Italian eats come via servers who "complement the food"; tabs are "reasonable", if "somewhat inflated because of the location", and critics complaining it's "overhyped" and "overcrowded" are countered by others opining about its "access" to "exceptional people-watching."

Carnivale *Nuevo Latino* 22 | 26 | 21 | $43

West Loop | 702 W. Fulton Mkt. (Union Ave.) | 312-850-5005 | www.carnivalechicago.com

"Festive", "loud" and "happening" sums up this "huge" West Loop "social arena" that "lives up to its name" thanks to "vibrant" decor ("colors explode at you"), "fabulous" drinks and Nuevo Latino dishes so "flavorful" some have a "foodgasm"; "knowledgeable" servers contribute to the "lively" atmosphere and prices are "reasonable" too, so even if a few sniff it's just "so-so", most agree it's "perfect for large groups."

Carson's *BBQ* 22 | 16 | 19 | $33

River North | 612 N. Wells St. (Ontario St.) | 312-280-9200
Deerfield | 200 Waukegan Rd. (bet. Kates & Lake Cook Rds.) | 847-374-8500
www.ribs.com

"Bring it on" say fans of the "delectable" ribs rubbed with "smoky, sweet" sauce, "mounds" of complimentary chicken liver pâté and other "classic" BBQ offerings (the stuff of "cardiologists' nightmares") served by "accommodating" staffers at this circa-1977 River North original and its Deerfield double; there's "not a great deal of atmosphere" (the River North "remodel doesn't matter"), and some find it "a bit pricey" "compared to the competition", but it's still "quite popular", nonetheless.

Catch 35 *Seafood* 24 | 22 | 23 | $49

Loop | Leo Burnett Bldg. | 35 W. Wacker Dr. (bet. Dearborn & State Sts.) | 312-346-3500
Naperville | 35 S. Washington St. (bet. Benton & Van Buren Aves.) | 630-717-3500
www.catch35.com

Afishionados catch "amazingly fresh" seafood at this "high-end" Loop and Naperville twosome turning out "solid", "well-executed" fare, including some dishes with "interesting" "Asian flair"; "elegant" decor and a "knowledgeable staff" are other pluses, so though "not for the faint of wallet", it's a "nice change of pace from all the beeferies"; P.S. Downtown has a "great piano bar."

Cellar at The Stained Glass *Eclectic* 22 | 19 | 21 | $42

Evanston | 820 Clark St. (bet. Benson & Sherman Aves.) | 847-864-8678 | www.thecellarevanston.com

There's "never a dull bite" assert acolytes of this "lively" Evanston hangout tended by "friendly" staffers where the "imaginative" Eclectic small plates are "big on flavor" and the "excellent" wine list is accompanied by an even "better beer selection"; prices are more "accessible" than its nearby Stained Glass sib, and though it can still be a "bit of a splurge" for some, it remains a "popular" "drop-in place" (though no reservations may result in a wait).

Cemitas Puebla *Mexican* 24 | 6 | 19 | $11

Humboldt Park | 3619 W. North Ave. (Monticello Ave.) | 773-772-8435 | www.cemitaspuebla.com

"Some of the best streetlike Mexican food" hails from this bargain-priced Humboldt Park "hole-in-the-wall" famous for its "phenomenal" namesake *cemitas* (sandwiches); a "friendly" staff that "treats you like family" provides another reason to brave the "dingy, dive"-like digs and somewhat "desolate" location.

Ceres' Table ⊠ *American* 24 | 17 | 22 | $44

Uptown | 4882 N. Clark St. (bet. Ainslie St. & Lawrence Ave.) | 773-878-4882 | www.cerestable.com

Set in an "unlikely location" on a "nondescript block", this Uptown New American is the "definition of a hidden gem" cheer fans who say chef-owner Giuseppe Scurato's "creativity shines" in the "delicious" seasonal fare that's further lifted by "varied, well-priced" wines; the "sleek, bordering on stark" decor "leaves something to be desired" (though recently added "sound boards help the noise level"), but "warm, welcoming" service and an "excellent price point for the quality" make it "worth knowing and worth visiting."

Chalkboard *American* 21 | 20 | 20 | $39

Lakeview | 4343 N. Lincoln Ave. (bet. Montrose & Pensacola Aves.) | 773-477-7144 | www.chalkboardrestaurant.com

The chalkboard displays chef-owner Gilbert Langlois' ever-changing menu at this "small" farm-to-table New American in Lakeview where comfort food faves (especially the "great fried chicken") make it "perfect on a cold winter night"; even if a few find the fare "overwrought", prices are moderate, and service is "warm" so most say it's a "worth-a-trip" "neighborhood place"; P.S. they also serve weekend afternoon tea and Sunday brunch.

☑ Charlie Trotter's ⊠Ⓜ *American* 28 | 26 | 28 | $152

Lincoln Park | 816 W. Armitage Ave. (bet. Dayton & Halsted Sts.) | 773-248-6228 | www.charlietrotters.com

"Well-heeled foodies worship" at this "first-rate" Lincoln Park "icon", the "grande dame of fine dining" with "jaw-dropping", "impeccably presented" New American tasting menus that "blend distinctive taste, color and texture", "reminding you of what perfection tastes like"; famed also for its "legendary wine list", "reverential", "exemplary service" and "beautiful" space, it's "extravagantly" priced, but those who insist "you'll leave feeling as though you've been on an amazing trip" commend it as a "classic choice for a big Chicago night out", and one that "will be missed", as it's set to close in August 2012.

Cheesecake Factory *American* 20 | 20 | 20 | $30

Streeterville | John Hancock Ctr. | 875 N. Michigan Ave. (bet. Chestnut St. & Delaware Pl.) | 312-337-1101 ◗

(continued)

Cheesecake Factory

Lincolnshire | Lincolnshire Commons | 930 Milwaukee Ave. (Aptakisic Rd.) | 847-955-2350

Skokie | Westfield Shoppingtown | 4999 Old Orchard Ctr. (Skokie Blvd.) | 847-329-8077

Schaumburg | Woodfield Shopping Ctr. | 53 Woodfield Rd. (Meacham Rd.) | 847-619-1090

Oak Brook | Oakbrook Center Mall | 2020 Spring Rd. (bet. Commerce St. & Harger Rd.) | 630-573-1800
www.thecheesecakefactory.com

For "loads of calories, lots of noise and a menu that does not quit", diners hit these links of the "busy, dizzy" "mass-market" chain where the "colossal portions" of "dependable" American eats can "feed a family of six"; service is "courteous" and prices are "reasonable", so "if you can tolerate the wait for a table" you'll "definitely get your money's worth."

Chef's Station Ⓜ American   25 | 21 | 22 | $54

Evanston | Davis Street Metro Station | 915 Davis St. (Church St.) | 847-570-9821 | www.chefs-station.com

At once "civilized", "quirky" and "charming", this "casual" "fine-dining" destination "hidden away" in an Evanston Metro station crafts "consistently outstanding" New American fare in an "unpretentious, comfortable-arty setting" that's "quiet and amenable to conversation"; if holdouts find it "overpriced", "excellent wine choices", "friendly" service and an "atmosphere that works for family or friends" have many vowing a "return trip."

Chens *Asian*   21 | 19 | 20 | $24

Wrigleyville | 3506 N. Clark St. (Addison St.) | 773-549-9100 | www.chenschicago.com

The "appealing mix" of "quality Chinese" and sushi "in a classy setting" makes this "inexpensive" Wrigleyville waystation "a welcome change" from the neighborhood "norm"; "energetic, personable" service adds further appeal, so even if it's "not the best food in town", it's "consistently good" "for a quick bite before a ball game" and a "go-to" for "delivery so fast, you'd swear they have a truck circling the block."

Chez Joël Ⓜ *French*   26 | 23 | 25 | $46

Little Italy/University Village | 1119 W. Taylor St. (May St.) | 312-226-6479 | www.chezjoelbistro.com

An "outstanding neighborhood gem" featuring "high-quality" "French comfort food", this "thriving", "comfortable" "Little Italy charmer" also wields a "nice wine list with a variety of grapes and prices"; throw in that it "feels like Paris" and tabs are "small for what you get", and loyalists laud it's "what a bistro should be."

Chicago Bagel Authority *Bakery/Sandwiches*   25 | 15 | 19 | $10

NEW Lakeview | 955 W. Belmont Ave. (bet. Sheffield & Wilton Aves.) | 773-549-1982

(continued)

(continued)

Chicago Bagel Authority
Lincoln Park | 953 W. Armitage Ave. (Sheffield Ave.) | 773-248-9606
www.eatcba.com

"Awesome" bagels plus a "huge menu with every sandwich combo under the sun" and baked goods like "big, soft" cookies brings noshers to this Lincoln Park "joint" (with a Lakeview sib); staffers "don't take themselves too seriously", and if "it takes awhile to steam your bagel", patient fans profess "perfection is worth the wait."

Chicago Chop House *Steak*
24 | 20 | 23 | $74

River North | 60 W. Ontario St. (bet. Clark & Dearborn Sts.) |
312-787-7100 | www.chicagochophouse.com

A "legend for major meat", this "true old-school steakhouse" set in a "comfortable" River North townhouse is considered "the ticket" by those craving "tender", "sumptuous" chops in "bustling", "authentic Chicago" environs decorated with photos of local celebrities; if some grouse "good grief it's gotten expensive", others counter service is "pleasant" and "knowledgeable", so when you "wish to eat where beef is king", "look no further."

Chicago Curry House *Indian/Nepalese*
20 | 15 | 20 | $29

South Loop | 899 S. Plymouth Ct. (9th St.) | 312-362-9999 |
www.curryhouseonline.com

For "something different", South Loopers visit this Indian-Nepalese offering a "huge" menu of "usual and unusual" dishes ("try the momo"); servers are "helpful" and the atmosphere "pleasant", so even if the space doesn't quite match, most appreciate the "inexpensive" prices fit for "lovers of deals"

Chicago Cut Steakhouse ❂ *Steak*
26 | 25 | 25 | $70

River North | 300 N. LaSalle St. (bet. Kinzie St. & Wacker Dr.) |
312-329-1800 | www.chicagocutsteakhouse.com

"Ridiculously good steaks and sides", "refreshing menu twists" and a "cool iPad wine list" make this "glossy" River North chophouse "truly memorable", ensuring its "see-and-be-seen dining room" is often "full of the city's power brokers"; "outstanding", "knowledgeable" servers and a "wow patio overlooking the river" are further reasons converts "could live there" – though you do "pay dearly" for it and so do your ears (the "crazy" noise level "makes shouting necessary"); P.S. chef Jackie Shen's post-Survey departure isn't reflected in the Food score.

Chicago Diner *Diner/Vegetarian*
23 | 15 | 22 | $19

Lakeview | 3411 N. Halsted St. (Roscoe St.) | 773-935-6696 |
www.veggiediner.com

A "vegetarian paradise", this "hippie-inspired" Lakeview diner has "stayed true to its mission" for nearly 30 years, providing "interesting", eco-conscious eats (many of which are vegan too) "cooked just right", plus "rich, flavorful" "milk-free milkshakes" (a "must-try"); there's a "cute staff" and the "divey" diner atmosphere befits the budget prices, so "long lines" are the "only downside" for most.

FOOD | DECOR | SERVICE | COST

Chicago Firehouse   *American*   22 | 22 | 21 | $47

South Loop | 1401 S. Michigan Ave. (14th St.) | 312-786-1401 | www.chicagofirehouse.com

A "pioneer of the South Loop renaissance", this revived "landmark with lots of history" does "delicious", "hearty" Traditional American food in a "charming" setting complete with the "old firehouse pole in the bar"; if a few hotheads assert it's merely "ordinary", it's still a "dependable" option especially given its "excellent wine-by-the-glass selection", "pleasing" service and "beautiful summer patio."

Chicago Pizza & Oven Grinder Co.   ♥ *Pizza*   25 | 18 | 21 | $24

Lincoln Park | 2121 N. Clark St. (bet. Dickens & Webster Aves.) | 773-248-2570 | www.chicagopizzaandovengrinder.com

The "upside-down pizza in a bowl" pot pies turn guests "giddy" at this cash-only "Lincoln Park institution", a "wood lodge look-alike" that also excels with "Italian grinders" and "amazing salads"; it's "not for the faint of heart" given the "long waits" (no reservations), quirky "seating system" (the host "somehow remembers your face") and "cramped" tables, but it's an affordable "treat" for something "different", especially with "out-of-towners" in tow.

Chicago Prime Steakhouse   *Steak*   - | - | - | E

Schaumburg | 1444 E. Algonquin Rd. (bet. Meacham Rd. & Thorntree Ln.) | 847-969-9900 | www.chicagoprimesteakhouse.com

"Fantastic" steaks star at this Schaumburg chophouse also known for its fortune 500 platter (lobster tails, oysters, crab cake, etc.) and "impressive" wine list; the dark wood–accented space is enhanced by a fireplace, and there's also a year-round outdoor patio.

Chicago Q   *BBQ*   22 | 23 | 21 | $37

Gold Coast | 1160 N. Dearborn St. (bet. Division & Elm Sts.) | 312-642-1160 | www.chicagoqrestaurant.com

"Chicago modern meets Southern BBQ" at pit-master Lee Ann Whippen's "cool" Gold Coast contender where diners with "an empty stomach and posh clothing" feast on "upscale" 'cue including "outta control" smoked ribs, "delicious" Kobe brisket and "rustic" sides set down by "friendly" servers in a "rocking, jam-packed" room; bean counters find prices "high" for what's on offer, but most don't mind since it's "total comfort-food heaven."

Chicago's Pizza   ● *Pizza*   16 | 10 | 16 | $19

Lakeview | 3114 N. Lincoln Ave. (bet. Ashland & Southport Aves.) | 773-477-2777
Lincoln Park | 3006 N. Sheffield Ave. (bet. Barry & Wellington Aves.) | 773-755-4030
Ravenswood | 1919 W. Montrose Ave. (bet. Damen & Ravenswood Aves.) | 773-348-1700
Old Irving Park | 4520 W. Irving Park Rd. (bet. Cicero & Kostner Aves.) | 773-427-0100
www.chicagos-pizza.com

"Slices hit the spot every time" at this "unpretentious" "long-lived" pizza quartet, a popular choice for "late-night drunk food" or "the next morning's hangover"; but sourpusses, wary of the "spartan environment", contend it's merely "ordinary" and "only good at 5 AM because it's the only thing open"; P.S. hours and BYO policy (some are, some aren't) vary by location.

Chief O'Neill's *Pub Food* | 17 | 20 | 18 | $24 |

Northwest Side | 3471 N. Elston Ave. (Albany Ave.) | 773-583-3066 | www.chiefoneillspub.com

A "warm Irish pub atmosphere" brings Northwest Siders to this "woody" bi-level bar where the eats are not always "exciting" but boast "occasional flashes of fried-food brilliance"; with solid service, frequent live music and a "fantastic outdoor area", it's the "perfect place to raise your glass after a hard week."

Chilam Balam 🛇 Ⓜ 🗡 *Mexican* | 25 | 16 | 20 | $34 |

Lakeview | 3023 N. Broadway (bet. Barry & Wellington Aves.) | 773-296-6901 | www.chilambalamchicago.com

"World-class", "super-seasonal" Mexican small plates wow guests at this "tiny" cash-only Lakeview "treasure" where the "basement atmosphere" is trumped by "penthouse food" and "BYO adds an extra draw" (though there's margarita mix and "luscious" virgin sangria); "insane waits" are downsides and the "reasonable" prices can "add up", but most agree it's "definitely worth it"; P.S. the Food score may not reflect chef Chuy Valencia's departure.

NEW Chilapan Ⓜ *Mexican* | ▽ 24 | 15 | 20 | $29 |

Ravenswood | 1522 W. Montrose Ave. (Ashland Ave.) | 773-878-1077 | www.tenangrypitbulls.com

Expect "authentic Mexican comfort food" at this Ravenswood storefront with a bright-blue facade and vibrant interior featuring mismatched seating; its BYO policy "is a plus", as are "warm, friendly" staffers and prices that won't break the bank.

Chizakaya 🛇 Ⓜ *Japanese* | 24 | 20 | 20 | $38 |

Lakeview | 3056 N. Lincoln Ave. (bet. Barry & Wellington Aves.) | 773-697-4725 | www.chizakaya.com

"Be adventuresome" and "open your eyes to Japanese pub cuisine" at this affordable izakaya in Lakeview where "inventive" fare including "delicious skewers" and starters like puffed pig's ears are matched with sake, shochu and other powerful libations; the lively space, with an open kitchen and both communal and smaller tables, is tended by a "helpful" staff, making it extra-accessible for the uninitiated.

C-House *Seafood* | 21 | 20 | 21 | $47 |

Streeterville | Affinia Chicago Hotel | 166 E. Superior St. (St. Clair St.) | 312-523-0923 | www.c-houserestaurant.com

Finatics (including self-proclaimed "suckers for a good raw bar") praise the seafood and other "high-quality" if somewhat pricey small plates at "celebrity chef" Marcus Samuelsson's Streeterville outpost further elevated by "knowledgeable" servers; "cool" decor and a rooftop terrace enhance the mood, though a few wish it were more "memorable."

Cité *American* | 19 | 24 | 19 | $69 |

Streeterville | Lake Point Tower | 505 N. Lake Shore Dr., 70th fl. (Navy Pier) | 312-644-4050 | www.citechicago.com

"Amazing views of the city" from the 70th floor of the Lake Point Tower lure diners to this elegant Streeterville New American where "romantic" environs trump the "fine" fare and service; still, the "fantastic" panoramic vistas make it "worth going" for "drinks at the bar around sunset", "an anniversary or a birthday" or when "you're in trouble with the wife", just "bring a fat wallet."

NEW City Farms
Market & Grill M *Sandwiches* | - | - | - | I |

North Center/St. Ben's | 147 W. Irving Park Rd. (Janssen Ave.) | 773-883-2767 | www.cityfarmsgrill.com

The brainchild of an ex-banker, this unfettered, farm-to-fork North Center sandwich slinger offers modern handhelds (and updated AM eats) in a space with an open kitchen and communal wood table seating; suppers and a companion food truck are also in the works.

City Park Grill *American* | 17 | 16 | 19 | $27 |

Highland Park | 1783 St. Johns Ave. (Central Ave.) | 847-432-9111 | www.thecityparkgrill.com

You can satisfy "any degree of hunger" at this "comfortable" and "relaxed" Highland Park American offering salads, sandwiches and other standbys for "reasonable" tabs; critics cite "so-so" victuals and suggest the decor needs "beefing up", but "friendly" service and a "varied" menu help "keep it in rotation", especially for the "older crowd."

City Provisions M *Deli* | ∇ 25 | 15 | 25 | $16 |

Ravenswood | 1818 W. Wilson Ave. (bet. Ravenswood & Wolcott Aves.) | 773-293-2489 | www.cityprovisions.com

"Everything is done the right way" at this bright, casual Ravenswood storefront that dishes "artisanal deli food" like "brilliant sandwiches", hearty entrees, soups and salads and also butchers, roasts and cures meats and bakes its own bread; service gets high marks, and there's also a counter for those looking to take out.

Claim Company *American* | 17 | 15 | 18 | $24 |

Northbrook | Northbrook Court Shopping Ctr. | 2000 Northbrook Ct. (bet. Lake Cook Rd. & Northbrook Court Dr.) | 847-291-9111 | www.theclaimcompany.com

An "excellent choice with children", this American in the Northbrook Court Shopping Center is famous for its "killer" salad bar and "huge shareable burgers"; "service is generally prompt" and tabs affordable, so though it's "not as notable as the original", it's still a "good place to stop while shopping" and "reliable" for "after-work drinks."

The Clubhouse *American* | 23 | 23 | 23 | $38 |

Oak Brook | Oakbrook Center Mall | 298 Oakbrook Ctr. (Rte. 83) | 630-472-0600 | www.theclubhouse.com

There's "something for everybody" at this "casual" American in Oak Brook mall where "well-prepared" "comfort food" comes in "hearty" portions "big enough to share"; "a lot of after-work action" takes place at the "busy" bar, while the quieter upstairs dining room is "special-occasion" worthy say fans who also take solid service and affordable tabs into consideration when deeming it an overall "reliable" pick.

Club Lucky *Italian*
22 | 18 | 21 | $33

Bucktown | 1824 W. Wabansia Ave. (Honore St.) | 773-227-2300 | www.clubluckychicago.com

Smells of "traditional" "homestyle Italian cooking" "waft for blocks" from this "'faux old-school" Bucktown "supper club" where there are "no surprises", just "huge portions", "solid" eats and "killer martinis"; "reasonable costs", "friendly" servers and a vibrant atmosphere" further explain why it's "managed to remain hip and fun" since its 1990 inception.

Coalfire Pizza Ⓜ *Pizza*
24 | 14 | 21 | $21

Noble Square | 1321 W. Grand Ave. (bet. Ada & Elizabeth Sts.) | 312-226-2625 | www.coalfirechicago.com

"Rich sauces", "fresh ingredients" and "light", "crispy" crusts charred "with a bit of black" "all come together", resulting in "sublime" pizzas at this "unpretentious" Noble Square pie house; "friendly" service "warms up the uninspired setting" and so regulars wish it "would become a chain."

Coast Sushi Bar ☽ *Japanese*
25 | 21 | 21 | $34

Bucktown | 2045 N. Damen Ave. (bet. Dickens & McLean Aves.) | 773-235-5775 | www.coastsushibar.com

Southcoast *Japanese*

South Loop | 1700 S. Michigan Ave. (bet. 16th & 18th Sts.) | 312-662-1700 | www.southcoastsushi.com

"You can rely on" this South Loop Japanese and its Bucktown BYO twin for "high-quality" sushi, "imaginative" rolls and "delicious entrees" in "modern" environs; service also gets high marks and tabs are "good", so they're often "hopping."

Coco Pazzo *Italian*
25 | 24 | 24 | $54

River North | 300 W. Hubbard St. (Franklin St.) | 312-836-0900 | www.cocopazzochicago.com

One of "Chicago's most sophisticated Italians" say fans of this River North "top bet" where the "delicious", "authentic Tuscan" offerings include both "solid" "classics" and more "creative" choices; "professional", "subtle service", "comfortable" velvet draped surroundings and a long Boot-based wine list featuring "a nice selection from various regions" are other assets that help make somewhat "high" prices feel "reasonable."

Coco Pazzo Café *Italian*
23 | 21 | 22 | $42

Streeterville | Red Roof Inn | 636 N. St. Clair St. (Ontario St.) | 312-664-2777 | www.cocopazzochicago.com

The "informal" "junior version of Coco Pazzo", this longtime Streeterville "favorite" maintains its "go-to" status with "thoughtfully prepared" Northern Italian fare, "helpful" service

	FOOD	DECOR	SERVICE	COST

and "fair prices"; inside features a "relaxed country atmosphere" and outside offers prime "people-watching", so "plan ahead" because it's often "busy."

Conte Di Savoia *Deli/Italian*　24 | 11 | 19 | $10

Little Italy/University Village | 1438 W. Taylor St. (bet. Laflin & Loomis Sts.) | 312-666-3471
West Side | 2227 W. Taylor St. (bet. Oakley Blvd. & Ogden Ave.) | 312-666-4335
www.contedisavoia.com

"High-quality meats and cheeses" make for "outstanding" sandwiches at this "super-authentic" Italian deli duo in Little Italy and the West Side; set in a "neighborhood grocery store", it has "few" "bare-bones tables" so though an outdoor patio (in both locales) adds more seats, many suggest it's "best for takeout", especially if you also take advantage of the "second-to-none" shopping selection; P.S. despite on-site liquor stores, alcohol isn't allowed in the dining area.

Convito Café & Market *French/Italian*　20 | 19 | 19 | $38

Wilmette | Plaza del Lago | 1515 Sheridan Rd. (bet. Westerfield Dr. & 10th St.) | 847-251-3654 | www.convitocafeandmarket.com
Set in the back of the market, this "charming" Wilmette cafe appeals with "trusty salads", pastas and other "usually well-prepared" French-Italian fare; a "wonderful selection of wine" leads to lingering in the "cozy" confines and tabs are "modest", so though it's "nothing exceptional", it's still a "dependable" "local go-to."

Coobah *Filipino/Nuevo Latino*　22 | 19 | 19 | $34

Lakeview | 3423 N. Southport Ave. (bet. Newport Ave. & Roscoe St.) | 773-528-2220 | www.coobah.com
"Flavorful, exciting" Filipino–Nuevo Latino "fusion food" in "sexy", "exotic" environs provide a "wonderful escape" from the "blahs" at this "affordable" Lakeview haunt; dissenters dub service "forgettable" and warn of "tables crammed next to each other", but fans focus instead on the "great" drinks and "fun atmosphere" that "adds to the experience."

Cooper's Hawk Winery & Restaurant *American*　21 | 22 | 22 | $37

Wheeling | 583 N. Milwaukee Ave. (Wolf Rd.) | 847-215-1200
NEW **Arlington Heights** | 798 W. Algonquin Rd. (bet. Embers Ln. & Goebbert Rd.) | 847-981-0900
South Barrington | 100 W. Higgins Rd. (Bartlett Rd.) | 847-836-9463
Burr Ridge | 510 Village Center Dr. (bet. Bridgewell & Lincolnshire Drs.) | 630-887-0123
Orland Park | 15690 S. Harlem Ave. (bet. 157th St. & Wheeler Dr.) | 708-633-0200
NEW **Naperville** | 1740 Freedom Dr. (bet. Diehl Rd. & Independence Ave.) | 630-245-8000
www.coopershawkwinery.com
Diners "unwind" at this "happening" American chain, a "gathering place for family and friends" with its "strong" menu of "wholesome"

"comfort food", "interesting variety" of wines made on-site and "prompt", "consistent" service; judges who "just don't get it" complain of "noisy", "conversation-challenged" digs and say it's "overpriced for the quality", but most find the tabs "reasonable" and like that there's "something for everyone in the group."

The Counter *Burgers*　　　　　　20 | 15 | 17 | $18

Lincoln Park | 666 W. Diversey Pkwy. (bet. Clark & Orchard Sts.) | 773-935-1995 | www.thecounterburger.com

It's "truly made your way" at this "laid-back" Lincoln Park chain link where it's an "intellectual exercise" to wade through the "unbelievable" array of options while "customizing everything" from burger to sauce to bun; service can be "spotty" and the "low-tech" space may not earn many points, but supporters say with "so many choices" it "never disappoints."

⛨ Courtright's Ⓜ *American*　　　　28 | 28 | 28 | $70

Willow Springs | 8989 S. Archer Ave. (Willow Springs Rd.) | 708-839-8000 | www.courtrights.com

A "beautiful, serene setting in the forest preserves" provides the backdrop for "well-prepared", "innovative" "foodie" fare at this "upscale" Willow Springs New American; "exemplary" treatment and a "well-decorated", "romantic" room further cement its "special-occasion" status.

Cozy Noodles & Rice *Thai*　　　　23 | 20 | 23 | $14

Lakeview | 3456 N. Sheffield Ave. (bet. Addison St. & Belmont Ave.) | 773-327-0100 | www.cozychicago.com

"Delicious Thai dishes" at "super-cheap" prices leave enthusiasts cheering this tiny Lakeview BYO "rocks"; "whimsical" and "quirky" toy store decor lends "charm" and service is "friendly" too, but with limited seating many opt for "very fast takeout."

🆕 Crêperie Saint-Germain Ⓜ *French*　－ | － | － | I

Evanston | 1512 Sherman St. (bet. Grove & Lake Sts.) | 847-859-2647 | www.creperiestgermain.com

Crêpes sweet and savory (the latter made with organic buckwheat), salads and hors d'oeuvres including classic onion soup and duck terrine come out of the kitchen at this midpriced French beneath a striped awning in Evanston; a massive map of the Paris Metro monopolizes one wall in the casual cafe setting with warm wood, butcher block tables and hanging window frames.

Crisp *Korean*　　　　　　　　　24 | 11 | 16 | $13

Lakeview | 2940 N. Broadway St. (Wellington Ave.) | 773-697-7610 | www.crisponline.com

"Decadent", "sinfully good" Korean "crispy fried chicken in spicy and savory flavors" stars at this "reasonably priced" Lakeview BYO where diners opting for other options like burritos and "tasty" rice bowls often find themselves "jealous for the rest of the meal"; the counter-service space offers "no real frills but no snobbery either", so many join the ranks of "satisfied diners with greasy fingers and smudged faces."

	FOOD	DECOR	SERVICE	COST

Cumin *Indian/Nepalese*   24 | 18 | 18 | $29

Wicker Park | 1414 N. Milwaukee Ave. (bet. Evergreen & Wolcott Aves.) | 773-342-1414 | www.cumin-chicago.com

"The smell of spices will draw you in" and the "delicious" fare will "keep you there" assure acolytes of this "casual yet modern" Wicker Park Indian-Nepalese offering "interesting" dishes filled with "exciting flavors"; toss in "friendly" service and "value" tabs and most "can't wait to go back."

Curry Hut Restaurant *Indian/Nepalese*   19 | 13 | 18 | $27

Highwood | 410 Sheridan Rd. (bet. Walker & Webster Aves.) | 847-432-2889 | www.curryhutrestaurant.com

Tasters "try new things" at this "value" Indian-Nepalese in Highwood offering "complex curries", "great veggie dishes" and other "solid" fare; the confines are "nothing fancy", but "servers are helpful", so if some shrug it "should be better", others find it a "nice change of pace."

Custom House Tavern *American*   26 | 25 | 24 | $51

Printers Row | Wyndham Blake | 500 S. Dearborn St. (Congress Pkwy.) | 312-523-0200 | www.customhouse.cc

"Custom-made for fine dining", this Printers Row New American in the Wyndham Blake is "not a run-of-the-mill hotel" eatery suggest supporters touting the "many interesting choices" and "top-notch" (if "limited") menu augmented by "innovative" cocktails; with "helpful", "dignified" service and a modern setting it's an "unexpected treat."

NEW Cyrano's Farm Kitchen *French*   - | - | - | M
(fka Cyrano's Bistrot & Wine Bar)

River North | 546 N. Wells St. (bet. Grand Ave. & Ohio St.) | 312-467-0546

This do-over of Gallic chef Didier Durand's long-standing River North bistro features, yes, a more farm-focused French menu – think lamb shank, boudin blanc and lots of fromage; the charming, barn-inspired decor includes farm tools, ceiling beams and vintage French chandeliers, and there's still sidewalk seating.

D & J Bistro Ⓜ *French*   25 | 19 | 24 | $44

Lake Zurich | First Bank Plaza Ctr. | 466 S. Rand Rd./Rte. 12 (Rte. 22) | 847-438-8001 | www.dj-bistro.com

"Still going strong after many years", this "true suburban gem" set in an "unlikely" Lake Zurich strip mall earns "bravos" for its "dependably outstanding" French bistro "classics" bolstered by a "fresh" wine list in "cozy" environs elevated by a "warm, friendly" staff; it also provides a "strong value", so while food is "better than the ambiance", unswerving supporters agree it's "aging gracefully."

Dan McGee Ⓜ *American*   - | - | - | M

Frankfort | 9975 W. Lincoln Hwy. (Locust St.) | 815-469-7750 | www.danmcgees.com

For "Downtown food in the far south suburbs", this Frankfort New American offers "well-considered", "original preparations" in an "intimate" space hidden behind a "nondescript" storefront; the "ur-

	FOOD	DECOR	SERVICE	COST

ban ambiance" and "good service" further add up to a "pleasurable" experience, though the pricing is "first-class" for the area.

☑ Davanti Enoteca *Italian* | 27 | 23 | 23 | $39 |

Little Italy/University Village | 1359 W. Taylor St. (Loomis St.) | 312-226-5550 | www.davantichicago.com

"Inventive" takes on "rustic" Italian cuisine, including small plates with "enormous taste" and "lick-the-bowl" pastas, come via restaurateur Scott Harris (Mia Francesca, The Purple Pig) at this "laid-back" Little Italy enoteca where patrons can choose from the "interesting", "well-priced" wine list or BYO from the attached retail shop (for a $7 corkage); no-reservations mean there's "typically a wait", but the "knowledgeable" staff aptly handles the "crowds", so customers call it "casual dining at its best."

Dave's Italian Kitchen *Italian* | 18 | 14 | 18 | $22 |

Evanston | 1635 Chicago Ave. (bet. Church & Davis Sts.) | 847-864-6000 | www.davesitaliankitchen.com

"A favorite for decades", this "Evanston classic" caters to families and the "Northwestern crowd" with "large" plates of "simple, unpretentious" Southern Italian food served up by "fast" staffers in basic "basement" digs; if gourmets gripe "mediocre" meals are "fine for children, not so fine for adults", diehards declare it's "consistent", "cheap" and has "endured more than 30 years for good reason."

David Burke's Primehouse *Steak* | 25 | 22 | 24 | $73 |

River North | James Chicago Hotel | 616 N. Rush St. (Ontario St.) | 312-660-6000

"Delight" in "dry-aged perfection" at this chophouse in River North's James Hotel where "showman" David Burke delivers "humongous" steaks complemented by a "supporting cast" of "imaginative" eats like pretzel-crusted crab cakes and "the best starter popovers" in a "beautiful" room that's "upscale without being too highfalutin"; add in carefully "choreographed" service and it all "comes at a price" – though the prix fixe lunch is an "awesome deal" and the "weekend brunch can't be beat."

Davis Street Fishmarket *Seafood* | 20 | 17 | 18 | $35 |

Evanston | 501 Davis St. (Hinman Ave.) | 847-869-3474 | www.davisstreetfishmarket.com

"Satisfied" fans cast their votes for the "comfortable, casual fish dining done well" at this midpriced Evanston old-timer with "a bit of a New Orleans theme" to its "solid" seafood; the service swings from "very good" to "lacking" and some anglers say it's "just meh", but most reckon "there's a reason you have to get here early to get in."

Dawali *Mediterranean/Mideastern* | 22 | 12 | 21 | $15 |

NEW **Lincoln Park** | 1625 N. Halsted St. (bet. Armitage Ave. & Willow St.) | 312-944-5800
Albany Park | 4911 N. Kedzie Ave. (Ainslie St.) | 773-267-4200
www.dawalikitchen.com

Diners get their "shawarma fix" at these Med–Middle Eastern sibs delivering "tasty, consistent" plates at "amazing prices"; Lincoln

FOOD DECOR SERVICE COST

Park is BYO and convenient to nearby theaters, while the Albany Park locale is alcohol-free, and at both, decor that doesn't "match the food quality" means fans at both often opt for carryout.

Deca Restaurant + Bar *French* | 22 | 22 | 23 | $51 |

Streeterville | Ritz-Carlton Chicago | 160 E. Pearson St, 12th fl. (N. Michigan Ave.) | 312-573-5160 | www.decarestaurant.com

Just off the redone 12th-floor lobby of the Streeterville Ritz-Carlton, this French brasserie provides a "lovely" art deco–inspired setting for a "wide range of fresh, well-prepared" fare (including "decadent desserts") to go along with the "obliging", "friendly" service and pleasant "people-watching"; few fault the fare as "middling" for hotel prices, but it couldn't be more convenient for pre-theater dining or breaks from "exercising your card at Water Tower Place."

De Cero 🅂🅼 *Mexican* | 21 | 18 | 19 | $34 |

West Loop | 814 W. Randolph St. (bet. Green & Halsted Sts.) | 312-455-8114 | www.decerotaqueria.com

Order the "mix and match" taco platter and "you can't go wrong" at this "trendy" yet "authentic" West Loop taqueria where the "broad" menu of "gourmet" Mex eats gets a boost from "killer margaritas"; the "casual" space has a "cantina-meets-warehouse" feel, and if a few find it "pricey" for the genre and "don't see the big deal", more claim the "flavorful food" will "keep you coming back."

Dee's *Asian* | 19 | 17 | 18 | $28 |

Lincoln Park | 1114 W. Armitage Ave. (Seminary Ave.) | 773-477-1500 | www.deesrestaurant.com

A "reasonable mix" of sushi and "basic but satisfying" Mandarin and Sichuan specialties comes "recommended" at this affordable Lincoln Park longtimer; the "owner's personal attention" and a "lovely" outdoor patio further qualify it for "neighborhood favorite" status.

Deleece *Eclectic* | 22 | 18 | 22 | $35 |

Lakeview | 3747 N. Southport Ave. (bet. Grace St. & Waveland Ave.) | 773-325-1710 | www.deleece.com

Enthusiasts exhort "every 'hood should have" a "charming little place" like this Lakeview "gem", recently relocated to a "brighter", "better" new indoor/outdoor space, but still "cozy, casual" and turning out "well-made" Eclectic fare; moderate tabs and "friendly" servers help seal the deal for a "family gathering, group of friends" or even "date night"; P.S. the new surroundings may not be fully reflected in the Decor score.

Deleece Grill Pub 🅼 *American* | ▽ 18 | 14 | 19 | $28 |

Lakeview | 3313 N. Clark St. (bet. Aldine Ave. & Buckingham Pl.) | 773-348-3313 | www.deleecegrillpub.com

"Simple" American comfort food "done well" (including the "popular" mac 'n' cheese) is doled out in "big portions" at this "busy", budget-priced pub sib to Deleece in Lakeview, run by a "helpful" team; there's also a nice selection of domestic craft beers and whiskeys, and an inviting patio for brunches with "good Bloody Marys and mimosas", to boot.

	FOOD	DECOR	SERVICE	COST

Del Rio ⊠ Ⓜ *Italian* | 21 | 17 | 21 | $42 |

Highwood | 228 Green Bay Rd. (Rte. 22) | 847-432-4608

"Time stands still" at this "family-run", "red-sauce Italian" that's been in Highwood "forever" (or at least since 1923), and that's fine with fans who say it's a "joy" to revisit for "properly priced", "classic" cooking, "old-school" service and "strong drinks" mixed by "great bartenders"; foodies who feel the fare is "not the draw" nod to "one of the most extensive and best" wine selections around and advise you "ask them about the cellar list they keep at the bar."

Del Seoul *Korean* | 24 | 10 | 15 | $13 |

Lakeview | 2568 N. Clark St. (Wrightwood Ave.) | 773-248-4227 | www.delseoul.com

Eaters have "endless love" for the Asian-Mexican "mashup" tacos (a "cultural fusion that works") at this "cheap", "quick-serve" Korean in Lakeview where revamped banh mi and more traditional specialties also "earn their place" on the "small menu"; the surroundings are "bare and bland" and the seating "isn't the most comfortable", but Seoul-searchers say you're here for the "amazing" food, "not the decor."

Demera Ethiopian *Ethiopian* | 20 | 15 | 17 | $26 |

Uptown | 4801 N. Broadway (Rosemont Ave.) | 773-334-8787 | www.demeraethiopianrestaurant.com

Surveyors swear "you can smell the sauces" cooking all the way from the Lawrence el stop at this "inexpensive" Uptown Ethiopian that offers a "nice variety" of "spicy meats" and veggie options served up in "generous portions" and followed by coffee from house-roasted beans; "so-so service and decor" don't deter pros who point to the "pleasant" outdoor seating and "fun atmosphere" (with occasional live music).

Depot American Diner *Diner* | ▽ 25 | 16 | 23 | $15 |

Far West | 5840 W. Roosevelt Rd. (bet. Mayfield & Monitor Aves.) | 773-261-8422 | www.depotamericandiner.com

For "well-done" American "comfort food", eaters hit up this Far West BYO, a "meatloaf heaven" also known for "wonderful" sandwiches and other dishes "as good and authentic as diner food gets"; bargain prices, nifty '50s decor and solid service round out the package.

Depot Nuevo *Nuevo Latino* | 17 | 19 | 20 | $32 |

Wilmette | 1139 Wilmette Ave. (bet. Central & Lake Aves.) | 847-251-3111 | www.depotnuevo.com

A "fun, inventive" take on Nuevo Latino eats, "creative", "delicious" cocktails and service "friendly to everyone from families to dates" add up to "lively" "crowds" at this affordable Wilmette spot in a converted train station; still, some deem it "nothing too impressive", citing "inconsistent" food and "cramped, noisy" digs, before conceding the "year-round covered porch" remains a draw; P.S. no reservations on weekends.

	FOOD	DECOR	SERVICE	COST

NEW Derby *American*
-|-|-|I

Lincoln Park | 1224 W. Webster Ave. (Magnolia Ave.) | 773-248-0900 | www.derbychicago.com

The venerable Lincoln Park Charlie's Ale House was gut-rehabbed to launch this neighborhood sports bar where burgers, sandwiches, flatbreads and specials jockey for position on the updated American pub food menu; the dining room features plush raised booths, an ornate bar with two dozen beer handles (and a hefty whiskey list) and front windows that open to outdoor seating.

NEW Deuce's & The Diamond Club *American*
-|-|-|M

Wrigleyville | 3505 N. Clark St. (bet. Cornelia Ave. & Eddy St.) | 773-644-5554 | www.deucesandthediamondclub.com

Designed by 555 (GT Fish & Oyster, Girl & The Goat), this sporty-sleek, bi-level Wrigleyville pad features a first-level dining room with exposed ductwork, retro athletic art on the walls and a cabana-and fountain-outfitted patio, while an upstairs lounge has its own bar and a balcony overlooking the bustle below; both scenes sate a neighborhood crowd, which swaps digits while diving into American eats like upscale burgers, mac 'n' cheese and gussied-up grilled cheese, accompanied by craft beers and oversize libations.

Devon Seafood Grill *Seafood*
21|21|21|$47

River North | 39 E. Chicago Ave. (Wabash Ave.) | 312-440-8660 | www.devonseafood.com

"Not just your basic seafood place" swear surveyors of these "upscale" chain links where the fin fare is "prepared in delicious ways" and "solid wine lists", generally "attentive service" and "fantastic happy-hour specials" add further appeal; the multilevel River North locale has a lively "bar scene", while the North Shore Milwaukee sib offers a Sunday brunch buffet to "fulfill every taste"; P.S. an Oak Brook outpost is slated for summer 2012.

Dimo's Pizza ● *Pizza*
23|13|20|$10
(fka Ian's Pizza)

Lakeview | 3463 N. Clark St. (bet. Cornelia & Newport Aves.) | 773-525-4580 | www.dimospizza.com/dimos_pizza.html

"Awesomely weird" (some say "ingenious") toppings like "steak and fries, mac 'n' cheese, etc." are "like every kid's dream" at this Lakeview BYO (recently converted from an Ian's Pizza); there's "not much ambiance" and late-night eaters should expect imbibers "coming from nearby bars", but service "moves quickly", so when you want to "experiment with funky" combinations, it fits the "inexpensive" bill.

Dining Room at Kendall College ⑤ *French*
▽ 23|20|23|$42

Near West | Kendall College | 900 N. North Branch St. (Halsted St.) | 312-752-2328 | www.kendall.edu

There's "something so charming" about this Near West "learning" ground turned "pleasant surprise", where Kendall College students prepare and "earnestly" (if "nervously") serve the New French "fine-

"dining" fare in modern digs where "big windows" provide "great views"; even supporters who say it's "nothing amazing" note "nothing beats the value."

Dinotto Ristorante *Italian* | 21 | 17 | 20 | $40 |

Old Town | 215 W. North Ave. (bet. Wells & Wieland Sts.) | 312-202-0302 | www.dinotto.com

This "cozy" Old Town "hideaway around the corner from Second City" ranks as "reliable" for "very good", "reasonably priced" Italian fare, "consistent" service and "great patio dining"; so if it's "not unique", it's still a "perfect neighborhood" spot – and "nice place to take a lady for dinner."

Di Pescara *Italian/Seafood* | 20 | 18 | 20 | $39 |

Northbrook | Northbrook Court Shopping Ctr. | 2124 Northbrook Ct. (Lake Cook Rd.) | 847-498-4321 | www.di-pescara.com

"Consistency is the word" at this Italian seafood specialist in Northbrook Court, a "local hangout" where the "extensive" menu, "relaxed" vibe and "reliable" service keep it a "go-to"; skeptics snark it "raises mediocrity to an art form" and what's "relatively cheap" to some is "kind of pricey" to others, but it's still "always packed."

DiSotto Enoteca ● *Italian* | ▽ 25 | 21 | 24 | $34 |

Streeterville | Mia Francesca | 200 E. Chestnut St. (bet. DeWitt Pl. & Michigan Ave.) | 312-482-8727 | www.disottoenoteca.com

A "welcome addition" from Scott Harris (Davanti Enoteca, Mia Francesca, The Purple Pig), this "casual" Streeterville Italian under Francesca's on Chestnut offers "delicious, well-prepared" Italian small plates to go with a large vino list; the "comfortable" "wine cellar"-like setting is elevated by "friendly", "knowledgeable" staffers and prices are affordable too, so it's a "fine option" for a "perfect first date."

Ditka's *Steak* | 22 | 21 | 22 | $49 |

Gold Coast | Tremont Hotel | 100 E. Chestnut St. (Michigan Ave.) | 312-587-8989

Oakbrook Terrace | 2 Mid America Plaza (bet. 16th & 22nd Sts.) | 630-572-2200

www.ditkasrestaurants.com

"Da coach gets it done" cheer fans of these "iconic" Gold Coast and Oakbrook Terrace steakhouses where you may "run into football legends" or Mike himself while feasting on "surprisingly good" fare including "Chicago-sized" cuts, "succulent" pork chops and "not-to-be-missed pot roast nachos" via "consistent" servers; if some say it's "kinda pricey", others find tabs "relatively reasonable", especially when considered part of a "sporting museum entrance fee" given all the "Bears memorabilia"; P.S. Downtown is "the place for game day."

Dixie Kitchen & Bait Shop *Cajun/Southern* | 19 | 16 | 18 | $22 |

Evanston | 825 Church St. (bet. Benson & Sherman Aves.) | 847-733-9030

Lansing | 2352 E. 172nd St. (Torrence Ave.) | 708-474-1378

www.dixiekitchenchicago.com

"A stuffed customer is a happy customer" at this "inexpensive" Evanston and Lansing duo where "large portions" of "down and delicious" Cajun-Southern fare including a "do-not-miss" brunch ("the best hangover cure") take devotees "as near to New Orleans" as they'll get "this far north"; the "noise level is generally high" and "service can be spotty", so fans focus their attention on the "whimsical, kitschy" decor; P.S. "expect a wait" on weekends

DMK Burger Bar *Burgers*　　　21 | 16 | 18 | $21

Lakeview | 2954 N. Sheffield Ave. (Wellington Ave.) | 773-360-8686 ☻
NEW Lombard | 2370 Fountain Square Dr. (bet. Butterfield & Meyers Rds.) | 630-705-9020
www.dmkburgerbar.com

"Eclectic gourmet burgers", including options for non-beef eaters, and "damn fine sides" like "addictive" "grown-up french fries" are "complemented incredibly well by a drink menu" featuring milkshakes, "well-made" craft cocktails and an "outstanding selection of microbrews" at the Lakeview original and Lombard spin-off from restaurateurs David Morton and Michael Kornick; a no-reservations policy often results in "long waits" and it's "loud" ("bring your earplugs"), but the "young and trendy" don't mind, especially because "service moves quickly" and "the price is right."

Don Juan's *Mexican*　　　19 | 16 | 18 | $28

Edison Park | 6730 N. Northwest Hwy. (Oshkosh Ave.) | 773-775-6438 |
www.donjuanschicago.com

"Open for decades", this family-run Edison Park "classic" offers "fairly ordinary" Mexican "standards" plus more "innovative" items in a "warm" space decorated with local art; "service can be hit-or-miss" and dissenters dub it "tired", but "cheap eats" and a "welcoming" "hospitable atmosphere" help keep it a "neighborhood favorite."

Dorado Ⓜ *French/Mexican*　　　25 | 16 | 23 | $34

Lincoln Square | 2301 W. Foster Ave. (bet. Claremont & Oakley Aves.) |
773-561-3780 | www.doradorestaurant.net

"A different twist on Mexican food" is the draw at this "creative" Lincoln Square BYO turning out "perfectly cooked" French-accented dishes ("two words: duck nachos") in "lively" environs; if the decor is a tad "lacking", satisfied diners point out it's an "excellent value" with solid service to boot.

Due Lire Ⓜ *Italian*　　　23 | 17 | 23 | $32

Lincoln Square | 4520 N. Lincoln Ave. (bet. Sunnyside & Wilson Aves.) |
773-275-7878 | www.due-lire.com

"Cozy" and "convivial (i.e. loud)", this "lovely" "little" Lincoln Square "storefront" "gem" serves "simple, wonderful" "authentic Italian fare" including "handmade pastas with delicious fresh sauces" alongside a "wine list to match"; "friendly" service and midscale prices help keep it a neighborhood "go-to."

Duke of Perth *Scottish*　　　20 | 18 | 20 | $22

Lakeview | 2913 N. Clark St. (Oakdale Ave.) | 773-477-1741 |
www.dukeofperth.com

"All that's missing is the dark and stormy night" at this "authentic" Scottish pub in Lakeview offering "flavorful, non-greasy pub grub" (including all-you-can-eat fish 'n' chips Wednesdays and Fridays) and a "tremendous selection of whiskeys and beers" in "cozy" surrounds where "the lack of TVs (and subsequent lack of bros) make it even better"; add in "rational prices" and "friendly" service and it's a "serious watering hole" "destination", especially when the back patio is open.

Ed Debevic's   *Diner*   16 | 19 | 19 | $21

River North | 640 N. Wells St. (Ontario St.) | 312-664-1707 | www.eddebevics.com

"Cheeky" servers "dance on the countertops and flirt with your date" at this affordable River North "hamburger joint" and shake shop where the "old-time diner" digs make you feel "like an extra in a '50s movie"; it's "popular with tourists" and young 'uns think it's "the greatest", so if you find the "kid cuisine" "meh" and think "the shtick is tired", at least "you can get an adult beverage."

Edelweiss   *German*   22 | 22 | 22 | $28

Norridge | 7650 W. Irving Park Rd. (Overhill Ave.) | 708-452-6040 | www.edelweissdining.com

"You'll waddle out" of this "authentic" German joint in Norridge after chowing down on "surprisingly good" sausages and schnitzels, throwing back Bavarian brews and listening to the live "oompah band"; the service earns high marks and the setting brings back "memories of the old country", so even those wondering if "maybe the beer makes everyone like the so-so specialties" still agree you'll leave "one happy camper."

NEW Eduardo's Enoteca   *Italian*   - | - | - | M

Gold Coast | 1212 N. Dearborn St. (bet. Division & Goethe Sts.) | 312-337-4490 | www.eduardosenoteca.com

In an "almost total reinvention", the same owners turned what was once the casual Edwardo's Natural Pizza into a more upscale Gold Coast offshoot, where a "polished" staff serves "delish" Italian dishes, "interesting", affordable small plates and "boutique" bottles; exposed rafters highlight the space's heritage as an old theater, and low lights make this wine bar a "charming date spot."

Edwardo's Natural Pizza   *Pizza*   20 | 11 | 15 | $19

Gold Coast | 1212 N. Dearborn St. (Division St.) | 312-337-4490
Lincoln Park | 2662 N. Halsted St. (Wrightwood Ave.) | 773-871-3400
Hyde Park | 1321 E. 57th St. (Kimbark Ave.) | 773-241-7960
South Loop | 521 S. Dearborn St. (bet. Congress Pkwy. & Harrison St.) | 312-939-3366
Skokie | 9300 Skokie Blvd. (Gross Point Rd.) | 847-674-0008
Wheeling | 401 E. Dundee Rd. (Milwaukee Ave.) | 847-520-0666
Oak Park | 6831 North Ave. (Grove Ave.) | 708-524-2400
www.edwardos.com

"Classic" deep-dish and "solid" thin-crust pies crafted with "emphasis on fresh, natural ingredients" please patrons of this "reliable, not awesome" series of "casual", wallet-friendly city and suburban pizza parlors; decor ranges from recently updated to "hole-in-the-wall", and snarks suggest you carry out or "put up with unskilled service."

☒ Edzo's Burger Shop Ⓜ Burgers   27 | 14 | 21 | $12

Evanston | 1571 Sherman Ave. (bet. Davis & Grove Sts.) | 847-864-3396 | www.edzos.com

"Simply awesome" "top-of-the-line" burgers with "tons of options for customization", plus a "fantastic selection" of "imaginative" "to-die-for" fries and "transcendent" "thick malts in terrific flavors" earn "wows" at this counter service Evanston joint; so even with "nonexistent" decor, "short hours" (till 4 PM) and "crazy long lines", it's still "really hard to complain."

Egg Harbor Café   American   22 | 17 | 21 | $17

Lincolnshire | 300 Village Green (bet. Half Day Rd. & Milwaukee Ave.) | 847-821-1515
Glenview | 2350 Lehigh Ave. (W. Lake Ave.) | 847-998-1101
Lake Forest | 512 N. Western Ave. (Deerpath Rd.) | 847-295-3449
Libertyville | 125 Lake St. (bet. Brainerd & Milwaukee Aves.) | 847-680-3610
Arlington Heights | 140 E. Wing St. (bet. Arlington Heights Rd. & Nothwest Hwy.) | 847-253-4363
Barrington | 210 S. Cook St. (bet. Lake & Station Sts.) | 847-304-4033
Downers Grove | 5128 Mochel Dr. (Curtiss St.) | 630-963-0390
Elmhurst | 140 Robert Palmer Dr. (bet. Park Ave & York St.) | 630-758-1010
Geneva | 477 S. Third St. (South St.) | 620-208-8940
Hinsdale | 777 N. York Rd. (Ogden Ave.) | 630-920-1344
www.eggharborcafe.com
Additional locations throughout the Chicago area

With service that seems pre-"screened by the polite police", things are "always sunny side up" at this "popular" suburban breakfast-and-lunch chain, where the "encyclopedic selection" of American eats is "done with care" and delivered in "generous portions" at "reasonable prices"; if not everyone appreciates the "gleeful country decor", and some consider the food "generic", it still doesn't prevent people from "coming back in droves."

Eggsperience Café   American   19 | 14 | 18 | $16

River North | Millennium Centre Condominiums | 35 W. Ontario St. (bet. Dearborn & State Sts.) | 312-870-6773
Bannockburn | Bannockburn Green Shopping Ctr. | 2545 Waukegan Rd. (Half Day Rd.) | 847-940-8444
Glenview | 2000 Tower Dr. (Aviator Ln.) | 847-998-5111
Park Ridge | 90 Northwest Hwy. (bet. Summit & Touhy Aves.) | 847-939-3976
Naperville | 2727 W. 75th St. (Beebe Dr.) | 630-548-1000
www.eggsperiencecafe.com

Fans say the "fluffy" omeletes are "a couple feet high" and pancakes "lighter than air" at this "bright, cheerful" chainlet, where "enthusiastic" if occasionally "inconsistent" servers ferry "hearty portions" of "above-average" daytime fare (River North is open 24 hours

Thursday–Saturday); pickier patrons protest it's just "meh", but "prices are good", so "waits are still not uncommon."

NEW Eggy's *Diner*

- | - | - | M

Streeterville | 333 E. Benton Pl. (Field Blvd.) | 773-234-3449 | www.eggysdiner.com

Redefining classic American diner fare with seasonal, locally sourced ingredients, this midpriced East Lakeshore BYO offers all-day breakfast and lunch items and family-style dinners, capped off with bakery throwbacks, such as pies, brownies and crumbles; the open, industrial space taps into nostalgia with counter seating and a soda fountain.

EJ's Place *Italian/Steak*

22 | 16 | 21 | $58

Skokie | 10027 Skokie Blvd. (Old Orchard Rd.) | 847-933-9800 | www.ejsplaceskokie.com

Solid "meat and potatoes fare" with an "Italian slant" is on offer at this Skokie steakhouse from the Gene & Georgetti crew, where "knotty pine paneling" creates a "rustic" "Wisconsin cabin" feel and service gets high marks; portions are "huge", so those who find prices "steep" are advised to "try splitting an entree – it works much better."

Elate *American*

23 | 23 | 20 | $48

River North | Hotel Felix | 111 W. Huron St. (Clark St.) | 312-202-9900 | www.elatechicago.com

"Innovative", "well-prepared" small and large plates grace the somewhat "pricey" menu at this New American "haven of tranquility" in River North's Hotel Felix; "stylish" industrial-meets-rustic decor and solid service further make it the place for a "quiet glass of wine", "fancy hotel brunch" or "soothing evening."

Elephant & Castle *Pub Food*

15 | 16 | 16 | $22

Loop | 111 W. Adams St. (bet. Clark & LaSalle Sts.) | 312-236-6656

Loop | 185 N. Wabash Ave. (Lake St.) | 312-345-1710 ◐

Near North | 160 E. Huron St. (bet. Chicago Ave. & Ontario St.) | 312-440-1180 ◐

www.elephantcastle.com

For "a touch of jolly old England" in Chicago, budget-watchers "grab a drink and a bite" at this "dependable" pub chain offering "lots of good beers on tap" alongside fish 'n' chips, shepherd's pie and other "genuine tastes of the mother country"; the less enthused take a "pass", citing "noisy" conditions, "inconsistent" service and fare that they find just "so-so."

Eleven City Diner *Diner*

19 | 18 | 18 | $21

South Loop | 1112 S. Wabash Ave. (11th St.) | 312-212-1112 | www.elevencitydiner.com

"Stacked sandwiches", "soothing" matzo ball soup and other "traditional" "Jewish deli" standards bring noshers to this "solid" South Looper in a "diner"-meets-"art deco"-styled space complete with a soda fountain ("you can get Green River [soda] and black cows"); service gets mixed marks ("fun" vs. "difficult") and some find "big

	FOOD	DECOR	SERVICE	COST

bills" surprising for the genre, but devotees kvell it's "well worth the price for the level of quality."

NEW EL Ideas 🏧Ⓜ *American* ▽ 29 | 21 | 28 | $143

Pilsen | 2419 W. 14th St. (bet. 15th St. & Ogden Ave.) | 312-226-8144 | www.elideas.com

Diners detect "real vision" at this "permanent pop-up" "hidden" in Pilsen where "you sit in the kitchen", an "intimate", "understated" 16-seat space, while "innovator" Phillip Foss (of the defunct Meatballs Mobile) turns out "wildly inventive", "delightfully delicious" New American cuisine on a spendy, "ever-changing" tasting menu; guests "get to talk with the chefs and even participate in prep and service", another reason it evokes an "underground dining experience", so even when "not every dish hits the mark", it still feels like "the coolest dinner party"; P.S. BYO makes it "more affordable than you'd expect."

El Jardin *Mexican* 18 | 13 | 17 | $25

Lakeview | 3401 N. Clark St. (bet. Newport Ave. & Roscoe St.) | 773-935-8155 | www.eljardinmexicancafe.com

Cubs fans come to this longtime Lakeview cantina "after games, to erase the memories" with "potent", "mind-bending margaritas" "soaked up" by "old-fashioned Mexican cooking"; affordable tabs and a "festive, lively" vibe help compensate for so-so decor and service, so it remains a "favorite" – just be prepared for "the worst hangover."

Elly's Pancake House *American* 19 | 14 | 21 | $15

Old Town | 101 W. North Ave. (N. Clark St.) | 312-643-2300 ◐
Mundelein | 435 Townline Rd. (Lake St.) | 847-837-8100
Arlington Heights | 372 E. Golf Rd. (Arlington Heights Rd.) | 847-364-4400
NEW Norridge | 5050 N. Cumberland Ave. (bet. W. Argyle St. & W. Foster Ave.) | 708-453-4500
www.ellyspancakehouse.com

Just "like sitting in mom's kitchen" note nibblers at this 24/7 Old Town American offering a "never-ending menu" of "consistently prepared breakfast staples" (plus lunch and dinner fare) via "friendly", "pleasant" servers; an "eclectic array of chairs" gives it a "quirky, festive feel", and with "value" tabs it's especially "popular with the young weekend brunch crowd"; sibs in Mundelein, Norridge and Arlington Heights are daytime-only.

Emilio's Tapas *Spanish* 24 | 20 | 22 | $35

Hillside | 4100 Roosevelt Rd. (Mannheim Rd.) | 708-547-7177
Emilio's Tapas Sol y Nieve *Spanish*
Streeterville | 215 E. Ohio St. (St. Clair St.) | 312-467-7177
www.emiliostapas.com

A "favorite" for "tip-top tapas", these "reasonable priced" Hillside and Streeterville siblings offer a "good diversity" of "well-made", "flavorful" Spanish dishes that are "both traditional and innovative"; "warm", "attentive" servers and "informal" Iberian-themed environs replete with "in-demand" outdoor seating further explain why they're "popular" "go-tos."

Emperor's Choice *Chinese*   ▽ 22 | 13 | 20 | $28

Chinatown | 2238 S. Wentworth Ave. (Cermak Rd.) | 312-225-8800

"An enduring Chinatown choice" with an "interesting, authentic menu" highlighting "creative seafood", this Cantonese longtimer also caters to guests with its "caring ownership and experienced servers"; though the decor doesn't earn raves despite white table-cloths and a fish tank, and it may be a tad "pricey" for the area, fans assure it's "always a step above the many others."

Epic Burger *Burgers*   19 | 13 | 16 | $13

Loop | University of Columbia | 517 S. State St. (bet. Congress Pkwy. & Harrison St.) | 312-913-1373
NEW **Streeterville** | 227 E. Ontario St. (bet. St. Clair St. & Fairbanks Ct.) | 312-257-3260
NEW **Gold Coast** | 40 E. Pearson St. (bet. Rush & State Sts.) | 312-257-3262
Lincoln Park | 1000 W. North Ave. (Sheffield Ave.) | 312-440-9700
NEW **Near South Side** | 550 W. Adams St. (Clinton & Jefferson Sts.) | 312-382-0400 ⑤
NEW **Skokie** | Westfield Old Orchard Mall | 4999 Old Orchard Ctr. (Skokie Blvd.) | 847-933-9013
www.epicburger.com

Hamburger hounds "heart" this quickly growing "high-end fast-food" mini-chain (with locations in the city and Skokie) for its all-natural beef patties served "with various toppings" like a cage-free fried egg or Wisconsin aged cheddar; "fresh-cut" fries and "fabu-lous" milkshakes compensate for the "utilitarian" "counter-service" settings, and while a frugal few contend they "could eat at a sit-down for the cost", most say "the price is right."

Epic Restaurant ⑤ *American*   - | - | - | E

River North | 112 W. Hubbard St. (bet. Clark St. & LaSalle Blvd.) | 312-222-4940 | www.epicrestaurantchicago.com

This swanky River Norther offers New American fine dining utilizing classic French technique and housemade ingredients; a winding staircase separates a second-floor dining room with soaring win-dows from an informal first-floor lounge (with a different menu) and seasonal outdoor dining on a vast rooftop.

Erie Cafe *Italian/Steak*   22 | 19 | 22 | $54

River North | 536 W. Erie St. (Kingsbury St.) | 312-266-2300 | www.eriecafe.com

A "solid contender in the steakhouse sweepstakes", this "oldie" in an "obscure" part of River North offers "a good hunk o' meat without the pretension" (and some say "even better" fish) served by a staff that "treats you like family"; it's not cheap, but the "lawyer crowd" in the cedar-lined "Sinatra-style" quarters and the "friendly regu-lars" in the bar don't seem to mind – plus there's "wonderful" river-side seating in summer.

	FOOD	DECOR	SERVICE	COST

Erwin, An American Cafe & Bar ⓜ *American*

| 23 | 20 | 23 | $41 |

Lakeview | 2925 N. Halsted St. (Oakdale Ave.) | 773-528-7200 | www.erwincafe.com

Chef Erwin Drechsler's Lakeview New American is a longtime "favorite" for "comfort food with a gourmet twist", using "fresh from the farmer's market" ingredients and offering "superb value" – especially the nightly three-course prix fixe; servers are "professional" and "welcoming", and the "rustic" setting is so "warm and friendly" that it almost "feels like home."

NEW Eshticken Pizza *Eclectic/Pizza*

| - | - | - | I |

Hoffman Estates | 4660 Hoffman Blvd. (Sutton Rd.) | 847-747-0000 | www.eshticken.com

Pizza patrons have a choice of hand-tossed crust or a proprietary, zero-carb (protein-based) option with various toppings, along with a smattering of sandwiches, pasta, calzone and family-recipe rice pudding, at this Suburban Northwestern; its setting is done up in black and red with flagstone walls, tile floors, communal high-top seating, banquettes and warm pendant lighting.

NEW Estate Ultra Bar ☻ *American*

| - | - | - | I |

River West | 1177 N. Elston Ave. (Division St.) | 312-582-4777 | www.estateultrabar.com

A long-empty piece of prime River West real estate has been transformed into this swanky lounge serving midpriced American shared plates, salads and sandwiches paired with signature cocktails, 20-ish draft brews and a compact wine list; inside the wood-clad bunker, multiple environments add a range of options from the spacious bar with TVs to plush lounge areas, refined dining tables, patios and a roofdeck, with design highlights include Sputnik light fixtures, mosaic tile and a fireplace; P.S. night-owl hours go til 2 AM during the week and 3 AM on Saturday.

Ethiopian Diamond *Ethiopian*

| 22 | 15 | 20 | $24 |

Edgewater | 6120 N. Broadway (Glenlake Ave.) | 773-338-6100

Ethiopian Diamond II *Ethiopian*

Rogers Park | 7537 N. Clark St. (bet. Howard St. & Rogers Ave.) | 773-764-2200

www.ethiopiandiamondcuisine.com

Those who have a "yen" for Ethiopian fare find it's "worth the trek" to this "authentic" duo, where the flavors are "tangy", the honey wine is "housemade" and the "bouncy-friendly" owner and "helpful" servers come to your aid "if you don't know the cuisine"; the "large" space "handles a party very well", and there is live "music to dine by" Friday night in Edgewater and Saturday night in Rogers Park.

ⓩ Everest ⓢⓜ *French*

| 27 | 28 | 27 | $115 |

Loop | One Financial Pl. | 440 S. LaSalle St., 40th fl. (Congress Pkwy.) | 312-663-8920 | www.everestrestaurant.com

Perched on the 40th floor of the Chicago Stock Exchange, this Loop longtimer with a "knockout" view of the city is deemed "perfection in the clouds" thanks to its "exquisite" Alsatian-influenced French prix fixe menus by chef Jean Joho, plus a "grand" wine list, all delivered with "exceptional" service in an "elegant supper-club setting"; though "not for the light-walleted", it's a "pinnacle" of "fine dining" befitting "special occasions."

NEW E wok Café *Japanese*
- | - | - | I

Northwest Side | 5056 W. Irving Park Rd. (bet. Lavergne & Leclaire Aves.) | 773-205-8335 | www.ewokcafe.com

BYO helps keep prices low at this Northwest Sider, which serves raw and cooked Japanese fare (including bento boxes and surf 'n' turf) plus a smattering of mixed Asian meals; the casual, modern setting features a granite sushi bar, an open kitchen and decorative knickknacks.

Exchequer *American/Pizza*
20 | 15 | 20 | $21

Loop | 226 S. Wabash Ave. (bet. Adams St. & Jackson Blvd.) | 312-939-5633 | www.exchequerpub.com

"Huge burgers" are among the inexpensive "bar food" "cooked up well" at this "ageless" Loop pub that's "not much to look at" but "has a certain character"; "attentive" staffers help make it a "local spot" for an "informal meal", or to "enjoy a drink, watch a game and unwind."

NEW Farmhouse *American*
∇ 22 | 22 | 21 | $36

Near North | 228 W. Chicago Ave. (bet. Franklin & Wells Sts.) | 312-280-4960 | www.farmhousechicago.com

"Homey" New American dishes (the "best cheese curds ever", "tasty" short ribs) meet an "incredible" Midwestern beer list at this midpriced "farm-to-table tavern" in Near North that also keeps it local with Michigan wine on tap and housemade sodas; salvaged decor across two stories and occasional live music add to the "welcoming", "convivial" vibe.

FatDuck Tavern & Grill *American*
(fka Duckfat Tavern & Grill)
19 | 15 | 18 | $22

Forest Park | 7218 Madison St. (Elgin Ave.) | 708-488-1493 | www.fatduckgrill.com

The signature duckfat fries are "the obvious highlight" and the burger is "pretty good" too at this Forest Park pub serving "hearty", low-cost American eats in digs with a "laid-back neighborhood" atmosphere; though some pooh-pooh it as "pedestrian", the patio's a sure bet for "a few pints in the sun."

Fat Willy's Rib Shack *BBQ/Southern*
20 | 14 | 18 | $22

Logan Square | 2416 W. Schubert Ave. (Western Ave.) | 773-782-1800 | www.fatwillysribshack.com

Customers "crave" the "just-right", "fall-off-the-bone" ribs and other "satisfying" BBQ eats at this "crowded", "real-deal" Southern smoke joint in Logan Square; a few gripe that delivery can be a "letdown", but more wager it's "worth checking out for a true 'cue experience."

Feast *American*
20 | 17 | 19 | $28

Gold Coast | 25 E. Delaware Pl. (bet. State & Wabash Sts.) | 312-337-4001

(continued)

Feast

Bucktown | 1616 N. Damen Ave. (North Ave.) | 773-772-7100
www.feastrestaurant.com

A "something-for-everyone" menu of "well-executed" New American "comfort food" makes this "reasonably priced" Bucktown and Gold Coast duo a "regular stop", especially during its "wonderful brunch" (the "best hangover cure"); service is generally "accommodating" if occasionally "slow" and the casual environs are "relaxed yet bustling", so if "disappointed" diners find it "inconsistent", it's nonetheless "popular" with "large groups", "young professionals" and the "stroller crowd."

NEW Felice's
Roman Style Pizza *Pizza*

| - | - | - | I |

Rogers Park | 6441 N. Sheridan Rd. (W. Arthur Ave.) | 773-508-7990 | www.loyolalimited.com/felices

Operated by Loyola students, this counter-service Rogers Park BYO puts out a rotating selection of affordable pizza preps by the pie or slice; red-and-white walls hung with student artwork decorate the casual space with an open kitchen and deli counter offering a few other grab-and-go foods; P.S. it's open til 2:30 AM on weekends.

The Fifty/50 ● *American*

| 19 | 13 | 16 | $20 |

Wicker Park | 2047 W. Division St. (bet. Damen & Hoyne Aves.) | 773-489-5050 | www.thefifty50.com

When the goal is "good-quality bar food" while "watching the game", this Wicker Park American scores with "some of the best wings in town" and plentiful flat-screens spread out over three levels (the "decor is sports"); the servers are "young and fun", just don't go in expecting "too much."

NEW Filini *Italian*

| ▽ 24 | 29 | 23 | $40 |

Loop | Radisson Blu Aqua Hotel | 221 N. Columbus Dr. (Wacker Dr.) | 312-477-0234 | www.filinichicago.com

This "beautiful" bi-level Italian with a "clever design" inside the Loop's curvaceous Radisson Blu Aqua Hotel dishes up hearty, midpriced fare bolstered by a Boot-based wine list and a "friendly" crew in tux jackets and jeans; downstairs, the "trendy" bar with a separate menu and "crispy" thin-crust pizza is a destination on its own.

Fireside Restaurant &
Lounge ● *American/Seafood*

| 22 | 20 | 20 | $26 |

Andersonville | 5739 N. Ravenswood Ave. (bet. W. Bryn Mawr & W. Peterson Aves.) | 773-561-7433 | www.firesidechicago.com

A "fireplace adds warmth" to this "dependable" Andersonville resto-pub with "surprisingly good" American fare (that "runs the gamut from pizza to fish"), a "huge" beer selection and somewhat of a "sports-bar" feel; it can get "noisy" at times, but service is "friendly" and the back patio (heated and enclosed in winter) "feels like the deck of a country club."

	FOOD	DECOR	SERVICE	COST

Fish Bar Ⓜ Seafood | 24 | 18 | 22 | $32 |

Lakeview | 2956 N. Sheffield Ave. (Wellington Ave.) | 773-687-8177 | www.fishbarchicago.com

Adjoining Lakeview's DMK Burger Bar, this "popular" "hybrid between a clam shack and New Orleans po' boy house" lures with "fantastic", "thoughtfully sourced" seafood, "lots of good beer" and a "relaxed", "unpretentious" atmosphere; a "small" space and "limited seating" mean there's often a "wait for a table" and you may need to shell out a bit to "fill up", "but it's seafood in Chicago, so what are you going to do?"; P.S. reservations taken for parties of three–four only.

Five Guys Burgers | 20 | 11 | 16 | $11 |

Lincoln Park | 2140 N. Clybourn Ave. (Wayne Ave.) | 773-327-5953
Lincoln Park | 2368 N. Clark St. (bet. Belden Ave. & Fullerton Pkwy.) | 773-883-8930
Rogers Park | The Morgan at Loyola Station | 1209 W. Arthur Ave. (Sheridan Rd.) | 773-262-9810
Libertyville | 147 N. Milwaukee Ave. (Rte. 176) | 847-549-0514
Naperville | 22 E. Chicago Ave. (Washington St.) | 630-355-1850
Oak Park | 1115 W. Lake St. (bet. Harlem Ave. & Marion St.) | 708-358-0856
www.fiveguys.com

"Honest", "juicy" burgers "with the right amount of grease", plus "mountains" of "heavenly fries" and "free peanuts while you wait" is "a formula that leaves patrons coming back for more" at this "cheerful", fast-growing chain; if faultfinders "don't see the fascination", those "addicted" to "all the free topping choices" simply insist "it works"; P.S. "many locations have those crazy cool Coke machines" with "a choice of 100-plus flavors."

Flat Top Grill Asian | 19 | 15 | 17 | $21 |

Loop | 30 S. Wabash Ave. (bet. Madison & Monroe Sts.) | 312-726-8400
Lakeview | 3200 N. Southport Ave. (Belmont Ave.) | 773-665-8100
Old Town | 319 W. North Ave. (Orleans St.) | 312-787-7676
West Loop | 1000 W. Washington Blvd. (Carpenter St.) | 312-829-4800
Evanston | 707 Church St. (bet. Orrington & Sherman Aves.) | 847-570-0100
Lombard | Shops on Butterfield | 305 Yorktown Ctr. (Highland Ave.) | 630-652-3700
Naperville | 218 S. Washington St. (bet. Chicago & Jefferson Aves.) | 630-428-8400
Oak Park | 726 Lake St. (Oak Park Ave.) | 708-358-8200
www.flattopgrill.com

"Get creative" in building "your own special stir-fry" and then "watch the show" as it's prepared at this Asian chain appealing to the "healthy" and "picky" with its "wide selection" of ingredients, "excellent sauces" and overall "flexibility"; though it "lacks in decor and ambiance", you "can't beat the price" and "kids love it."

Fleming's Prime Steakhouse & Wine Bar Steak | 24 | 22 | 23 | $61 |

Near North | 25 E. Ohio St. (bet. State & Wabash Sts.) | 312-329-9463

(continued)

Fleming's Prime Steakhouse & Wine Bar

Lincolnshire | Lincolnshire Commons | 960 Milwaukee Ave.
(Aptakisic Rd.) | 847-793-0333
www.flemingssteakhouse.com

An "excellent selection" of "high-quality" "steaks of all types" are "well prepared and mouthwatering" at this "upscale" city and suburban chophouse chain where 100 wines by the glass (a "fabulous concept"), "consistent", "prompt" service and "dark", "clubby" surrounds with the "requisite wood paneling" also win praise; "everything is costly" as per the category, so "go hungry and pay off your credit card beforehand."

Flight ⊠ *Eclectic* | 23 | 20 | 20 | $38 |

Glenview | 1820 Tower Dr. (Patriot Blvd.) | 847-729-9463 |
www.flightwinebar.com

Whether it's the "wonderful wine flights" or "opportunity to try a little of this and a little of that", this Eclectic small-plater "in the heart of the Glen" fits the bill when you want to sample "something new"; service is "fast" and the modern space pleasant, if a "tad crowded", so despite a few grumbles of "overpriced" tabs, most agree it's "just different enough" to please.

Flight 1551 *American* | - | - | - | M |

Old Town | 1551 N. Wells St. (bet. North Ave. & Schiller St.) |
312-944-1551 | www.flight1551.com

This modern wine bar and restaurant in Old Town serves moderately priced New American small plates, some arranged in flights (burgers, grilled cheese, cheeses), along with thin-crust pizza and mini desserts; the long, narrow digs, open lunch through late-night (2 AM daily), include a fireplace and a crescent-shaped back bar offering more than 50 glass pours from an elaborate tap system.

Flo Ⓜ *Southwestern* | 22 | 15 | 20 | $19 |

Noble Square | 1434 W. Chicago Ave. (bet. Bishop & Noble Sts.) |
312-243-0477 | www.flochicago.com

Fans find this "solid" Southwestern joint in Noble Square a "cool drink of water", thanks to "creative" cuisine and a "knock your boots off" brunch complete with "incomparable" (and "strong") Bloody Marys"; the "no-frills, low-budget" setting is matched by wallet-friendly tabs and enlivened by "colorful characters" and a "courteous" staff.

The Florentine *Italian* | 22 | 22 | 22 | $51 |

Loop | JW Marriott Chicago | 151 W. Adams St. (bet. LaSalle & Wells Sts.) | 312-660-8866 | www.the-florentine.net

"Delicious" "contemporary" Italian cuisine paired with an "impressive" wine list draws the "expense-account" set to this "sleek, giant" venue inside the Loop's JW Marriott Chicago; tables "spaced far apart" make for "gracious" "fine dining", and that plus a "ready-to-please" staff further make it a "hot spot for business breakfasts, lunches or dinners."

Fogo de Chão *Brazilian/Steak* | 25 | 22 | 25 | $59 |

River North | 661 N. La Salle Dr. (Erie St.) | 312-932-9330 |
www.fogodechao.com

"Bring on the meat coma" chant diners at this River North link of the
all-you-can-eat Brazilian churrascaria chain, an "ultimate pig-out
place for carnivores" who feast on an "unending parade" of "uniformly delicious" cuts that "just keep coming until you say 'uncle'"
plus "extensive" options from the "decadent" salad bar ("a meal in
itself"); "running" servers "grant wishes like genies" in the "elegant
dining room" – just "bring a big appetite to justify the expense."

☑ Fontano's Subs *Sandwiches* | 28 | 9 | 19 | $10 |

Loop | 20 E. Jackson Blvd. (bet. State St. & Wabash Ave.) |
312-663-3061 ☑
Hinsdale | 9 S. Lincoln St. (Chicago Ave.) | 630-789-0891
Naperville | 1767 W. Ogden Ave. (Aurora Ave.) | 630-717-7821
Naperville | 2879 W. 95th St. (Cedar Glade Rd.) | 630-305-8010
www.fontanossubs.com

"It's all in the bread" (and "finest deli meats") at this "native"
Chicago chainlet cranking out "awesome" subs "the way they
should be" ("no wimpy" offerings); "you know it's good because all
the cops eat here", but plenty opt for takeout since "it's a slice of life,
not a fine-dining atmosphere."

Foodlife *Eclectic* | 19 | 13 | 14 | $18 |

Streeterville | Water Tower Pl. | 835 N. Michigan Ave. (bet. Chestnut &
Pearson Sts.) | 312-335-3663 | www.leye.com

NEW Foodease *Eclectic*

Streeterville | Water Tower Pl. | 835 N. Michigan Ave.
(bet. Chestnut & Pearson Sts.) | 312-335-3663 |
foodeasechicago.com

"Combining convenience with class", this "fab food court" at Water
Tower Place "impresses" with "so many stations" ("think sushi next
to barbecue next to Mexican") and works well for "feeding a group"
or just taking a "shopping break"; "reliable if a bit unexciting", it's
pegged as "pricey" by some, but others assure "you can eat here
cheaply if you want"; P.S. across the mezzanine, a new area called
Foodease adds even more options.

NEW Forza ● *Italian* | – | – | – | M |

Lincoln Park | 2476 N. Lincoln Ave. (Altgeld St.) | 773-248-7888 |
www.barforza.com

At this dark, funky Lincoln Park 'gastrobar', expect creative, midpriced Italian small plates and pizza plus a classic antique bar issuing an extensive wine list, craft cocktails and 10 draft brews; a
Piaggio motorcycle greets patrons at the front of the long, narrow
space, which has high-top and banquette seating.

Fountainhead *Japanese* | 21 | 22 | 22 | $30 |

Ravenswood | 1970 W. Montrose Ave. (bet. Damen & Winchester Aves.) |
773-697-8204 | www.fountainheadchicago.com

"Unpretentious" yet "not too lowbrow", this "packed" Ravenswood
pub with "damn near the best beer list in the city" goes "beyond typ-

ical bar food" with dishes ranging from a "simple" burger to more "extravagant" duck confit pasta; guests also go for the whiskey selection and "love the feel" of the mahogany bar and rooftop garden.

NEW 4Suyos Peruvian | - | - | - | I |

Logan Square | 2727 W. Fullerton Ave. (bet. California & Washtenaw Aves.) | 773-278-6525 | www.4suyos.com

Peruvian plates like rellenas and ceviche, steamed fish and marinated tofu lure Logan Square locals to this budget-friendly BYO whose name means 'four directions'; the humble storefront setting features bare tables, tile floors and walls and a scattering of framed posters.

Fox & Obel Cafe Eclectic | 20 | 13 | 15 | $20 |

Near North | 401 E. Illinois St. (McClurg Ct.) | 312-379-0112 | www.fox-obel.com

Nestled within a "gourmet" "food palace", this "cafeteria-style" Near North cafe is a "nice place to relax" while enjoying "tempting" Eclectic fare like "tasty" breakfast offerings, "flavorful" sandwiches and "incredible" salads; those bothered by "crowded" conditions and somewhat "slow" service go "during off-peak hours" for a "quality snack" or glass of "delicious wine."

☒ Francesca's Amici Italian | 22 | 19 | 21 | $36 |

Elmhurst | 174 N. York St (2nd St.) | 630-279-7970

☒ Francesca's Bryn Mawr Italian

Edgewater | 1039 W. Bryn Mawr Ave. (Kenmore Ave.) | 773-506-9261

☒ Francesca's by the River Italian

St. Charles | 200 S. Second St. (Illinois St.) | 630-587-8221

☒ Francesca's Fiore Italian

Forest Park | 7407 Madison St. (Harlem Ave.) | 708-771-3063

☒ Francesca's Forno Italian

Wicker Park | 1576 N. Milwaukee Ave. (North Ave.) | 773-770-0184

☒ Francesca's Intimo Italian

Lake Forest | 293 E. Illinois Rd. (Western Ave.) | 847-735-9235

☒ Francesca's North Italian

Northbrook | Northbrook Shopping Plaza | 1145 Church St. (bet. Keystone Ave. & Shermer Rd.) | 847-559-0260

☒ Francesca's on Chestnut Italian

Streeterville | Seneca Hotel | 200 E. Chestnut St. (Mies van der Rohe Way) | 312-482-8800

☒ Francesca's on Taylor Italian

Little Italy/University Village | 1400 W. Taylor St. (Loomis St.) | 312-829-2828

☒ La Sorella di Francesca Italian

Naperville | 18 W. Jefferson Ave. (bet. Main & Washington Sts.) | 630-961-2706
www.miafrancesca.com
Additional locations throughout the Chicago area

"Reliably solid" for Italian fare "done right", this Chicago-based chain (with a few out-of-state sibs) is a "family favorite" thanks to an "affordable" menu that "continues to change", highlighting "well-prepared" standards alongside some "unexpected dishes"; if doubters dub it merely "fair" and complain some locales are "too noisy", fans single out "prompt", "pleasant" service and say it's "always a good option."

Francesco's Hole in the Wall *Italian*   23 | 15 | 21 | $36

Northbrook | 254 Skokie Blvd. (Frontage Rd.) | 847-272-0155 | www.francescosholeinthewall.com

The pasta is "always al dente" at this "tiny", "real-deal" Northbrook Italian known for its "handwritten menus" of "terrific", midpriced dishes proffered by a "friendly" staff; though "not fancy", it's a "longtime favorite" as evidenced by the "noisy", "jammed" dining room and "long waits" (no reservations).

Frankie's Scaloppine & 5th Floor Pizzeria *Italian/Pizza*   19 | 18 | 20 | $29

Gold Coast | 900 Shops | 900 N. Michigan Ave., 5th fl. (bet. Delaware & Walton Pls.) | 312-266-2500 | www.leye.com

"Pizzas and pastas are tasty with enough variety to satisfy a group of picky eaters" at this "cozy" Italian spot to "rest your tired feet" located on the fifth floor of the 900 North Michigan Shops; even "locals" "love the view", "reasonable prices" and "friendly" service.

Franks 'N' Dawgs Ⓜ *Hot Dogs*   26 | 12 | 19 | $14

Lincoln Park | 1863 N. Clybourn Ave. (bet. Kenmore & Sheffield Aves.) | 312-281-5187 | www.franksndawgs.com

"Wonderfully creative", "indulgent" hot dogs and sausages with "refined toppings" and "delightful flavor combinations" are the "epicurean" "love child of Oscar Mayer and Alice Waters" at this Lincoln Park BYO, where "sides that are works of beauty" also grab attention; it may be "pricey" for wieners, but the staff is "always welcoming, even when there are crowds" and a patio provides "plenty of seating in nice weather."

Fred's *American*   20 | 22 | 20 | $45

Gold Coast | Barneys New York | 15 E. Oak St. (Rush St.) | 312-596-1111 | www.barneys.com

It's "quite the scene" for "people-watching" at this "swanky" Gold Coaster that's "hidden" on the top floor of Barneys and "good looking, like most of the diners"; even if opinions vary over the New American fare – "fabulous" vs. "overpriced" – it still comes "alive at lunch" and the terrace is "unbeatable on a gorgeous summer night."

ＮＥＷ French Quarter New Orleans Kitchen ◗ *Cajun*   - | - | - | M

Lombard | Yorktown Ctr. | 44 Yorktown Ctr. (bet. Grace St. & Highland Ave.) | 630-495-2700 | www.fqrestaurant.com

Situated on the outskirts of Yorktown Mall, this upscale Cajun in Lombard transports diners to N'Awlins by way of purple and gold hues, Mardi Gras beads hung from chandeliers and bayou-themed artwork; the native Louisiana chef hits all the basics with both small and large plates (gumbo, étouffée, jambalaya), and there's also a menu of late-night bar bites, served in a front lounge where live jazz plays on Saturdays.

Freshii *American* 18 | 11 | 15 | $11

NEW Loop | 161 N. Clark St. (bet. Lake & Randolph Sts.) | 312-332-4151
Loop | 200 W. Monroe St. (bet. La Salle St. & Wacker Dr.) | 312-269-0995 ☒
NEW Loop | 200 W. Randolph St. (Wells St.) | 312-578-1470
Loop | 311 S. Wacker Dr. (bet. Jackson Blvd. & Van Buren St.) | 312-435-0311 ☒
Near North | 835 N. Michigan Ave. (Chestnut St.) | 312-202-9009
NEW West Loop | 111 W. Jackson Blvd. (S. Clark St.) | 312-588-5998
www.freshii.com

Downtowners on-the-go benefit from "fresh", "giant" salads "tossed to order", as well as wraps, bowls and other "healthyish" American eats done "your way" at this eco-minded global chain; some call the customizable menu "totally confusing" and merely "passable", but boosters brand it a "brilliant concept, perfectly executed."

Froggy's French Cafe ☒ *French* 25 | 21 | 24 | $49

Highwood | 306 Green Bay Rd. (Highwood Ave.) | 847-433-7080 | www.froggysrestaurant.com

"One of the hidden jewels of the North Shore", this Highwood Frenchie turns out "succulent" bistro fare blending classic and modern styles while also offering a "good selection of wine" and "solid, attentive" service; if the brick-lined setting strikes some as "a bit faded", tabs are "reasonable" (thanks in part to a "great" prix fixe) and devotees still "love it" over "30 years later."

NEW Frog n Snail ☒ *American/French* - | - | - | M

Lakeview | 3124 N. Broadway St. (Rosemont Ave.) | 773-661-9166 | www.frognsnail.com

Dale Levitski (Sprout) puts his spin on bistro fare at this midpriced American-French in Lakeview turning out classic plates like beef stroganoff and steak frites – plus the namesake frog and snail dish of course; the space is awash in rustic wood and cool stone with a crêpes-and-coffee bar in the front.

Frontera Fresco *Mexican* 24 | 13 | 15 | $16

Loop | 111 N. State St. (Washington St.) | 312-781-4483 ☒
Skokie | Old Orchard | 4909 Old Orchard Ctr. (Lamon Ave.) | 847-329-2638
www.fronterafresco.com

Tortas Frontera ☒☒ *Mexican*

Loop | 10 S. Dearborn St. (bet. Madison & Monroe Sts.) | no phone
Pilsen | O'Hare Int'l Airport | Terminal 1 | no phone
www.rickbayless.com

"An easy way to get a taste of chef Rick Bayless' creations" "without the wait or prices", this Loop quick-serve in the Macy's food court (with a Skokie sib) offers "amazingly good" tacos, tortas and other "quality" Mexican fare that's "way better than any cafeteria has any right to be"; groupies who admit "going to the mall just to come here" also say "don't miss the fresh lime-based drinks"; P.S. the newer sandwich-focused Tortas Fronteras opened post-Survey.

	FOOD	DECOR	SERVICE	COST

☑ Frontera Grill 🄢🄜 *Mexican* | 27 | 22 | 24 | $44 |

River North | 445 N. Clark St. (bet. Hubbard & Illinois Sts.) | 312-661-1434 | www.fronterakitchens.com

"Celeb" chef-owner Rick Bayless' "deep passion" shows at his "legendary" River North flagship that "elevates Mexican cuisine to a higher order", offering "perfectly executed", "imaginative" dishes with the "right balance of flavor and spice" plus "heavenly margaritas", all set down by "consistently efficient", "well-informed" servers in "festive", "artwork-themed" digs; limited reservations mean it's "very difficult to get a table" and waits are "extremely long", but believers call it "the gold standard" for the genre (adjacent "Topolobampo is the platinum standard"), so "if it isn't worth the wait, what is?"

Frontier ● *American* | ▽ 23 | 21 | 18 | $33 |

Noble Square | 1072 N. Milwaukee Ave. (bet. Noble & Thomas Sts.) | 773-772-4322 | www.thefrontierchicago.com

You can eat just about "any part of any animal" at this American Noble Square gastropub where a "wild-game concept" plays out in "rustic, lodgy" environs featuring a taxidermy bear behind the bar; on the down side, it can be "really crowded" and "crazy loud" with "spotty service", but a "diverse" midpriced menu including some 20 kinds of oysters adds to reasons it's "very enjoyable", "if you get a seat"; P.S. there's a seasonal beer garden.

🆕 Fuji Sushi Buffet *Japanese* | - | - | - | M |

Lakeview | 3026 N. Ashland Ave. (bet. Nelson St. & Wellington Ave.) | 773-327-7000 | www.fujisushibuffet.com

A massive (and MSG-free) spread of all-you-can-eat sushi, seafood, grilled meats, Japanese classics and salad and dessert bars lures Lakeview locals and fish fans to this affordable, alcohol-free strip-mall spot (à la carte items are also offered); wood dividers break up a dining room populated with booths and ornate chairs, a recessed ceiling with colorful, clubby backlighting and – oddly – a meandering mural of the Great Wall of China; P.S. toddlers under three dine for free.

Fulton's on the River 🄢 *Seafood/Steak* | 19 | 21 | 20 | $45 |

River North | 315 N. LaSalle Dr. (Wacker Dr.) | 312-822-0100 | www.fultonsontheriver.com

"Location, location, location" is the reason to visit this "solid" River North steak and seafood spin-off of Disney's Orlando riverboat version, where the patio provides "awesome" views, the "slabs of beef" are "big" and the "dynamite" deviled eggs are "topped with a generous helping of caviar"; still, sticklers say it's "a bit overpriced" for food that "doesn't quite measure up" to the setting and service.

Gabriel's 🄢🄜 *French/Italian* | 25 | 22 | 25 | $75 |

Highwood | 310 Green Bay Rd. (Highwood Ave.) | 847-433-0031 | www.egabriels.com

A "welcoming" "occasion restaurant", this Highwood French-Italian "continues to earn its reputation" say surveyors touting the "interesting", "tasty" cooking from chef-owner Gabriel Viti and "warm,

	FOOD	DECOR	SERVICE	COST

"friendly" servers who are particularly "helpful" when navigating the "extensive wine list"; quibblers say "not much has changed in the last 15 years (including the decor)" and the menu could stand a "refresh", but loyalists wax it "never gets old" – especially if you have an "expense account."

Gaetano's Ⓢ Italian   ∇ 28 | 21 | 24 | $60

Forest Park | 7636 Madison St. (bet. Ashland & Lathrop Aves.) | 708-366-4010 | www.gaetanos.us

If fans "could take a restaurant to a desert island", this smallish Forest Park Italian "would be it", thanks to "a marvelous chef" whose "outstanding" food "continually gets more inventive"; given that it's also a "great bargain" with "friendly" service that "loves feeding the customers", it "never disappoints."

The Gage ◗ American   24 | 22 | 22 | $41

Loop | 24 S. Michigan Ave. (bet. Madison St. & Monroe Dr.) | 312-372-4243 | www.thegagechicago.com

"In a row of ordinary eateries", this "über-hip" gastropub is an "upscale surprise", "really delivering" with chef Dirk Flanigan's "adventurous", "awe-inspiring" New American eats and a "phenomenal beer selection" in "just plain cool" Loop digs featuring an "excellent view of Millenium Park"; enthusiasts justify the "packed and loud" conditions as "part of its charm" and give "attentive" service props too, so most excuse prices that may be a "tad high" for the genre; P.S. "if you value your hearing, wait for summer and eat outdoors."

Gale Street Inn American   22 | 17 | 21 | $30

Jefferson Park | 4914 N. Milwaukee Ave. (Lawrence Ave.) | 773-725-1300 | www.galestreet.com

"Fall-off-the-bone", "perfectly tender" ribs and other "consistently good" Traditional American fare in "generous portions" have made this moderate Jefferson Park "supper club type of joint" a "Chicago tradition" since 1963; "friendly" service lends a "welcoming" vibe, so even those who find the "old-school" decor "lacking" say "don't let that stop you."

Gaylord Fine Indian Cuisine Indian   22 | 18 | 20 | $34

Gold Coast | 100 E. Walton St. (bet. Michigan Ave. & Rush St.) | 312-664-1700
Schaumburg | 555 Mall Dr. (Higgins Rd.) | 847-619-3300
www.gaylordil.com

"Complex, aromatic and flavorful" Indian "classics" delivered with "amicable" service make for "happy" campers at this "authentic", moderately priced twosome; the newer Gold Coast location is more "upscale" than the Schaumburg branch, but both offer a lunch buffet.

Geja's Cafe Fondue   22 | 24 | 22 | $54

Lincoln Park | 340 W. Armitage Ave. (Orleans St.) | 773-281-9101 | www.gejascafe.com

"Perfect for a first date", this "pricey" Lincoln Park "throwback" provides an "intimate setting with dark lights, heavy curtains" and "guitar serenades" as a backdrop for "tasty" fondues of cheese, beef, seafood and chocolate; an "extensive wine list" and "attentive" service stoke the "romantic" vibe, though neatniks warn the "haze of candles and cooking oil" means "dry cleaning is required"; P.S. no children under 10.

🆕 Gemellato Ristorante Ⓜ *Italian* | – | – | – | M |

Bridgeport | 260 W. 26th St. (Princeton Ave.) | 312-706-8081

Bridgeport locals and Sox fans should cheer this upscale, tri-level Italian from the Ricobene's crew serving hearty, traditional entrees, plus steaks, chops and fresh pastas, all paired with a concise, Boot-centric wine list; the handsome setting sports red leather uphol-stered chairs and barstools plus granite and marble surfaces, while the third-floor 260 Sports Bar offers a casual menu, great city views and free parking with a shuttle to Sox games.

Gemini Bistro Ⓜ *American* | 22 | 20 | 22 | $44 |

Lincoln Park | 2075 N. Lincoln Ave. (Dickens Ave.) | 773-525-2522 | www.geminibistrochicago.com

Chef Jason Paskewitz's "approachable" New American fare with French-Med inflections is "designed to please" at this Lincoln Park bistro where a "friendly" staff and simple, "classy" decor including a big marble bar add to the "warm atmosphere"; some call it "solid but not stellar" but given the fair prices and "interesting" bites, locals deem it "worth going back to."

❎ Gene & Georgetti 🅑 *Steak* | 25 | 19 | 23 | $61 |

River North | 500 N. Franklin St. (Illinois St.) | 312-527-3718 | www.geneandgeorgetti.com

"Lusty carnivores" crowd this "venerable" 1940s steakhouse "under the el" in River North to dig into "chops done perfectly" and "porterhouse that falls over the plate"; "crusty" waiters who've "been there forever" are deemed "part of the ambiance" in the "old-school" "men's club" setting, and while skeptics say it's "tired" and that "regulars get better service", it's still considered "worth the experience" and price.

Gene & Jude's Red Hot Stand ❶🏁 *Hot Dogs* | 24 | 8 | 20 | $7 |

O'Hare Area | 2720 River Rd. (Grand Ave.) | 708-452-7634

A "very old-school", "super-affordable" O'Hare Area "institution" since 1950 (and Chicago's No. 1 Bang for the Buck), this pup-house puts out "meaty, squeak-on-your-teeth" hot dogs, plus "fresh-cut fries, tamales and drinks, period!" handed out by "great characters" in "dive" digs (stand-up only); "yes, the line really is that long", but it "moves fast", so dogged diners swear "they still get it right every time, whether it's noon or 2 AM" (closes at 1 Sunday–Thursday); P.S. "do not ask for ketchup if you know what's good for you."

❎ Gibsons Bar & Steakhouse *Steak* | 26 | 22 | 25 | $66 |

Gold Coast | 1028 N. Rush St. (Bellevue Pl.) | 312-266-8999 ❶
Rosemont | Doubletree O'Hare | 5464 N. River Rd. (bet. Balmoral & Bryn Mawr Aves.) | 847-928-9900 ❶

(continued)

Gibsons Bar & Steakhouse

Oak Brook | 2105 S. Spring Rd. (22nd St.) | 630-954-0000
www.gibsonssteakhouse.com

A "first-class icon", this Gold Coast "beef palace" and its suburban sequels tempt "serious steak lovers" with "flavorful" meat and "all the trimmings", "towering" desserts, "stiff drinks" and a "wide wine selection"; the "cost, of course, goes with the quality" (it's more "reasonable for lunch"), and "the wait can be long, long, long – even with reservations" – but service "makes you feel like a regular whether it's your first time or 55th" and the "bustling" crowd of "heavy-hitters" is prime for "people-watching"; P.S. all locations feature live music.

Gilt Bar ●🛭Ⓜ *American*

| 26 | 26 | 22 | $44 |

River North | 230 W. Kinzie St. (bet. Franklin & Wells Sts.) | 312-464-9544 | www.giltbarchicago.com

The name fits at this "stylish", "see-and-be-seen" River North gastropub from Brendan Sodikoff (Au Cheval, Maude's Liquor Bar), where a "decadent", "inspired" New American menu of "exceptional" small and large plates "will melt you to the floor", especially when paired with "imaginative", "delicious" craft cocktails; service is "friendly and laid-back", and while it's not cheap, the "sexy" setting of low lights, ornate chandeliers and leather booths "can't miss" as a "special date-night spot."

Gioco *Italian*

| 22 | 21 | 21 | $42 |

South Loop | 1312 S. Wabash Ave. (13th St.) | 312-939-3870 | www.gioco-chicago.com

"Solid" Northern Italian fare "true to the authentic flavors of Italy" does it for diners who recommend the "perfectly cooked pastas with complex and satisfying sauces" and "excellent" pizza at this "rustic" South Looper set in a circa-1890 building; "friendly service", a "thoughtful wine list" and moderate tabs also help ensure it's a "keeper."

Giordano's *Pizza*

| 22 | 16 | 18 | $22 |

Loop | 135 E. Lake St. (Upper Michigan Ave.) | 312-616-1200
Loop | 225 W. Jackson Blvd. (Franklin St.) | 312-583-9400
River North | 730 N. Rush St. (Superior St.) | 312-951-0747 ●
Lakeview | 1040 W. Belmont Ave. (Kenmore Ave.) | 773-327-1200
Logan Square | 2855 N. Milwaukee Ave. (Wolfram St.) | 773-862-4200
Northwest Side | 5927 W. Irving Park Rd. (Austin Ave.) | 773-736-5553
Hyde Park | 5311 S. Blackstone Ave. (53rd St.) | 773-947-0200
Southwest Side | 5159 S. Pulaski Rd. (Archer Ave.) | 773-582-7676 ●
Southwest Side | 6314 S. Cicero Ave. (63rd St.) | 773-585-6100 ●
Greektown | 815 W. Van Buren St. (Halsted St.) | 312-421-1221
www.giordanos.com
Additional locations throughout the Chicago area

Pie partisans maintain they make "magic" at this string of "classic" "stuffed pizza" specialists (the "scrumptious thin crust" has its supporters too) known for "consistency, extremely fresh sauce", "cheesy goodness" and "overflowing toppings"; service may come "with a smile" but "doesn't rise above the neighborhood pizza joint" genre, and ambiance varies by location, but the price is "decent" and most deem it an overall "crowd-pleaser"; P.S. you can "expect to wait" during prime time, so "order ahead to speed things up."

☑ Girl & The Goat *American*   27 | 24 | 25 | $55

West Loop | 809 W. Randolph St. (bet Green & Halsted Sts.) | 312-492-6262 | www.girlandthegoat.com

"Energetic" chef Stephanie Izard "balances flavors like Monet did with his color palette", creating "top-notch nose-to-tail cuisine" ("duck tongues, lamb hearts" and "pig face, anyone"?), vegetables that "will blow your mind" and other "innovative" small plates that "grab the brass ring" at her "cozy", surprisingly "reasonable" West Loop New American where the "passionate" staff's suggestions will "never lead you astray"; "incredibly noisy" digs are easily overlooked by "foodies" who insist it's the "future of dining"; P.S. "good luck getting a reservation."

Glenn's Diner and Seafood House *Diner*   25 | 16 | 22 | $32

Ravenswood | 1820 W. Montrose Ave. (Honore St.) | 773-506-1720 | www.glennsdiner.com

Rapt raters rave "about half the ocean's on the menu" at this "crowded" Ravenswood waystation that's "quietly serving up" "an incredible selection" of "superbly prepared" seafood alongside Traditional American diner fare and "one-price-fits-all wines" (there's also a "bustling brunch with fabulous Bloody Marys"); "accommodating" service helps many overlook "tightly spaced tables" and a "nondescript setting", especially since some speculate "in another location the food would be 30% more"; P.S. Tuesday's "all-you-can-eat king crab leg is the bomb."

NEW Glenview House ● *American*   19 | 18 | 21 | $29

Glenview | 1843 Glenview Rd. (bet. Lehigh Ave. & Waukegan Rd.) | 847-724-0692 | www.theglenviewhouse.com

The "solid" menu featuring some "interesting" "twists" ("like pot roast nachos") attracts diners "young and old" to this Glenview American, while an "awesome drink selection" including "bourbons galore" and more than 100 beers add "hangout" appeal; set in a recently renovated 18th-century house, it has an "inviting" main downstairs area and an upstairs whiskey bar (typically open Thursday–Saturday only), featuring a "cozy fireplace", and that plus "friendly" service help explain why it often gets "packed."

Goddess & Grocer *Sandwiches*   21 | 11 | 16 | $16

Gold Coast | 25 E. Delaware Pl. (bet. State St. & Wabash Ave.) | 312-896-2600
Bucktown | 1646 N. Damen Ave. (North Ave.) | 773-342-3200
Northwest Side | 2222 N. Elston Ave. (bet. Ashland & Fullerton Aves.) | 773-292-7100
www.goddessandgrocer.com

"Exemplary to-go salads" and "delicious" sandwiches and baked goods win fans at this upscale "deli-style" trio; "friendly" service can be "a little bit slow" and the basic environs have limited seats, but it's still a "great neighborhood spot" to "pick up a gourmet dinner or stop for lunch."

Gold Coast Dogs *Hot Dogs*

17	7	13	$10

Loop | 159 N. Wabash Ave. (bet. Lake & Randolph Sts.) | 312-917-1677
Loop | Union Station | 225 S. Canal St. (bet. Adams St. & Jackson Blvd.) | 312-258-8585
O'Hare Area | O'Hare Int'l Airport | Terminal 3 (I-190) | 773-462-7700
O'Hare Area | O'Hare Int'l Airport | Terminal 5 (I-190) | 773-462-0125
www.goldcoastdogs.net

For the "indulgence" of a "tasty Chicago dog" or other "quick bites", like burgers and sandwiches, these "consistent", counter-serves "hit the spot" – and are easy on the wallet too; despite some who bark it's a "subpar local chain" with merely "adequate" grub and "grumpy" service, supporters say it's still a "convenient" standout for sustenance "on the run."

NEW Goosefoot ⊠Ⓜ *American*

-	-	-	VE

Lincoln Square | 2656 W. Lawrence Ave. (Washtenaw Ave.) | 773-942-7547 | www.goosefoot.net

Chris Nugent made a highly rated splash at old-school French bastion Les Nomades before opening this "impressive" fine-dining "BYO foodie haven" "off the beaten path" in Lincoln Square that offers a "gorgeous, creative" New American tasting menu; expect artisan ingredients, artful presentations, "stellar service" and the high prices that go with them, plus no corkage fee and menus printed on plantable seed paper.

Goose Island Brewing Co. *Pub Food*

17	16	18	$23

Wrigleyville | 3535 N. Clark St. (Addison St.) | 773-832-9040
Lincoln Park | 1800 N. Clybourn Ave. (Sheffield Ave.) | 312-915-0071
www.gooseisland.com

Quaffers honk approval for the "terrific" beer selection at these brewpub twins, where "well-priced" "standard bar fare" meets "some surprisingly upscale options" and service is "friendly" and "efficient"; Lincoln Park offers weekend brewery tours, while fans flock to Wrigleyville "before and after Cubs games" or to watch on the 20 TVs.

Gordon Biersch Brewery
Restaurant *Pub Food*

17	17	15	$25

Bolingbrook | Promenade Bolingbrook | 639 E. Boughton Rd. (Janes Ave.) | 630-739-6036 | www.gordonbiersch.com

"A good place to have a beer with friends in a relaxed atmosphere", this midpriced Bolingbrook chain link offers locally produced microbrews ("some of the seasonal selections are a nice change of pace") paired with some generally "solid" pub grub ("fish and shrimp tacos, burgers and specialty pizzas"); service is "efficient" and the "modern setting" populated by "good people", plus there's "a great patio during warmer weather."

	FOOD	DECOR	SERVICE	COST

The Grafton Pub & Grill *Pub Food*   ▽ 23 | 23 | 21 | $21

Lincoln Square | 4530 N. Lincoln Ave. (bet. Sunnyside & Wilson Aves.) | 773-271-9000 | www.thegrafton.com

A "classic Irish" pub setting sets the stage for a "great beer selection" and solid bar eats like "wonderful burgers" at this affordable Lincoln Square hangout; "friendly" staffers contribute to an atmosphere that "makes you want to pop in on a cold winter evening and stay indefinitely", and concertgoers advise checking it out "before a show" at nearby Old Town School of Folk Music.

Graham Elliot *American*   25 | 22 | 23 | $82

River North | 217 W. Huron St. (bet. Franklin & Wells Sts.) | 312-624-9975 | www.grahamelliot.com

After a post-Survey kitchen shakeup, the "imaginative" New American fare is offered via tasting menus only at Graham Elliot Bowles' "flashy" River Norther known for "expertly prepared" plates "filled with wit and whimsy"; "attentive but not overbearing" service and a "vibrant" setting help make it "upscale without the snottiness", so though a few find it "overpriced", and it's certainly "not for the financially faint of heart", devotees deem it a "dining experience you'll always remember."

Grahamwich *Sandwiches*   19 | 15 | 16 | $16

River North | 615 N. State St. (bet. Ohio & Ontario Sts.) | 312-265-0434 | www.grahamwich.com

Surveyors split over this "affordable" River North concept from Graham Elliot Bowles, with supporters calling it a "charming take on the sandwich joint" and talking up the "to-die-for" sides and "inventive" "upscale" sammies highlighting "unique" "flavor combinations", while the "bummed" bemoan "cramped" environs, "limited seating" and say the "ideas are better than the execution."

Grand Lux Cafe *Eclectic*   21 | 23 | 21 | $31

River North | 600 N. Michigan Ave. (Ontario St.) | 312-276-2500 | www.grandluxcafe.com

A more "upscale" version of the Cheesecake Factory, this River North Eclectic offers a similar "monstrous-sized menu" in "glitzy" grand cafe-style environs "overlooking Michigan Avenue"; it's "touristy, yes", but "fair prices" given the "oversized portions" earn favor as does "fast", "genuinely friendly" service, so as with the original, "plan to wait and wait."

NEW Grange Hall   - | - | - | I
Burger Bar 🖪 🅼 *American/Burgers*

West Loop | 844 W. Randolph St. (bet. Green & Peoria Sts.) | 312-491-0844 | www.grangehallburgerbar.com

Burgers get the farm-to-table treatment at this West Loop joint offering gourmet patties (think grass-fed beef, free-range turkey, veggie and bean) with a variety of local cheeses and toppings, paired with snacks, sides and homemade pies and ice creams, plus cocktails, classic American canned beers and a rotating vino selection; touches like cowbells, barn lamps and mismatched antique linens lend charm in the rustic farmhouse setting, and breakfast is in the works.

	FOOD	DECOR	SERVICE	COST

NEW Gratto Pizzeria &

- | **-** | **-** | **M**

Deli *Pizza/Sandwiches*

Wicker Park | 1341 N. Damen Ave. (bet. Evergreen Ave. & Schiller St.) | 773-904-7455 | www.wickerparkpizza.com

This Wicker Park entry delivers (literally and figuratively) a dozen or so rustic thin-crust pizza creations plus selections of classic Italian cold subs and hot sandwiches, with a BYO policy that helps keep prices moderate; the quaint vintage brick storefront with a handful of tables features a photo wall of fame and a deli case stocked with meats, cheese and olives.

Great Lake ⑤ Ⓜ *Pizza*

27 | **14** | **15** | **$28**

Andersonville | 1477 W. Balmoral Ave. (bet. Clark St. & Glenwood Ave.) | 773-334-9270

"Beautifully chewy and fragrant pies come out of the oven" at this organic-focused Andersonville BYO known for "interesting" combinations, "crust so good you could eat it plain" and "crazy waits" (though most promise "your patience is rewarded"); "decor is spartan, service is basic" and a few find it "just so-so", but more insist it's got some of the "best pizza in the city" – "too bad" it's seldom open (Wednesday–Saturday).

Greek Islands *Greek*

22 | **19** | **22** | **$29**

Greektown | 200 S. Halsted St. (Adams St.) | 312-782-9855 ●
Lombard | 300 E. 22nd St. (Highland Ave.) | 630-932-4545
www.greekislands.net

Hellenophiles hail these "welcoming" Greektown and Lombard "go-tos" for "authentic", "down-to-earth Greek comfort food" (including "flaming cheese") "consistently well-prepared" "in the traditional way"; generally "efficient service" and "reasonable prices" are other pluses, so it's often "packed" and also "perfect for family dining"

Green Zebra *Vegetarian*

28 | **23** | **25** | **$49**

Noble Square | 1460 W. Chicago Ave. (Greenview Ave.) | 312-243-7100 | www.greenzebrachicago.com

"Creativity reigns" at Shawn McClain's "sophisticated" Noble Square stop, "the best vegetarian in town" say surveyors touting the "high-quality", "beautifully presented" small plates with "flavors incredible enough to thrill carnivores"; extras like "impeccable service", a "sleek" setting and "great wine list" add allure, and if it's "a little expensive, you definitely get what you pay for", so acolytes advise "open your mind and go – immediately."

The Grill on the Alley *American*

21 | **20** | **21** | **$48**

Streeterville | Westin Michigan Ave. | 909 N. Michigan Ave. (Delaware Pl.) | 312-255-9009 | www.thegrill.com

"Solid" "standard American fare" awaits at this "dependable, clubby" Beverly Hills spin-off in Streeterville's Westin Michigan Avenue where "reliable steaks" and other "enjoyable" dishes mean you may "not have a gastronomique festivale of an experience but you won't go away hungry"; it's not cheap, but "attentive service" and a "low-key" vibe make it a "quiet place to meet friends or business associates."

	FOOD	DECOR	SERVICE	COST

GT Fish & Oyster *Seafood* | 26 | 24 | 24 | $54 |

River North | 531 N. Wells St. (Grand Ave.) | 312-929-3501 | www.gtoyster.com

Fish practically "swim right onto the plate" at this "trendy" River North "marine dream" ("all that's missing is the brine in the air") where chef Giuseppe Tentori's "inventive" "small-plate seafood" offerings display "depth of skill", the "cocktails are perfection" and service is "engaging"; the nautical-themed space is "kitschy" but "chic" with communal tables and floor-to-ceiling windows, and though a little "pricey" for some, most have "no complaints except for the difficulty of getting reservations."

NEW Gyro-Ména ● *Greek* | - | - | - | I |

Lakeview | 905 W. Belmont Ave. (bet. Clark St. & Wilton Ave.) | 773-935-2600 | www.gyro-mena.com

This fresh idea in casual dining brings build-your-own gyros to Lakeview, offering a meat choice of spit-roasted chicken, pork or 'American' ground beef and lamb, 15 toppings and 10 sauces (or fries stuffed inside), along with classics like Greek chicken, saganaki and spanakopita; the casual, counter-service space features butcher block tables, high-top stools at counters and TVs showing belly dancers, and a 2 AM closing time Friday–Saturday should please night owls.

Gyu-Kaku *Japanese* | 23 | 19 | 20 | $33 |

Streeterville | 210 E. Ohio St. (St. Clair St.) | 312-266-8929 | www.gyu-kaku.com

If you want to "try something new" and like to "play with your food", head to this Streeterville link of an international Japanese yakiniku chain for "mouthwatering appetizers" and "nicely spiced meat and vegetables" that you cook yourself on in-table grills amid industrial, wood-accented stylings; "friendly" service "helps explain the procedure" and "the price is right", so it's a "great destination for a group dining experience."

Hackney's *Burgers* | 19 | 15 | 19 | $22 |

Printers Row | 733 S. Dearborn St. (bet. Harrison & Polk Sts.) | 312-461-1116
Glenview | 1241 Harms Rd. (Lake Ave.) | 847-724-5577
Glenview | 1514 E. Lake Ave. (bet. Sunset Ridge & Waukegan Rds.) | 847-724-7171
Lake Zurich | 880 N. Old Rand Rd. (Rand Rd.) | 847-438-2103
Palos Park | 9550 W. 123rd St. (La Grange Rd.) | 708-448-8300
www.hackneys.net

"When you're craving a burger" that "soaks through the dark rye", "drips down your arm" and is elevated by the "cardiac indulgence" of "don't-miss" onion rings, plus "interesting beers on tap" and "mean martinis", fans suggest these "reasonably priced" "local institutions" tended by "friendly" staffers; complainers citing "dated", "divey" decor and fare that's "only average" are drowned out by die-hards deeming them the "real deal" and "better than" newer joints "by a country mile."

Hai Yen *Chinese/Vietnamese*
22 | 13 | 17 | $22

Lincoln Park | 2723 N. Clark St. (Diversey Pkwy.) | 773-868-4888
Uptown | 1055 W. Argyle St. (bet. Kenmore & Winthrop Aves.) | 773-561-4077
www.haiyenrestaurant.com

"Authentic" Vietnamese eats plus Mandarin specialties make for "great comfort food" at this "bargain-priced" Uptown and Lincoln Park duo; "helpful" staffers "make it easy to navigate the menu" and though decor is "minimal", so is the noise, so many "don't understand why it's not more crowded"; P.S. Uptown is closed on Wednesdays.

Half Shell ●⇗ *Seafood*
24 | 9 | 18 | $34

Lakeview | 676 W. Diversey Pkwy. (bet. Clark & Orchard Sts.) | 773-549-1773 | www.halfshellchicago.com

"Crab legs are the big draw" of this cash-only Lakeview "dungeon" where finatics who "don't care about the atmosphere" fill up on "huge portions" of "well-prepared" seafood at prices much "lower" than found elsewhere; sure, the "basement locale" is "divey" and service can be "rough", but it's all "part of the charm" for "an experience" that's "well worth" it; P.S. no reservations.

Hamburger Mary's *Burgers*
19 | 18 | 22 | $20

Andersonville | 5400 N. Clark St. (Balmoral Ave.) | 773-784-6969 | www.hamburgermaryschicago.com

"A spectacle of a dining experience" say fans of this "playful", "funky" Andersonville "must" dishing "inventive" (some say "crazy") "giant hamburgers", plus other "reliable comfort food" all "served up with a little sass" by the staffers in drag; it's nothing "fancy", but returners call it "fun at all times" – including when a "stiletto lands on the table with the bill"; the adjacent Rec Room sports bar serves the full menu.

Hannah's Bretzel *Sandwiches*
23 | 16 | 18 | $13

Loop | 131 S. Dearborn St. (bet. Adams St. & Marble Pl.) | 312-621-1111
Loop | 180 W. Washington St. (bet. La Salle & Wells Sts.) | 312-621-1111 🖲
Loop | Illinois Ctr. | 233 N. Michigan Ave. (Wacker Pl.) | 312-621-1111 🖲
NEW **River North** | 400 N. LaSalle St. (bet. Kinzie & Hubbard Sts.) | 312-621-1111
www.hannahsbretzel.com

"Delicious pretzel bread", "exciting flavor combinations" and "fresh, healthy options" add up to "addicting", "mouthwatering" sammies at these Downtown spots where "quality" organic ingredients keep them "a step ahead of the competition" and justify "higher than average costs"; the spaces differ by locale (Washington Street has very limited seating and Dearborn is "roomy"), but "don't let the long lines fool you", because "friendly"service at each "gets you in and out quickly."

Han 202 Ⓜ *Asian/Eclectic*
25 | 23 | 23 | $32

Bridgeport | 605 W. 31st St. (bet. Lowe Ave. & Wallace St.) | 312-949-1314 | www.han202.com

"Unusual but delicious" say surveyors of this Bridgeport BYO offering an "innovative", "well-presented" prix fixe menu of Eclectic-influenced Asian dishes; tabs are "unbelievably inexpensive", staffers "friendly" and the digs "serene" and "conversation-friendly", so many say it's one of the "best deals in town."

Happ Inn Bar & Grill   *American*   17 | 16 | 19 | $32

Northfield | 305 Happ Rd. (bet. Mt. Pleasant St. & Orchard Ln.) | 847-784-9200 | www.thehappinn.com

"You name it, you can get it" at this "welcoming" Northfield resto-bar offering a "wide-ranging" menu from burgers, salads and other American "standards" to pizza and Mexican specialties like tacos and enchiladas; despite "close-together" tables and "noisy" conditions that make it "difficult to hear your table companions", "regulars" say it "fills a void", which explains why it's "popular" and "always packed."

Hard Rock Cafe ● *American*   14 | 22 | 15 | $29

River North | 63 W. Ontario St. (bet. Clark & Dearborn Sts.) | 312-943-2252 | www.hardrockcafe.com

If dining among "rock 'n' roll memorabilia" sounds like "paradise" to you, then "the ambiance is worth the visit" to this "noisy", "touristy" River North chain link offering "typical" American fare ("you won't find epicurean food"); it's "spendy" for what you get and critics scoff "been to one city, been to 'em all", but "music fans" still mark it a "must stop", and hey, at least "the drinks are good."

Harry Caray's   *Italian/Steak*   23 | 22 | 22 | $45
(aka Harry Caray's Italian Steakhouse)

River North | 33 W. Kinzie St. (Dearborn St.) | 312-828-0966
Rosemont | O'Hare International Ctr., Holiday Inn | 10233 W. Higgins Rd. (Orchard Pl.) | 847-699-1200
Lombard | Westin Lombard | 70 Yorktown Ctr. (Butterfield Rd.) | 630-953-3400

Harry Caray's Seventh Inning Stretch   *Italian/Steak*
Southwest Side | Midway Int'l Airport | 5757 S. Cicero Ave. (55th St.) | 773-948-6300
www.harrycarays.com

Diners who "like steak and sports memorabilia" find this midpriced trio (with a Midway sib) a "true Chicago treat", with "surprisingly good" "high-quality" chops plus "solid Italian staples" and "ample drinks" in "old-fashioned" surroundings displaying a "massive collection" of "interesting" baseball paraphernalia; foes crying foul over "predictable" eats and "tourist trap" vibes are outmatched by fans insisting the "laid-back" setting and "crowd-watching" capabilities are "endlessly entertaining"; P.S. there's also a more casual Navy Pier tavern offshoot.

Harry Caray's Tavern   *American*   19 | 20 | 18 | $37

River North | Navy Pier | 700 E. Grand Ave. (Lake Shore Dr.) | 312-527-9700 | www.harrycaraystavern.com

"Consistently good" American standards (burgers, salads, pasta) offered at "reasonable" prices make this more casual River sib to the Harray Caray steakhouses the "valedictorian in a wasteland of sub-par" Navy Pier dining options; critics complain it's a "tourist trap", but its "sports bar" vibe appeals to others who find it a "comfortable" choice, especially for "people-watching" on the patio.

Haymarket Pub & Brewery ❶ *Pub Food*   18 | 18 | 19 | $22

West Loop | 737 W. Randolph St. (Halsted St.) | 312-638-0700 |
www.haymarketbrewing.com

"A changing list of house beers", "plus guest brews" "add to the lure" of this West Looper where "better then average pub food" is served by "nice people" in a "rustic room" with "old Chicago style" and a "large rooftop with a view of the skyline"; while some sippers wish they'd "improve" the "limited menu" selection, realists reckon "it's not the hautest place in the area, but it's good and affordable."

HB Home Bistro Ⓜ *American*   25 | 21 | 24 | $37

Lakeview | 3404 N. Halsted St. (Roscoe St.) | 773-661-0299 |
www.homebistrochicago.com

"Connoisseurs delight" in the "sublime" New American bistro fare at Joncarl Lachman's small Lakeview "gem" – "one of the most affordable upscale restaurants around" thanks to a BYO policy and an "amazing" Wednesday prix fixe; with a "cozy", "noisy" atmosphere and service that's "charming" and "relaxed", you'll feel "like you're family – but one of those cool families."

Heartland Cafe *Eclectic/Vegetarian*   17 | 16 | 18 | $20

Rogers Park | Heartland Bldg. | 7000 N. Glenwood Ave. (Lunt Ave.) |
773-465-8005 | www.heartlandcafe.com

"Real hippies" favor this affordable, "longtime" veggie "institution" in Rogers Park for "healthy" Eclectic eats including "some decent carnivore options" in a "down-home" setting "with authentic character"; malingerers who say "meh", however, are "baffled" by the "mystique", citing occasionally "dodgy service", musing its "few" nearby "competitors" may account for its popularity; P.S. you can "sit outside and enjoy the sunshine."

Hearty Ⓜ *American*   23 | 19 | 22 | $40

Lakeview | 3819 N. Broadway (Grace St.) | 773-868-9866 |
www.heartychicago.com

Former Food Network stars, the Hearty Boys "definitely bring it" at this "inventive", midpriced New American in Lakeview, serving "rich" yet "refined" comfort food with a "modern" Southern accent; "easygoing" if a bit "slick", it comes through with "solid" service and "consistent" cooking that devotees say "has yet to disappoint."

Heaven on Seven *Cajun/Creole*   21 | 17 | 19 | $26

Loop | Garland Bldg. | 111 N. Wabash Ave., 7th fl. (Washington Blvd.) |
312-263-6443 🗷⇗

River North | AMC Loews | 600 N. Michigan Ave., 2nd fl. (bet. Ohio &
Ontario Sts.) | 312-280-7774

Naperville | 224 S. Main St. (bet. Jackson & Jefferson Aves.) |
630-717-0777

www.heavenonseven.com

For a "'N'Awlins fix" of Cajun–Creole "delights", fans hit this "festive", "kitschy" mini-chain that "maintains its kick" with "authentic" "toothsome" fare (plus a "wall of hot sauces") and "killer cocktails" like "spicy Bloody Marys", all ferried by generally "professional" servers; while some score it simply a "solid approximation" of the "real deal", most appreciate the "reasonable prices" and are especially loyal to the cash-only Loop original with a "lunch counter vibe" (it's not open for dinner).

Hecky's Barbecue *BBQ*

22 | 5 | 15 | $17

Evanston | 1902 Green Bay Rd. (Emerson St.) | 847-492-1182 | www.heckys.com

The "sauce is the secret" at this "iconic" Evanston BBQ joint, a "long-time local favorite" for "smoky, crunchy rib tips", "massive turkey legs" and "standout" sides, all at "reasonable prices"; it's takeout and delivery only, so no matter that its "divey" ambiance "leaves something to be desired", since only those looking to "see a Chicago Bear" find reason to linger.

Hema's Kitchen *Indian*

22 | 14 | 18 | $25

Lincoln Park | 2411 N. Clark St. (Fullerton Pkwy.) | 773-529-1705
West Rogers Park | 2439 W. Devon Ave. (bet. Artesian & Campbell Aves.) | 773-338-1627
www.hemaskitchen.com

"Solid", "authentic" Indian cooking including "stellar vegetarian standards" "satisfies" at these Lincoln Park and West Rogers Park BYOs where the "variety"of offerings is reminiscent of dining with "your grandma making sure you don't lose weight"; sure, the decor "could use some sprucing up", but service is "earnest" and prices "affordable", so most "will definitely come back."

☑ Henri *American*

27 | 27 | 26 | $69

Loop | 18 S. Michigan Ave. (Monroe St.) | 312-578-0763 | www.henrichicago.com

"A lavish surprise" awaits at this "high-end" Loop New American, where chef Dirk Flanigan's French-inflected menu boasting "regional ingredients combined in fresh, innovative ways" is complemented by "top-notch" wines and "tasty" craft cocktails; the "peaceful", "visually stunning" space sets a tone of "refinement without stuffiness" and "service is superb", so "everything is fit for a queen", including the tab.

Home Run Inn Pizza *Pizza*

25 | 17 | 22 | $21

Southwest Side | 4254 W. 31st St. (bet. Kildare & Tripp Aves.) | 773-247-9696 | www.hrichicagosbestpizza.com ◗
Southwest Side | 6221 S. Archer Ave. (Moody Ave.) | 773-581-9696 | www.homeruninn.com
Addison | 1480 W. Lake St. (Foxdale Dr.) | 630-775-9696 | www.hrichicagosbestpizza.com
Bolingbrook | 1280 W. Boughton Rd. (Weber Rd.) | 630-679-9966 | www.hrichicagosbestpizza.com
Westmont | 605 N. Cass Ave (Ogden Ave.) | 630-789-0096 | www.hrichicagosbestpizza.com

Outlying areas lay claim to these "time-enduring" pie parlors that "pay homage to the past" with "addicting" "old-style" "thin pizza" "with a sweet crispy crust" "loaded" with so many ingredients "it's almost not thin any more"; prized as much for being "neighborhood anchors" (some for "generations") as for their "reasonable prices", they hit a home run as fan "favorites."

Honey 1 BBQ Ⓜ BBQ   21 | 7 | 18 | $16

Bucktown | 2241 N. Western Ave. (Lyndale St.) | 773-227-5130 | www.honey1bbq.com

"Your mouth waters from the smell of the meat slow cooking" attest admirers of this Bucktown BYO "cranking out" "authentic" BBQ offerings like "standout" ribs "smoked to perfection" via "friendly" staffers; it's "not a romantic spot for a first date", but the "no-frills" setting matches the budget-friendly tabs.

Hop Häus ❶ Burgers   19 | 16 | 16 | $19

River North | 646 N. Franklin St. (Erie St.) | 312-467-4287
Rogers Park | 7545 N. Clark St. (Howard St.) | 773-262-3783
www.thehophaus.com

A "wide selection of beer will quench your thirst" at this River North and Rogers Park duo specializing in "all kinds" of "gourmet" burgers available in "every type of meat imaginable" (plus veggie too) and in "every possible combination"; the spacious digs have many wide-screen televisions, so even if a few complain of "inconsistent" grub and "slow" service, supporters say "if you want to eat and watch a sporting event", "you've come to the right haus."

Hopleaf Belgian   24 | 19 | 19 | $30

Andersonville | 5148 N. Clark St. (Foster Ave.) | 773-334-9851 | www.hopleaf.com

The "staggering" beer list "impresses even the most experienced connoisseur" and the "excellent" Belgian-focused menu "shows range" with "plenty" of "inventive" "tasty twists" (try the "kick-ass mussels") at this affordable Andersonville gastropub populated by a "young, lively crowd" (21 and older only); "knowledgeable" service can border on smug" and no ressies often means "painful" waits, but it's still "almost always packed" – though an impending expansion should help.

NEW Hota Ⓜ Spanish   - | - | - | M

Evanston | 2545 Prairie Ave. (bet. Central & Harrison Sts.) | 847-733-0899 | www.hotarestaurant.com

New owners have transformed Evanston's Jacky's On Prairie into this moderately priced Spanish with an eclectic, Latin-influenced menu offered in small and large plates; the tony setting features multiple seating areas, gleaming wood floors, stained butcher block tables and rotating local artwork.

Hot Chocolate Ⓜ American   24 | 21 | 21 | $34

Bucktown | 1747 N. Damen Ave. (Willow St.) | 773-489-1747 | www.hotchocolatechicago.com

"Sweet and savory are both done to perfection" at chef-owner Mindy Segal's Bucktown American where the midpriced menu of "imaginative" entrees and "divinely inspired" desserts has been given a heavier seasonal focus following a post-Survey revamp and accompanying renovation; the new digs have a more industrial look, and additional seats may help alleviate "crowded" conditions.

❷ Hot Doug's 🈲🚭 *Hot Dogs*   26 | 14 | 21 | $13

Avondale | 3324 N. California Ave. (Roscoe St.) | 773-279-9550 | www.hotdougs.com

"Genius" owner Doug Sohn often "greets everybody personally" and takes orders at the counter of his "iconic" Avondale "shrine to encased meats", bringing franks to "unbelievable heights" with "incredibly creative" gourmet concoctions like foie gras–topped Sauternes duck sausage and "scrumptious" Friday and Saturday-only duck fat fries, all for under $10; guests wait in "huge" lines to visit the "cramped", "tacky" ketchup-colored shop, but it is "well worth the wait" for these "pedigreed pups."

Hot Woks Cool Sushi *Asian*   19 | 17 | 19 | $24

Loop | 30 S. Michigan Ave. (bet. Madison & Monroe Sts.) | 312-345-1234
Loop | 312 W. Adams St. (bet. Franklin St. & Wacker Dr.) | 312-220-0011 🈲
Old Irving Park | 3930 N. Pulaski Rd. (Dakin St.) | 773-282-1818
Roscoe Village | 2032 W. Roscoe St. (Seeley Ave.) | 773-880-9800
www.hotwokscoolsushi.com

"Delicious" noodles, "creative sushi rolls" (like the Obama-nami) and other "flavorful" Asian dishes "come out fast" thanks to "efficient" staffers at this "reasonably priced" city quartet; it's often "nice and quiet" too, though some cite "uneven" results, warning "what's good is very good", but what's bad is . . .", well, "stick with the standards"; P.S. Irving Park is BYO.

Hubbard Inn 🈲 *American*   21 | 23 | 19 | $36

River North | 110 W. Hubbard St. (bet. Clark & LaSalle Sts.) | 312-222-1331 | www.hubbardinn.com

Diners "spend time wandering around just looking" at the "interesting" art and "beautiful people scattered" throughout the "variety of areas" (including the first-floor lounge that looks like a "rustic version of a Harry Potter library") at this multilevel River North American; the moderately priced menu is anchored by "very good" snacks and "shared plates", with a selection of craft brews and "fantastic cocktails" and "happy servers" contribute to an overall "warm", "lively" atmosphere, but since it can get "noisy", some leave it to "the younger set."

Hub 51 ◐ *American/Eclectic*   21 | 20 | 19 | $35

River North | 51 W. Hubbard St. (Dearborn St.) | 312-828-0051 | www.hub51chicago.com

The "seen-and-be-seen-set" pack this "trendy" River North American-Eclectic serving "diverse" "upgraded bar food" (sushi, burgers, tacos) in addition to a "fantastic" brunch; "informed" staffers tend the "modern" space where "twentysomething scenesters" "tweet", "watch a game" or enjoy a "night on the town" that continues on to the "hopping" club Sub 51 downstairs, and if detractors don't see the appeal, buffs "could stay here all day."

Z Hugo's Frog Bar & Chop House ◐ *Seafood/Steak* 25 | 22 | 24 | $56

NEW Des Plaines | Rivers Casino | 3000 S. River Rd. (Devon Ave.) | 847-768-5200

Z Hugo's Frog Bar & Fish House ◐ *Seafood*

Gold Coast | 1024 N. Rush St. (bet. Bellevue Pl. & Oak St.) | 312-640-0999

Naperville | Main Street Promenade Bldg. | 55 S. Main St. (Van Buren Ave.) | 630-548-3764

www.hugosfrogbar.com

"Steaks and seafood, done simply" star at this "upscale" trio affiliated with Gibsons (which supplies the beef) that's also known for "succulent frogs' legs doused in garlic butter" and desserts "gigantic" enough to "feed a small village"; "friendly", "attentive" service leaves most with "no complaints" and the "boisterous" "convivial atmosphere" adds "night out" (but "not quiet date") appeal, so though it's "pricey", those looking for a "great feasting experience" put it on the "repeat list"; P.S. the Des Plaines outpost in the Rivers Casino is 21 and older only.

NEW Hutong Fresh Asian Café *Asian* - | - | - | I

Oak Park | 1113 Lake St. (bet. Harlem Ave. & Marion St.) | 708-383-9888 | www.hutongcafe.com

At this Oak Park entry from Sushi House vets, the budget-friendly Pan-Asian menu includes plenty of nods to Beijing street fare; the earth-toned, counter-serve digs feature multihued banquettes, wood seating and moody lantern lighting.

Il Mulino New York *Italian* 25 | 25 | 24 | $72

Gold Coast | 1150 N. Dearborn St. (bet. Division & Elm Sts.) | 312-440-8888 | www.ilmulino.com

For a "romantic" rendezvous over "fine Italian cuisine" in a "charming atmosphere" enhanced by service that "makes you feel special", this "classy" NYC-bred contender in the Gold Coast's historic Biggs Mansion is "hard to beat"; fence-sitters deem it an "uninspired" experience that's just "too expensive", but they're outvoted by enthusiasts who describe it as "exquisite all around."

Ina's *American* 23 | 18 | 21 | $21

West Loop | 1235 W. Randolph St. (Elizabeth St.) | 312-226-8227 | www.breakfastqueen.com

"Breakfast heaven" declare diners of "friendly Chicagoan" Ina Pinkney's West Loop New American that delivers "good old-fashioned comfort food" (offered at lunch too) via "warm" staffers known to "treat you like a relative who is actually liked"; the "simple" space "lined with an eclectic collection of mistmatching salt and pepper shakers" is complemented by a "happy", "welcoming" vibe, and that plus affordable prices help ensure it comes "highly recommended."

	FOOD	DECOR	SERVICE	COST

India House *Indian*
22 | 18 | 19 | $31

River North | 59 W. Grand Ave. (bet. Clark & Dearborn Sts.) | 312-645-9500
Arlington Heights | 721 W. Golf Rd. (bet. Algonquin Rd. & Fernandez Ave.) | 847-278-0760
Buffalo Grove | Buffalo Grove Town Ctr. | 228-230 McHenry Rd. (Lake Cook Rd.) | 847-520-5569
Oak Brook | 2809 Butterfield Rd. (Meyers Rd.) | 630-472-1500
www.indiahousechicago.com

A "tremendous" selection of "authentic" Indian dishes at "reasonable prices" has fans branding this chain a "solid performer", especially since it "adjusts spice levels to Midwestern palates" and the "large portions will keep you full"; devotees also cheer the "helpful" staff and "tasteful" surroundings, and the few who find tabs "a bit too expensive" concede the "high-quality" lunch buffet is a "huge plus."

Indian Garden *Indian*
20 | 18 | 17 | $32

Streeterville | 247 E. Ontario St. (Fairbanks Ct.) | 312-280-4910 | www.indiangardenchicago.com

Set on the second floor in a "quiet" room "with huge windows", this Streeterville Indian garners praise for "well-seasoned" sometimes "spicy" fare that "transports you straight to India"; "reasonable prices" and generally "attentive" service are also appreciated by frequenters as is the "good lunch buffet"; P.S. the West Rogers Park outpost is separately owned.

Indie Cafe *Japanese/Thai*
23 | 20 | 21 | $22

Edgewater | 5951 N. Broadway (bet. Elmdale & Thorndale Aves.) | 773-561-5577 | www.indiecafe.us

"Gorgeous" presentations stand out at this "consistent" Edgewater "go-to" bringing together "quality" Thai and Japanese (including "excellent" sushi) in a simple, "unassuming" setting; customers also commend the "prompt" service and "outrageously affordable" tabs.

Ing ⑤Ⓜ *American*
23 | 22 | 21 | $78

West Loop | 951 W. Fulton Mkt. (Morgan St.) | 855-834-6464 | www.ingrestaurant.com

A "flavor tripping menu" awaits at this "extremely creative" West Loop New American from Homaro Cantu (Moto) where the molecular gastronomy fare is mostly "very good", though a few say the "fussy" "experiments" could use "some fine-tuning"; some also find it "overpriced", though admit the high ceilings and red walls contribute a "cool" feel and service is "attentive."

Inovasi ⑤ *American*
26 | 23 | 25 | $44

Lake Bluff | 28 E. Center Ave. (Scranton Ave.) | 847-295-1000 | www.inovasi.us

"Lake Bluff is now on the inventive fine-dining map" thanks to "passionate" chef John des Rosiers' "refreshing" New American "foodie find" where "sustainable, organic "small plates are "innovative and delicious" and the "über-local" produce may come from the rooftop garden, making prices "reasonable" for the "quality"; items are "expertly served" in a "bistro" atmosphere, so it's an overall "joyous" place for a "green night out."

Intelligentsia Coffee *Coffeehouse* 23 | 18 | 21 | $9

Loop | 53 W. Jackson Blvd. (bet. S. Michigan & S. Wabash Aves.) | 312-253-0594 🗷

Loop | 53-55 E. Randolph St. (bet. N. LaSalle & N. State Sts.) | 312-920-9332

NEW **River North** | Merchandise Mart | 222 W. Merchandise Mart Plaza, 12th fl. (bet. Orleans & Wells Sts.) | 312-340-4443 🗷 M

Lakeview | 3123 N. Broadway St. (bet. Barry Ave. & Briar Pl.) | 773-348-8058

www.intelligentsiacoffee.com

"Coffee snobs" clamor for "craftsmanship in a cup", like "amazing lattes", "properly well-made drip" and the "best espresso", at this city foursome where "exacting baristas know their stuff"; "while prices are higher" than at other places, the "casual hipster crowd" doesn't mind, especially since the comfortable digs feel like a "second living room", making it an overall "ideal place to caffeinate."

Irazu 🗷 🗭 *Costa Rican* 23 | 12 | 19 | $17

Bucktown | 1865 N. Milwaukee Ave. (Western Ave.) | 773-252-5687 | www.irazuchicago.com

"Fantastic" "traditional" Costa Rican food offered at "cheap" prices makes this "vegetarian-friendly" Bucktown BYO a "favorite"; an "unimpressive" building is bettered by the "cantinalike" atmosphere, a "warm" staff and "improved outdoor seating", just note no reservations and cash-only; P.S. "try the oatmeal shake", it's "the best."

Itto Sushi 🌑🗷 *Japanese* 24 | 17 | 24 | $35

Lincoln Park | 2616 N. Halsted St. (Wrightwood Ave.) | 773-871-1800 | www.ittosushi.com

A "total real-deal that predates the sushi craze", this circa-1982 Lincoln Park Japanese proffers plates so "authentic" and "well prepared" that aficionados advise you "forget the trendy spots"; "entertaining chefs" engage with a "good local crowd" ("regulars, Japanese expats") in the simple space, and with patio seating and late service (till midnight), it's an "all-time fave."

Jack's on Halsted 🌑 *American* 16 | 16 | 17 | $37

Lakeview | 3201 N. Halsted St. (Belmont Ave.) | 773-244-9191 | www.jacksonhalsted.com

Loyalists find this "useful" Lakeview New American to be "one of the few good restaurants" in the area, citing a "fun" atmosphere, "thoughtful menu" and "well-priced wine list"; naysayers, however, hesitate over "hit-or-miss" meals and find the whole affair "overpriced for what you get."

Jake Melnick's Corner Tap 🌑 *Pub Food* 19 | 19 | 20 | $24

Gold Coast | 41 E. Superior St. (Wabash Ave.) | 312-266-0400 | www.jakemelnicks.com

"Above-average" bar food and "tons of beer options" does it for those who tap this "dependable" Gold Coast pub; many TVs make it a "safe choice for watching sporting events", and with solid service and "reasonable prices", it also draws those simply looking for a "comfy place to hang out."

J. Alexander's *American* | 21 | 19 | 21 | $34 |

Lincoln Park | 1832 N. Clybourn Ave. (bet. Willow & Wisconsin Sts.) | 773-435-1018
Northbrook | 4077 Lake Cook Rd. (bet. I-294 & Sanders Rd.) | 847-564-3093
Oak Brook | 1410 16th St. (Rte. 83) | 630-573-8180
www.jalexanders.com

Chain-averse "foodies make an exception" for these "well-managed" "meeting spots" that "aim to please" with "quick", "consistent" service and a "large, diverse" American menu of "reliable food at decent prices"; still, foes find them "average" and say "the only thing not mediocre is the bill at the end of the meal", while also conceding they "work when you need to sit down with a bunch of friends."

Jam ⊅ *American* | ▽ 28 | 24 | 24 | $21 |

Logan Square | 3059 W. Logan Blvd. (bet. Milwaukee & Sacramento Aves.) | 773-292-6011 | www.jamrestaurant.com

After relocating from Ukrainian Village to Logan Square, this affordable New American BYO known for "interesting, consistent" dishes offered at its "crazy good breakfasts" and "excellent brunches" now serves dinner too; the stainless-steel–accented space with an upscale diner feel gets much improved marks and service is "friendly" to boot, so it's a "don't-miss" kinda place.

Jane's Ⓜ *American/Eclectic* | 24 | 20 | 22 | $33 |

Bucktown | 1655 W. Cortland St. (Paulina St.) | 773-862-5263 | www.janesrestaurant.com

The "chef strives to make every dish original and usually succeeds" at this "quaint" New American–Eclectic in a "tucked away" Bucktown locale; service that warrants no complaints, moderate prices and cozy, "relaxed" surrounds "convince" most it's an overall "charming place for brunch, lunch or dinner."

Japonais *Japanese* | 24 | 26 | 21 | $58 |

River North | 600 W. Chicago Ave. (Larrabee St.) | 312-822-9600 | www.japonaischicago.com

"Beautiful people" flock to this "swanky" River North "hot spot" to visit the "Zen-like" dining room, "hip" downstairs bar or dreamy riverside terrace and dine on "inventive" sushi and other "excellent, creative" Japanese choices; service can be uneven, and some complain it's "painfully noisy" ("if you value your hearing pick a weekday"), but others who don't mind bringing "big money" like the energetic "buzz."

Jerry's *Sandwiches* | 21 | 17 | 16 | $19 |

Wicker Park | 1938 W. Division St. (Damen Ave.) | 773-235-1006 | www.jerryssandwiches.com

"A sandwich for everyone" appears to be the motto of this Wicker Park deli offering what seems like the "largest menu of all time", with "over 100" "creative" sammies, plus salads, sides and more

FOOD | DECOR | SERVICE | COST

served alongside milkshakes, craft beers and wines by the glass; there's also a "nice outdoor area to people-watch", so even if service can tend toward "inconsistent", it's still a "charming" "hangout."

Jerry's Restaurant *American*   23 | 20 | 21 | $43

Winnetka | 507 Chestnut St. (bet. Elm & Oak Sts.) | 847-441-0134 | www.cornercooks.com

A suburban "gem" up Winnetka way, this "interesting" American offers a "delicious" if slightly expensive menu of "excellent-quality" fare that makes it a "special-occasion favorite", especially for "ladies who lunch"; it can get "noisy" at "prime times" so those in the know "ask to sit in the side room" when they want to "get away from the crowd gathered at the bar."

Jilly's Cafe Ⓜ *American/French*   21 | 16 | 22 | $43

Evanston | 2614 Green Bay Rd. (Central St.) | 847-869-7636 | www.jillyscafe.com

An "unexpected find in Evanston" say supporters of this longtime New American–New French proffering "solid", "well-executed" dishes in an "unassuming" space with a "pleasant adult atmosphere"; "personable" service and "good prices" help compensate for a room so "small" it can feel "cluttered", and insiders advise "the best deal is the champagne brunch."

NEW Jimbo's Top Gun Red Hots/   – | – | – | I
Signature Pizza ●🖼Ⓜ *Hot Dogs/Pizza*

Wrigleyville | 3617 N. Broadway (bet. Addison St. & Patterson Ave.) | 773-868-9700 | www.signaturepizzachicago.com

This double-duty, 24-hour BYO in Wrigleyville offers two casual favorites – hot dogs and pizza – plus burgers, a handful of hearty Italian pastas and sandwiches, and a full breakfast menu; the space is split into counter-service sections with a scattering of tables, plasma TVs and Chicago memorabilia.

Jin Ju *Korean*   ∇ 22 | 18 | 21 | $30

Andersonville | 5203 N. Clark St. (Foster Ave.) | 773-334-6377 | www.jinjurestaurant.com

"Knowledgeable" staffers and "well-prepared, tasty" plates make this midpriced Andersonville "surprise" a "perfect place to introduce someone to Korean food"; devotees also "can't say enough good things about the soju martinis", so even if the "dark, sexy" decor doesn't win over quite as many, it still "won't disappoint."

NEW Jin Thai *Thai*   – | – | – | I

Edgewater | 5458 N. Broadway (Catalpa Ave.) | 773-681-0555 | www.jinthaicuisine.com

Thai classics, whole snapper and a handful of mixed Asian staples (sweet and sour, ginger and teriyaki dishes) mix on the menu at this Edgewater corner storefront, where dessert also gets more attention than your standard Thai spot; you can BYO or indulge in some interesting juices (longan, lemongrass, fresh coconut) in a spare setting of blond wood floors, gray walls, black tables and chairs and a stand of bamboo.

	FOOD	DECOR	SERVICE	COST

Joe's Crab Shack ● *Seafood*   20 | 18 | 20 | $42

Gurnee | 5626 Northridge Dr. (Plaza Dr.) | 847-662-4801
Schaumburg | 2000 E. Golf Rd. (McConnor Pkwy.) | 847-517-1212
www.joescrabshack.com

"Seafood heaven" insist the initiated at this Schaumburg chain link offering up "fresh" fin fare "of all kinds" in "casual" environs that "remind you of a day at the beach"; one person's "inexpensive" is another's "pricey", but "service is generally friendly" so even if a few find it merely "adequate", it's still "satisfying", especially "with a group"; P.S. there's also a Gurnee outpost.

☑ Joe's Seafood, Prime Steak &   27 | 23 | 26 | $66
Stone Crab *Seafood/Steak*

River North | 60 E. Grand Ave. (Rush St.) | 312-379-5637 |
www.joes.net

"Some of the sunshine from Miami Beach" shines at this River North surf 'n' turf "half sister" to the Florida flagship where "grilled-to-perfection" steaks, "tasty, tender stone crab claws as big as your hand" and other "lip-smackingly good" fare is ferried by "professional", "amiable" servers in dark wood–accented digs; it's "noisy and touristy" with "prime prices" but "who cares" when it "consistently delivers" say fans whose "only problem is getting a reservation at a decent time."

John Barleycorn *Pub Food*   17 | 18 | 15 | $23

Wrigleyville | 3524 N. Clark St. (bet. Addison St. & Sheffield Ave.) |
773-549-6000 ●ⓈⓂ
Lincoln Park | 658 W. Belden Ave. (Lincoln Ave.) | 773-348-1570
Schaumburg | 1100 American Ln. (bet. Commons Dr. & National Pkwy.) |
847-619-5540 ●
www.johnbarleycorn.com

An "institution" since 1960, this Lincoln Park American (with Wrigleyville and Schaumburg sibs) vends "well-priced" American "pub food" to "college students, yuppies and cops"; even skeptics admit the "lively cast of characters" helps "offset" complaints about decor, service and merely "average" fare.

John's Place Ⓜ *American*   18 | 16 | 19 | $24

Lincoln Park | 1200 W. Webster Ave. (Racine Ave.) | 773-525-6670
Roscoe Village | 2132 W. Roscoe St. (Hamilton Ave.) | 773-244-6430
www.johnsplace.com

"Kudos to John" praise patrons of this "steady" Lincoln Park original and its Roscoe Village sequel where "solid" American eats, "accommodating" staffers and affordable prices make them ripe for "family dining even if you don't have your own"; even doubters who dub them merely "fair" concede they're "good places to be relaxed with kids."

Joy's Noodles & Rice *Thai*   22 | 15 | 21 | $16

Lakeview | 3257 N. Broadway St. (bet. Aldine Ave. & Melrose St.) |
773-327-8330 | www.joysnoodlesandrice.com

"Meals are always inexpensive" at this "reliable" Lakeview BYO, a "favorite local haunt" for "solid" noodles and other "consistently "tasty" Thai plates ferried by "attentive" servers; a "nice patio in back" is an appealing alternative to the no-frills storefront space, so most agree it's a "staple for good reason."

Joy Yee's Noodle Shop *Asian* 21 | 12 | 17 | $19

Chinatown | 2139 S. China Pl. (Archer Ave.) | 312-328-0001
South Loop | 1335 S. Halsted St. (bet. Liberty & W. Maxwell Sts.) | 312-997-2128
Evanston | 521 Davis St. (bet. Chicago & Hanman Aves.) | 847-733-1900
Naperville | Iroquois Shopping Ctr. | 1163 E. Ogden Ave. (Iroquois Ave.) | 630-579-6800

Joy Yee Plus Shabu Shabu *Asian*

Chinatown | 2159 S. China Pl. (Archer Ave.) | 312-842-8928
www.joyyee.com

"It can take a half hour" to read through the "dizzying array of Chinese, Japanese, Vietnamese and Thai" dishes offered at these BYO noodleries turning out "huge portions" of "well-crafted" plates served alongside"flavorful" fresh fruit smoothies and teas; many get "crowded" and "noisy", and what's "amazingly fast service" to some means feeling "rushed out" to others but given the "great prices for the amount of food you get" ("share or plan to tote home mega left-overs"), most agree you "can't go wrong"; P.S. the Chinatown Shabu Shabu also serves sushi.

Julius Meinl *Austrian* 21 | 19 | 18 | $17

Lakeview | 3601 N. Southport Ave. (Addison St.) | 773-868-1857
Lincoln Square | 4363 N. Lincoln Ave. (Montrose Ave.) | 773-868-1876

NEW Julius Meinl Coffee Bar & Patisserie 🗷Ⓜ *Austrian*

Ravenswood | 4115 N. Ravenswood Ave. (bet. Belle Plaine & Berteau Aves.) | 773-883-1862
www.northamerica.meinl.com

"Quainlicious" ("quaint" plus "delicious") proclaim patrons of these coffeehouse twins in Lakeview and Lincoln Square offering a mix of Austrian fare and cafe standards including "truly authentic" Viennese pastries, "well-proportioned" sammies and "imaginative, filling" breakfast items; "gracious" service and "calming" settings with a "European vibe" also win favor, and there's live music Fridays and Saturday nights; P.S. a Ravenswood triplet opened post–Survey.

Jury's *Pub Food* 18 | 15 | 20 | $21

North Center/St. Ben's | 4337 N. Lincoln Ave. (Montrose Ave.) | 773-935-2255 | www.jurysrestaurant.com

"Staffers bend over backwards to accommodate guests" at this North Center watering hole, a "warm" "neighborhood spot" for "good" pub eats including "one of the better burgers in town"; jurors dismissing it as merely "average" are overruled by defendants pointing to its "back beer garden", low tabs and "overall" "friendly" vibe.

Kamehachi *Japanese* 22 | 17 | 19 | $37

Loop | 311 S. Wacker Dr. (bet. Jackson Blvd. & Van Buren St.) | 312-765-8700 🗷

(continued)

(continued)

Kamehachi

River North | Westin River North | 320 N. Dearborn St. (bet. Carroll Ave. & Wacker Dr.) | 312-744-1900

Old Town | 1531 N. Wells St. (bet. North Ave. & Schiller St.) | 312-664-3663 ◐

Northbrook | Village Green Shopping Ctr. | 1320 Shermer Rd. (bet. Church St. & Meadow Rd.) | 847-562-0064
www.kamehachi.com

A "longtime anchor of the sushi scene", this recently relocated Old Town original (now "roomier") and its sister spin-offs are "community staples" where "authentic", "traditional" fare gets a boost from "innovative specials", "good sake" and "craft beer selections"; "the service doesn't measure up to the food", but prices are fairly "reasonable" and it's "reliable", so most "plan on going back."

Karma *Asian*   ▽ 23 | 27 | 22 | $40

Mundelein | Doubletree Libertyville-Mundelein | 510 E. Rte. 83 (Rte. 45) | 847-970-6900 | www.karmachicago.com

"Beautiful decor" – including a "cool" pond in the middle of the dining room – "sets the mood" for "flavorful" Asian fusion fare at this "sleek" "gem" in Mundelein's Doubletree Hotel; "booths and low noise make it conversation friendly", service gets high marks and tabs are moderate, so devotees dub it "amazing for the suburbs" and wonder "why it isn't crowded."

Karyn's Cooked *Vegan/Vegetarian*   21 | 17 | 18 | $27

River North | 738 N. Wells St. (Superior St.) | 312-587-1050

Karyn's Fresh Corner *Vegan/Vegetarian*

Lincoln Park | 1901 N. Halsted St. (Armitage Ave.) | 312-255-1590
www.karynraw.com

An "interesting dining adventure awaits" at this River North and Lincoln Park duo, the former mainly vegan, the latter raw, where those "in the mood" to go veggie are "not let down" by the "innovative" fare; still, doubters declare "nothing on the menu stands out", and what's "reasonable" to some is "pricey" to others, but supporters are soothed by the solid "customer service" and laid-back atmosphere.

Karyn's on Green Ⓜ *American/Vegan*   23 | 25 | 23 | $33

Greektown | 130 S. Green St. (bet. Adams & Monroe Sts.) | 312-226-6155 | www.karynsongreen.com

"Beautiful", "posh" surroundings with white walls and wood accents provide the backdrop for "tasty", "high-quality" New American-vegan fare at this more upscale Greektown sib to Karyn's Cooked and Karyn's Fresh; "inventive cocktails", moderate prices and "attentive" service add to the appeal, so even non-vegetarians are "sold."

⊠ Katsu Japanese Ⓜ *Japanese*   29 | 19 | 24 | $57

Northwest Side | 2651 W. Peterson Ave. (bet. Talman & Washtenaw Aves.) | 773-784-3383

"Utterly authentic" Japanese fare "spoils" diners at this Northwest Side longtimer, "one of the best traditional sushi bars in Chicago" where chef-owner Katsu Imamura transforms "quality ingredients"

FOOD | DECOR | SERVICE | COST

into "beautifully prepared" plates; "enthusiastic", "knowledgeable" staffers elevate the "serene", "minimalist" space, so though it's not cheap (or for "fans of crazy over-stuffed rolls"), it's "hands down" a place to "visit again and again."

Keefer's 🗷 American
25 | 23 | 25 | $61

River North | 20 W. Kinzie St. (Dearborn St.) | 312-467-9525 | www.keefersrestaurant.com

"There's no flash or drama, just the real thing" – "top-notch" chops, "strong drinks" – at this spacious River North American in a "modern", "adult" setting enhanced by an "active" bar scene and patio for "prime people-watching"; "accommodating", "standout" service further broadens the appeal, so many say it's an "ideal" (if costly) choice for "eating with clients" or just "hanging with the guys."

Kiki's 🗷 French
25 | 22 | 24 | $48

Near North | 900 N. Franklin St. (Locust St.) | 312-335-5454 | www.kikisbistro.com

An "old standby" that "refuses to bend to current trends", this "welcoming" Near North Frenchie appeals with "well-prepared" "authentic" bistro fare and "high-quality wine" served by "friendly" staffers who "treat you as family"; the "cozy", "charming" space has a "happy buzz" and tabs are moderate, so Kiki-philes wanting an "escape from the city hustle bustle" return "again and again."

Kinzie Chophouse Steak
23 | 20 | 23 | $44

River North | 400 N. Wells St. (Kinzie St.) | 312-822-0191 | www.kinziechophouse.com

A River North "staple" "with a real Chicago feel", this chophouse offers "consistently good" fare and "generous drinks" from an "attentive" staff that "tries hard" and "knows its stuff"; the spacious dining room "never lacks for charm and ambiance" and prices are "fair", so even if it's "not spectacular", it's still a "favorite."

Kitsch'n on Roscoe Eclectic
▽ 21 | 18 | 20 | $20

Roscoe Village | 2005 W. Roscoe St. (bet. Damon & Seeley Aves.) | 773-248-7372 | www.kitschn.com

"Original", "updated comfort food" stars at this Roscoe Village Eclectic where the appropriately "kitschy", "funky" decor (lava lamps, vintage lunchboxes, action figures) "takes you back to a simpler time"; "friendly service" and affordable tabs also ensure it's a "classic"; P.S. it closes at 3 PM.

Klay Oven Indian
19 | 16 | 17 | $28

River North | 414 N. Orleans St. (bet. Hubbard & Kinzie Sts.) | 312-527-3999

Oak Park | 734 Lake St. (bet. N. Euclid & N. Oak Park Aves.) | 708-386-3999
www.klayovenrestaurant.com

"Solid" Indian fare including a "bargain" lunch buffet boasting a "cornucopia of dishes" curries favor with fans of this River North and Oak Park duo; the "relaxed" ambiance suits "both business meals and dining out with friends", but critics find prices "expensive" for just "ok" food and say service could be improved.

	FOOD	DECOR	SERVICE	COST

Koda Bistro Ⓜ *French*   ▽ 23 | 18 | 19 | $45

Far South Side | 10352 S. Western Ave. (bet. 103rd & 104th Sts.) | 773-445-5632 | www.kodabistro.com

"Tasty" "tapas-style" offerings plus "lovely" mains woo Far South Siders to this midpriced French bistro; "classy" surrounds, "warm" service and a "welcoming environment" further ensure supporters can "count on" an "enjoyable" "fine-dining" experience.

Koi *Asian*   18 | 18 | 17 | $30

Evanston | 624 Davis St. (bet. Chicago & Orrington Aves.) | 847-866-6969 | www.koievanston.com

Sushi, Chinese and Thai food share the "wide-ranging" menu at this "reliable" Evanston Pan-Asian, where "well-executed" rolls and some "unique" dishes come via "friendly" servers in a "bright, airy" space that becomes "cozy" during winter when the fireplace is lit; still, holdouts hint it's "pricer than others" nearby and sometimes "hit-or-miss."

🮱 Kuma's Corner ⬤ *Burgers*   27 | 16 | 18 | $22

Avondale | 2900 W. Belmont Ave. (Francisco Ave.) | 773-604-8769 | www.kumascorner.com

For "awesome", "hard-core burger creations" (plus "killer" mac 'n' cheese) served up with "a side of pounding metal music" this midpriced Avondale "dive bar" remains the "gold standard"; "two-hour waits" (no reservations), "borderline X-rated" decor and the "sassiest servers in Chicago" might keep "conservative elderly relatives at home" but it's "well worth" bringing "some earplugs and a thick skin" (or getting takeout) for the beefy "experience of a lifetime."

Kuni's *Japanese*   ▽ 26 | 18 | 22 | $33

Evanston | 511-A Main St. (bet. Chicago & Hinman Aves.) | 847-328-2004 | www.kunisushi.com

Some of the "freshest fish around" features in the "marvelous" "traditional sushi" served alongside other "excellent Japanese dishes" at this "old-school" Evanston "standard-bearer" that's "still more interested in quality than trendiness"; sure, there's "zero decor", but with "extremely reasonable" tabs and "attentive service", it's still a "favorite."

La Bocca della Verità *Italian*   22 | 15 | 20 | $31

Lincoln Square | 4618 N. Lincoln Ave. (Eastwood Ave.) | 773-784-6222 | www.laboccachicago.com

"Outstanding pastas" and other "authentic" Italian dishes, "not the Americanized versions" pair with a "wide assortment of wines" at this "reasonably priced" Lincoln Square "gem"; "service is leisurely" in the "charming" space with "mismatched chairs", and "sidewalk seating provides for a perfect meal on a warm afternoon."

Labriola Bakery Café & Neopolitan Pizzeria *Italian/Pizza*   25 | 19 | 21 | $19

Oak Brook | 3021 Butterfield Rd. (Meyers Rd.) | 630-574-2008 | www.labriolabakerycafe.com

The "broad" Italian-focused menu includes everything from "welldone" pizzas, "fantastic soups and sandwiches" and a burger to

FOOD | DECOR | SERVICE | COST

"boast" of to "delicious" baked goods including "out-of-this-world" bread at this Oak Brook cafe; "great service" and affordable tabs further make it solid for "any meal", but insiders acquainted with the "horrible lunch cram go at a different time."

La Casa de Isaac *Mexican*   21 | 15 | 20 | $27
Highland Park | 431 Temple Ave. (Waukegan Ave.) | 847-433-5550 | www.lacasadeisaac.com

La Casa de Isaac & Moishe *Mexican*
Highland Park | 2014 First St. (bet. Elm Pl. & Green Bay Rd.) | 847-433-7400 | www.isaacandmoisherestaurant.com

Isaac & Moishe DFV *Mexican*
Highwood | 311 Waukegan Ave. (Temple Ave.) | 847-433-0557 | www.isaacandmoishedeli.com

"Not your run-of-the-mill Mexican eatery" advise admirers of this midpriced Highland Park duo (with a Highwood deli sib) where the "solid", "well-prepared" fare comes with a few "interesting" "twists" and the margaritas are "outstanding"; the bright decor is "evocative of Mexico" and service is "cordial", so though "crowds can be tough", most give it a hearty *"bueno"*; P.S. it closes early Friday afternoons through sundown Saturday for Shabbat.

La Crêperie ⓜ *Crêpes/French*   21 | 17 | 19 | $23
Lakeview | 2845 N. Clark St (bet. Diversey Pkwy. & Surf St.) | 773-528-9050 | www.lacreperieusa.com

The 40-year longevity "speaks to customer approval" of this "intimate" and "enduring" Lakeview kitchen offering "reasonably priced" "classic French crêpes with high-quality ingredients" ("chocolate, chicken, whatever they are serving") plus a "good wine list to accompany them"; "decor needs updating" but service is "friendly" and it "feels like a true Paris cafe" with a "gorgeous" garden "oasis in the spring/summer/fall."

NEW Lady Gregory's *American/Irish*   19 | 20 | 20 | $28
Andersonville | 5260 N. Clark St. (Berwyn Ave.) | 773-271-5050 | www.ladygregorys.com

"Soul-warming" Irish and American pub grub, an "excellent" beer list and a "whiskey list as long as the River Shannon" are offered in "warm", "homey" environs complete with a sizable patio at this "upscale" Andersonville bar; service is "helpful" and tabs moderate, so the few who find it "formulaic" are overruled by those insisting "you won't find another like it."

La Gondola *Italian*   20 | 12 | 19 | $28
Lakeview | 1258 W. Belmont St. (Lakewood Ave.) | 773-935-9011
Lakeview | Wellington Plaza | 2914 N. Ashland Ave. (Wellington Ave.) | 773-248-4433
www.lagondolachicago.com

"Homestyle" cooking at "value" prices is the calling card of these "red-sauce joints" in Lakeview known for "comforting pastas" and other Italian "basics" served by "friendly" staffers; the quaint" original in Wellington Plaza is "tiny", while the newer, BYO spin off has roughly double the seats, and if the digs don't appeal, both are "recommended for carryout."

La Lagartija Taqueria 🗷 *Mexican*   `- | - | - | I`

West Loop | 132 S. Ashland Ave. (bet. Adams & Monroe Sts.) | 312-733-7772 | www.lalagartijataqueria.com

Laura Cid-Perea, tres leches queen and founder of Pilsen's former Bombon Bakery, is co-owner of this "friendly" lizard-themed West Loop taqueria where the budget-minded menu majors in "excellent" tacos (including the requisite al pastor, breakfast and build-your-own options) and minors in everything else casual Mex – from burritos and quesadillas to desserts; it now offers full bar service with a focus on, of course, margaritas.

La Madia *Italian/Pizza*   `24 | 23 | 22 | $29`

River North | 59 W. Grand Ave. (bet. Clark & Dearborn Sts.) | 312-329-0400 | www.dinelamadia.com

"Delicious wood-fired pizza" "featuring a good selection of ingredients" is served alongside "interesting salads" and other "well-thought-out" offerings plus a "wine list that works" at this "trendy" yet "classy" River North Italian; "knowledgeable" service is another feature, and "honest prices" make it "one of the better, affordable options" in the area.

Lao Beijing *Chinese*   `24 | 12 | 16 | $23`

Chinatown | Chinatown Mall | 2138 S. Archer Ave. (Cermak Rd.) | 312-881-0168

Lao Shanghai *Chinese*

Chinatown | 2163 S. China Pl. (Princeton Ave.) | 312-808-0830

Lao Sze Chuan *Chinese*

Chinatown | 2172 S. Archer Ave. (Princeton Ave.) | 312-326-5040 ◗

Downers Grove | 1331 W. Ogden Ave. (Oakwood Ave.) | 630-663-0303

Lao You Ju ◗ *Chinese*

Chinatown | Richmond Ctr. | 2002 S. Wentworth Ave. (bet. Archer Ave. & Cullerton St.) | 312-225-7818
www.tonygourmetgroup.com

"Local foodies" "travel to the Far East" courtesy of Tony Hu's "authentic", "high-quality" Chinese cuisine at these "cheap" "favorites" known for "encyclopedialike menus" and "beautifully spiced", "intensely" flavored dishes (including some so "hot" they'll "melt your socks off"); sure, "the service is iffy" and "the decor is nonexistent", "but so what" ask fans who advise you simply "close your eyes and savor the tastes"; P.S. clubby You Ju is more posh and modern than its predecessors.

🆕 Lao Hunan *Chinese*   `▽ 28 | 14 | 19 | $23`

Chinatown | 2230 S. Wentworth Ave. (bet. Alexander St. & 22nd Pl.) | 312-842-7888 | www.tonygourmetgroup.com

Tony Hu's Chinatown "empire" now includes this "amazing addition" where the "incredible" renditions of "true Hunan dishes" are "different than standard Chinese" offerings – and "not for the timid" (a "high tolerance for spicy food" is helpful); the no-frills "Maothemed" decor extends to the "kitschy" Red Army uniforms worn by the "welcoming" staff, and with affordable tabs, most rank it "definitely worth a visit."

NEW La Parrilla Colombian Steak House   Colombian/Steak

| – | – | – | M |

Northwest Side | 6427 W. Irving Park Rd. (bet. Narragansett & Natchez Aves.) | 773-777-7720

You can fuel up on grilled churrascaria meats, empanadas, arepas, sandwiches and traditional Colombian entrees (the menu bears QR codes linking to food and travel info) at this Northwest Side steakhouse; the small, casual digs, done up in red and gold, include a bar dispensing signature cocktails, and there are beer towers on the cherry-stained tables.

La Petite Folie   M French

| 26 | 22 | 24 | $51 |

Hyde Park | Hyde Park Shopping Ctr. | 1504 E. 55th St. (Lake Park Blvd.) | 773-493-1394 | www.lapetitefolie.com

"Tops in Hyde Park for delicious brasserie standards", this "elegant" "jewel" turns out "classically prepared" French fare backed by an "excellent" wine list in a "serene", "civilized" dining room; it's not cheap, but it offers a "good price-quality ratio", and service is "friendly" too, so fans say it's "such a relief" to have it in the 'hood.

La Sardine   ⊠ French

| 25 | 22 | 24 | $44 |

West Loop | 111 N. Carpenter St. (bet. Randolph St. & Washington Blvd.) | 312-421-2800 | www.lasardine.com

"Consistently first-rate bistro food with a distinctly French feel" can be found at this "moderate" West Loop Parisian, where the menu boasts "ample" portions of "comfort food your *grand-mère* would make", including "to-die-for" soufflés; "no-pretense" service and a "warm", "crowded" space that is "larger and easier to navigate" than sister restaurant Le Bouchon further lead fans to "highly recommend it."

La Scarola   Italian

| 26 | 16 | 22 | $38 |

River West | 721 W. Grand Ave. (bet. Halsted St. & Union Ave.) | 312-243-1740 | www.lascarola.com

A "very small but high-powered place", this River West "hole-in-the-wall" "transports you back in time" to "grandma's Sunday afternoon Italian" meal with "plentiful" portions of "authentic and amazing" fare via "old-school" servers you can "laugh and have fun with"; tabs that "won't break the budget" are another reason it can get "crowded" and "loud", so "reservations are a must" – though "even with one, you could be waiting for a while."

Las Palmas   Mexican

| ∇ 22 | 17 | 19 | $33 |

Bucktown | 1835 W. North Ave. (Honore St.) | 773-289-4991 | www.laspalmaschicago.com

A "refreshingly creative take on Mexican food" wins praise at this Bucktowner with a breezy back atrium and outdoor patio; it may be "on the pricier side" for the genre but it's "well worth it" say supporters who suggest it's a "good dining experience when you want a little nicer than a taco and burrito joint."

Las Tablas *Colombian/Steak*   23 | 19 | 20 | $29

Lakeview | 2942 N. Lincoln Ave. (Wellington Ave.) | 773-871-2414

Northwest Side | 4920 W. Irving Park Rd. (bet. Lamon & Laporte Aves.) | 773-202-0999 ⑤

www.lastablas.com

For some of the "best Colombian food around", diners visit these steakhouse "alternatives" in Northwest Side and Lakeview offering "tender" cuts and other "wonderfully spiced fare" that "you can smell from a block away"; service is "friendly", and with "high-energy vibes" they're "great places with friends" for a "satisfying night out."

La Tasca *Spanish*   22 | 19 | 19 | $37

Arlington Heights | 25 W. Davis St. (Vail Ave.) | 847-398-2400 | www.latascatapas.com

A "great variety" of "authentic" tapas offers "so many tastes in one evening" at this midpriced Arlington Heights Spaniard in a festive "hustle-and-bustle" filled dining room with colorful murals; it can get "a little loud on the weekends" and service swings from "good" to "slow", but those who appreciate the "citylike ambiance" and "excellent", if "potent" sangria consider it a "fave."

Lawry's The Prime Rib *American/Steak*   26 | 23 | 26 | $54

River North | 100 E. Ontario St. (Rush St.) | 312-787-5000 | www.lawrysonline.com

A "history-filled temple to prime rib", this "classic" River North link of the Beverly Hills–based chophouse chain offers its "excellent" namesake dish "served old-world style" "right from a roasting cart" in portions ranging from "manageable to football-player sized"; "accommodating" staffers are "on-point" in the "comfortable" former McCormick mansion setting, so despite a few grumbles about "dated" decor and tabs "a bit on the expensive side", most rank it a "stop not to be missed."

NEW La Z De Oro ⦿ *Mexican*   - | - | - | M

Berwyn | 6241 Cermak Rd. (bet. Harvey & Highland Aves.) | 708-788-7602 | www.lazdeororestaurant.com

A revamp of Los Jarritos, this three-squares Mexican in Berwyn takes an upscale-casual, sit-down approach with art-adorned walls, a full bar and large, family-friendly portions of standbys like enchiladas, tacos and tortas; there are also shakes, including a signature avocado flavor, plus hangover-abating weekend specials like pozole and menudo.

Le Bouchon ⑤ *French*   23 | 19 | 20 | $43

Bucktown | 1958 N. Damen Ave. (Armitage Ave.) | 773-862-6600 | www.lebouchonofchicago.com

"As close to a Parisian bistro as you can get in Chicago", this "fairly priced" Bucktown boîte on "Rue Damen" serves "tasty", "traditional" dishes in a "cozy" wood-trimmed space; all in all it has "real French character without the server attitude", so though "tables are a bit cramped and it can get a little noisy", most swear that's "a small price to pay" for a "wonderful" meal, especially if you go on Tuesday for the "pretty awesome" prix fixe.

Le Colonial *Vietnamese*

23 | 24 | 22 | $49

Gold Coast | 937 N. Rush St. (bet. Oak & Walton Sts.) | 312-255-0088 | www.lecolonialchicago.com

You'll be "transported to pre-war Vietnam" at this "posh" Gold Coast "must" where the "elegantly exotic" "tropical" setting with ceiling fans, bamboo and palms sets the stage for "succulent", "well-balanced" Vietnamese fare ferried by "helpful" staffers; tables can get "a little crowded and the noise level can rise", but an up-stairs bar area and balcony add appeal, and though it's not cheap, the majority finds tabs "reasonable" given the "high quality", adding a "repeat" visit is "in the near future."

Leopold Ⓜ *Belgian*

23 | 20 | 23 | $41

Noble Square | 1450 W. Chicago Ave. (bet. Bishop St. & Greenview Ave.) | 312-348-1028 | www.leopoldchicago.com

"Unique twists" elevate the "truly tasty" Belgian pub eats ("if you see rabbit anything, order it") at this "slightly upscale" Noble Square "gem" where the "flavorful" fare, including "fabulous frites, of course", is paired with an "extensive beer list" and "amazing specialty cocktails"; "friendly", "knowledgeable" service and a "warm", "charming" space decorated with photos and stained-glass windows make it a "perfect date place", so supporters say go – and "definitely share plates."

ⓩ Les Nomades Ⓢ Ⓜ *French*

28 | 27 | 28 | $123

Streeterville | 222 E. Ontario St. (bet. Fairbanks Ct. & St. Clair St.) | 312-649-9010 | www.lesnomades.net

"A refuge of civility", this Streeterville French evokes "a more elegant era" with its "superbly attentive, efficient" servers, "serene" "flower-filled townhouse" setting and "sublime" "haute cuisine" from recently returned "master" chef Roland Liccioni; a "remarkable" wine list further elevates it to "special-occasion" status, so though "pricey", fans say it's "worth every centime."

ⓩ Le Titi de Paris Ⓜ *French*

27 | 24 | 25 | $65

Arlington Heights | 1015 W. Dundee Rd. (Kennicott Ave.) | 847-506-0222 | www.letitideparis.com

Chef-owners Michael and Susan Maddox "know their craft" at this Arlington Heights longtimer where "carefully prepared" French classics, an "excellent" wine selection and "infinitely charming" service have acolytes "feeling like pampered monarchs"; the "elegant room" further makes it an "epitome of fine dining", though the "not inexpensive" prices mean many save it for "special-occasions"; P.S. it's reportedly set to close in June 2012.

Le Vichyssois Ⓜ *French*

▽ 26 | 19 | 26 | $58

Lakemoor | 220 Rand Rd. (bet. Hollywood Terr. & Willow Rd.) | 815-385-8221 | www.levichyssois.com

"Always top notch" laud loyalists of chef-owner Bernard Cretier's "classic French" cooking at this circa-1976 Lakemoor longtimer where "knowledgeable, efficient" staffers tend to guests in an antiquey country home setting that some find a bit "dated"; surveyors who snark "for the cost, you can join the 21st century at other restaurants" are drowned out by devotees who call it a "consistent", "well-worth-it" "favorite"; P.S. it's closed Mondays and Tuesdays.

NEW Libertad Ⓜ *Nuevo Latino* ▽ 24 | 17 | 24 | $35

Skokie | 7931 Lincoln Ave. (bet. Babb Ave. & Niles Center Rd.) | 847-674-8100 | www.libertad7931.com

A "revelation" swoon fans of the "flavorful" Nuevo Latino small plates at this "little" Skokie "hideaway"; "service could not be friendlier or more attentive" and tabs are affordable, so even if the spare storefront setting doesn't reach the same heights, its "booming business" reflects its "special-gem" status.

Lillie's Q *BBQ/Southern* 22 | 18 | 19 | $27

Bucktown | 1856 W. North Ave. (Wolcott Ave.) | 773-772-5500 | www.lilliesq.com

"Get sauced (BBQ sauced, that is)" at chef-owner Charlie McKenna's Bucktown 'cue joint, a "meat lover's" "heaven" say fans fawning over the "luscious" pulled pork, "scarf"-worthy ribs and other "Southern favorites", plus 'moonshine' cocktails and an "awesome beer selection", all served in rustic, wood-accented digs; service gets mixed marks ("terrific" vs. "unreliable"), the "no-reservations policy is annoying" and a few find it just "so-so", but with moderate prices most agree it's still a "solid choice."

NEW Linkin House Restaurant ● *Burgers/Pub Food* - | - | - | I

Lincoln Park | 2142 N. Clybourn Ave. (bet. Southport & Wayne Ave. S.) | 773-857-1111 | www.linkin-house.com

Nightlife denizens and sports fans meet at this vast, tri-level Lincoln Park purveyor of exotic burgers (including one topped with Nutella) and other inexpensive pub fare, accompanied by a rotating selection of seasonal draft beers; done up in all black, the environs boast two separate bar areas, three dozen TVs (with no cover for pay-per-view events) and a DJ spinning house tracks.

Lloyd's Chicago Ⓩ *American* 16 | 17 | 20 | $29

Loop | 1 S. Wacker Dr. (Madison St.) | 312-407-6900 | www.lloydschicago.com

A "convenient" Loop locale coupled with solid service and a varied menu of American standards make this midpriced option "dependable" for a "business lunch" or "pre-opera dinner"; though critics find it merely "average", its spacious white-tablecloth dining room is often still "crowded", and occasionally a "madhouse"; P.S. closed Saturdays unless the Lyric's in session.

LM *French* 25 | 23 | 24 | $47

Lincoln Square | 4539 N. Lincoln Ave. (bet. Sunnyside & Wilson Aves.) | 773-942-7585 | www.lmrestaurant.com

A "limited" yet "diverse enough" menu of "delicious", "expertly prepared" plates whet *appétits* at this Lincoln Square New French, where "charming, attentive" servers tend to diners in a "stylish" "bistro-style" space complete with a glassed-in patio that's "one of the loveliest in the city"; some warn it can feel "pricey" for "portions that are more European than American", but it's still "perfect for a special night out"; P.S. a South Loop sib, Brasserie by LM, opened post-Survey.

The Lobby *European/Seafood*   24 | 26 | 25 | $58

River North | Peninsula Chicago | 108 E. Superior St., 5th fl. (bet. Michigan Ave. & Rush St.) | 312-573-6760 | www.peninsula.com
The "expansive", "airy" setting featuring floor-to-ceiling windows makes it hard to "concentrate on your meal" say wowed diners at this "upscale" Euro seafood specialist in River North's Peninsula Hotel that delivers "top-notch" fare, including a "fabulous brunch" and "popular high tea" further enhanced by "attentive" service; so it's no surprise that those on a "tight budget" should "bring an expense account."

Lockwood *American*   22 | 23 | 21 | $51

Loop | Palmer House Hilton | 17 E. Monroe St (bet. State St. & Wabash Ave.) | 312-917-3404 | www.lockwoodrestaurant.com
Set in the "famed" Palmer House Hotel lobby, this "upscale" Loop New American is a "sight to be seen" with its "modern" elegant stylings that set the stage for "solid" sometimes "imaginative" fare backed by wines "uniformly good both in selection and price"; service is generally "courteous", and though its "location can make it rather pricey", you can't beat its "good proximity to downtown theaters."

☒ Longman & Eagle ❶ *American*   27 | 22 | 23 | $41

Logan Square | 2657 N. Kedzie Ave. (Schubert Ave.) | 773-276-7110 | www.longmananddeagle.com
"Off the charts for original fare" typifies praise for this Logan Square "hipster" "hot spot" where the "bordering-on-brilliant" New American menu "mixes game and offal with traditional comfort food" and the "pitch-perfect cocktails" from bartending "ar-teests" are "wonderful as well"; service is "knowledgeable" and "friendly" and the setting "relaxed", so though a no-reservations policy ("whatever happened to that civilized custom?") often results in a wait, most say it's "worth fighting the crowds"; P.S. it's also an inn, so if you overdo it, "they've got rooms upstairs."

Los Nopales Ⓜ *Mexican*   23 | 15 | 19 | $25

Lincoln Square | 4544 N. Western Ave. (bet. Sunnyside & Wilson Aves.) | 773-334-3149 | www.losnopalesrestaurant.com
"Authentic" "homestyle" Mexican *comida* at "reasonable prices" has fans swearing they'll "come back again and again" to this Lincoln Square BYO ($2 corkage); "accommodating" service helps distract from the bare-bones "storefront" setting, so those complaining it's "not noteworthy" are drowned out by fans deeming it a "go-to spot."

☒ Lou Malnati's Pizzeria *Pizza*   25 | 16 | 20 | $22

River North | 439 N. Wells St. (Hubbard St.) | 312-828-9800
Lincoln Park | 958 W. Wrightwood Ave. (Lincoln Ave.) | 773-832-4030
(continued)

(continued)

Lou Malnati's Pizzeria

Far South Side | 3859 W. Ogden Ave. (Cermak Rd.) |
773-762-0800
Printers Row | 805 S. State St. (8th St.) | 312-786-1000
Evanston | 1850 Sherman Ave. (University Pl.) | 847-328-5400
Lincolnwood | 6649 N. Lincoln Ave. (Prairie Rd.) | 847-673-0800
Buffalo Grove | 85 S. Buffalo Grove Rd. (Lake Cook Rd.) | 847-215-7100
Elk Grove Village | 1050 E. Higgins Rd. (bet. Arlington Heights &
Busse Rds.) | 847-439-2000
Schaumburg | 1 S. Roselle Rd. (Schaumburg Rd.) | 847-985-1525
Naperville | 131 W. Jefferson Ave. (bet. Main & Webster Sts.) |
630-717-0700
www.loumalnatis.com
Additional locations throughout the Chicago area

"Come with an appetite" to this "iconic" chain, "the place to go if you want to experience Chicago-style deep-dish" say pie-zanos "omg"-ing over the "thick", "incredible" butter crust, "ooey gooey, nicely stretchy cheese" and sausage plenty "enough to feed an army", plus "respectable" thin-crust pies and "fantastic" "large" salads too; the staff is "casual and friendly", and though the decor strikes some as "humble", most barely notice, wishing only that "made-to-order" 'zas didn't result in "a bit of a wait."

Lou Mitchell's *Diner*   24 | 13 | 20 | $17

Loop | 565 W. Jackson Blvd. (Jefferson St.) | 312-939-3111 ⊟
O'Hare Area | O'Hare Int'l Airport | Terminal 5 (I-190) |
773-601-8989 ●
www.loumitchellsrestaurant.com

Eaters advise "come hungry" to this Loop "king of breakfast", a "quintessential" "Chicago icon" since 1923 where "oversized" portions of "hearty", "high-quality" diner fare like "lighter than air scrambled eggs" and "amazing French toast" are served morning through afternoon via "friendly" staffers who "have been working there for 20 years or more"; "you'll rub elbows with workers from the stock exchange and other executives" in the "crowded" "old-time" environs, just bring cash (the airport quick-serve takes credit cards) and "get there early to avoid the lines" – though late-risers are "treated to donut holes and Milk Duds" while they wait.

Lovells of Lake Forest *American*   22 | 24 | 23 | $56

Lake Forest | 915 S. Waukegan Rd. (Everett Rd.) | 847-234-8013 |
www.lovellsoflakeforest.com

The "beautiful, quaint house setting" decorated with "out-of-this-world (literally) artifacts" from the chef-owner's father, Apollo 13 astronaut Jim Lovell, provides the backdrop for a "wonderful selection" of "tasty" New American plates at this pricey Lake Forester; "standout" service contributes to a "soothing ambiance", and if a few snipe you're "paying for a famous name", more find it a "magical place to dine"; P.S. try the downstairs Capatain's Quarters "for a more casual evening with some additional bar food selections" and live music Friday and Saturday nights.

	FOOD	DECOR	SERVICE	COST

☑ L2O *Seafood* | 25 | 28 | 26 | $152 |

Lincoln Park | Belden-Stratford Hotel | 2300 N. Lincoln Park W. (Belden Ave.) | 773-868-0002 | www.l2orestaurant.com

"Get dressed up and wear your good jewelry" to this "swanky" dining room inside Lincoln Park's Belden-Stratford Hotel that delivers an "opulent experience", from the "inventive" seafood tasting menus and "deep" wine list to the "strikingly beautiful" space further elevated by "attentive", "professional" servers; tabs may "bring tears to your eyes", so many say it's "for special occasions only" – unless of course you "go on someone else's dime."

☑ Lula Cafe *Eclectic* | 27 | 21 | 23 | $31 |

Logan Square | 2537 N. Kedzie Blvd. (bet. Fullerton Ave. & Logan Blvd.) | 773-489-9554 | www.lulacafe.com

Noshers have "nothing but praise" for chef-owners Jason Hammel and Amalea Tshilds at their "charming" Logan Square Eclectic serving "inventive", "worship"-worthy farm-to-table fare "while maintaining a humble spirit" evidenced by "fair" prices, "laid-back" service and "funky" environs decorated with "creative artwork"; it "gets packed with hipsters" (especially during the "well-known" brunch), but a recent renovation should help alleviate the "crowded" conditions that come with being a "top-notch" "institution."

LuLu's Dim Sum & Then Sum *Asian* | 22 | 16 | 21 | $22 |

Evanston | 804 Davis St. (Sherman Ave.) | 847-869-4343 | www.lulusdimsum.com

"Big portions" of "deeply flavored", occasionally "inventive" dim sum, noodles and more make for a "solid, filling meal" at this "kid-friendly" Evanston Asian; "busy but efficient" staffers tend the "spunky, quirky" storefront space, and though it's probably "not the most authentic" option, it's "affordable" with a number of all-you-can-eat specials ("flavorful great deals").

Lupita's ⓜ *Mexican* | 20 | 15 | 21 | $24 |

Evanston | 700 Main St (Custer Ave.) | 847-328-2255 | www.lupitasmexicanrestaurant.com

You'll "never leave hungry" at this "family-friendly" Evanston Mexican offering a "mostly standard menu" of "delicious" fare via "caring" staffers in a "cheerful room" decorated with pictures and artwork; weekend guitar music is another plus, and though a few deem it "pedestrian", it's still a "favorite with locals."

LuxBar ◑ *American* | 19 | 19 | 20 | $34 |

Gold Coast | 18 E. Bellevue Pl. (Rush St.) | 312-642-3400 | www.luxbar.com

"Classic" American grub like burgers, salads and steaks offered at "reasonable" prices in "lively", "seriously hip" surrounds make this "neighborhood joint" a "great choice for the budget-conscious who don't want to sacrifice the see-and-be-seen atmosphere of the Gold Coast"; it's a "crazy noisy zoo" on weekends and during "big sport events", but service remains generally "prompt", so even snarkers saying there's "nothing d-lux" about it concede it's a "reliable" "pit stop", especially when "people-watching outdoors in the summer."

	FOOD	DECOR	SERVICE	COST

L. Woods Tap & Pine Lodge *American* | 20 | 18 | 20 | $32 |

Lincolnwood | 7110 N. Lincoln Ave. (Kostner Ave.) | 847-677-3350 | www.lwoodsrestaurant.com

An "ersatz Wisconsin supper club", this "reasonably priced" Lincolnwood waystation is a "prototypical Lettuce Entertain You joint", delivering "gargantuan" portions of "consistently good" American fare, including "tasty barbecue", via "experienced and friendly" servers; the "casual" wood-paneled environs are bedecked with "a lot of fish and antlers", and those who say "nothing is going to blow your mind" are countered by "crowds" that suggest it's a "favorite of many."

NEW M ⑤M *American* | - | - | - | M |

Highland Park | 675 Central Ave. (Green Bay Rd.) | 847-748-8954 | www.mrestaurant.net

This Highland Parker aims to provoke 'mmm's with seasonal American cuisine from the 'sea' and 'prairie', accompanied by a compact wine list; the clean architectural design features plate-glass windows, molded ceilings, white tablecloths, a bar and an out-door seating with a fire pit.

Macello *Italian* | - | - | - | M |

West Loop | 1235 W. Lake St. (bet. Elizabeth St. & Racine Ave.) | 312-850-9870 | www.macellochicago.com

Cognoscenti say the "authentic", "well-prepared" cuisine "brings you right back to Italy" at this midpriced West Loop Italian; the "modern" decor (devoid of "cheesy stuff" like "tacky tablecloths") exudes "warmth", and so the "out-of-the-way" locale doesn't deter those who are left wondering why "it's not more crowded" and suggesting diners "give it a try.

Macku Sushi *Japanese* | 26 | 22 | 23 | $46 |

Lincoln Park | 2239 N. Clybourn Ave. (bet. Greenview & Webster Aves.) | 773-880-8012 | www.mackusushi.com

So "fresh" are the "mind-blowing sashimi", "inventive sushi" and "amazing specials" at this "pricey but worth it" Lincoln Park Japanese that patrons wonder if there's "a fish market in the backyard"; "attentive" servers and a "trendy" yet "inviting" modern space also earn admiration from those who "cannot say enough" about it.

Maggiano's Little Italy *Italian* | 22 | 20 | 21 | $33 |

River North | 516 N. Clark St. (bet. Grand Ave. & Illinois St.) | 312-644-7700

Skokie | Westfield Shoppingtown | 4999 Old Orchard Ctr. (Skokie Blvd.) | 847-933-9555

Schaumburg | 1901 E. Woodfield Rd. (Rte. 53) | 847-240-5600

Naperville | 1847 Freedom Dr. (Diehl Rd.) | 630-536-2270

Oak Brook | Oakbrook Center Mall | 240 Oakbrook Ctr. (Rte. 83) | 630-368-0300

www.maggianos.com

"Popular" for "family-style" dining, this "consistent" chain satisfies "both big and little kids" with "humongous portions" of "familiar", "reliable" Italian dishes, "served quickly" and "with cheer" in a "lively", "comfortable" setting; dissenters dubbing it merely "decent" are outnumbered by fans focusing on its "phenomenal value" and insisting the "whole experience will uplift your spirits" – which may stay uplifted since "you can eat for a week on the leftovers."

Magnolia Cafe M *American*   23 | 19 | 22 | $38

Uptown | 1224 W. Wilson Ave. (Magnolia Ave.) | 773-728-8785 | www.magnoliacafeuptown.com

"Delicious" cuisine bolstered by a wine list that "works well with the menu" brings Uptowners to this "cozy" New American set in a "small, but comfortable" candlelit room; service gets high marks and prices are "fair" too, so it "makes for a fun escape" in an "underserved" part of town.

Mago *Mexican*   ∇ 25 | 21 | 25 | $27

Arlington Heights | 115 W. Campbell St. (Vail Ave.) | 847-253-2222
Bolingbrook | 641 E. Boughton Rd. (Feather Sound Dr.) | 630-783-2222
www.magodining.com

"Definitely not your typical Mexican restaurant" enthuse fans of this "reasonably" priced Bolingbrook and Arlington Heights duo where "innovative" touches offer a "different spin" on standards ("even the tacos are interesting"); "bitchin' margaritas", "cool" Aztec-inflected decor and "excellent" service further leave devotees warning "keep it to yourself or we'll have to wait in long lines to get in."

Maijean M *French*   ∇ 26 | 23 | 23 | $53

Clarendon Hills | 30 S. Prospect Ave. (Park Ave.) | 630-794-8900 | www.maijean.com

Some of the "best French food around" comes from this "top" Clarendon Hills bistro say fans saluting the "quality" offerings, solid service and romantic art nouveau setting; there's also a working fireplace and outdoor patio, so though not cheap, it's still "trek"-worthy.

NEW Mama Milano *Italian/Pizza*   – | – | – | I

Old Town | 1419 N. Wells St. (bet. North Ave. & Schiller St.) | 312-787-3710 | www.mamamilano.com

Old-school Italian Papa Milano's fathered this budget-friendly Old Town pizzeria offering classic pies and a handful of salads and sandwiches, all washed down by beer, wine and coffee drinks; it's cozy, narrow space features vintage light fixtures, posters, rustic brickwork and a long communal dining bar with a TV.

Mana Food Bar *Eclectic/Vegetarian*   26 | 20 | 22 | $33

Wicker Park | 1742 W. Division St. (bet. Hermitage & Wood Sts.) | 773-342-1742 | www.manafoodbar.com

"Creatively prepared" Eclectic-vegetarian small plates are so "delicious" "you don't even realize you aren't eating meat" swear "discerning diners" of this no-reservations Wicker Park veggie "heaven"; service is "friendly" and prices are "reasonable" too, so the "only problem" is the "small" size of the "modern" wood-lined space, leading patrons to plead "please open in a bigger location."

	FOOD	DECOR	SERVICE	COST

Manny's Cafeteria & Delicatessen *Deli*

24 | 9 | 17 | $18

South Loop | 1141 S. Jefferson St. (bet. Grenshaw St. & Roosevelt Rd.) | 312-939-2855 ⑤

Southwest Side | Midway Int'l Airport | 5700 S. Cicero Ave. (55th St.) | 773-948-6300

www.mannysdeli.com

"Don't let the linoleum fool you" because "they don't make restaurants like this anymore" attest admirers of this "legit" South Loop "institution" (with a Midway outpost) where "monstrous sandwiches", "hard-to-choose-from" steam trays and other deli "classics" ("talk about comfort food") are the path to "gastro heaven" – and an "awesome value for your money" too; the "sparse" "cafeteria-style" environs are full of "characters" who make "people-watching a highlight", and "old-school" (some say "rude") service is "part of the fun", so just make sure to "clear out your afternoon to take a big nap after imbibing."

Margie's Candies *American*

23 | 17 | 20 | $12

Bucktown | 1960 N. Western Ave. (Armitage Ave.) | 773-384-1035 | www.margiescandies.nv.switchboard.com ☽

Logan Square | 1813 W. Montrose Ave. (Ravenswood Ave.) | 773-348-0400

"Treat yourself" to a "scoop of nostalgia" at these "old-timey" ice cream and candy "classics" serving up "amazing" splits and sundaes topped by hot fudge that's "not too sweet" and "not to rich" (but "so thick you need to cut it with a knife"), plus Traditional American fare, though most suggest "sticking to the desserts"; the circa-1921 Bucktown "institution" often has "lines around the block" so some try the newer Logan Square sequel, as both "hit the spot" and are "completely worth the time and money" for a "step back in time."

Marigold Ⓜ *Indian*

23 | 19 | 20 | $35

Uptown | 4832 N. Broadway (Rosemont Ave.) | 773-293-4653 | www.marigoldrestaurant.com

"Modern Indian food" is the draw at this affordable Uptowner, proving an "interesting alternative" to the usual South Asian fare with a "wide variety" of "consistently good" unique dishes including some truly "addictive" offerings; they "make great cocktails too" and service is "friendly" in the warm space, though purists pouting it "lacks traditional flair" suggest getting your "authentic" eats fix elsewhere.

NEW Marmalade *American*

▽ 26 | 17 | 24 | $18

North Center/St. Ben's | 1969 W. Montrose Ave. (Damen Ave.) | 773-883-9000 | www.marmaladechicago.com

"Every dish delivers" at this fairly "cheap" American BYO in "out-of-the-way" North Center offering an "extensive, imaginative" daytime menu of "decidedly upscale" "sweet and savory options"; "attentive" staffers tend to diners in a "bare-bones, but clean and modern" milieu, and regulars warn that "long waits" on weekends will only increase "unless we can keep it quiet."

NEW Masa Azul Ⓜ *Southwestern* — | — | — | M

Logan Square | 2901 W. Diversey Ave. (bet. Francisco Ave. & Richmond St.) | 773-687-0300 | www.masaazul.com

Expect moderately priced regional Southwestern fare with a modern chef's imprint at this Logan Square spot; the airy, urban setting features an orange-and-blue color scheme, funky light fixtures and a concrete bar serving a monster tequila 'library' and craft cocktails (including some made with the lesser known Mexican spirit sotol).

Mastro's Steakhouse ● *Steak* 26 | 23 | 25 | $77

River North | 520 N. Dearborn St. (Grand Ave.) | 312-521-5100 | www.mastrosrestaurants.com

"Buttery", "well-prepared" meat, "overflowing martinis and towering seafood appetizers" put this "decadent" and "very expensive" River North outpost of the "Arizona über-steakhouse" "near the top" of local chops spots; "excellent" servers will leave guests "pampered and satiated" in "posh" bi-level environs replete with chandeliers and white linens, and live piano nightly means "the bar atmosphere rocks."

Maude's Liquor Bar ●ⓍⓂ *French* 25 | 25 | 23 | $49

West Loop | 840 W. Randolph St. (bet. Green & Peoria Sts.) | 312-243-9712 | www.maudesliquorbar.com

"Bring a date" to Brendan Sodikoff's "super-sexy" West Loop restolounge where the house cocktails are "ridiculously delicious" and the "modernized old-school French" bistro fare is "tantalizing" enough to "make up for the limited menu"; the "dimly lit", "romantic" setting evokes "dining in vintage Paris" and the "cool staffers" are "helpful", so the only complaint is that it can be a "challenge to get in"; P.S. "unless you bring your night vision glasses, try to sit downstairs."

Maya Del Sol *Nuevo Latino* 23 | 22 | 23 | $33

Oak Park | 144 S. Oak Park Ave. (bet. Pleasant St. & South Blvd.) | 708-358-9800 | www.mayadelsol.com

"Creative fusion" fare and an "unbelievable drink menu" fuel a "festive, relaxed" atmosphere at this affordable Oak Park Nuevo Latino that's especially good for allergic eaters with its many dairy-, gluten- and meat-free offerings; service remains solid despite "constantly busy" environs and "the outdoor area is the place to be in the summer", so those complaining it's just "ok" are in the minority.

M Burger *Burgers* 17 | 8 | 16 | $11

NEW Loop | Thompson Ctr. | 100 W. Randolph St. (Clark St.) | 312-578-1478
River North | 5 W. Ontario St. (State St.) | 312-428-3548
Streeterville | 161 E. Huron St. (bet. Michigan Ave. & St. Clair St.) | 312-254-8500
NEW Gold Coast | Water Tower Place | 835 N. Michigan Ave. (Pearson St.) | 312-867-1549
www.mburgerchicago.com

For "fast food, gourmet-style", this LEYE chow chain has some moaning "mmmm burger", declaring it "very good for what it is" – a "casual" sandwich supplier with "addicting fries" and "great shakes" at a "reasonable price"; eaters who were "expecting a lot more" due to the "hype" say it's "not the best burger in town, but it's not the worst either" and it helps "if you can handle the long wait and have a place to eat it" (some locations have a "few outdoor tables" in summer).

McCormick & Schmick's *Seafood*   20 | 21 | 21 | $46

Loop | 1 E. Wacker Dr. (bet. State St. & Wabash Ave.) | 312-923-7226
Gold Coast | 41 E. Chestnut St. (Rush St.) | 312-397-9500
Rosemont | 5320 N. River Rd. (bet. Foster Ave. & Technology Blvd.) | 847-233-3776
Skokie | Westfield Shoppingtown | 4999 Old Orchard Ctr. (Skokie Blvd.) | 847-763-9811
Oak Brook | 3001 Butterfield Rd. (Meyers Rd.) | 630-571-3700
www.mccormickandschmicks.com

Those praising the "wide choice" of "reliably good" seafood and "quality" steaks say this "upscale" chain's "formula works"; granted it's "not a foodie's dream" and tabs aren't low, but "comfortable, clubby" environs and generally solid service make it "old faithful" for business meetings, and plus, its "happy-hour deals can't be beat."

MC Restaurant Ⓜ *French/Vietnamese*   - | - | - | I

Wicker Park | 1401 N. Ashland Ave. (Blackhawk St.) | 773-489-5600 | www.mcrestaurantandlounge.com

Julie Mai (of the former Julie Mai's Le Bistro) is behind this intimate, wallet-friendly Wicker Park entry serving French-influenced Vietnamese bites, plus a burger and basic sandwich offerings for the less adventurous (not to mention a dozen bubble-smoothie options); the brightly decorated corner space boasts walls of windows, with artwork and food-market photography adding cultural accents.

Medici on 57th *American*   19 | 16 | 17 | $18

Hyde Park | 1327 E. 57th St. (bet. Kenwood & Kimbark Aves.) | 773-667-7394 | www.medici57.com

A "classic U of Chicago hangout" since 1963, this "reasonably priced" Hyde Park BYO "satisfies" with "large portions" of American fare including dishes featuring "quirky variations", like the "awesome" garbage pizza; somewhat hit-or-miss service barely registers with the "varied and interesting clientele" that deems it a "reliable" "staple."

Melting Pot *Fondue*   19 | 19 | 20 | $42

River North | Millennium Center Towers | 609 N. Dearborn St. (bet. Ohio & Ontario Sts.) | 312-573-0011 ◗
Buffalo Grove | 1205 W. Dundee Rd. (Arlington Heights Rd.) | 847-342-6022
Schaumburg | 255 W. Golf Rd. (bet. Higgins & Roselle Rds.) | 847-843-8970
Downers Grove | 1205 Butterfield Rd. (bet. Finley Rd. & Highland Ave.) | 630-737-0810
Naperville | 4931 S. Rte. 59 (111th St.) | 630-717-8301
www.meltingpot.com

For a "girls' night or a romantic interlude" that's "fun without seeming forced", dippers try "something different", cooking their own "craveworthy" food ("melted cheese and chocolate? Yes, please!") at this "relaxed" fondue chain; "helpful" service is a plus, though "baffled" skeptics wonder "why people flock" here for what they consider "overpriced" offerings.

NEW Melt Sandwich Shop 🚫 *Sandwiches*

– | – | – | I

Bucktown | 1840 N. Damen Ave. (bet. Churchill & Moffat Sts.) | 773-292-6358 | www.meltsandwichshoppechicago.com

Nightlife impresario Dion Antic goes cheesy with this cash-only Bucktown sandwich mecca riffing on that childhood fave grilled cheese with charcuterie items and Cuban, Turkish and even Canadian influences, accompanied by soup, salad and kids' options; the space is tongue-in-cheek schoolroom, with menus in a 'World History' folder, food served on trays, colorful molded cafeteria chairs and a blackboard hung with empty picture frames; P.S. there's no alcohol service.

Mercadito ● *Mexican*

22 | 21 | 18 | $39

River North | 108 W. Kinzie St. (bet. Clark & LaSalle Sts.) | 312-329-9555 | www.mercaditorestaurants.com

"Delicious", "schmancy tacos" and other "unique", "upscale" Mexican dishes go with "killer" cocktails at this "popular River North hangout"; "beautiful people" are part of the "inviting" modern decor, so despite service that's "somewhat compromised" when "noisy" and crowded, it's a "cool" place just "to be seen."

Mercat a la Planxa *Spanish*

26 | 24 | 23 | $54

South Loop | Blackstone Hotel | 636 S. Michigan Ave. (Balbo Ave.) | 312-765-0524 | www.mercatchicago.com

Get an "introduction to the vitality of Spanish food" at this "swanky", "high-energy" South Loop Catalan in the "beautifully restored" Blackstone Hotel where "creativity abounds" in chef Jose Garces' "authentic", "amazing" tapas offered alongside "inventive cocktails" and a "deep", "well-paired" wine list; "attentive" but "not intrusive" service adds to the "wow"-worthy experience, and as for cost, it varies since "you can eat a few tapas for very little money or spend quite a bit on the tasting menus."

Merlo la Salumeria Ⓜ *Italian*

24 | 21 | 22 | $54

Lincoln Park | 2638 N. Lincoln Ave. (Wrightwood Ave.) | 773-529-0747

Merlo on Maple *Italian*

Gold Coast | 16 W. Maple St. (bet. Dearborn & State Sts.) | 312-335-8200
www.merlochicago.com

"Authentic", "well-prepared" North Italian cooking like "sumptuous fresh pastas and ragouts" and "to-die-for risottos" please partisans of this "civilized" Gold Coast and Lincoln Park duo dubbed "the antidote to today's restaurant-group conglomerates"; though it "can feel overpriced at times", "knowledgeable" staffers and "pleasant" environs help ensure it's still a "comfortable meal kind of place."

	FOOD	DECOR	SERVICE	COST

Mesón Sabika *Spanish*

25 | 24 | 23 | $39

Naperville | 1025 Aurora Ave. (bet. River Rd. & West St.) | 630-983-3000 | www.mesonsabika.com

Tapas Valencia *Spanish*

South Loop | 1530 S. State St. (bet. 15th & 16th Sts.) | 312-842-4444 | www.tapasvalencia.com

The "amazing variety" of "flavorful", "well-prepared" tapas "encourages sampling" at this "solid" Naperville and South Loop duo tended by "cordial" servers; the suburban locale is set in a "charming old mansion" with an outdoor "garden paradise" for "dining under the stars", and the city post has patio seating, and though the "cost can add up quickly", most agree they're still a "go-to" for parties and events or just a romantic dinner."

Mexique Ⓜ *Mexican*

24 | 20 | 22 | $45

Noble Square | 1529 W. Chicago Ave. (bet. Armour St. & Ashland Ave.) | 312-850-0288 | www.mexiquechicago.com

For "inventive", "unexpected" fare boasting "flavors you won't taste anywhere else" surveyors swear by "personable" chef-owner Carlos Gaytan's "delicious" French-influenced Mexican cooking at this "lively", somewhat "out-of-the-way" Noble Square stop; "accommodating service" and a "clean, modern" setting also work in its favor, so bean-counters complaining of "high prices" are drowned out by fans insisting "you won't be disappointed"; P.S. many "wish it served cocktails" (beer, wine and sangria only).

M Henry Ⓜ *American*

25 | 20 | 21 | $23

Andersonville | 5707 N. Clark St. (Hollywood Ave.) | 773-561-1600 | www.mhenry.net

M Henrietta Ⓜ *American*

Edgewater | 1133 W. Granville Ave. (Broadway) | 773-761-9700 | www.mhenrietta.com

A "top option for brunch", these midpriced Andersonville and Edgewater New American BYOs offer "consistently outstanding" "sweet and savory" breakfast and lunch fare that forces "delicious decisions" – and lots of "salivating" – in the "bright, sunny" digs helmed by "friendly" servers; both have weekend waits, though Henry's is more "epic", and Henrietta also serves a "tasty" dinner with appeal for "both vegetarian and carniverous diners."

Mia Francesca *Italian*

24 | 19 | 21 | $38

Lakeview | 3311 N. Clark St. (School St.) | 773-281-3310 | www.miafrancesca.com

After more than 20 years this "moderately priced" Lakeview Italian is "still at the top of its game" say fans saluting the "standout", "homestyle" "comfort food", "expansive yet approachable wine list" and "professional" service; "tables are close together" in the "vibrant", "bustling" space, so it can get "loud" ("what? I can't hear you"), but adherents still "come back time and time again" for one of "the best all-around deals in town"; P.S. check out the "lovely" patio.

	FOOD	DECOR	SERVICE	COST

Z Michael **M** *French* — 27 | 23 | 26 | $71

Winnetka | 64 Green Bay Rd. (Winnetka Ave.) | 847-441-3100 | www.restaurantmichael.com

"Classic" French cooking gets a "modern" update at chef-owner Michael Lachowicz's "elegant but not snobby" Winnetka dining room turning out "delicious" "first-class" plates heightened by "imaginative touches"; "professional", "helpful" servers inspire high praise too, and patrons can "actually speak to one another without shouting" in the "upscale bistro" environs, so though it's "not inexpensive", devotees still deem it a "culinary treat" and suggest you "put it on your to-do list"; P.S. the Decor score may not reflect a recent remodeling.

NEW Michael Jordan's Steak House *Steak* — 23 | 23 | 24 | $66

Streeterville | InterContinental Chicago | 505 N. Michigan Ave. (bet. Grand Ave. & Illinois St.) | 312-321-8823 | www.mjshchicago.com

"Warm", "helpful" staffers contribute to the "all-star performance" at this booth-enhanced dining room in Streeterville's InterContinental where supporters cheer a surprisingly "innovative menu for a steakhouse", deeming it "expensive but worth it for a special night out"; reticent refs, however, say "there are better options" in the city, though they concede it's still a "great stop for any fan of the Bulls or Jordan."

Milk & Honey *American* — 23 | 19 | 21 | $15

Wicker Park | 1920 W. Division St. (bet. Damen & Wolcott Aves.) | 773-395-9434 | www.milkandhoneycafe.com

"Grab your morning paper and get a quick bite" at this counter-service Wicker Park American that "tempts" diners with a "simple" affordable menu of breakfast and lunch eats, like "outstanding housemade oatmeal" and "fresh" sandwiches; the "small" space can get "busy", but "friendly" staffers, a "chill vibe" and "welcoming atmosphere" all "encourage you to linger and work on your computer" – though if "noisy", "crowded" environs are "not your idea of a relaxing brunch, go before or after a rush" (or when "it's nice enough to sit outside").

Miller's Pub *American* — 18 | 16 | 19 | $27

Loop | 134 S. Wabash Ave. (bet. Adams & Monroe Sts.) | 312-263-4988 ●
Southwest Side | Midway Int'l Airport | 5700 S. Cicero Ave. (55th St.) | 773-948-6300
www.millerspub.com

A "Chicago institution" with a "wealth of history on its walls", this "venerable" Loop American puts out "traditional, satisfying" eats and drinks at "decent prices"; "servers who seem to have been here for years" tend to a "rotating cast of characters" in the "festive", "seedy looking" digs, so even if it offers "nothing exciting", loyalists say it's still an "ol' standby"; P.S. there's a small Midway airport outpost.

	FOOD	DECOR	SERVICE	COST

☑ Mirai Sushi *Japanese* | 27 | 22 | 22 | $49 |

Wicker Park | 2020 W. Division St. (bet. Damen & Hoyne Aves.) | 773-862-8500 | www.miraisushi.com

Try it once and you will "return again and again" promise patrons of this "quality" Wicker Park Japanese delivering "excellent", "inventive" sushi plus other "flavorful preparations" to go along with the "snazzy sake, wine and cocktail options"; solid service and a "cool, trendy ambiance" make it a "good date spot", so if a few find tabs "steep", many don't notice, noting they could "eat here everyday."

Miramar Bistro *French* | 17 | 18 | 18 | $46 |

Highwood | 301 Waukegan Ave. (Highwood Ave.) | 847-433-1078 | www.miramarbistro.com

Paris meets Havana at this somewhat costly Highwood Frenchie turning out "good" bistro standards alongside a few Cuban-accented dishes in banquette-enhanced digs with a "great bar" that helps make it a "fun place for drinks"; still, critcs remain unmoved, complaining of "tables on top of each other", "inconsistent" service and "hit-or-miss" fare, even as fans cite "fantastic" outdoor seating that "reminds of Paris."

NEW Mitad del Mundo ● *Mexican* | – | – | – | M |

Logan Square | 2833 W. Armitage Ave. (Mozart St.) | 773-661-1150 | www.mitaddelmundorestaurant.com

Prolific mole master Geno Bahena returns to Logan Square with this moderately priced arrival serving fresh multiregional Mexican, including wood-grilled tacos, unusual desserts, specialty coffee drinks and margaritas shaken at the table; the cozy, warmly lit setting with bare wood tables and a bar is decorated with multicolored paper and food-themed artwork, and there's live music on weekends.

Mity Nice *American* | 19 | 15 | 18 | $27 |

Streeterville | Water Tower Pl. | 835 N. Michigan Ave., Mezzanine level (bet. Chestnut & Pearson Sts.) | 312-335-4745 | www.leye.com

"Comfort food to the max" is the draw of this "reasonably priced" American inside Streeterville's Water Tower Place mall, where the meal starts with a "cordial" welcome from servers and "buttery" popovers in lieu of a bread basket; while regulars regret the remodel from "woody lodge" to "contemporary coffee shop", others insist it's still a "reliable" "place to pause between shopping."

☑ Mixteco Grill Ⓜ *Mexican* | 27 | 18 | 22 | $32 |

Lakeview | 1601 W. Montrose Ave. (Ashland Ave.) | 773-868-1601 | www.mixtecogrill.com

"Uniformly superb" apps, "to-die-for" mole sauces and "out-of-this-world" entrees make this Lakeview Mexican a "standout", especially since BYO further tempers the "reasonably priced" tabs; service is "friendly" and the art "eye-catching", so the "only negative is that it can get quite noisy."

▣ MK *American* | 28 | 25 | 26 | $73 |

Near North | 868 N. Franklin St. (bet. Chestnut & Locust Sts.) | 312-482-9179 | www.mkchicago.com

"Among the finest in Chicago", this Near North New American from Michael Kornick has "all the right ingredients", with "thoughtful, unique" meals that "reflect the seasons", "show-stealing" desserts and a "spectacular" wine list all offered by "accommodating" staffers; the "swanky" loftlike area is "bustling", the mezzanine "more intimate" and "everyone leaves happy – except the guy stuck with the tab."

NEW Mo Dailey's Pub & Grille ● *Pub Food* | - | - | - | I |

Northwest Side | 6070 N. Northwest Hwy. (bet. Newark Ave. & Raven St.) | 773-774-6121 | www.modaileys.com

A neighborhood hangout, this Norwood Parker offers an affordable menu of classic pub fare along with more substantial entree plates; vintage police and firefighter memorabilia highlight the first responder theme (in honor of the owner's father), and it has 27 TVs screening sports, plus an elevated seating area with a fireplace.

NEW Moderno *Italian* | - | - | - | M |

Highland Park | 1850 Second St. (bet. Elm Pl. & Central Ave.) | 847-433-8600

This midpriced Highland Park Italian from John des Rosiers (Inovasi) pours 200 boutique bottles, perfect for pairing with shareable, scratch-made small plates, salads, pizzas and pastas all arranged by complexity of flavors; its clean-lined space is flooded with natural light and outfitted with modern, mismatched seating, and there's also a small bar area and expansive outdoor patio.

Mon Ami Gabi *French* | 24 | 23 | 24 | $44 |

Lincoln Park | Belden-Stratford Hotel | 2300 N. Lincoln Park W. (Belden Ave.) | 773-348-8886
Oak Brook | Oakbrook Center Mall | 260 Oakbrook Ctr. (Rte. 83) | 630-472-1900
www.monamigabi.com

"A little slice of France" in Chicagoland, this "reasonably priced" French duo offers "consistently excellent", "well-prepared" bistro dinners via "attentive" service that "breaks the Gallic stereotype"; the outpost in Oak Brook's Center Mall also serves lunch and is "delightful" during or "after a day of shopping", and the Lincoln Park locale "fits perfectly" in the "grand, old Parisian-styled" Belden-Stratford Hotel.

Montarra Ⓜ *American* | - | - | - | E |

Algonquin | 1491 S. Randall Rd. (County Line Rd.) | 847-458-0505 | www.montarra.com

"Beautifully presented" "cutting-edge" fare "rewards" diners who discover this Algonquin New American set in an "easily missable strip mall"; "knowledgeable" staffers, a "well-chosen" wine list and modern environs round out the "pleasureable" (if somewhat pricey) package.

	FOOD	DECOR	SERVICE	COST

NEW Monti's 🏷️Ⓜ️ *American/Sandwiches* | - | - | - | I |

Lincoln Square | 4757 N. Talman Ave. (bet. Lawrence & Leland Aves.) | 773-942-6012 | www.ilovemontis.com

A former Rockit chef is behind this wallet-friendly, Philly cheesesteak-focused 'wichery that also serves salads, hoagies and pizzas, accompanied by house cocktails and craft brews; the remodeled Cinners space in Lincoln Square has a funky bar vibe with exposed brick and high-top tables, and it's open till 12 AM Thursday through Saturday.

Moody's Pub ● *Pub Food* | 20 | 16 | 16 | $19 |

Edgewater | 5910 N. Broadway (Thorndale Ave.) | 773-275-2696 | www.moodyspub.com

"It hasn't changed a bit" since its 1959 opening say regulars of this "basic but reliable" Edgewater pub, where "fast, friendly" servers offer "well-priced" bites, like "delish" burgers and "fresh-cut" fries "washed down with pitchers of beer"; many prefer it in summer for the "unbeatable" outdoor patio, deeming the inside "dingy and uninviting" despite the "roaring" fireplace in winter.

NEW Morso *American* | - | - | - | M |

Lincoln Park | 340 W. Armitage Ave. (bet. Lincoln Ave. & Orleans St.) | 773-880-9280 | www.morsochicago.com

Matt Maroni (ex Gaztro-Wagon) is behind this moderate Lincoln Park New American where the "quirky" small plates–focused menu is divided into six sections (veg, shellfish, offal, etc.) and paired with craft cocktails and "good beers on tap"; the bi-level space has polished wood floors, an open kitchen and an upstairs lounge offering bar nibbles (there's also seasonal seating on a covered patio).

🄩 Morton's The Steakhouse *Steak* | 26 | 23 | 25 | $72 |

Loop | 65 E. Wacker Pl. (bet. Michigan & Wabash Aves.) | 312-201-0410
Gold Coast | Newberry Plaza | 1050 N. State St. (Maple St.) | 312-266-4820
Rosemont | 9525 Bryn Mawr Ave. (N. River Rd.) | 847-678-5155
Northbrook | 699 Skokie Blvd. (Dundee Rd.) | 847-205-5111
Schaumburg | 1470 McConnor Pkwy. (bet. Golf & Meacham Rds.) | 847-413-8771
Naperville | 1751 Freedom Dr. (Diehl Rd.) | 630-577-1372
www.mortons.com

"Perfect for closing the big deal or celebrating a major milestone", this "original power brokers' steakhouse" (with locations area-wide, including the vintage-1978 State Street original) "sets the standard and maintains it" when it comes to "melt-in-your-mouth" chops and "super-fresh" seafood, all served via "truly professional" staffers in "hushed, formal" surroundings; "pricey" (some say "overpriced") tabs are tempered by "huge" portions and "bargain bar bites", so for many it's an all-around "favorite."

🄩 Moto 🏷️Ⓜ️ *Eclectic* | 27 | 23 | 27 | $158 |

West Loop | 945 W. Fulton Mkt. (Sangamon St.) | 312-491-0058 | www.motorestaurant.com

"Extraordinary" molecular gastronomy brings "new surprises around every corner" at this Eclectic West Loop "delight", exhibiting Homaro

Cantu's "insane creativity" via a "playful" prix fixe; "steep prices make it event dining for sure", but "attentive" service, "minimalist" decor and "very private" booths mean it's all the more "worth it."

Mr. Beef ●☒⇄ *Sandwiches* 24 | 8 | 14 | $11

River North | 666 N. Orleans St. (bet. Erie & Huron Sts.) | 312-337-8500 | www.mrbeefonorleans.com

"Loyal devotees" seeking "authentic" "Chicago street food done well" dig this "real-deal" River North "mecca" for its "damn good", "gut filling" sandwiches at bargain prices; though it "looks like it should be condemned" and service seems to be "declining", you're "there to have a great Italian beef, not a dining experience"; P.S. cash-only and on weekends it reopens at 10:30 PM to serve late-night diners (till 4 AM Friday, till 5 AM Saturday).

Mt. Everest Restaurant *Indian/Nepalese* 22 | 16 | 19 | $28

Evanston | 630 Church St. (bet. Chicago & Orrington Aves.) | 847-491-1069 | www.mteverestrestaurant.com

"Nicely prepared" Indian plates satisfy "all sort of palates" and the "flavorful" Nepali dishes are "an added attraction" at this "reasonably priced" Evanston eatery where devotees say "go with a group in order to sample many dishes" or try the "most excellent" lunch buffet "full of tasty choices"; "prompt" service makes up for unremarkable decor, and imbibers who feel the "bar selection leaves something to be desired" are advised to try the "don't-miss" beers.

Mundial Cocina ▽ 26 | 17 | 24 | $35
Mestiza ☑ *Eclectic/Mexican*

Pilsen | 1640 W. 18th St. (bet. Marshfield Ave. & Paulina St.) | 312-491-9908 | www.mundialcocinamestiza.com

"Innovative" globally influenced Mexican eats draw diners "off the beaten path" to this rustic Pilsen storefront; "value" prices, solid service and an interesting wine selection further make it a "worth-the-trip" "gem."

⬛NEW My Mother's Kitchen ☑ *Southern* – | – | – | M

Elmwood Park | 6818 W. North Ave. (Newcastle Ave.) | 773-887-4368 | www.mymotherskitchenchicago.com

The menu changes daily at this quaint Southern charmer in Elmwood Park offering soulful standbys (fried chicken, meatloaf, smothered pork chops) and classic sides; the cozy earth-toned setting includes an enclosed patio, and the BYO policy further results in moderate tabs.

Myron & Phil Steakhouse ☑ *Steak* 20 | 16 | 23 | $45

Lincolnwood | 3900 W. Devon Ave. (Springfield Ave.) | 847-677-6663 | www.myronandphil.com

"Nostalgia abounds" at this moderate Lincolnwood steakhouse, where "consistently good" beef and seafood are "prepared like they were in the Rat Pack days"; "steady" servers tend to a "'60s supper club" space that "takes you back a generation", and though what's "retro" to some is "tired" to others naysaying a "senior citizens only" vibe, it's still "never empty."

	FOOD	DECOR	SERVICE	COST

Nabuki *Japanese* ▽ 26 | 24 | 24 | $52

Hinsdale | 18 E. First St. (bet. Garfield Ave. & Washington St.) | 630-654-8880 | www.nabukihinsdale.com

"Finally, city-quality sushi in the 'burbs" exult enthusiasts of this "high-end" Hinsdale Japanese, where "very solid", "elegant" eats are enhanced by Latin accents and delivered by "involved" staffers amid "colorful" decor; some wish for less "pricey" tabs and "a little more legroom", but admit it's "worth a trip."

Nacional 27 Ⓢ *Nuevo Latino* 22 | 22 | 21 | $46

River North | 325 W. Huron St. (Orleans St.) | 312-664-2727 | www.n27chicago.com

"The flavors of South and Central America come alive" at this contemporary River North Nuevo Latino where "well-prepared" dishes are "great for sharing", servers "take the time to explain it all" and "you can dance the calories off after dinner" with music from DJs and live bands (Thursdays–Saturdays); while fussers who "expected better" say "save your money", fans who "love" the "tasty" drinks and "lovely sidewalk patio" say it's a "reliable" choice "for something different."

Z Naha Ⓢ *American* 27 | 24 | 25 | $73

River North | 500 N. Clark St. (Illinois St.) | 312-321-6242 | www.naha-chicago.com

"Imaginative" dishes featuring "complex combinations of ingredients" are chef-owner "Carrie Nahabedian's gift to all of us" effuse enthusiasts "astonished" by the "well-composed", "perfectly prepared" plates at this "top-notch" River North New American; "the staff is engaging in the best way" ("like that one brother-in-law you actually like") and the "contemporary" space "impresses" too (even when "noisy"), so most overlook "steep prices" and soak in the "Zen experience."

NEW Native Foods Café *Vegan* 23 | 18 | 23 | $16

Loop | 218 S. Clark St. (Quincy St.) | 312-332-6332 Ⓢ
Lakeview | 1023 W. Belmont Ave. (bet. Kenmore & Sheffield Aves.) | 773-549-4904
Wicker Park | 1484 N. Milwaukee Ave. (Honore St.) | 773-489-8480
www.nativefoods.com

"Gorge yourself without the guilt" at this California-based chain, a "wholesome" "addition to Chicago's vegan" scene known for "creative" meatless fare that's both "flavorful and satisfying"; "enthusiasm" is the hallmark of the "personally invested staff" and digs are generally "pleasant" too.

NEW Nellcôte ❶ *American* – | – | – | M

West Loop | 833 W. Randolph St. (Green St.) | 855-635-5268 | www.nellcoterestaurant.com

Old Town Social's Jared Van Camp unleashes his culinary imagination at this West Loop New American where the midpriced menu showcases handcrafted ingredients (even the flour is house-ground); the posh setting has soft chandelier lighting, an elevated mezzanine area and a marble staircase; P.S. it's named for the Riviera site where some Rolling Stones recording sessions happened.

NEW New England Seafood Company Fish Market *Seafood*

| – | – | – | M |

Lakeview | 3341 N. Lincoln Ave. (bet. Roscoe & School Sts.) | 773-871-3474 | www.neseafoodcompany.com

Lobster traps, netting and a fish tank set the tone at this East Coast-style counter-service seafood shack inside a Lakeview market where the fish is flown in daily; the moderately priced menu features clams, crabs and lobsters in all the familiar formats, as well as chowders and bisques, baked fish dinners and fried combos; P.S. no reservations and no alcohol.

ⓩ Next Ⓜ *Eclectic*

| 29 | 26 | 29 | $164 |

West Loop | 953 W. Fulton Mkt. (bet. Morgan & Sangamon Sts.) | 312-226-0858 | www.nextrestaurant.com

"Genius" Grant Achatz "breaks the mold", completely redesigning the themed fixed-price menu every three months at his "dazzling" West Loop Eclectic, an "unparalleled culinary experience" where enjoying "life-changingly delicious food" offered in "thought-provoking presentations" is "more like being part of a story than simply eating"; "flawless" staffers (rated No. 1 for Service in Chicago) enhance the "cozy", modern confines, so despite "über-expensive" tabs and a "bizarre ticketing system" "requiring feats of psychological endurance" it's still "worth every penny and then some."

Next Door Bistro Ⓜ *American/Italian*

| 21 | 16 | 21 | $42 |

Northbrook | 250 Skokie Blvd. (Frontage Rd.) | 847-272-1491 | www.nextdoorbistro.com

"Regulars" head to this casual Northbrook Italian-American for an "extensive" menu of "delicious" fare ferried by "friendly, quick" servers; holdouts hint "preferred customers" often get better treatment, but "great prices" help take the edge off.

Niche ⓏⓂ *American*

| ▽ 27 | 25 | 28 | $66 |

Geneva | 14 S. Third St. (bet. James & State Sts.) | 630-262-1000 | www.nichegeneva.com

"Attentive", "personable" service, "wonderful" New American fare and a "stellar wine list" highlighting limited batch offerings add up to a "fine-dining" experience at this Geneva "must-try"; add in "relaxed, inviting" environs and it's a "great option for special-occasion or romantic dining" – just "fill your wallet" in preparation.

Nick's Fishmarket Ⓩ *Seafood*

| 25 | 22 | 24 | $60 |

Rosemont | O'Hare International Ctr. | 10275 W. Higgins Rd. (Mannheim Rd.) | 847-298-8200

Nick's Fishmarket Grill & Bar Ⓩ *Seafood*

River North | Merchandise Mart | 222 W. Merchandise Mart Plaza (bet. Orleans & Wells Sts.) | 312-621-0200
www.nicksfishmarketchicago.com

Diners "craving seafood" choose this duo for "fabulously fresh fish" and "choices galore"; the newer River North outpost has urban stylings and a blue-lit bar, while the Rosemont longtimer looks more "old-school", and though you'll "pay a lot" at both, loyalists remain undeterred, especially since the "staffs work to provide some of the best service you'll find."

NEW Nieto's *American*

— | — | — | M

Highland Park | 429 Temple Ave. (Waukegan Ave.) | 847-432-0770 | www.nietosrestaurant.com

Carlos and Debbie Nieto have reconcepted their long-standing Highland Park fine-dining destination Carlos' into this more informal American with a midpriced menu of burgers, classic entrees and old-school desserts; the warm wood paneling remains in a cozy, softly lit room with rows of frames to post customer photos; P.S. they serve separate gluten-free and kids' menus.

☑ Nightwood *American*

27 | 23 | 25 | $41

Pilsen | 2119 S. Halsted St. (21st St.) | 312-526-3385 | www.nightwoodrestaurant.com

A "constantly evolving menu" of "inventive, exciting" "farm-to-table" fare is on offer at this New American "standout" where "deliciously prepared, reasonably priced" dinners and an "outstanding" Sunday brunch featuring "donuts to weep over" "compel you to take the trip to Pilsen"; "fantastic" staffers attend to "pretty, shiny people" in the "hip, down-to-earth" digs, and there's a "delightful" patio when "inside is so noisy that you can't hear yourself, much less your companions."

90 Miles Cuban Cafe *Cuban*

23 | 18 | 21 | $18

Lakeview | 3101 N. Clybourn Ave. (Barry Ave.) | 773-248-2822
Logan Square | 2540 W. Armitage (Rockwell St.) | 773-227-2822
www.90milescubancafe.com

Champions cheer the "authentic", "filling" "Cuban comfort food" including "spot-on" empanadas, "delicious" ropa vieja and "fantastic coffee" at these "cheap" BYOs in Logan Square ("more comfortable") and Lakeview (a "tiny hut") where you "bring your own rum" and they supply "sangria, mimosa and mojito mixers"; "fast, friendly" servers contribute to the "festive atmosphere", and both offer outdoor seating.

Niu Japanese Fusion Lounge *Asian*

23 | 21 | 18 | $33

Streeterville | 332 E. Illinois St. (bet. Columbus Dr. & McClurg Ct.) | 312-527-2888 | www.niusushi.com

"Creative Asian flavor combinations" win fusion fans at this affordable Streeterville stop offering "quality" sushi, plus stir-fry, noodles and more, boosted by an extensive cocktail list; service is generally "quick" in the modern, minimalist space, and the theater-adjacent location makes it a pick "before or after the movies."

N9ne Steakhouse ☒ *Seafood/Steak*

22 | 24 | 21 | $61

Loop | 440 W. Randolph St. (Canal St.) | 312-575-9900 | www.n9ne.com

Though the steaks at this "upscale" Loop chophouse are "surprisingly good considering how hip it once was", many say the real "reason to go is to enjoy views" of the "beautiful young ones" and assorted "arm candy" that fill the "trendy, high-styled" room along with "groups of bussinessmen on expense accounts"; the less enthused complain it's "pricey" for "average" food and leave it to those looking for a "people-watching place."

Ⓩ NEW NoMI Kitchen *American*   26 | 27 | 25 | $72

Gold Coast | Park Hyatt Chicago | 800 N. Michigan Ave., 7th fl. (bet. Michigan Ave. & Rush St.) | 312-239-4030 | www.parkchicago.hyatt.com

After a "remake", the "more relaxed" yet still "elegant" space "passes the test for excitement" say those revisiting this "top-drawer" New American in the Gold Coast's Park Hyatt where the "inventive", "wide-ranging" menu also inspires high praise; "service remains excellent" too, and with "magnificent city views" and an "extensive" wine list most agree it's "special-occasion"-worthy, "especially if you have an expense account"; P.S. the outdoor roof garden remains, and is now visible from inside through a glass wall.

Noodles by Takashi Yagihashi ● ☒ *Japanese*   ▽ 23 | 11 | 17 | $14

Loop | 111 N. State St. (Washington St.) | 312-781-4483 | www.visitmacyschicago.com

"One of the standouts" at the upscale Macy's food court in the Loop, this Japanese "step up from your typical fast-food noodle shop" via namesake chef Takashi Yagihashi (Takashi, The Slurping Turtle) serves "fabulous" ramen topped by "fresh" ingredients; its nondescript shopping-mall setting means supporters "can't give props for decor", but that's ok for most given affordable tabs.

Nookies *Diner*   21 | 13 | 20 | $17

NEW Edgewater | 1100 W. Bryn Mawr Ave. (Winthrop Ave.) | 773-516-4188

Old Town | 1746 N. Wells St. (bet. Lincoln & North Aves.) | 312-337-2454

Nookies Too *Diner*

Lincoln Park | 2114 N. Halsted St. (bet. Dickens & Webster Aves.) | 773-327-1400

Nookies Tree *Diner*

Lakeview | 3334 N. Halsted St. (Buckingham Pl.) | 773-248-9888 www.nookiesrestaurants.net

A "huge variety" of "classic" American "comfort food" keeps "everyone from twentysomethings to big families" "returning to sample more" at these "friendly" BYO "staples" famous for "monster" breakfasts and lunches at the "right prices"; they're especially popular on weekends, but "unpretentious" service ensures "long lines move quickly"; P.S. Lincoln Park and Lakeview are open 24 hours on Fridays and Saturdays, while Old Town and Edgewater also serve dinner.

Noon-O-Kabab *Persian*   24 | 17 | 19 | $25

Albany Park | 4661 N. Kedzie Ave. (Leland Ave.) | 773-279-8899 | www.noonokabab.com

"Grilled kebabs are the main attraction" at this Albany Park Persian, though it's "great for vegetarians as well", with Middle Eastern salads and other "satisfying" vittles offered at a "good price"; service can be "a tiny bit slow" when "busy", but is otherwise "warm" and "friendly" in the "cozy", "recently expanded and redecorated" space, so most ultimately qualify it "a true find."

Nori *Japanese* 24 | 19 | 19 | $25

Lakeview | 954 W. Diversey Pkwy. (Sheffield Ave.) | 773-904-1000
NEW Rogers Park | 1237 W. Devon Ave. (Magnolia Ave.) | 773-262-5216
NEW Wicker Park | 1393 N. Milwaukee Ave. (Wood St.) | 773-292-9992
www.norichicago.com

"Delicious" and "creative rolls" including the "amazing dragon roll" top the menu at this "busy" Japanese threesome; if a few feel the "decor leaves much to be desired", "efficient" service helps distract, especially since BYO further lessens already "reasonable" tabs (though the full-service Lakeview branch has a corkage fee).

Z North Pond M *American* 26 | 28 | 26 | $74

Lincoln Park | 2610 N. Cannon Dr. (bet. Diversey & Fullerton Pkwys.) | 773-477-5845 | www.northpondrestaurant.com

Gourmets "get their locavore on" at this "ever-innovative" New American where chef Bruce Sherman's "inspiring" and "refined farm-to-table" fare "dazzles" and the "pastoral" setting "hidden" inside Lincoln Park offers "breathtaking views" of North Pond and the city skyline; yes, you'll "pay quite a lot", but "unpretentious, welcoming" service completes the "exquisite" picture, making it a "total package" and "refuge from the urban din."

Norton's Restaurant *American* 19 | 14 | 22 | $27

Highland Park | 1905 Sheridan Rd. (Central Ave.) | 847-432-3287 | www.nortons-restaurant.com

"Highland Park's version of *Cheers*", this "family-friendly" American delivers "solid" eats, but really scores with service "so friendly" and "personal" the food tastes better; the "casual" digs can be "cramped", but they make "you feel like you're always dining with friends", so most don't mind.

Oak Tree Bakery and Restaurant *American* 16 | 16 | 16 | $24

Gold Coast | Bloomingdale's Bldg. | 900 N. Michigan Ave., 6th fl. (bet. Delaware & Walton Pls.) | 312-751-1988 | www.oaktreechicago.com

An "oasis of quiet" since 1991, this midpriced Gold Coast American woos shoppers and "ladies who lunch" with "reliable" "comfort food" offered until 5 PM daily; "the seating is comfortable" and the service "good", so even if the "years have taken their toll", it's still a "pleasant stop" while "spending on the Magnificent Mile."

Oceanique Z *French/Seafood* 25 | 20 | 24 | $70

Evanston | 505 Main St. (bet. Chicago & Hinman Aves.) | 847-864-3435 | www.oceanique.com

"Purveying foodie fare" since 1989, this "upscale" Evanston "fish mecca" still "dazzles" with "expertly prepared" New French dishes bolstered by an "exceptional" wine list; "fine service" adds to

FOOD | DECOR | SERVICE | COST

the "first class" feel, and if some deem it "overpriced" given its the "storefront" feel, it doesn't stop others from insisting its "ship always comes in."

NEW The Ogden *American*

– | – | – | I

West Loop | 1659 W. Ogden Ave. (bet. Adams & Monroe Sts.) | 312-226-1888 | www.theogdenchicago.com

This 'chef-driven sports bar' near United Center serves budget-friendly New American – think popcorn cooked in chicken fat, brandade tacos and smoked mushroom grinders – accompanied by vintage-inspired cocktails and 50 or so beers; the urban-industrial environs boast exposed brick, booths with inset TVs and a fireplace.

Old Jerusalem Restaurant *Mideastern*

20 | 8 | 18 | $18

Old Town | 1411 N. Wells St. (bet. North Ave. & Schiller St.) | 312-944-0459 | www.oldjerusalemrestaurant.com

"Really basic, but well-made" Middle Eastern chow is "always a value" at this "reasonably priced" Old Town longtimer tended by "friendly" staffers; just "don't look up from your plate" because the "harsh lighting" "doesn't make your date look too good" warn diners who prefer outdoor seating or getting takeout.

NEW Old Town Pour House 🅂🅼 *American*

– | – | – | M

Old Town | 1419 N. Wells St. (bet. Burton Pl. & Schiller St.) | 312-477-2800 | www.oldtownpourhouse.com

Located in the former 33 Club space, this Old Town arrival offers a midpriced menu of American pub food plus 90 draft beers and wine on tap; the handsome, swanky digs include a long bar, multiple TVs, front windows that open to sidewalk seating and a grand staircase leading up to a loungey mezzanine.

Old Town Social ◑ *American*

24 | 22 | 17 | $34

Old Town | 455 W. North Ave. (Cleveland Ave.) | 312-266-2277 | www.oldtownsocial.com

Chef Jared Van Camp's "kick-ass" New American noshes and "mind-blowing charcuterie" go well with "dozens of esoteric beers" and "inventive cocktails" at this "fancy sports bar" in Old Town "that morphs into a dance club late"; the wood-accented "loft space" with many TVs also has a "cool lounge area in front if you don't feel like standing in the crowded main bar", and that plus "nice outside seating" and moderate prices help make it "a must-stop" – "just don't expect much by way of service."

Olive Mediterranean Grill *Mediterranean*

– | – | – | I

Loop | Clark & Lake | 201 N. Clark St. (bet. Lake St. & Wacker Dr.) | 312-726-1234 🅂

NEW Old Town | 1001 W. North Ave. (Sheffield Ave.) | 312-274-5525 www.eatomg.com

All-day dining on inexpensive Mediterranean classics (shawarma, kebabs, falafel, salads, baklava) comes to Old Town in the form of this casual, alcohol-free outpost of the Loop food-court original; the colorful setting features pendant lighting, reclaimed wood tables and industrial ductwork.

| | FOOD | DECOR | SERVICE | COST |

NEW Ombra *Italian*

| - | - | - | M |

Andersonville | 5310 N. Clark St. (bet. Berwyn & Summerdale Aves.) | 773-506-8600 | www.barombra.com

Part of sibling restaurant Acre has been converted into this Andersonville cicchetti bar serving small Italian plates that are meant to be shared; as for the interior, expect a clever amalgamation of salvaged materials, like vintage newspaper wallpaper and leather jacket-covered seats, plus rustic wood accents and an aerial view of Florence suspended from the ceiling in panels; P.S. no reservations.

One North ☒ *American*

| 16 | 16 | 15 | $35 |

Loop | UBS Bldg. | 1 N. Wacker Dr. (Madison St.) | 312-750-9700 | www.restaurants-america.com

"Solid if not spectacular" eats and moderate tabs make this "comfortable" Loop New American a "dependable spot" for "business lunches" and dinners before the Lyric Opera (open Saturdays in show season only); fence-sitters, however, feel it's merely "serviceable", especially considering the "indifferent" service – but many agree its "convenient" location trumps all, keeping it a "standby."

Opa! Estiatorio *Greek*

| 23 | 20 | 21 | $39 |

Vernon Hills | 950 Lakeview Pkwy. (Hawthorn Pkwy.) | 847-968-4300 | www.oparestaurant.com

"Delicious" Greek fare at moderate prices is the lure of this Vernon Hills Hellenic tended by "pleasant, efficient" servers who make diners "feel like welcomed guests"; the "airy", white-walled dining room and "gorgeous" outdoor patio overlooking Bear Lake also add appeal.

Opart Thai House *Thai*

| 24 | 17 | 21 | $19 |

Lincoln Square | 4658 N. Western Ave. (Leland Ave.) | 773-989-8517
South Loop | 1906 S. State St. (Archer Ave.) | 312-567-9898
www.opartthai.com

"Authentically prepared dishes are aromatic and flavorful" at this Thai duo in Lincoln Square and the South Loop where "converts" also preach about the "nuanced spicing" and all around "delicious", "quality" fare; "decor is nothing to look at", but with "relatively inexpensive tabs" and solid service, loyalists still find it "hard to resist" and feel "lucky to live close" by; P.S. Lincoln Square is BYO.

Orange *Eclectic*

| 20 | 14 | 17 | $19 |

River North | 738 N. Clark St. (bet. Chicago Ave. & Superior St.) | 312-202-0600
Lincoln Park | 2413 N. Clark St. (Fullerton Pkwy.) | 773-549-7833
Roscoe Village | 2011 W. Roscoe St. (Damen Ave.) | 773-248-0999
Near West | 730 W. Grand Ave. (bet. Halsted St. & Union Ave.) | 312-942-0300
www.orangerestaurantchicago.com

"The creativity works" at these Eclectic "masters of breakfast" known for "tasty pancake flights", "funky, freakin' good" frushi (fruit sushi) and other "kooky" offerings (lunch is more "ordinary") served alongside the "gulpable" orange-infused coffee; occasionally "frantic" service and digs that "seem decorated with the leftovers from a low-rent basement" don't deter supporters who make it a "favorite non high-end" option.

Original Gino's East *Pizza*   21 | 15 | 16 | $24

River North | 633 N. Wells St. (Ontario St.) | 312-943-1124 | www.ginoseast.com
Streeterville | 162 E. Superior St. (Michigan Ave.) | 312-266-3337 | www.ginoseast.com
Lincoln Park | 2801 N. Lincoln Ave. (Diversey Pkwy.) | 773-327-3737 | www.ginoseastlakeview.com
O'Hare Area | 8725 W. Higgins Rd. (bet. Cumberland & East River Rds.) | 773-444-2244 | www.ginosonhiggins.com
Deerfield | Embassy Suites Hotel | 1445 Lake Cook Rd. (Kenmore Ave.) | 847-945-4300 | www.ginoseastdeerfield.com
Libertyville | 820 S. Milwaukee Ave. (bet. Condell & Valley Park Drs.) | 847-362-1300 | www.ginoseast.com
Barrington | 352 Kelsey Rd. (Main St.) | 847-381-8300 | www.ginoseast.com
Rolling Meadows | 1321 W. Golf Rd. (Algonquin Rd.) | 847-364-6644 | www.ginoseastrollingmeadows.com
St. Charles | Tin Cup Pass Shopping Ctr. | 1590 E. Main St. (Tyler Rd.) | 630-513-1311 | www.ginoseast.com
Wheaton | 315 W. Front St. (bet. West St. & Wheaton Ave.) | 630-588-1010 | www.ginoseast.com
Additional locations throughout the Chicago area

"Deep-dish reigns supreme" at these "landmark pizza emporiums" judged "just plain good" for their "Chicago-style" pies and "out-of-this-world" cornmeal crusts; they "don't waste any money" on the "pleasantly grungy" surrounds and service can be "inconsistent", but fans insist you still "can't go wrong", so "bring your sharpie" to "graffiti the walls" – after the "food coma" wears off of course.

The Original Pancake House *Diner*   24 | 14 | 20 | $17

Gold Coast | 22 E. Bellevue Pl. (bet. Michigan Ave. & Rush St.) | 312-642-7917 | www.walkerbros.net
Lincoln Park | 2020 N. Lincoln Park W. (Clark St.) | 773-929-8130 | www.walkerbros.net
Far South Side | 10437 S. Western Ave. (bet. 104th & 105th Sts.) | 773-445-6100 | www.walkerbros.net
Hyde Park | Village Ctr. | 1517 E. Hyde Park Blvd. (bet. 51st St. & Lake Park Blvd.) | 773-288-2322 | www.walkerbros.net
Park Ridge | 106 S. Northwest Hwy. (Touhy Ave.) | 847-696-1381 | www.walkerbros.net
Oak Forest | 5148 W. 159th St. (bet. Laramie & Le Claire Aves.) | 708-687-8282 | www.walkerbros.net
Orland Park | 15256 S. La Grange Rd. (Orland Park Pl.) | 708-349-0600 | www.originalpancakehouse.com
Forest Park | 7255 Madison St. (bet. Elgin & Marengo Aves.) | 708-771-5411 | www.originalpancakehouse.com

Walker Bros. Original Pancake House *American*
Lincolnshire | 200 Marriott Dr. (Milwaukee Ave.) | 847-634-2220

(continued)

(continued)

Walker Bros. Original Pancake House

Glenview | 1615 Waukegan Rd. (Woodlawn Ave.) | 847-724-0220
Highland Park | 620 Central Ave. (2nd St.) | 847-432-0660
Wilmette | 153 Green Bay Rd. (Isabella St.) | 847-251-6000
Arlington Heights | 825 W. Dundee Rd. (Ridge Ave.) | 847-392-6600
Lake Zurich | Lake Zurich Theatre Development | 767 S. Rand Rd. (June Terr.) | 847-550-0006
www.walkerbros.net
Additional locations throughout the Chicago area

"Carbo loading" commenters who "crave a breakfast stacked high with buttermilk pancakes, huge pieces of ham and crunchy bacon" washed down with "excellent coffee" swear by these "conventional" diner "classics" for "breakfast all day long" (closing times vary); the staff is "friendly and considerate, especially of kids and parents", and while the "kitschy" country decor "leaves a bit to be desired", you "can't beat the price", so "there's always a crowd."

NEW Osteria de Pizza
- | - | - | I

Metro *Italian/Pizza*
Lakeview | 2863 N. Clark St. (bet. Diversey Pkwy. & Surf St.) | 773-472-6411 | www.osteriadepizzametro.com

Square-cut Roman-style pizza is the centerpiece of the wallet-friendly menu at this Lakeview BYO also vending appetizers, salads, fresh pasta, panini and a couple of classic entrees; the charming neighborhood setting is decorated with a black-and-white tile floor and vintage prints.

Osteria Via Stato *Italian*
23 | 21 | 22 | $42

River North | 620 N. State St. (Ontario St.) | 312-642-8450
Pizzeria Via Stato *Pizza*
River North | 620 N. State St. (Ontario St.) | 312-337-6634
www.osteriaviastato.com

"Well-presented", "consistently good" "Italian comfort food" available à la carte or in a prix fixe "family-style" option draws dinner-time diners to this "lively" River North osteria in "pleasant", archway-enhanced environs, while "solid", "über-thin" pizza with "toppings to please kid and grown-up tastes" alike makes for a "relaxing" meal at the adjacent pie parlor (open for lunch too); service is generally "accommodating" and most have no complaints about the tabs, so both will "easily satisfy a group."

Over Easy Café M *American*
▽ 27 | 22 | 23 | $15

Ravenswood | 4943 N. Damen Ave. (bet. W. Ainslie & W. Argyle Sts.) | 773-506-2605 | www.overeasycafechicago.com

"Get ready to eat" at this "busy" Ravenswood BYO offering "massive portions" of "filling, indulgent" American breakfast, lunch and brunch fare upgraded by "interesting" and "unusual combinations"; "small" digs mean waits can be "long", but "accommodating" staffers offer complimentary coffee to those in line, and since tabs "go over easy on your wallet", most find it "must-go" worthy.

Owen & Engine *British*

23 | 23 | 24 | $33

Logan Square | 2700 N. Western Ave. (Schubert Ave.) | 773-235-2930 | www.owenandengine.com

The "outrageously good fish 'n' chips" and other "insanely delicious" offerings are "some of the best high-concept pub food in town" applaud aficionados of this midpriced Logan Square Brit that also "makes a splash" with an "unmatched" selection of cask-conditioned and craft brews; "knowledgeable" staffers include some of the "friendliest, funnest bartenders" and the cozy wood-accented space has an upstairs area with a fireplace, so don't be surprised if it's "crazy crowded."

Oysy *Japanese*

23 | 20 | 21 | $31

River North | 50 E. Grand Ave. (bet. Rush St. & Wabash Ave.) | 312-670-6750
South Loop | 888 S. Michigan Ave. (9th St.) | 312-922-1127
www.oysysushi.com

"Excellent quality sushi, sashimi and other Japanese fare" find favor at this "trendy" South Loop and River North twosome with "really pretty rolls, inventive combos" and "great lunch specials"; the "spare" "modern" space gets a boost from "polite" service, and with "reasonable prices", it's "highly recommended" "for a date or a group."

The Palm *Steak*

24 | 21 | 23 | $69

Loop | Swissôtel Chicago | 323 E. Wacker Dr. (bet. Columbus St. & Lake Shore Dr.) | 312-616-1000 | www.thepalm.com

"An old standby", this Loop link of the "old-fashioned" chophouse chain "continues to shine" with "soft, juicy filets", "huge lobsters" and other "consistently well-executed fare" delivered in "warm" surrounds enhanced by caricatures of local celebrities; "professional", "adult" service helps "make every meal an occasion", so regulars say bring your "expense account" and "eat like no one is watching."

Pane Caldo *Italian*

23 | 21 | 21 | $62

Gold Coast | 72 E. Walton St. (bet. Michigan Ave. & Rush St.) | 312-649-0055 | www.pane-caldo.com

"Unusual and fresh" Northern Italian dishes are prepared with a "wonderful attention to detail" at this "cozy", "romantic" Gold Coaster; an "older crowd" lends a "quiet vibe" and service is generally "attentive", so even if there's debate about whether the "food warrants the price", most have an overall "good experience."

Pappadeaux Seafood Kitchen *Seafood*

23 | 21 | 21 | $39

Westmont | 921 Pasquinelli Dr. (Oakmont Ln.) | 630-455-9846 | www.pappadeaux.com

"When you can't go to NOLA" head here suggest surveyors of this affordable Westmont seafood specialist where the "flavorful" dishes feature a "nice Cajun kick", "making you feel like being in the Big Easy"; "fast and friendly" service helps create a "positive vibe" in the spacious, wood-accented environs, and when it gets too "crowded" and "noisy", a seasonal patio provides another option.

Paris Club ● *French* | 21 | 21 | 20 | $42

River North | 59 W. Hubbard St. (bet. Clark & Dearborn Sts.) | 312-595-0800 | www.parisclubchicago.com

A "chic" "urban" space "packed with beautiful young people" provides the backdrop for chef Jean Joho's "approachable", "well-executed" "bistro classics" at this "relatively affordable" River North Frenchie from the brothers Melman; "capable service" navigates the "always jumping" space, and if critics call it "more club than Paris" and say "sightseeing" is the real "draw", that's fine by most who find it a "welcome addition to the nightlife scene", jokingly asking "what did we do before it came along?"

Park Grill *American* | 19 | 19 | 18 | $43

Loop | Millennium Park | 11 N. Michigan Ave. (bet. Madison & Washington Sts.) | 312-521-7275 | www.parkgrillchicago.com

"You can't beat the setting" at this Loop American in "gorgeous" Millennium Park where the "broad" menu of "remarkably good" fare gets a boost from "views of skaters at the rink" in winter and "people-watching" on the "delightful" patio in summer; service gets mixed marks ("attentive" vs. "spotty"), and critics who fault merely "decent" fare and "overpriced" tabs leave it to the "tourists", but plenty of pleased patrons note just being there "is a thrill."

Parthenon ● *Greek* | 21 | 16 | 19 | $33

Greektown | 314 S. Halsted St. (bet. Jackson Blvd. & Van Buren St.) | 312-726-2407 | www.theparthenon.com

For a bit of "the Med translocated to Halsted", fans "take a crowd" to this circa-1968 Greektown "standard" to sup on "delicious" "traditional" Hellenic fare, including the "must-eat" "flaming" *saganaki* (cheese); "hustling" servers are "friendly", and you get "a lot for little money", so though it "could use a decor upgrade" supporters say that's the price you pay for "soul."

NEW Pasteur ☒ *French/Vietnamese* | - | - | - | M

Edgewater | 5525 N. Broadway St. (bet. Bryn Mawr & Catalpa Aves.) | 773-728-4800 | www.pasteurrestaurantchicago.com

This veteran Edgewater French-Vietnamese has reopened with two chefs cooking non-fusion fare from both countries – pho to foie – for lunch and dinner, accompanied by exotic craft cocktails; the space has been updated in chic neutrals and white tablecloths, with wicker and leather chairs, plush banquettes and gyroscope-inspired chandeliers.

NEW Patron's Hacienda ● *Mexican/Steak* | - | - | - | M

River North | 316 W. Erie St. (bet. Franklin & Orleans Sts.) | 312-642-2400 | www.patronschicago.com

Expect authentic, moderately priced Mexican meals and chophouse favorites (with options for vegetarians), signature margaritas and a massive tequila menu (including flights) at this River North arrival; the high-ceilinged, sports-barlike digs feature a kaleidoscope of color, funky furnishings, wall hangings, murals and multiple TVs.

	FOOD	DECOR	SERVICE	COST

Pegasus ◐ Greek
21 | 18 | 19 | $31

Greektown | 130 S. Halsted St. (bet. Adams & Monroe Sts.) |
312-226-4666 | www.pegasuschicago.com

Pegasus on the Fly ◐ Greek

Southwest Side | Midway Int'l Airport | 5700 S. Cicero Ave. (55th St.) |
773-581-1522 | www.pegasusonthefly.com

"Delicious" "Greek comfort food" has patrons saying "*opa!*" at this
"lively" yet "conversation-friendly" Greektowner "notable for its fabulous rooftop" "with impressive city views"; though "service varies between very good and just good", it's "less rushed" than some of its
neighbors and that plus affordable tabs help explain why it comes
"recommended"; P.S. the Midway Airport sib offers a limited menu.

☑ Pelago Ristorante Italian
26 | 25 | 26 | $72

Streeterville | Raffaello Hotel | 201 E. Delaware Pl.
(Mies van der Rohe Way) | 312-280-0700 | www.pelagorestaurant.com

For "Italian fine-dining bliss", talliers tout the "fantastic" homemade
pasta, "excellent sauces" and "extensive wine selection" at this
"under-the-radar" "find" in Streeterville's Raffaello Hotel, where
service is yet another "highlight"; "you can smell the love in the air"
in the "sleek" room filled with an "elegant, well-heeled clientele" –
just "expect prices to match" (or try the "great lunch deals").

Penny's Noodle Shop Asian
21 | 13 | 19 | $15

Lakeview | 3400 N. Sheffield Ave. (Roscoe St.) | 773-281-8222 Ⓜ
Lincoln Park | 950 W. Diversey Pkwy. (Sheffield Ave.) |
773-281-8448
Wicker Park | 1542 N. Damen Ave. (North Ave.) | 773-394-0100 Ⓜ
Northfield | 320 Happ Rd. (Orchard Ln.) | 847-446-4747
Oak Park | 1130 Chicago Ave. (Harlem Ave.) | 708-660-1300
www.pennysnoodleshop.com

A "favorite for a cheap eat", this Asian mini-chain offers "plentiful"
portions of "satisfying", "flavorful" fare – and "way more than just noodles"; it may "lack ambiance" and is "not the most authentic" option,
but it's still a "reliable standby", especially appreciated for "fast service when you're in a hurry"; P.S. Lakeview and Northfield are BYO.

Pensiero Ristorante Ⓜ Italian
▽ 21 | 21 | 19 | $48

Evanston | Margarita European Inn | 1566 Oak Ave. (Davis St.) |
847-475-7779 | www.pensieroitalian.com

Despite a series of chef changes at this somewhat expensive resurrection of the former Va Pensiero, this Italian in Evanston's Margarita
European Inn maintains an "interesting menu" ("don't expect lasa-
gna") paired with a "wide-ranging" wine list; service is "attentive",
and some note the "recent redecoration seems to have upped the
noise level, but not to an extreme."

Pequod's Pizzeria ◐ Pizza
25 | 15 | 19 | $19

Lincoln Park | 2207 Clybourn Ave. (bet. Greenview & Webster Aves.) |
773-327-1512 | www.pequodspizza.com

"What dreams are made of" effuse enthusiasts of the "salty,
cheesy" "caramelized crust" (a "revelation") that along with "sweet

sauce" makes this Lincoln Park pizza pub "stand out" in a crowded field; "service is ok", the surrounds "divey" and there's "no ambiance", but really, "who cares" ask fans who wonder "why people waste time eating anything else."

NEW Perennial Virant *American* `26` `23` `24` `$54`

Lincoln Park | Hotel Lincoln | 1800 N. Lincoln Ave. (Clark St.) | 312-981-7070 | www.perennialvirant.com

"Incredibly well-executed", "inventive seasonal cuisine" displays the "tremendous talent" of chef Paul Virant (Vie) at this revamped New American in Lincoln Park's newly reopened Hotel Lincoln where the "flawlessly presented" fare is served in an "inviting" space filled with "trendy" "beautiful people"; "knowledgable, attentive" service and a "great bar scene" enhance the "lively ambiance", and while somewhat "pricey" tabs might make it "more of a special-occasion destination than a weekly jaunt", most maintain it "should be on every Chicago foodie's list."

Pete Miller's Seafood & `22` `20` `20` `$49`
Prime Steak *Seafood/Steak*

Evanston | 1557 Sherman Ave. (bet. Davis & Grove Sts.) | 847-328-0399 ●

Wheeling | 412 N. Milwaukee Ave. (bet. Mayer Ave. & Wolf Rd.) | 847-243-3700

www.petemillers.com

Loyalists who say these "high-end" suburban sibs are "surviving the onslaught of chain steakhouses with flying colors" cite their "prime" cuts, "delicious" seafood and "memorable sides" all served by an "engaged" staff; classy surrounds with dark-wood accents are livened by "fantastic live jazz" most nights; P.S. to avoid the "crowded, noisy" weekends try lunch at the Wheeling outpost, which also boasts a "fantastic outdoor patio."

Petterino's *American* `19` `21` `22` `$42`

Loop | Goodman Theatre Bldg. | 150 N. Dearborn St. (Randolph St.) | 312-422-0150 | www.petterinos.com

Service "knows how to get you to the show on time" (and "valet is a huge plus") at this "swanky" Italian-tinged American that's "a must" for the Loop theater crowd with "dependably tasty" "Wisconsin supper club food" for a "reasonable price"; though some find the offerings "uninspired" and say it's "there to soak the tourists", it remains "popular", especially for its business lunch and Sunday brunch; P.S. "have a martini and dream about being a star" at the "unique" Monday night open mike.

P.F. Chang's China Bistro *Chinese* `20` `20` `20` `$31`

River North | 530 N. Wabash Ave (Grand Ave.) | 312-828-9977
Northbrook | Northbrook Court Shopping Ctr. | 1819 Lake Cook Rd. (Northbrook Court Dr.) | 847-509-8844
Schaumburg | Woodfield Mall | 5 Woodfield Mall (Frontage & Golf Rds.) | 847-610-8000
Orland Park | Orland Park Crossing | 14135 S. La Grange Rd. (143rd St.) | 708-675-3970

(continued)

P.F. Chang's China Bistro

Lombard | 2361 Fountain Square Dr. (bet. Butterfield & Meyers Rds.) | 630-652-9977
www.pfchangs.com

The "assortment of Americanized Chinese food" "may not be authentic, but boy is it good" say fans of this "consistent chain" where the atmosphere is "inviting", the environs "comfortable" and the service "faster than high speed rail"; critics sneer it's "overpriced and oversalted", but even skeptics are "surprised" it's "actually pretty good."

Philly G's *Italian*   21 | 23 | 23 | $37

Vernon Hills | 1252 Rte. 45 E. (Evergreen Dr.) | 847-634-1811 | www.phillygs.com

A "quaint" and "elegant country home setting" sets the stage for "dependably tasty" "authentic" fare at this Vernon Hills Italian run by "friendly folks" who make diners feel personally "invited to their house"; moderate tabs and a "pleasant" atmosphere further ensure it's a "family favorite."

NEW Phil's Last Stand ❶ *Burgers/Hot Dogs*   - | - | - | I

Ukrainian Village | 2258 W. Chicago Ave. (Oakley Blvd.) | 773-245-3287 | www.philslaststand.com

Blogger Phil Ashbach is behind this Ukrainian Village upgrade on the standard dog house where the likes of char dogs and 'Fatso' burgers, fried shrimp, salami and mac 'n' cheese are served in a spiffier-than-usual setting with counter service, barstools and industrial lighting; P.S. late-night eats are offered until 4 AM Thursday–Saturday.

Phil Stefani's 437 Rush Ⓩ *Italian/Steak*   23 | 22 | 24 | $53

River North | 437 N. Rush St. (Hubbard St.) | 312-222-0101 | www.stefanirestaurants.com

A "can-do attitude" and "friendly" vibe pervade this "elegant" Italian steakhouse in River North where the staff treats diners like "old friends" while ferrying "homespun" dishes and "generous cuts of well-prepared meat"; black-and-white photos of the city decorate the "quintessential Chicago" space, and if it's too costly for some, regulars say "try lunch for better prices."

Phoenix *Chinese*   24 | 12 | 15 | $27

Chinatown | 2131 S. Archer Ave., 2nd fl. (Wentworth Ave.) | 312-328-0848 | www.chinatownphoenix.com

"Yum, yum dim sum" chant diners at this "cheap" Chinatown "standby", a "popular" place to "stuff yourself" on "numerous" "authentic" offerings from the carts plus other "top-notch" Chinese dishes; sure, the "decor is pretty worn" and service can be "spotty", but loyalists insist it still "always works" for a "high-quality meal."

Pho 777 Ⓜ *Vietnamese*   23 | 10 | 18 | $17

Uptown | 1065 W. Argyle St. (bet. Kenmore & Winthrop Aves.) | 773-561-9909

Set out on a "culinary adventure" at this BYO "hole-in-the-wall" Uptown "where your dollar goes amazingly far" with the "vast"

Vietnamese menu of "flavorful" phos and other "authentic" basics; if the decor doesn't quite match, fans focus instead on the "awesomely bad" "Asian pop music" and "friendly" staff.

Phò Xe Tång *Vietnamese*　　∇ 26 | 9 | 16 | $14

Uptown | 4953-55 N. Broadway (Argyle St.) | 773-878-2253 | www.tank-noodle.com

"The secret is out" about this "authentic" Uptown BYO delivering some of "the most flavorful pho around (which is saying a lot)" plus other "delicious" Vietnamese dishes, all at bargain prices; service is "fast, considering how busy they are" ("even at 3 in the afternoon"), and despite bare-bones surrounds, slurpers insist it "never fails to please"; P.S. closed Wednesdays.

☑ Piccolo Sogno *Italian*　　26 | 24 | 23 | $54

Near West | 464 N. Halsted St. (Grand Ave.) | 312-421-0077 | www.piccolosognorestaurant.com

Tony Priolo's "divine", "flavorful" fare is "impeccably prepared with fresh ingredients" and paired with a "very deep wine list" at this "authentic" Near West Italian; "elegant surroundings" include a "serene" garden featuring "twinkling lights and flowing vines", service is "lovely no matter how busy" and prices are "reasonable" given the "quality" – no wonder devotees dub it a "dream come true"; P.S. its River North sequel, Piccolo Sogno Due, is set to open at press time.

Piece *Pizza*　　25 | 19 | 19 | $22

Wicker Park | 1927 W. North Ave. (Damen Ave.) | 773-772-4422 | www.piecechicago.com

"Don't let the appearance fool you" say fans of this Wicker Park pizzeria, because though the "sports bar" decor may "say pub grub", the "mouthwatering" thin-crust pizza is "high quality" with "infinitely customizable toppings" that "make it possible to get anything you might be craving"; the "crazy vast array of different beers" (including "excellent" ones brewed on-site) also "impresses" and service is "friendly", so though "it's a little loud", it's "worth braving the often lengthy wait"; P.S. there are "live bands and karaoke some nights – you decide if that's a benefit or liability."

Pierrot Gourmet *French*　　24 | 22 | 22 | $27

River North | Peninsula Chicago | 108 E. Superior St. (bet. Michigan Ave. & Rush St.) | 312-573-6749 | www.peninsula.com

Francophiles get "whisked away to France" courtesy of "authentic" cooking, a "well-chosen" wine list and "warm farmhouse decor" at this "lovely Parisian bistro" inside River North's Peninsula Hotel; despite moderate tabs detractors deem it "overpriced" for what's on offer, but most still salute the "charmingly delightful" vibe that's further enhanced by seamless service.

The Piggery *American/BBQ*　　∇ 19 | 13 | 18 | $24

Lakeview | 1625 W. Irving Park Rd. (Marshfield Ave.) | 773-281-7447 | www.thepiggerychicago.com

"If you like pork", this casual Lakeview "barbecue joint" "is the place" say 'cue cravers who tout the "expansive" American menu

	FOOD	DECOR	SERVICE	COST

with its pig-centric spins on dishes from chili to pot roast; "lots of TVs" and a "nice beer selection" contribute to the "sports bar" vibe (it's "no place to bring a first date"), and if a few find it "average", solid service and wallet-friendly tabs make up for it; P.S. complimentary shuttles are offered to Bulls and Blackhawks games.

Pine Yard *Chinese*

| 17 | 13 | 14 | $24 |

Evanston | 1033 Davis St. (Oak St.) | 847-475-4940 | www.pineyardrestaurant.com

"When you want some good old Chinese" this sprawling Evanston longtimer is a "dependable" choice, offering Mandarin-Sichuan specialties via service so "fast" plates arrive "before you've had one sip of drink"; decor is "cold" and some say it's "gone downhill", but "fair" prices help keep it a "multidecade favorite for takeout."

Pinstripes *American/Italian*

| 17 | 18 | 18 | $29 |

Northbrook | 1150 Willow Rd. (Founders Dr.) | 847-480-2323
Barrington | 100 W. Higgins Rd. (Rte. 59) | 847-844-9300
www.pinstripes.com

A "fun place for kids and adults alike" these "sporty", "upscale" bocce court/bowling alleys in Northbrook and Barrington score a "definite strike", delivering "reliably tasty" American-Italian pub fare (including an "amazing" Sunday buffet brunch) in "friendly" environs elevated by "wonderful" outdoor patios; "reasonable" tabs help silence those who deem it just "ok" with "hit-or-miss" service.

Pita Inn *Mediterranean/Mideastern*

| 24 | 10 | 17 | $12 |

Glenview | 9854 N. Milwaukee Ave. (bet. Central & Golf Rds.) | 847-759-9990
Skokie | 3910 Dempster St. (Crawford St.) | 847-677-0211
Wheeling | 122 S. Elmhurst Rd. (Jenkins Ct.) | 847-808-7733
www.pita-inn.com

Diners willing to brave the "long lines" at these "bare-bones" North Suburban "madhouses" are rewarded with "huge portions" of "consistently delish" Med–Middle Eastern eats including "wonderfully smoky" baba ghanoush, "mouthwatering" shawarma and "some of the best falafel around"; with "extremely fast" service and "cheap" tabs to "fit everyone's budget", a "strong following" keeps them "deservedly packed."

Pizano's Pizza & Pasta *Italian/Pizza*

| 21 | 16 | 18 | $23 |

Loop | 61 E. Madison St. (Michigan Ave.) | 312-236-1777 ◐
NEW River North | 800 N. Dearborn St. (Chicago Ave.) | 855-749-2667 ◐
Gold Coast | 864 N. State St. (Chicago Ave.) | 312-751-1766 ◐
Glenview | 1808 N. Waukegan Rd. (Chestnut Ave.) | 847-486-1777
www.pizanoschicago.com

"Stuff yourself silly" at these "credible joints" where enthusiasts taste its "Malnati heritage" in the "buttery, flaky" deep-dish pies offered alongside "tasty thin-crust (gasp!)" 'zas, plus "generous servings of homemade pasta" and other Italian standards; a few finger-waggers fuss "it doesn't stand out from the rest" and warn of "tables too close together", but most cheer "friendly" service, affordable tabs and say with one visit "you'll immediately understand why Chicago is known for its pizza"; P.S. River North is carryout only.

Pizza D.O.C. *Italian/Pizza*   24 | 18 | 20 | $28

Lincoln Square | 2251 W. Lawrence Ave. (bet. Bell & Oakley Aves.) | 773-784-8777 | www.mypizzadoc.com

"They're serious about their pies" at this affordable Lincoln Square Italian that disciples declare "pope-worthy" thanks to a "wide selection" of wood-fired thin-crust pizzas that will "transport you right to Napoli"; warm staffers help create a "family-friendly" vibe, and an all-you-can-eat Sunday brunch adds more kid appeal.

Pizzeria Uno ● *Pizza*   23 | 15 | 18 | $25

River North | 29 E. Ohio St. (Wabash Ave.) | 312-321-1000

Pizzeria Due ● *Pizza*

River North | 619 N. Wabash Ave. (bet. Ohio & Ontario Sts.) | 312-943-2400
www.unos.com

"Forsake all other Unos" order pie purists who declare these "world famous" River North "originals" "about nine miles ahead of the chains around the country" thanks to "classic deep-dish" pizzas "laden with cheese and tomatoes" and balanced by "crispy", "pastry-like "crusts; sure, they're "not much for decor", but "out-of-town guests" appreciate the "old-time feel", and despite "long waits" (Due is "less crowded"), most agree "you have to go at least once."

P.J. Clarke's *American*   18 | 15 | 18 | $27

Streeterville | Embassy Suites Hotel | 302 E. Illinois St. (Columbus Dr.) | 312-670-7500

Gold Coast | 1204 N. State Pkwy. (Division St.) | 312-664-1650
www.pjclarkeschicago.com

Sports "saloons" "known for their burgers" and other "reasonably priced" "comfort food", these Gold Coast and Streeterville Americans are also "good for people-watching" and "lively atmospheres"; critics say "little stands out" and the environs could use a "face-lift", but "reliable" service and "consistent quality" still make them"standbys."

Pockets *Sandwiches*   18 | 8 | 14 | $10

Loop | 309 W. Lake St. (Franklin St.) | 312-641-0949 🛂
Loop | 329 S. Franklin St. (Jackson Blvd.) | 312-922-9255 🛂
Loop | 555 S. Dearborn St. (W. Harrison St.) | 312-554-8155
Streeterville | 205 E. Ohio St. (St. Clair St.) | 312-923-9898
Lakeview | 3001 N. Lincoln Ave. (Southport Ave.) | 773-528-2167
Northwest Side | 3927 W. Belmont Ave. (Milwaukee Ave.) | 773-481-3535
Northwest Side | 4301 N. Lincoln Ave. (Cullom Ave.) | 773-755-4111
Hyde Park | 1307 E. 53rd St. (S. Kimbark Ave.) | 773-667-1313
West Loop | 1009 W. Madison St. (S. Morgan St.) | 312-738-0080
Aurora | 1330 N. Orchard Rd. (Indian Trl.) | 630-907-0011
www.pocketsonline.com
Additional locations throughout the Chicago area

When you want to "feel healthy while consuming a sandwich as big as your head", these quick serves favored for "saladlike" pitas and "delicious" calzones fit the "affordable" bill; though with small, no-frills surroundings most opt for "great carryout."

[NEW] The Point ●☒Ⓜ *American*

| - | - | - | I |

West Loop | 401 N. Milwaukee Ave. (Kinzie St.) | 312-666-1600 | www.pointbarchicago.com

Upgraded New American bar food (short rib nachos, polenta cakes, truffle, Swedish meatball hoagies) pairs with craft brews, new and vintage-inspired cocktails and Julius Meinl coffee at this casual West Loop corner spot named for its noteworthy angled building; its funky environs are outfitted with an elaborate parquet floor, leather banquettes, modern art and sexy photomurals.

Pompei Pizza *Italian*

| 19 | 16 | 17 | $15 |

Streeterville | 212 E. Ohio St. (bet. Fairbanks Ct. & St. Clair St.) | 312-482-9900

Lakeview | 2955 N. Sheffield Ave. (bet. Oakdale & Wellington Aves.) | 773-325-1900

Little Italy/University Village | 1531 W. Taylor St. (bet. Ashland Ave. & Laflin St.) | 312-421-5179

Oakbrook Terrace | 17 W. 744 22nd St. (bet. Butterfield Rd. & Summit Ave.) | 630-620-0600

www.pompeipizza.com

A "smorgasbord" of "filling" Italian eats awaits diners at this "cafeteria-style" quartet where "consistent" pastas, specialty strudel pizzas and a "wide selection of salads" make it "good for a quick bite"; there may be "nothing in the way of atmosphere" and staffers can be occasionally "ornery", but "poor students" say it's still "excellent for the money" and an all around "easy", "reliable" choice.

Pork Shoppe Ⓜ *BBQ*

▽ | 19 | 12 | 18 | $16 |

Avondale | 2755 W. Belmont Ave. (California Ave.) | 773-961-7654 | www.porkshoppechicago.com

'Cue-lovers confess they'd "knock down old ladies and children" for the "savory", "decadent" "pork belly pastrami" (a "can't-miss item") at this counter-service Avondale BBQ joint set in a minimalist storefront featuring butcher-block communal tables and farm tools; "warm" (if "spotty") service and affordable tabs are further draws.

Portillo's Hot Dogs *Hot Dogs*

| 23 | 18 | 20 | $12 |

Near North | 100 W. Ontario St. (N. Lasalle St.) | 312-587-8910

Addison | 100 W. Lake St. (Addison Rd.) | 630-628-0358

Arlington Heights | 806 W. Dundee Rd. (bet. Kennicott & Ridge Aves.) | 847-870-0870

Crystal Lake | 855 Cog Circle (Chalet Dr.) | 815-788-0900

Schaumburg | 611 E. Golf Rd. (bet. Basswood St. & Plum Grove Rd.) | 847-884-9020

Batavia | 531 N. Randall Rd. (bet. South Dr. & Mill St.) | 630-482-9600

Forest Park | 7740 W. Roosevelt Rd. (Des Plaines Ave.) | 708-383-7557 ●

Naperville | 1992 W. Jefferson St. (Rte. 59) | 630-420-7156 ☒Ⓜ

www.portillos.com

"How can you not love" this chain "legend" ask admirers drooling over the "classic Chicago-style hot dogs", Italian beef so "awesome" it "fixes things in the universe" and "infamous", "knock-your-socks-off" chocolate cake; praise also goes out to the "snappy service" and "cheap" tabs, making it both a de rigueur "outing for all guests to the area" and a "perennial" local "favorite."

Potbelly Sandwich Shop *Sandwiches* | 18 | 13 | 17 | $11 |

Loop | One Illinois Ctr. | 111 E. Wacker Dr. (Michigan Ave.) | 312-861-0013 🖼

Loop | Insurance Exchange | 175 W. Jackson Blvd. (bet. Financial Pl. & Wells St.) | 312-588-1150 🖼

Loop | 190 N. State St. (Lake St.) | 312-683-1234 🖼

Loop | 303 W. Madison St. (Franklin St.) | 312-346-1234 🖼

Loop | 55 W. Monroe St. (bet. Clark & Dearborn Sts.) | 312-577-0070 🖼

River North | 508 N. Clark St. (bet. Grand Ave. & Illinois St.) | 312-644-9131

River North | Shops at North Bridge | 520 N. Michigan Ave., 4th fl. (Grand Ave.) | 312-644-1008

Lakeview | 3424 N. Southport Ave. (bet. Newport Ave. & Roscoe St.) | 773-289-1807

Lincoln Park | 1422 W. Webster Ave. (Clybourn Ave.) | 773-755-1234

Lincoln Park | 2264 N. Lincoln Ave. (bet. Belden & Webster Aves.) | 773-528-1405

www.potbelly.com

Additional locations throughout the Chicago area

"So many sandwiches, so little time" muse champions of the "best damn" sammies "toasted fresh" at this "cheap", "reliable" chain where "tasty" salads, "don't-miss" milkshakes and "fresh baked cookies" also contribute to its "cult" following; frequent "live lunch-time music" and "friendly" staffers pep up the otherwise bare-bones surroundings, and though a few call the "cattle chute" experience "tedious", at least the "lines always move quickly."

Prairie Grass Cafe *American* | 22 | 19 | 20 | $42 |

Northbrook | 601 Skokie Blvd. (bet. Dundee & Henrici Dr.) | 847-205-4433 | www.prairiegrasscafe.com

"Home cooking with flair and panache" comes courtesy of chef-owners Sarah Stegner and George Bumbaris at this "pleasant" Northbrook New American where "rethought" "comfort food" "draws on local ingredients"; the "comfortable" "mess hall"–like space gets "crowded" and "noisy at prime times", but guests generally find "the service and kitchen keep up", delivering a "good value for the quality."

Prasino *American* | 23 | 22 | 20 | $33 |

NEW **Wicker Park** | 1846 W. Division St. (Marion Ct.) | 312-878-1212

La Grange | 93 S. La Grange Rd. (Cossitt Ave.) | 708-469-7058

www.prasino.com

"Bold flavors" define the "extensive", "innovative" American menu at this midpriced duo in Wicker Park and suburban La Grange with a "green theme" (Prasino is Greek for green) that extends from the "locally sourced" ingredients and organic wines to the "modern", eco-friendly surroundings featuring reclaimed materials; "friendly, polite" servers add to the "laid-back" vibe, and fans say it's an especially "fabulous" choice for breakfast.

	FOOD	DECOR	SERVICE	COST

NEW Premise M *American*
(fka In Fine Spirits)

| - | - | - | M |

Andersonville | 5420 N. Clark St. (bet. Balmoral & Rascher Aves.) |
773-334-9463 | www.premisechicago.com

Former Andersonville wine bar In Fine Spirits has been reconcepted into this New American featuring inventive, moderately priced seasonal plates from a Graham Elliot vet, along with wine flights and craft cocktails; there's a main-floor dining room with a tin ceiling and a bar, plus a posh, soothing second-floor salon with a fireplace.

Pret A Manger 🖂 *Sandwiches*

| 19 | 12 | 18 | $12 |

Loop | 100 N. LaSalle St. (bet. Randolph & Washington Sts.) |
312-660-9494
Loop | 211 W. Adams St. (Wells St.) | 312-546-8270
www.pret.com

"The Brits invade Chicago" with these "serviceable" "takeaways" where "darn tasty, fresh" sandwiches including "many veggie selections" plus other "healthy choices" like soups and salads make them "nice variations from the standard"; if a few question the "big hoopla", most appreciate "quick" service that makes for "easy eating" "when you're in a hurry."

Prosecco 🖂 *Italian*

| 24 | 24 | 24 | $59 |

River North | 710 N. Wells St. (bet. Huron & Superior Sts.) |
312-951-9500 | www.prosecco.us.com

A "complimentary taste of Prosecco" provides a fitting welcome to this "beautiful" and "romantic" River North Italian, a little "piece of Venice" boasting "authentic", "well-prepared" dishes that "aren't outrageously priced"; "warm", "professional" staffers offer "spot-on" wine recommendations, and though "busy" nights can be "noisy" with "tight seating", devotees revel in the "energetic vibe."

Province 🖂 *American*

| 25 | 24 | 25 | $51 |

West Loop | 161 N. Jefferson St. (bet. Lake & Randolph Sts.) |
312-669-9900 | www.provincerestaurant.com

Chef-owner Randy Zweiban "uses Latin and Asian techniques" to "enhance locally sourced ingredients" with "bold and spicy flavors" at this somewhat pricey West Loop New American turning out "creative", "original" fare in "varying sizes of plates, from small to large"; the LEED-certified building offers an "open and airy yet intimate" setting and service is "friendly", so it works for both "a casual dinner or a special occasion."

Z The Publican *American*

| 26 | 23 | 23 | $49 |

West Loop | 837 W. Fulton Mkt. (Green St.) | 312-733-9555 |
www.thepublicanrestaurant.com

A "slam dunk" gush groupies of Paul Kahan's West Loop New American, a "temple to the pig" with its pork-centered, "finger-lican' good" eats plus a "wonderful selection" of "quality" oysters, one of the "best, smartest" beer lists in the city – and plenty of "deliciously prepared" veggies too; communal tables lend a "hip cafeteria" feel, service is "helpful" and while "prices aren't crazy", you can

	FOOD	DECOR	SERVICE	COST

"spend a lot to get filled up", but as long as "you don't mind loud", you'll still "look forward to eating here again."

NEW Publican Quality Meats *American/Sandwiches*

| - | - | - | I |

West Loop | 825 W. Fulton Market (Green St.) | 312-445-8977 | www.publicanqualitymeats.com

A white-tiled, blue-tinged butcher, market and American cafe, Paul Kahan's West Loop haunt hawks the likes of house-cured charcuterie and fresh-baked bread, as well as ingredient-driven sandwiches and signature-blend coffee; there's also a display kitchen for hosting dinners and hands-on events, while a walk-in meat locker serves as inspiration.

Public House ❶ *American*

| 19 | 19 | 17 | $29 |

River North | 400 N. State St. (Kinzie St.) | 312-265-1240 | www.publichousechicago.com

"Check out the table taps" at this midpriced River North drinking den, a "lively" American "sports bar" with a "lounge feel" where "upscale" pub grub, "tons of beers" and "plenty of TVs" for "watching the game" provide "hangout" appeal; those averse to "packed" conditions say it's "way better on weeknights" when a late-night menu is offered until 1 AM (2 AM on weekends).

☑ Pump Room *American*

| 21 | 27 | 24 | $59 |

Gold Coast | Public Hotel | 1301 N. State Pkwy. (bet. Banks & Goethe Sts.) | 312-229-6740 | www.pumproom.com

The "gorgeous", "chic" revamp of this Public Hotel–based landmark is "classy with a capital C" say habitués of Jean-Georges Vongerichten's "celebratory" Gold Coast arrival, where "upbeat", "personable" staffers relay "creative" New American dishes in a "glitzy" "see-and-be-seen" setting; you can still "plow through the throngs" to Sinatra's table, and while a few tut it "doesn't compare" to its "revered" predecessor, the masses "welcome" it back, adding "you never know who you'll run into" at the bar.

☑ The Purple Pig ❶ *Mediterranean*

| 26 | 21 | 21 | $42 |

River North | 500 N. Michigan Ave. (Illinois St.) | 312-464-1744 | www.thepurplepigchicago.com

"Adventurous" foodies scarf "every part of the pig but the oink" at Jimmy Bannos Jr.'s midpriced River North Med where "thought-provoking", "richly flavored small plates eat large", making it a "favorite after two or three bites"; it's "very small and does not take reservations", but the "young and soon to be deaf" don't mind, as the wine list is "killer", the service "unpretentious yet attentive" and the overall "buzz justified"; P.S. don't miss "glorious outside seating by the Chicago River."

Quartino ❶ *Italian*

| 22 | 20 | 21 | $32 |

River North | 626 N. State St. (Ontario St.) | 312-698-5000 | www.quartinochicago.com

"The more people in your party to share dishes, the better" at this "hip", "always crowded" River North Italian where "authentic", "way-above-average" "big and little bites" (including "wonderful house-cured meats"), "many wine options" by the carafe and "genuinely good" service "completely outweigh" the "astounding noise"; the "rustic" bi-level environs can get "tight", but with "prices so reasonable you can go back the next night" – and many do.

NEW Quay *American*   19 | 22 | 20 | $43

Streeterville | 465 E. Illinois St. (bet. Lake Short Dr. & McClurg Ct.) | 312-981-8400 | www.quaychicago.com

Three venues in one – a "sports bar, restaurant and lounge" – this "expansive" addition to Streeterville offers an "attractive", "group"-friendly setting for "well-prepared" New American meals, or just "cocktails and apps"; the staff does a solid job too, but a few critics would like to see more "competitive" drink pricing, and argue it's "trying to do too many things at once."

Quince Ⓜ *American*   25 | 23 | 26 | $58

Evanston | Homestead Hotel | 1625 Hinman Ave. (Davis St.) | 847-570-8400 | www.quincerestaurant.net

"Serious contemporary cuisine" full of "gourmet surprises" and "impeccable" service make this "charming, romantic" New American in the "historic" Homestead Hotel one of "Evanston's finest"; despite a few who find the "aristocratic atmosphere" somewhat "stilted", most dub it a "quiet success" (though a "pricey" one).

Ras Dashen *Ethiopian*   ▽ 27 | 23 | 24 | $27

Edgewater | 5846 N. Broadway (bet. Ardmore & Rosedale Aves.) | 773-506-9601 | www.rasdashenchicago.com

"It's fun to eat with your hands" at this midpriced Edgewater Ethiopian, the "real thing" for "well-spiced", "full-of-flavor" fare and "traditional" injera bread used as a "scooper"; "consistently gracious" servers work the casual room decorated with paintings, so all in all most "leave happy."

RA Sushi *Japanese*   18 | 18 | 17 | $29

Gold Coast | 1139 N. State St. (Elm St.) | 312-274-0011
Glenview | 2601 Aviator Ln. (Patriot Blvd.) | 847-510-1100
Lombard | Shops on Butterfield | 310 Yorktown Ctr. (Highland Ave.) | 630-627-6800
www.rasushi.com

"Always buzzing" with a "mostly young crowd", this "trendy" sushi chain provides "innovative" rolls and other bites "mixing traditional and newer flavors"; despite its shortcomings on "authenticity", the "party" atmosphere and "awesome" happy-hour "deals" that encourage "imbibing sake swiftly" are incentive enough for some.

Real Urban Barbecue *BBQ*   21 | 14 | 16 | $21

Highland Park | Port Clinton Square Shopping Ctr. | 610 Central Ave. (2nd St.) | 224-770-4227 | www.realurbanbbq.com

'Cue fans go "hog wild" for the "tangy" brisket at this "cafeteria-style" Highland Park pit stop also offering "juicy" pulled pork, "savory" sides "worth standing in line for" and other BBQ standards; though a few cite "underwhelming" results and "wish for table service at these prices", it still provides "refuge for those too tired to drive into the city" for "porcine cuisine."

Z NEW Red Door *Eclectic*   - | - | - | M

Bucktown | 2118 N. Damen Ave. (Charleston St.) | 773-235-6434
Marked by a scarlet entryway, Troy Graves' clever Bucktown gastropub keeps things affordable with a group-friendly array of Eclectic small plates and globally inspired libations; wood-trimmed environs come with a large, tree-shaded patio where themed brunches will be held.

NEW Red Violet *Chinese*   - | - | - | M

River North | 121 W. Hubbard St. (LaSalle St.) | 312-828-0222 | www.redvioletchicago.com
Upscale, multiregional Chinese chow, paired with exotic cocktails, craft beers and a compact wine list, makes up the massive menu at this modern River North 200-seater; the bi-level, low-lit space offers a range of seating options (lounge and armchair groupings, bar, banquettes and dining tables), funky furnishings and cultural curios.

Reel Club *Seafood*   23 | 23 | 22 | $44

Oak Brook | Oakbrook Center Mall | 272 Oakbrook Ctr. (Rte. 83) | 630-368-9400 | www.leye.com
"Worth hunting for" in the "sprawling" Oakbrook Center mall, this "elegant" Lettuce Entertain You seafooder nets props for "fine fish", "watchful service" and a wine list that "sparkles with variety"; the "pleasant, modern" space holds a "sizable" bar, helping to accommodate the "hordes of wealthy shoppers" who make it a regular "go-to", especially for Sunday brunch.

Retro Bistro Ⓜ *French*   25 | 18 | 23 | $44

Mt. Prospect | Mount Prospect Commons | 1746 W. Golf Rd. (Busse Rd.) | 847-439-2424 | www.retrobistro.com
The "high-quality" cooking "executed with creativity and care" "defies logic" say fans acknowledging the strip-mall setting of this "reasonably priced" Mount Prospect Frenchie and advising you to "get over it"; add in "charming" service and a "homey, welcoming" atmosphere and most concede it "wins us over every time."

Revolution Brewing ☻ *American*   23 | 21 | 21 | $26

Logan Square | 2323 N. Milwaukee Ave. (bet. California & Fullerton Aves.) | 773-227-2739 | www.revbrew.com
"The beer makes your toes curl" promise patrons of this Logan Square American also vending "consistent", "inventive" bar bites "with class" including "surprisingly robust vegetarian" choices; set in a spacious restored space with tin ceilings and a fireplace, it's usually "packed", but "pleasant service in a sea of hipsters" keeps most happy.

Reza's *Mediterranean/Mideastern*   19 | 15 | 18 | $27

River North | 432 W. Ontario St. (Orleans St.) | 312-664-4500
Andersonville | 5255 N. Clark St. (Berwyn Ave.) | 773-561-1898 ☻
NEW Lincoln Park | 2423 N. Clark St. (bet. Arlington Pl. & Fullerton Ave.) | 773-244-0300

	FOOD	DECOR	SERVICE	COST

(continued)

Reza's

Oak Brook | 40 N. Tower Rd. (Butterfield Rd.) | 630-424-9900
www.rezasrestaurant.com

The saying "come hungry, leave happy applies" to this "steady" Med-
Mideastern trio (with a newer Lincoln Park sib) crow converts who insist you "can't go wrong" with "huge portions" of "reasonably good"
Persian fare (also offered in buffet form); some feel the surroundings
could use a "major refresh" and service can be inconsistent, but "if
you're looking for quantity" and "great value" it "won't disappoint."

Rhapsody *American*   21 | 23 | 20 | $47

Loop | Symphony Ctr. | 65 E. Adams St. (bet. Columbus St. &
Lake Shore Dr.) | 312-786-9911 | www.rhapsodychicago.com

A "sophisticated" space with "many windows" and "lots of light"
provides the backdrop for "solid", "well-prepared" plates at this
Loop New American adjacent to Symphony Center; surveyors split
over whether tabs are "expensive" or "reasonable for the quality",
but most applaud "efficient" pre-concert service and a patio that's a
"garden oasis" in summer.

Z Ria 🗷 **M** *American*   27 | 27 | 27 | $142

Gold Coast | Waldorf-Astoria Chicago | 11 E. Walton St. (bet. Rush &
State Sts.) | 312-880-4400 | www.riarestaurantchicago.com

"In a word, brilliant" say fans of the "impressively elegant dining" at
this Gold Coast New American in the Waldorf-Astoria where chef
Danny Grant's "flawlessly executed", "exquisitely" presented fare is
"consistently rewarding", especially when augmented by some of
"the most creative wine pairings in the universe"; the "pitch-
perfect" staffers are "down-to-earth" yet "professional" in the
"soothing", "serene" space, so though it "hurts a lot to pay", acolytes assert it "should be near the top of every Chicago foodie's list."

Z Riccardo Trattoria *Italian*   28 | 21 | 25 | $49

Lincoln Park | 2119 N. Clark St. (bet. Dickens & Webster Aves.) |
773-549-0038 | www.riccardotrattoria.com

"Best Italian in the city" honors go to this "small" and "casual" yet
"urbane" Lincoln Park "gem", house of "homemade everything" offered in "breathtaking" "upscaled" "traditional dishes" that are further enhanced by a "well-varied wine list"; with "no airs", "friendly,
attentive service" and "prices well below its competitors", it's un-
surprisingly "tough to get a table."

Ricobene's ● *Italian*   24 | 12 | 19 | $12

Bridgeport | 252 W. 26th St. (Wells St.) | 312-225-5555
Far South Side | 5160 S. Pulaski Rd. (bet. 51st St. & 52nd Pl.) |
773-284-2400
www.ricobenesfamoussteaks.com

The breaded steak sandwich is "to die for", the "famous" french
fries are "delicious" and the pizza is "worth the wait" declare diners
who advocate a trip to this Italian-leaning "staple" on the Far South
Side and in Bridgeport "when you want to cheat on your diet"; no-

	FOOD	DECOR	SERVICE	COST

frills surroundings may not standout, but solid service and cheap tabs make up for it.

NEW Ripasso Ⓜ *Italian*   — | — | — | E

Bucktown | 1619 N. Damen Ave. (bet. Cortland & Homer Sts.) | 773-342-8799 | www.ripassochicago.com

Chef-owner Theo Gilbert (of defunct Terragusto) helms this somewhat costly Bucktown Italian where "silky ribbons" of handmade pasta "dressed in Sunday's finest" team with a Boot-centric wine list; cozy digs feature a tin ceiling, wood booths and butcher-block communal tables good for large groups.

Riva *Seafood*   20 | 23 | 20 | $48

Streeterville | Navy Pier | 700 E. Grand Ave. (Lake Shore Dr.) | 312-644-7482 | www.rivanavypier.com

"Get a window seat" for "spectacular views of Lake Michigan and the Downtown skyline" at this "classy" seafooder on Streeterville's Navy Pier, where the "good to very good" fin fare satisfies for "long business lunches" and dining "before or after" the Shakespeare Theater; doubters warn you'll rub elbows with "tourists" and may encounter "rushed" service, but the "relaxing" vista helps compensate.

R.J. Grunts *American*   20 | 18 | 21 | $23

Lincoln Park | 2056 N. Lincoln Park W. (bet. Armitage & Dickens Aves.) | 773-929-5363 | www.rjgruntschicago.com

"Where it all began" for the Lettuce Entertain You "empire", this "moderately priced" Lincoln Park "institution" tended by "friendly" staffers is known for "huge" portions of American "comfort food", an "endless" salad bar (it "looks like a farmer's market") and "one of the best" weekend brunch buffets; "photos of former waitresses paper the walls" of the "cramped" space, and a "cool, nostalgic" "hippie vibe" that "hasn't changed" since the '70s helps ensure it "stays popular."

RL *American*   24 | 27 | 24 | $54

Gold Coast | 115 E. Chicago Ave. (Michigan Ave.) | 312-475-1100 | www.rlrestaurant.com

It's like "dining at the home of a wealthy Ivy League friend" note noshers of this "classy" Gold Coast American, a "sophisticated" Ralph Lauren offshoot where "surprisingly good", "runway-ready" dishes, "impeccable" service and "clubby" leather-accented surroundings make guests "feel special"; the "tucked-and-pulled" clientele doesn't raise eyebrows at tabs a few find "overpriced", so it's generally "crowded", especially during the "executive-filled" weekday lunch.

Robinson's No. 1 Ribs *BBQ*   20 | 10 | 14 | $22

Loop | Union Station | 225 S. Canal St. (bet. Adams St. & Jackson Blvd.) | 312-258-8477 | www.rib1.com

Lincoln Park | 655 W. Armitage Ave. (Orchard St.) | 312-337-1399 | www.ribs1.com Ⓜ

Oak Park | 940 W. Madison St. (Clinton St.) | 708-383-8452 | www.rib1.com

"Regulars" at these cost-conscious BBQ BYOs are "hooked" on ribs slathered with "out-of-this-world" sauce and other "satisfying" plates;

critics who say it's "coasting" have a bone to pick with sometimes "subpar" service and "sad" decor, adding that it's better for "carryout."

Rock Bottom Brewery *American* | 19 | 18 | 19 | $23 |

Near North | 1 W. Grand Ave. (State St.) | 312-755-9339
Orland Park | 16156 S. La Grange Rd. (163rd St.) | 708-226-0021
Lombard | 94 Yorktown Ctr. (Highland Ave.) | 630-424-1550
Warrenville | 28256 Diehl Rd. (Winfield Rd.) | 630-836-1380
www.rockbottom.com

The house's "ever-changing" microbrews attract hopsheads to this "better-than-average" brewpub chain, a "safe choice" thanks to "good portions" of American "classics", affordable tabs and "friendly" service; even those who find the grub merely "ordinary" concede it's solid for "after-work happy hours."

Rockit Bar & Grill ❷ *American* | 19 | 17 | 17 | $28 |

River North | 22 W. Hubbard St. (bet. Dearborn & State Sts.) | 312-645-6000 | www.rockitbarandgrill.com

Rockit Burger Bar ❷Ⓜ *Burgers*

Wrigleyville | 3700 N. Clark St. (Waveland Ave.) | 773-645-4400 | www.rockitburgerbar.com/

"Bring your entourage" for a "blast" at this "affordable" River North American and its revamped, burger-focused Wrigleyville sib scoring with "high-quality" "pub fare" and "efficient" service in "unpretentious" "sports bar" environs; if they're "too much of a scene" for some, others "dig the Bloody Mary bar" offered at the "above-par" weekend brunch and note the Wrigleyville outpost is "perfect" pre or post-Cubs games.

Roditys ❷ *Greek* | 22 | 18 | 22 | $29 |

Greektown | 222 S. Halsted St. (bet. Adams St. & Jackson Blvd.) | 312-454-0800 | www.roditys.com

"Get your Greek fix" at this circa-1973 Greektowner that transports diners to the isles ("close your eyes and go to Greece") with the "authentic, just plain good" Hellenic fare; accommodating service, "moderate prices" and a "soothing" yet group-friendly atmosphere complete the picture.

NEW Roka Akor *Japanese/Steak* | 24 | 26 | 22 | $64 |

River North | 111 W. Illinois St. (Clark St.) | 312-477-7652 | www.rokaakor.com

"From raw to seared, everything is on point" say boosters of this River North steakhouse, a Scottsdale transplant showcasing "creative, beautifully presented" Japanese fare like sushi and items from the robata grill in "hip, modern" digs tended by "unintrusive" staffers; though faultfinders cite an "overactive bar scene" and "exorbitant" prices, those in search of a "big night out" or "ultimate date" place keep it "busy" and "bustling."

Ron of Japan *Japanese/Steak* | 24 | 20 | 24 | $44 |

Near North | 230 E. Ontario St. (bet. Fairbanks Ct. & St. Clair St.) | 312-644-6500

(continued)

(continued)

Ron of Japan

Northbrook | 633 Skokie Blvd. (Dundee Rd. & Henrici Dr.) | 847-564-5900
www.ron-of-japan.com

For "dinner and a show" patrons "highly recommend" these moderate Japanese steakhouse twins in Near North and Northbrook where "showboat servers" "do tricks" while cooking the "quality" teppanyaki-focused fare "right in front of you"; the "spectacle" makes it a "fun experience for the kids", just be prepared to sit at communal tables.

NEW Roots Handmade Pizza ● *American/Pizza*

▽ 23 | 20 | 21 | $20

West Town | 1924 W. Chicago Ave. (Winchester Ave.) | 773-645-4949 | www.rootspizza.com

Piezanis "welcome" this West Town pizzeria, cheering its "unique" scissor-cut pies that are "done to perfection" with Quad Cities–style malted crust and a "wonderful alternative to deep-dish"; affordable American fare like salads and sausages extends the menu, and while a "massive" all-Midwestern beer list is alone "worth the visit", the "large" space and "comfortable booths" also make it appealing for "watching the game or just hanging out."

Rootstock Wine & Beer Bar ● *American*

24 | 20 | 20 | $32

Humboldt Park | 954 N. California Ave. (Augusta Blvd.) | 773-292-1616 | www.rootstockbar.com

Admirers insist you'll "fall in love" with this approachable Humboldt Park boîte for its charcuterie, "beautiful" cheese plates and other "light, tasty" New American bites complemented by "diverse" wines by the glass and an "excellent" beer selection; it also promises commendable service and a "casual" yet "cool living-room" vibe, so though a few voice concerns about the "sketchy" neighborhood, most agree "you won't be disappointed."

Rosal's Italian Kitchen 🅱 *Italian*

▽ 29 | 18 | 26 | $38

Little Italy/University Village | 1154 W. Taylor St. (Racine Ave.) | 312-243-2357 | www.rosals.com

If you're "not going to Rome", you should come "without delay" to this "authentic" Little Italy "enticer" advise admirers heaping praise on the "tremendous" Sicilian cooking full of "big flavors" and "friendly" staffers who "work hard"; surroundings are "small" and "sparse", but "budget-friendly" tabs mean "you get a lot for your money", so no one minds much.

Rose Angelis 🅜 *Italian*

26 | 20 | 23 | $31

Lincoln Park | 1314 W. Wrightwood Ave. (bet. Racine & Southport Aves.) | 773-296-0081 | www.roseangelis.com

"Enormous" portions of "delicious" "homemade" Italian fare offered at "beyond reasonable" tabs make this Lincoln Park long-timer a "favorite" while the "romantic", "cozy house" setting ensures it a "date destination"; add in "friendly" service and regulars say it "never disappoints."

Rosebud Italian Specialties & Pizzeria *Italian*

22 | 18 | 21 | $40

Naperville | 22 E. Chicago Ave. (bet. State St. & Wabash Ave.) | 630-548-9800

Rosebud Old World Italian *Italian*

Schaumburg | 1370 Bank Dr. (Meacham Rd.) | 847-240-1414

Rosebud on Rush *Italian*

Streeterville | 720 N. Rush St. (Superior St.) | 312-266-6444

Rosebud Theater District 🖪 *Italian*

Loop | 3 First National Plaza | 70 W. Madison St. (bet. Clark & Dearborn Sts.) | 312-332-9500

Rosebud Trattoria *Italian*

River North | 445 N. Dearborn St. (Illinois St.) | 312-832-7700

The Rosebud *Italian*

Little Italy/University Village | 1500 W. Taylor St. (Laflin St.) | 312-942-1117

www.rosebudrestaurants.com

"Popular with the tourists" but still "too good for locals to pass up", this "little-changed" Taylor Street "landmark" and its empire of metro area eateries specializes in "huge portions" of "well-executed", "traditional" Italian and "thoughtful wine lists" presented by a "smart" crew; even if they're slightly "expensive", "loud" and "crowded to a fault", their "consistent" quality still wins kudos.

Rosebud Prime *Steak*

24 | 21 | 23 | $57

Loop | 1 S. Dearborn St. (Madison St.) | 312-384-1900

Rosebud Steakhouse *Steak*

Streeterville | 192 E. Walton St. (Mies van der Rohe Way) | 312-397-1000

www.rosebudrestaurants.com

"In a city with great steaks", this Loop and Streeterville duo may be "overshadowed by glitzier" chophouses, but it still "really produces" with a "wide selection" of "top-quality" cuts set down by "dependable" "old-school" staffers; an "elegant" setting and "pleasant" atmosphere lend "business-hangout" appeal, while softening expectedly "pricey" tabs.

Rosewood Restaurant & Banquets Steakhouse *Steak*

∇ 26 | 19 | 25 | $52

Rosemont | 9421 W. Higgins Rd. (bet. N. River Rd. & Willow Creek Dr.) | 847-696-9494 | www.rosewoodrestaurant.com

It may "look like the typical banquet facility", but fans say the "prime meats" and "awesome sauces" "far exceed the first impression" at this "old-school" Rosemont chophouse; highly rated staffers and a "retro supper club" feel attract "business-lunchers", and if some find it a "bit pricey for the locale", jet-setters counter there's "no better dining near O'Hare."

Roti Mediterranean Grill *Mediterranean*

22 | 14 | 18 | $12

Loop | 310 W. Adams St. (bet. Franklin St. & Lower Wacker Dr.) | 312-236-3500 | www.roti.com 🖪

(continued)

(continued)

Roti Mediterranean Grill

Loop | 33 N. Dearborn St. (bet. Calhoun Pl. & Washington St.) | 312-263-9000 | www.roti.com Ⓢ

River West | 10 S. Riverside Plaza (bet. Madison & Monroe Sts.) | 312-775-7000 | www.rotiusa.com

Northbrook | 984 Willow Rd. (Three Lakes Dr.) | 847-418-2400 | www.roti.com

Vernon Hills | 1240 Rte. 45 E. (bet. Ranney Ave. & Stone Fence Rd.) | 847-883-8800 | www.rotiusa.com

"Build-your-own fast food" at this "Mediterranean answer to Chipotle", a "cheap" chain where "everything tastes fresh" and "has tons of flavor"; despite the "many ways to customize", a scattering squawks there's too much "sameness" to the preparations, but more point to "efficient" service and say it's "great for takeout and complete meals on the go."

Roy's *Hawaiian*

25 | 23 | 24 | $52

River North | 720 N. State St. (Superior St.) | 312-787-7599 | www.roysrestaurant.com

It seems the "fish have leapt out of the ocean and onto the grill" at this River North rendition of the "upscale" "Hawaiian fusion" chain where dishes are "innovative but not fufu", "presentations are creative" and the "drinks are delectable"; further, the "relaxed" ambiance is "great for conversation" and service is "attentive" so most are left with "no complaints", except for the "pricey but oh-so-worth-it" tabs.

NEW RPM Italian ◑ *Italian*

- | - | - | M

River North | 52 W. Illinois St. (Dearborn St.) | 312-222-1888 | www.rpmitalian.com

TV personalities Giuliana and Bill Rancic are behind this Melman-backed River North Italian where housemade pasta, plus steaks and seafood, lure scene-sated daters and groups, while cicchetti, antipasti and tipples issued from two bars give night owls incentives to linger; the sprawling, black-and-white-hued digs feature leather accents and sweeping, round banquettes.

Ruby of Siam *Thai*

22 | 14 | 19 | $21

Loop | 170 W. Washington St. (bet. LaSalle & Wells Sts.) | 312-609-0000 | www.rubyofsiam.com

Skokie | Skokie Fashion Sq. | 9420 Skokie Blvd. (Gross Point Rd.) | 847-675-7008 | www.rubyofsiamskokie.com

Siam Splendour *Thai*

Evanston | 1125 Emerson St. (Ridge Ave.) | 847-492-1008 | www.siamsplendour.com

An "extensive" menu of "flavorful, satisfying" Thai "standards", including "plenty of vegetarian options", makes this "accommodating" city and suburban trio (Evanston is separately owned) a regular "go-to" for dine-in or carryout; "friendly" service helps compensate for "basic" "nondescript" digs, especially since the "price is right" (and even more "reasonable" at the BYO Loop and Skokie outposts).

	FOOD	DECOR	SERVICE	COST

Russell's Barbecue *BBQ*
19 | 11 | 15 | $13

Elmwood Park | 1621 N. Thatcher Ave. (North Ave.) | 708-453-7065 | www.russellsbarbecue.com

A "family favorite" since 1930, this "old-fashioned" Elmwood Park "tradition" "keeps people coming back" with its beef sandwiches and other "reasonably priced" BBQ specialties; service can be "spotty" and decor "isn't special", but it "brings back memories of childhood", so habitués still "drop in."

Russian Tea Time *Russian*
22 | 21 | 22 | $40

Loop | 77 E. Adams St. (bet. Michigan & Wabash Aves.) | 312-360-0000 | www.russianteatime.com

Convenient to the Art Institute and CSO, this "comfy", "old-world" Loop Russian proffers "boldly flavored" "dacha comfort food" and other "well-prepared" specialties via servers with "discretion and elan worthy of any haute Muscovite"; "exquisite teas" and "house-infused vodkas" round out the meal, though "prices on the high side" are part of the package.

NEW Rustic House Ⓜ *American*
▽ 22 | 22 | 19 | $47

Lincoln Park | 1967 N. Halsted St. (bet. Armitage Ave. & Willow St.) | 312-929-3227 | www.rustichousechicago.com

You may "dream about the rotisserie chicken" and other solid responsibly sourced meats at this "inviting" Lincoln Park American (sister to Gemini Bistro), where farm-inspired decor and an "above-par" wine list keep it "warm and comfortable while still being upscale"; a few feel the service could use some work, but many agree it's "fantastic without being overly fussy."

Ruth's Chris Steak House *Steak*
26 | 22 | 24 | $66

River North | 431 N. Dearborn St. (Hubbard St.) | 312-321-2725
Northbrook | Renaissance North Shore Hotel | 933 Skokie Blvd. (Sunset Ridge Rd.) | 847-498-6889
South Barrington | Arboretum Mall | 100 W. Higgins Rd. (Bartlett Rd.) | 847-551-3730
www.ruthschris.com

"Reliably excellent", these "civilized" triplets "honor" their "venerable" steakhouse franchise with "tender, flavorful" chops, "delicious" sides "large" enough to share and service that "could not be better"; so maybe it's "a bit corporate" and lacking "the character" of a local spot, but devotees insist the overall "consistent quality" still makes it "splurge"-worthy.

Ⓩ Ruxbin Ⓜ *Eclectic*
28 | 23 | 24 | $45

Noble Square | 851 N. Ashland Ave. (Pearson St.) | 312-624-8509 | www.ruxbinchicago.com

Tasters are "transported into a culinary adventure" courtesy of chef-owner Edward Kim and his "delicious, innovative" Eclectic cooking at this "freakin' awesome" Noble Square BYO; the "small" space offers a "fascinating lesson in creative recycling" – "repurposed" decor includes "bench backs made of seat belts" – and service is "incredibly friendly", so grumps groaning "only the young can tolerate two-hour waits" (no reservations) are overuled by those who simply "love everything", including the "coolest bathroom", "hands down."

Sabatino's ❶ *Italian*   25 | 19 | 23 | $35

Old Irving Park | 4441 W. Irving Park Rd. (Kenneth Ave.) | 773-283-8331 | www.sabatinoschicago.com

"It does not get any more old school than this" attest admirers of this Old Irving Park "time machine" where you "get your money's worth" with "plentiful" portions of "delicious", "well-prepared" Italian "classics" served in "throwback" "supper club" surrounds"; "friendly" servers "done up" in white shirts and bow ties contribute to the "charm", just be warned it can be "crazy crowded" on weekends when there's piano music.

Sable Kitchen & Bar ❶ *American*   24 | 23 | 23 | $49

River North | Hotel Palomar | 505 N. State St. (Illinois St.) | 312-755-9704 | www.sablechicago.com

"Inventive", "fun-to-share" American "small and medium bites" from former *Top Chef*-testant Heather Terhune "just click" at this River North hangout in the Hotel Palomar where the "creative", "quality" cocktails "match the food" and fuel a "high-energy" bar scene; it's a "bit pricey" for some faultfinders who find it "just ok" given the "hype", but the majority concludes "there's little room for disappointment here."

Sabor Saveur Ⓜ *French/Mexican*   21 | 18 | 21 | $44

Ukrainian Village | 2013 W. Division St. (Damen Ave.) | 773-235-7310 | www.saborsaveur.com

Though it may seem like a "strange concept", the "unique" French-Mex fusion is "great in execution" assure *amis* of this "spirited" Ukie Village contender with a whitewashed, art gallery feel; given the "attentive" service and "reasonable" tabs, many "would go back", especially those who "like trying new things."

NEW Sacco Bruno *Italian/Sandwiches*   - | - | - | I

Bucktown | 2151 W. Armitage Ave. (Leavitt St.) | 773-278-8028 | www.saccobruno.com

With a name that means 'brown bag', this Bucktown arrival whips up Italian deli sandwiches and grinders (including a create-your-own option from a big ingredient list), salads and focaccia pizza; the brick corner space, done up with open ductwork and wood floors, offers counter-service dining with high-top seating, a bar with TVs and a retail grocery area.

Ⓩ Sai Café *Japanese*   27 | 17 | 23 | $36

Lincoln Park | 2010 N. Sheffield Ave. (Armitage Ave.) | 773-472-8080 | www.saicafe.com

There's "nothing crazy or too creative" because "it's all about the fish" at this "steady" Lincoln Park Japanese turning out "pristinely fresh", "spectacular" sushi and other "high-quality" fare via "efficient" servers; the "pleasant" enough decor doesn't inspire the same praise, but it still "can't be beat", especially given such "reasonable prices."

	FOOD	DECOR	SERVICE	COST

Saigon Sisters ⓧ *Vietnamese*   24 | 18 | 21 | $31

West Loop | 567 W. Lake St. (bet. Clinton & Jefferson Sts.) |
312-496-0090 | www.saigonsisters.com

"Banh mi me, baby!" implore "blown-away" boosters of this West
Loop Vietnamese sister to the French Market stall where "interesting" fare boasting "bright flavors" tastes "upscale" but comes at
"downscale prices"; "helpful" servers elevate the "basic" wood and
steel space, but with limited seating, you may need to "get there in
off hours" to snag a spot.

Salatino's *Italian*   – | – | – | M

Little Italy/University Village | 626 S. Racine Ave. (Harrison St.) |
312-226-9300

Scott Harris of Francesca's is behind this Little Italy trattoria for red-
sauce Italian, offering family recipes revived from the onetime neighborhood favorite Gennaro's; the warm setting features old-school
checkered tablecloths, a tin ceiling and '50s-era photography.

Saloon Steakhouse *Steak*   23 | 19 | 21 | $55

Streeterville | Seneca Hotel | 200 E. Chestnut St. (Mies van der Rohe Way) |
312-280-5454 | www.saloonsteakhouse.com

A "hidden gem" in Streeterville's Seneca Hotel, this "clubby" "old
Chicago steakhouse" matches the "solid" meat and seafood of some
"famous-name" competitors, minus the "attitude" and "overcrowded
tables"; as a "neighborhood hangout" it's "expensive", but carnivores
contend it's still "a value for the dollar" considering the "quality."

Salpicón *Mexican*   25 | 22 | 24 | $53

Old Town | 1252 N. Wells St. (bet. Goethe & Scott Sts.) |
312-988-7811 | www.salpicon.com

A "standout", thanks to chef Priscila Satkoff's "command of regional
cuisine", this "extraordinary" Old Town Mexican "hits all the notes"
with "inventively prepared" "authentic cuisine" paired with "tremendous margaritas", "tequilas galore" and an "outstanding wine
list"; "helpful" staffers lend a "warm" feel in the "colorful" newly remodeled space, so somewhat costly tabs barely register for those
deeming it an "all around winner."

Salsa 17 *Mexican*   23 | 20 | 22 | $33

Arlington Heights | 17 W. Campbell St. (bet. Dunton & Vail Aves.) |
847-590-1122 | www.salsa17.com

It's no wonder there's a "vibrant bar scene" since margaritas
come in "virtually every flavor" at this "popular" Arlington
Heights hacienda, serving "savory", somewhat "upscale" Mexican
food, including "terrific moles" and guacamole "made to order"
at your table; live Wednesday night mariachi performances add to
the festive atmosphere.

San Soo Gab San ⓓ *Korean*   26 | 10 | 14 | $26

Lincoln Square | 5247 N. Western Ave. (Foster Ave.) | 773-334-1589

A generous variety of "appetizing" small dishes pairs with an "excellent", "endless supply of cook-your-own-meats" at this budget-

friendly Lincoln Square Korean BBQ where it's "speedy" ("you don't come for service with a smile") – and open 24 hours a day; "the whole restaurant swims in smoke" and "your hair will smell for days", but regulars still rate it "well worth it."

Santorini ● *Greek/Seafood*   22 | 19 | 20 | $40

Greektown | 800 W. Adams St. (Halsted St.) | 312-829-8820 | www.santorinichicago.com

From "great grilled octopus" and "expertly deboned" whole fish to other "hearty" Hellenic fare (both "traditional" and "modern"), "there's not a bum dish on the menu" assure aficionados of this Greektown seafooder; "lively" service and a "giant stone hearth" enhance the "casual" ambiance, and it's a strong "value" too – especially if you "go with a crowd" and order family-style.

Sapori Trattoria *Italian*   26 | 20 | 25 | $35

Lincoln Park | 2701 N. Halsted St. (Schubert Ave.) | 773-832-9999 | www.saporitrattoria.net

"Authentic" "down-home" cooking is "guaranteed to delight" at this Lincoln Park Italian, a "small neighborhood trattoria" where the food is "high quality", the "service always friendly" and the prices "fair"; sure, "decor could be better", but it's still "charming" – and there's "always a crowd."

NEW Saranello's *Italian*   ∇ 24 | 24 | 21 | $41

Wheeling | 601 N. Milwaukee Ave. (Wolf Rd.) | 847-777-6878 | www.saranellos.com

Cognoscenti croon about the "wonderful Italian food" ("love the meatballs") and rolling wine cart at this "reasonably priced" Lettuce Entertain You newcomer in Wheeling's Westin Chicago North Shore; the "warm, welcoming" exposed-brick dining room adds allure, so even carpers who indicate it's still "working out the kinks" "like it" nonetheless.

Sayat Nova *Armenian*   23 | 20 | 21 | $29

Streeterville | 157 E. Ohio St. (bet. Michigan Ave. & St. Clair St.) | 312-644-9159 | www.sayatnovachicago.com

"They have a way with lamb" and other "delicious" specialties at this "affordable" Streeterville Armenian, a "charming" "urban oasis" that's been feeding "Magnificent Mile shoppers" since 1970; atmospheric lantern lighting and mosaic alcoves lend a "gorgeous" touch, and while it's "not all that exotic" for everyone, it still works as a "change of pace" or just a "cozy" respite on those "cold Chicago nights."

⚡ Schwa ⊠Ⓜ *American*   28 | 16 | 24 | $107

Wicker Park | 1466 N. Ashland Ave. (Le Moyne St.) | 773-252-1466 | www.schwarestaurant.com

Willing "guinea pigs" devour the "mindbendingly creative" New American "experiments" of "punk rock cooking genius" Michael Carlson at his "cutting-edge" Wicker Park BYO where the "seriously amazing" prix fixe menu is served by the chefs; "there's no atmosphere" but those who consider it "fine dining without the stuffiness" don't mind, suggesting you "bring an open mind, some booze" (and some big bucks) and strap in for an "exhilarating" night out; P.S. "make reservations far in advance – and good luck with that."

NEW Scofflaw ● *Pub Food*

| – | – | – | I |

Logan Square | 3201 W. Armitage Ave. (bet. Kedzie & Sawyer Aves.) | 773-252-9700

Expect a ramshackle farm-meets-parlor vibe – complete with tractor seat barstools, ornate settees and intimate nooks – at this Logan Square drinking den, where a Longman & Eagle alum turns out gussied-up, pubby small plates; meanwhile, its tipples pay homage to gin, which appears in modern, carefully crafted cocktails, sipped before a roaring fireplace or in sweeping, semicircular booths.

Scoozi! *Italian*

| 21 | 21 | 21 | $37 |

River North | 410 W. Huron St. (bet. Hudson Ave. & Sedgwick St.) | 312-943-5900 | www.leye.com

It "keeps getting better" laud loyalists of this "vibrant", "crowded-all-the-time" River North Italian, a midpriced Lettuce Entertain You stalwart for "homestyle" pastas and brick-oven pizzas (plus new gluten-free offerings) delivered by "professional" staffers in a "huge" space where groups and families can "spread out"; so while it may offer "nothing daring", it's a "consistent" choice that keeps most "happy."

NEW Scout Waterhouse & Kitchen ● *American*

| – | – | – | M |

South Loop | 1301 S. Wabash Ave. (13th St.) | 312-705-0595 | www.thescoutchicago.com

This upscale sports bar occupies the South Loop's onetime Opera space serving beyond-your-basic American burgers, sandwiches (including grilled cheese that serves four), flatbreads and small plates; the rustic setting is full of reclaimed wood, dozens of TVs and copper dividers, with additional assets including a long beer list, signature cocktails, weekend DJs and patio seating.

Seasons 52 *American*

| 26 | 24 | 26 | $39 |

Schaumburg | 1770 E. Higgins Rd. (bet. Mall Dr. & Martingale Rd.) | 847-517-5252 | www.seasons52.com

A "fantastic concept" rave regulars of this "moderately priced", "über-healthy" Schaumburg chain link where the "creative" New American "concoctions" "change with the seasons" and weigh in at 475 calories or less, resulting in "incredible", "guilt-free dining"; "comfortable" upscale-casual environs and the "most attentive" servers further explain why it's "well patronized"; P.S. an Oakbrook Center outpost is set to open around press time.

NEW 2nd Street Bistro Ⓜ *American*

| ∇ 21 | 19 | 24 | $39 |

Highland Park | 1825 Second St. (bet. Central Ave. & Elm Pl.) | 847-433-3400 | www.2ndstreethp.com

A "welcome addition" to Highland Park, this BYO American bistro turns out solid contemporary cooking with a farm-to-table bent in "pretty", countrylike surroundings; service gets high marks and tabs are moderate, making it an overall "good" choice; P.S. the owners also operate a quick-serve eatery (Stashs) with a sprawling American menu and an Italian BYO (2nd Street Enoteca) out of the same space.

Sepia *American*   26 | 26 | 25 | $60

West Loop | 123 N. Jefferson St. (bet. Randolph & Washington Sts.) | 312-441-1920 | www.sepiachicago.com

"Chef Andrew Zimmerman is a wizard" trumpet tasters touting the "creative", "divinely executed" fare at this "upscale", locally focused West Loop New American where the cocktails are "expertly made", "service is impeccable" and "the room is stylish and cool without being pretentious"; it's not cheap, but bean counters wondering whether they "got their money's worth" are overruled by those calling it a "perfect place" to bring "people you want to impress."

NEW Seven Ocean *Asian*   - | - | - | M

Oak Park | 122 N. Marion St. (bet. Lake St. & North Blvd.) | 708-524-7979 | www.sevenocean.us

Understated and elegant, this midpriced West Suburban Pan-Asian offers two seasonally changing prix fixe menus plus à la carte options from Tatsu chef-owner Tanapat Vannopas; the uncluttered, quiet dining room features globe lighting, upholstered seating and dark-wood tables.

1776 ⓢ *American*   26 | 19 | 24 | $42

Crystal Lake | 397 W. Virginia St./Rte. 14 (bet. Dole & McHenry Aves.) | 815-356-1776 | www.1776restaurant.com

Elk, boar, ostrich and bison are just some of the "unique" specials starring on the "excellent" and "interesting" New American menu at this "charming" Crystal Lake "jewel" also offering a "magnificent wine list" ("the owner, Andy, will help you choose"); "decor is lacking, but who cares" say patriots who point to the "warm", "knowledgeable" staffers and moderate tabs, insisting "John Hancock, Thomas Jefferson and the rest would be proud to dine here."

NEW 720 South Bar & Grill *American*   - | - | - | M

South Loop | Hilton Chicago | 720 S. Michigan Ave. (bet. Balbo Ave. & 8th St.) | 312-922-4400

Seasonal American fare, including small plates, seafood and steaks, plus updated dessert classics and creative breakfasts are what to expect at this midpriced grill in the South Loop Hilton; the sophisticated setting combines various woods, fibers and natural stone alongside white leather chairs, shimmery banquettes, drum light fixtures and a wine storage room.

▣ Shanghai Terrace ⓢ *Chinese*   27 | 28 | 25 | $71

River North | Peninsula Chicago | 108 E. Superior St., 4th fl. (bet. Michigan Ave. & Rush St.) | 312-573-6744 | www.chicago.peninsula.com

"Each dish is a masterpiece" at this "upscale" Chinese off the lobby of River North's Peninsula Hotel where the "exquisite" cuisine is matched by "astounding decor" and a "beautiful" '30s-style dining room that earns it top Decor honors in Chicago; "elegant, polite" service and a "terrace perfect for summer days and nights" further ensure a "top experience", so "expensive" tabs come as no surprise.

⚡ Shaw's Crab House *Seafood*   25 | 21 | 23 | $53

River North | 21 E. Hubbard St. (bet. State St. & Wabash Ave.) | 312-527-2722
Schaumburg | 1900 E. Higgins Rd. (Frontage & Woodfield Rds.) | 847-517-2722
www.shawscrabhouse.com

The "quality is as high as ever" at this "lively" River North "institution" and its Schaumburg sib, where fin fans feast on an "excellent array of seafood" from "terrific fish" and "perfectly fresh oysters" to "surprisingly great sushi"; the city sib has an "old-school", "clubby" feel echoed in the "retro" decor of the 'burbs outpost, and service at both is "spot-on", so while tabs cost "an arm and a (crab) leg", they're "less expensive than a trip to Cape Cod or Maine"; P.S. many "love the Sunday brunch and Bloody Mary bar."

Shula's Steakhouse *Steak*   21 | 20 | 21 | $64

Streeterville | Sheraton Chicago Hotel & Towers | 301 E. North Water St. (Columbus Dr. & News St.) | 312-670-0788
Itasca | Westin Chicago NW | 400 Park Blvd. (Thorndale Ave.) | 630-775-1499
www.donshula.com

"In a crowded field", "football nuts" befriend these Itasca and Streeterville links of the national steakhouse chain, where mementos nod to the undefeated 1972 Miami Dolphins and "nice" servers "show cuts of meat" – including a behemoth porterhouse – tableside "before you order"; if some call the "caricature" concept ("menus on footballs?") a bit "goofy", swains support it, even despite Bears-leaning "regional partisanship."

Signature Room *American*   17 | 26 | 19 | $60

Streeterville | John Hancock Ctr. | 875 N. Michigan Ave., 95th fl. (bet. Chestnut St. & Delaware Pl.) | 312-787-9596 | www.signatureroom.com

"The sky's the limit" at this "iconic", 95th-floor New American perched atop the Hancock, where "breathtaking" vistas "day and night" (even from the "powder room") tend to outshine "competent" service and a "no-surprises" menu; since you're largely "paying for the view", most advise reserving it for "entertaining out-of-town guests" or "eating till you drop" at the Sunday brunch buffet or Friday/Saturday lunch buffets.

Silver Seafood ➊ *Chinese/Seafood*   ∇ 27 | 10 | 19 | $23

Uptown | 4829 N. Broadway (Lawrence Ave.) | 773-784-0668 | www.silverseafoodrestaurant.com

"Terrific" Cantonese "comfort food" and seafood specialties are the draw at this affordable Uptown "favorite" where regulars recommend skipping the Americanized fare and trying "something different from the real Chinese menu"; the "simple setting" harkens "back to the '50s" and "service can vary", but "your taste buds will appreciate" the experience; P.S. open daily until 1 AM.

	FOOD	DECOR	SERVICE	COST

Simply It *Vietnamese*
| 22 | 13 | 20 | $20 |

Lincoln Park | 2269 N. Lincoln Ave. (Belden Ave.) | 773-248-0884 | www.simplyitrestaurant.com

An "extensive menu" of "authentic" Vietnamese dishes greets guests at this "reliable" Lincoln Park BYO "bargain"; if the decor lags behind, "attentive" service makes up for it, so most simply have a "lovely" meal.

❷ Sixteen *American*
| 25 | 28 | 24 | $91 |

River North | Trump International Hotel & Tower | 401 N. Wabash Ave., 16th fl. (Kinzie St.) | 312-588-8030 | www.trumpchicagohotel.com

A "striking" setting on the 16th floor of Trump International Hotel & Tower offers "drop-dead" city views that enhance the "unusual" yet "delicious" New American plates at this "world-class" River North dining room; service is highly rated too, but the bill may "leave you breathless" so most save it for "special occasions" – or "go on some-one else's expense account"; P.S. the Food score may not reflect the arrival of Thomas Lents (ex Joël Robuchon in Las Vegas).

NEW Slurping Turtle ❶ *Japanese/Noodles*
| 22 | 22 | 19 | $27 |

River North | 116 W. Hubbard St. (bet. Clark & LaSalle Sts.) | 312-464-0466 | www.slurpingturtle.com

Diners can "slurp down" a "comforting bowl of steaming ramen" or "dive into" more adventurous "noshes" at chef Takashi Yagihashi's "hip" River North izakaya starring "casual Japanese food with mod-ern flair"; if the service can seem a touch "iffy" to some, fans instead focus on the "funky" ultramod decor, advising wafflers to just "do it" and go.

Small Bar ❶ *American*
| 21 | 17 | 21 | $19 |

Logan Square | 2956 N. Albany Ave. (Wellington Ave.) | 773-509-9888
Ukrainian Village | 2049 W. Division St. (bet. Damen & Hoyne Aves.) | 773-772-2727
www.thesmallbar.com

Regulars "never tire" of these "low-key" gastropubs in Logan Square and Ukrainian Village where the "menu is a notch above everyday bar food" and "inventive specials" complement an im-pressive selection of craft beers; service that's "helpful without be-ing overbearing" and easy-on-the-wallet tabs also enhance their "true neighborhood" appeal.

Smashburger *Burgers*
| 19 | 13 | 19 | $15 |

NEW **Darien** | 2425 W. 75th St. (bet. Centerbury Pl. & Webster St.) | 630-427-1788 🅂 Ⓜ
NEW **Arlington Heights** | 115 W. Rand Rd. (bet. Arlington Heights Rd. & Crestnut Ave.) | 224-232-8323
NEW **Schaumburg** | 687 E. Golf Rd. (bet. Basswood St. & Plum Grove Rd.) | 847-519-3679
NEW **Oak Lawn** | 5139 W. 95th St. (bet. 52nd & Tully Aves.) | 708-422-2952
Batavia | Trader Joe's Shopping Ctr. | 842 N. Randall Rd. (Fabyan Pkwy.) | 630-593-5030
NEW **Bloomingdale** | 148 S. Gary Ave. (Stratford Ave.) | 224-232-8326

(continued)

Smashburger

Bolingbrook | 149 N. Weber Rd. (bet. Jennifer Ln. & Thackeray Dr.) | 630-759-2781
Elmhurst | 538 W. Charles Rd. (West Ave.) | 630-592-4878
NEW **Wheaton** | 1 Rice Lake Sq. (Loop Rd.) | 630-871-3392
www.smashburger.com

"Juicy", "special-sauced" burgers and chicken sandwiches get a "build-your-own" boost with complimentary toppings at this "pleas-ant", "fast"-casual "surprise", a Denver-based, all-American chain with counter-service outposts suburbia-wide; shakes and rosemary-laced "fresh-cut" fries also inspire praise, save a few objections about "average" results.

Smith & Wollensky *Steak*

23 | 22 | 24 | $64

River North | 318 N. State St. (Upper Wacker Dr.) | 312-670-9900 | www.smithandwollensky.com

Join the "business expense crowd" for "celebrity-watching" at this NYC transplant in River North, where "big-portioned", "cooked-as-ordered" "prime" meats are served in "happening" wood-accented digs; "helpful" staffers "take their responsibilities seriously" and the "lovely outdoor patio" offers "wonderful views", so dissenters dub-bing it "underwhelming" are in the minority.

Smoke Daddy *BBQ*

22 | 15 | 18 | $24

Wicker Park | 1804 W. Division St. (Wood St.) | 773-772-6656 | www.thesmokedaddy.com

"Tender", "slowly smoked" meat, "from pulled chicken and pork, through ribs and brisket", make this midpriced Wicker Parker a "BBQ lovers' paradise"; the surroundings are "just divey enough", service is solid and "live music adds to the experience", so 'cuen-noisseurs say it's "worth putting in the rotation."

☑ Smoque BBQ ⓜ *BBQ*

26 | 11 | 18 | $20

Old Irving Park | 3800 N. Pulaski Rd. (Grace St.) | 773-545-7427 | www.smoquebbq.com

"Lines out the door" attest that this Northwest Side BYO has "achieved BBQ perfection" in the form of "outrageous", "smoky" brisket "burst-ing with flavor", "the best" "juicy" ribs and "equally good" sides that "blow other joints out of the water"; it's "truly a dive" with eaters packed in at "community tables", but "friendly" staffers "manage the crowds well" (the "table juggling is fascinating") and it's "cheap to boot", so the "addicted" dub it "worth any wait, in any weather."

Socca *French/Italian*

23 | 21 | 23 | $38

Lakeview | 3301 N. Clark St. (Aldine Ave.) | 773-248-1155 | www.soccachicago.com

"Robust" French-Italian fare and "courteous" service shine at this "cozy" Lakeview bistro where the "specials are a highlight", rates are "reasonable" and the staff "remembers" you; "versa-tile" enough for special occasions or "random nights", it's an overall "neighborhood fave."

	FOOD	DECOR	SERVICE	COST

Sola *American*   24 | 22 | 23 | $45

Lakeview | 3868 N. Lincoln Ave. (Byron St.) | 773-327-3868 |
www.sola-restaurant.com

"Say aloha to fresh, local flavors with an island twist" at chef-owner Carol Wallack's Hawaiian-inspired Lakeview New American that's "an eating experience to share" with "imaginative preparations" set down by "helpful" servers in "comfortable", contemporary digs; while quibblers claim it's "not particularly memorable", most insist it "rises above" the rest – and boasts a "gem of a brunch" on weekends.

NEW Soulwich Ⓢ *Asian/Sandwiches*   - | - | - | I

Evanston | 1634 Orrington Ave. (bet. Davis St. & Elgin Rd.) |
847-328-2222 | www.soulwich.com

Budget-friendly sandwiches of mixed Asian influence (predominantly Singapore and Burma – not your typical banh mi) tickle Evanston taste buds with traditional curries, spices, organic local produce and housemade sauces; the casual counter-service setting is brightly colored with space-age seating and framed posters.

South Branch   ▽ 22 | 22 | 18 | $28
Tavern Grille Ⓢ *American*

Loop | 100 S. Wacker Dr. (Monroe St.) | 312-546-6177 |
www.southbranchchicago.com

Whether for business lunches or "after-work drinks in the Loop", this "popular" New American fuels go-getters with a "vast", moderately priced menu and thoughtful beer list; solid service and an open, airy dining room further the year-round appeal, while scenic riverside seating makes it a "great venue in the summer"; P.S. weekdays only.

The Southern ⦁Ⓜ *Southern*   21 | 21 | 20 | $30

Wicker Park | 1840 W. North Ave. (bet. Honore St. & Wolcott Ave.) |
773-342-1840 | www.thesouthernchicago.com

"Winner winner, fried chicken dinner" chant cheerleaders who are "happy to be surrounded by Southern favorites" like "juicy, crisp" bird, "fluffy" biscuits and "gravy that will put your mama to shame" at this rustic, approachable Wicker Park hangout; artful cocktails and a "beautiful" rooftop deck (complete with cabanas) are reasons to linger.

NEW Southern Mac &   18 | 10 | 18 | $10
Cheese Store Ⓢ *Southern*

Loop | 60 E. Lake St. (bet. Garland Ct. & Wabash Ave.) |
312-262-7622

Southern Mac Ⓢ *Southern*

Location varies | no phone
www.thesouthernmac.com

Converts "didn't believe that mac 'n' cheese was a meal" until visiting this inexpensive Loop home base and its food truck sib known for "insanely rich" helpings in "varieties you'd never try otherwise" (plus salads and desserts at the brick-and-mortar operation); with catering and delivery options to further their fix, most muse "what's not to love?"

South Gate Cafe *American*

18 | 19 | 19 | $36

Lake Forest | 655 Forest Ave. (Deerpath Rd.) | 847-234-8800 | www.southgatecafe.com

The "wonderful" patio is the "perfect place to partake" of casual, "varied" "American bistro cuisine" at this "popular" Lake Forester set in a circa-1901 building; a few wish the food were "better" and service gets mixed marks ("friendly" vs. "snooty"), but many still "love the garden room at lunch" and sitting outdoors on a "clear summer night."

NEW Southport & Irving 🅂🅜 *Burgers*

− | − | − | M

North Center/St. Ben's | 4002-4004 N. Southport Ave. (Irving Park Rd.) | 773-857-2890 | www.southportandirving.com

From the Broadway Cellars folks comes this Napa-nuanced North Center bistro, an American wine bar offering a seasonally informed menu of specialty burgers and comforting, eclectic mains; affordable drink specials, Sunday suppers and a Tuesday prix fixe add extra incentive for a visit.

Southport Grocery & Café *American*

24 | 16 | 19 | $21

Lakeview | 3552 N. Southport Ave. (bet. Addison & Eddy Sts.) | 773-665-0100 | www.southportgrocery.com

"If you can climb over the strollers" and endure "long waits on weekends", you'll be rewarded with "creative", "consistently good" brunch/lunch fare, like "grown-up pop tarts" and "yummy" sandwiches all delivered by "friendly" staffers at this midpriced Lakeview New American; perusing the "super-cool dry goods" passes time while queued for "limited seating" in the "small", "crowded" space, and regulars who "don't skip the cupcakes" warn you may need a "double workout" afterward.

South Water Kitchen *American*

15 | 16 | 17 | $33

Loop | Hotel Monaco | 225 N. Wabash Ave. (Lake St.) | 312-236-9300 | www.southwaterkitchen.com

"Comfortable surroundings", "quick service" and "simple" American food draw "after-work" tipplers and a "mature", "pre-theater" crowd to this midpriced, "bistro-like" Looper adjacent to the Hotel Monaco; if some find it "uninspired" all around, they concede the patio seating's an "upside."

Spacca Napoli Pizzeria 🅜 *Pizza*

26 | 20 | 22 | $25

Ravenswood | 1769 W. Sunnyside Ave. (bet. Hermitage & Ravenswood Aves.) | 773-878-2420 | www.spaccanapolipizzeria.com

"Get here as fast as you can" advise admirers of this midpriced Ravenswood pizzeria dishing "true thin-crust" Neopolitan-style pies that reach "superlative" levels with "well-sourced ingredients"; the rustic space is "sparsely decorated but comfortable", service is "friendly" and patio seating is "divine", so it's "perfect for a casual dinner, family party or cozy date."

Z Spiaggia *Italian* **26** **27** **26** **$105**

Gold Coast | One Magnificent Mile Bldg. | 980 N. Michigan Ave.
(Oak St.) | 312-280-2750 | www.spiaggiarestaurant.com

An "ultimate special-occasion place", this Gold Coast "destination" "leaves nothing to be desired", from Tony Mantuano's "exquisite", "beautifully presented" "haute Italian" plates and the "deeply
varied wine list" to the "warm, discreet" service known to treat
guests "like royalty"; "spectacular views of the lake" feature in the
"elegant", "sterling setting", so though you need "a bag of gold to
pay the bill", acloytes insist it's "worth the splurge", "hands down";
P.S. jackets required.

Z Sprout **M** *American* **28** **25** **25** **$77**

Lincoln Park | 1417 W. Fullerton Ave. (bet. Janssen & Southport Aves.) |
773-348-0706 | www.sproutrestaurant.com

Chef-"magician" Dale Levitski "excites taste buds" at his Lincoln
Park New American, a "showplace for creative cuisine" with "innovative combinations", "clean flavors" and "outstanding tastes"; service is "warm and knowledgable" and the stone-walled space
"pleasant", which helps quiet those who find it "overpriced";
P.S. "brunch is a highlight."

Stained Glass Wine Bar Bistro *American* **25** **22** **24** **$54**

Evanston | 1735 Benson Ave. (bet. Church & Clark Sts.) | 847-864-8600 |
www.thestainedglass.com

At once "comfortable" and "classy", this "high-end" Evanston New
American turns out "creative", "uniformly delicious" cuisine complemented by "an extraordinary wine selection" (including "imaginative flights"); you can "trust the advice" from "helpful servers"
and prices are deemed "reasonable" given the "quality", so in sum,
it's a "very returnable place"; its Cellar at The Stained Glass sibling
is a more affordable option.

NEW Standard Grill **⊠M** *American* **–** **–** **–** **M**

Westmont | Standard Market | 333 E. Ogden Ave. (Blackhawk Dr.) |
630-366-7030 | www.standardmarket.com

Set within the gleaming-white, barnlike Standard Market in
Westmont, this sleek American uses artisanal, local ingredients
in its affordable menu of salads, sandwiches, pizza and more; to
drink are house cocktails, wine and beer (bottles from the bev sec-
tion can be imbibed, corkage fee-free) plus an array of on-display,
fruit-infused waters.

Stanley's Kitchen & Tap *American* **19** **14** **17** **$21**

Lincoln Park | 1970 N. Lincoln Ave. (Armitage Ave.) | 312-642-0007 |
www.stanleyskitchenandtap.com

Affordable American "comfort food" ("well-executed" fried
chicken, "to-die-for" mac 'n' cheese) is a draw at this "casual" Lincoln Park "institution" that's "always a good time", especially when
it morphs into a "lively" scene after dinner; meanwhile, reviewers
who relish the brunch and its hangover-abating Bloody Mary bar call
weekends the "best time to visit" for a "Southern fix."

	FOOD	DECOR	SERVICE	COST

Star of Siam *Thai* — 22 | 18 | 20 | $22

River North | 11 E. Illinois St. (State St.) | 312-670-0100 | www.starofsiamchicago.com

It's "hard to find" given the area's "double-decker streets", but this "low-key" River North Thai is "worth the expedition" for "fragrant rice dishes" (with the "best peanut sauce around") and other picks from a "reliably decent" roster; "fast" service, "soothing" surrounds and overall "value" for lunch and takeout make it a "go-to" for folks who've "loved it for years."

State and Lake *American* — 17 | 17 | 17 | $34

Loop | theWit Hotel | 201 N. State St. (Lake St.) | 312-239-9400 | www.stateandlakechicago.com

Not quite a "cookie-cutter hotel" hang, this "well-decorated", afford-able Loop American offers a bit of a "respite" from the "aggressively hip theWit", coupling "tasty", locally sourced food with Midwestern beers and "good cocktails"; it's accommodating to "yuppies" after-work and the "pre- and post-theater" set, though too "pretentious" and "blah" for those who feel the dining's an "after-thought."

Steve's Deli *Deli* — 21 | 11 | 15 | $19

River North | 354 W. Hubbard St. (bet. Kingsbury & Orleans Sts.) | 312-467-6868 | www.stevesdeli.com

"Almost as good as the original" near Detroit, this checkered-floor River North deli satisfies with its "terrific", hefty sandwiches, homey soups and other "old-time" staples; so-so service and sur-rounds don't derail belly busters, who advise "bring your wallet and your appetite", since tabs can add up.

Stir Crazy *Asian* — 20 | 17 | 19 | $24

Northbrook | Northbrook Court Shopping Ctr. | 1186 Northbrook Ct. (Lake Cook Rd.) | 847-562-4800

Schaumburg | Woodfield Mall | 5 Woodfield Mall (Frontage & Golf Rds.) | 847-330-1200

Oak Brook | Oakbrook Center Mall | 105 Oakbrook Ctr. (Rte. 83) | 630-575-0155

Warrenville | 28252 Diehl Rd. (Winfield Rd.) | 630-393-4700 www.stircrazy.com

"You choose the protein, veggies and sauce" for "appealing" cus-tomized stir-fries, or order from a "wide selection" of other "fresh", "healthy" Asian dishes at these "cut-above" chain links with "kid-friendly" settings; though a few DIY-doubters cite "uneven" results, low prices and "quick" service keep it "bustling."

NEW Storefront Company ● *American* — - | - | - | E

Wicker Park | 1941 W. North Ave. (bet. Damen & Winchester Aves.) | 773-661-2609 | www.thestorefrontcompany.com

Acclaimed chef Bryan Moscatello (ex DC's Zola and Potenza) is cooking up modern American farm-to-table plates small and large with a seasonal slant in Wicker Park's famed Flat Iron Building, where patrons can make a moderately priced meal or full-blown ex-pensive dining experience (bonus for night owls: it's open until 2 AM);

seating options within the sleek digs include communal tables, a cozy dining room and a massive bar issuing updates on classic cocktails, and there's also a chef's open kitchen 'counter' showcasing four-course tasting menus.

Sullivan's Steakhouse *Steak*

| 24 | 22 | 22 | $61 |

River North | 415 N. Dearborn St. (Hubbard St.) | 312-527-3510
Lincolnshire | 250 Marriott Dr. (Milwaukee Ave.) | 847-883-0311
Naperville | 244 S. Main St. (bet. Chicago & Jackson Aves.) | 630-305-0230
www.sullivanssteakhouse.com

"Sizzling steaks melt in your mouth", at this "high-end" chophouse chain boasting "well-executed" presentations and a staff that's "always at the ready"; "dark, masculine" stylings and frequent live jazz add to the "throwback atmosphere", and while a few feel it's not quite "top tier", most are happy to shell out for "special occasions."

Sultan's Market *Mideastern*

| 21 | 13 | 16 | $11 |

Lincoln Park | 2521 N. Clark St. (Deming Pl.) | 312-638-9151
Wicker Park | 2057 W. North Ave. (Hoyne Ave.) | 773-235-3072 ⊅
www.chicagofalafel.com

An "endless" salad bar "full of nowhere-else selections" is a draw at this counter-service BYO duo in Lincoln Park and Wicker Park also offering "fresh", "light" Middle Eastern fare like lentil soup and falafel; service and decor may lag a bit behind, but with wallet-friendly tabs (Wicker Park is cash-only), they're a "perfect lunch place for every day."

Sunda *Asian*

| 24 | 25 | 21 | $51 |

River North | 110 W. Illinois St. (bet. Clark & LaSalle Sts.) | 312-644-0500 | www.sundachicago.com

One of "the best combinations of food, cocktails and people-watching" can be found at this "hip" River North "hot spot" where the "stunning" "modern" room "with lovely lighting" attracts "celebs and normal folk alike" who fill up on "interesting sushi" and other "pricey-but-worth-it" Asian fusion fare; it can get "crazy busy" and "loud" ("bring a microphone"), but service "does its best to accommodate", so scenesters "can't stop going back."

Sun Wah BBQ *Chinese*

| 25 | 12 | 15 | $23 |

Uptown | 5039 N. Broadway (bet. Argyle & Winona Sts.) | 773-769-1254 | www.sunwahbbq.com

"If you haven't had the duck dinner, you ain't living" ("don't forget to order ahead") insist regulars of this Uptown Chinese "favorite", where "it's hard to go wrong" when the other "authentic" dishes, especially the "Hong Kong–style BBQ" offerings, are so "chopstick licking good"; the "atmosphere is nothing special" and when "it's packed, and that's often", service can be "hurried", but "it's all worth it with cheap prices" – and of course "incredible food."

Superdawg Drive-In *Hot Dogs*

| 21 | 17 | 18 | $11 |

Northwest Side | 6363 N. Milwaukee Ave. (Devon Ave.) | 773-763-0660 ◐

(continued)

Superdawg Drive-In

Wheeling | 333 S. Milwaukee Ave. (Mors Ave.) | 847-459-1900
www.superdawg.com

Car hops say "hiya" while handing out "Whoopercheesies", "crispy, light" fries and "juicy" Chicago-style dogs at this "classic" Northwest Side drive-in "legend" (a "must-see" for its rooftop mascots) and its "fantastic" spin-off in Wheeling; "steeped in tradition", it's the "ultimate" for lifers, and even skeptics say "try it once to check it off your bucket list."

Sushi Naniwa *Japanese*   ▽ 23 | 13 | 23 | $37

River North | 607 N. Wells St. (bet. Ohio & Ontario Sts.) | 312-255-8555 | www.sushinaniwa.com

Regulars have "no complaints" about this Japanese "go-to" in River North, with moderately priced, "fresh sushi rolls done well", "attentive" service and all-around "neighborhood-joint" appeal; though it has "zero atmosphere" compared to Bob San (its more upscale sib), the patio gives it a boost in the summer.

Sushi Para *Japanese*   20 | 11 | 14 | $24

Palatine | 1268 E. Dundee Rd. (Baldwin Ln.) | 847-202-9922 | www.sushiparachicago.com

Sushi Para D *Japanese*

Lincoln Park | 543 W. Diversey Pkwy. (bet. Lampden & Lehmann Cts.) | 773-248-1808 | www.sushiparachicago.com

Sushi Para II *Japanese*

Lincoln Park | 2256 N. Clark St. (bet. Belden Ave. & Grant Pl.) | 773-477-3219 | www.sushiparachicago.com

Sushi Para M *Japanese*

Bucktown | 1633 N. Milwaukee Ave. (bet. Damen & North Aves.) | 773-252-6828 | www.sushiparachicago.com

Sushi Sai *Japanese*

Loop | 123 N. Wacker Dr. (bet. Franklin St. & Wacker Dr.) | 312-332-8822 | www.sushisaionline.com

"Go hungry and order as much as you can" advise the initiated at this perennially "packed" Japanese mini-chain where the "quality", "all-you-can-eat" sushi "never stops" (a "long enough" à la carte menu is also offered); sure, there's "not much atmosphere" and service can be "indifferent", but devotees still insist the "bargain" is "hard to beat"; P.S. the Bucktown and Lincoln Park locations are BYO.

Sushisamba Rio ● *Japanese/S American*   22 | 25 | 20 | $50

River North | 504 N. Wells St. (bet. Grand Ave. & Illinois St.) | 312-595-2300 | www.sushisamba.com

"Fashionista"-friendly digs (including a chic rooftop bar) set the stage for "inventive" sushi and "eclectic" Japanese–South American plates (ceviche, robata-grilled meats) at this "trendy" River North "scene"; servers keep the "fun drinks" coming, so revelers overlook pricey tabs to "impress" a date or simply soak in the "cool atmosphere."

	FOOD	DECOR	SERVICE	COST

NEW Sutherlands Food & Spirits ● *American/Burgers*

-	-	-	I

Northwest Side | 5353 W. Irving Park Rd. (bet. Lockwood & Long Aves.) | 773-930-4790

At this neighborhood hangout Portage Parkers can partake of classic bar fare – think burgers and sandwiches, salads and wraps, mac 'n' cheese wedges and ice cream pies – accompanied by a generous draft and bottled beer list; the cozy tavern atmosphere features exposed brick, a massive bar, a tin ceiling, TVs and a digital jukebox.

Sweet Maple Café *American*

25	14	22	$20

Little Italy/University Village | 1339 W. Taylor St. (bet. Loomis & Racine Sts.) | 312-243-8908 | www.sweetmaplecafe.com

Known for "wonderful breakfast and lunch" fare, this no-frills, Little Italy American does "bountiful egg dishes" and some of the "best" pancakes and biscuits around; strong service and modest tabs help account for the waits, but diners deem it "worth standing in line for."

Swordfish *Japanese*

▽ 27	21	22	$44

Batavia | 207 N. Randall Rd. (McKee St.) | 630-406-6463 | www.swordfishsushi.com

Some of the "best sushi in the Western 'burbs" can be found at this moderate Japanese offering a large, "interesting" menu of creative rolls and grilled dishes; modern decor and a solid staff also add appeal.

Table Fifty-two *American/Southern*

25	23	24	$56

Gold Coast | 52 W. Elm St. (bet. Clark & Dearborn Sts.) | 312-573-4000 | www.tablefifty-two.com

Art Smith's "elegant" "soul food", like the "ballyhooed fried chicken", "ethereal biscuits" and other "Southern comforts to die for", is "cooked exactly how you want" at this "unpretentious" Gold Coast American in a "homey" "old house setting" enhanced by "low-key" yet "excellent" service; some surmise you're "paying for the chef's name" (he worked for Oprah), but converts consider it a "favorite."

Taco Grill *Mexican* (fka Fonda Isabel)

-	-	-	M

Lombard | 18 W. 333 Roosevelt Rd. (bet. Finley Rd. & Lincoln St.) | 630-691-2222

Westmont | 111 W Ogden Ave. (bet. Warren & Washington Sts.) | 630-353-0964

The original Westmont taqueria and its Lombard sib, a conversion from Fonda Isabel, are a "step up from the average", offering Mexican mainstays that diners customize with offerings from the sizable salsa and condiment bar; the spare settings match the affordable prices.

Taco Joint Urban Taqueria & Cantina *Mexican*

24	16	19	$22

Lincoln Park | 1969 N. Halsted St. (bet. Armitage Ave. & Willow St.) | 312-951-2457 | www.tacojoint.com

"Tantalizing" tacos with "interesting flavors" plus other inexpensive Mexican street eats send "taste buds into a fury of joy" at this

Lincoln Park sister to Zocalo; colorful cantina surrounds, "fast" service and a full bar including 50 agave tequilas make it a happy-hour natural, but meal-goers should be advised it doesn't take ressies.

☑ TAC Quick *Thai* | 27 | 17 | 18 | $19 |

Wrigleyville | 3930 N. Sheridan Rd. (bet. Dakin St. & Irving Park Rd.) | 773-327-5253 | www.tacquick.net

For "out-of-the-ordinary Northern Thai dishes", go with the "secret menu, all the way" say seekers of "cheap eats, deliciously done" at this "authentic" Wrigleyville BYO; black-and-white decor, sidewalk seating and a "convenient location close to public transport" enhance the "way-better-than-average" experience.

☑ Takashi Ⓜ *American/French* | 28 | 23 | 25 | $66 |

Bucktown | 1952 N. Damen Ave. (Armitage Ave.) | 773-772-6170 | www.takashichicago.com

"Meticulously crafted" New American–New French dishes featuring an "excellent melding" of "delicate", "complex" flavors highlight chef-owner Takashi Yagihashi's "magic" touch at this "exceptional" Bucktown "gem"; there's an "understated elegance" to the "cozy" space and servers "clearly take pride in their work", so it's "habit-forming" to those who can afford the pricety tabs; P.S. the River North Slurping Turtle sib is a less costly alternative.

☑ Tallgrass Ⓜ *French* | 27 | 25 | 28 | $87 |

Lockport | 1006 S. State St. (10th St.) | 815-838-5566 | www.tallgrassrestaurant.com

The "fabulous" "old-school" French fare takes diners on "a trip back in time" at this prix fixe-only Lockport "destination" where "surprising innovations" elevate "classic" dishes; set in a "handsome, historic" building, it "delivers a complete dining experience" with "knowledgeable, attentive" staffers and environs that are "elegant but not stuffy", so many agree you "can't beat it for a world-class evening" – even if "it'll take years before you can afford to return."

🆕 Tandoor Char House *Indian/Pakistani* | – | – | – | I |

Lincoln Park | 2652 N. Halsted St. (bet. Diversey Pkwy. & Wrightwood Ave.) | 773-327-2652 | www.tandoorchicago.com

A big menu of Indo-Pak eats includes classic apps and grill and tandoor specialties (meats are all halal), plus updated salads and wraps at this bargain-priced Lincoln Park BYO; the spare but inviting space is decorated with warm yellow walls and framed photos.

Tango Sur *Argentinean/Steak* | 24 | 18 | 19 | $30 |

Lakeview | 3763 N. Southport Ave. (Grace St.) | 773-477-5466 | www.folklorechicago.com

"Serious meat lovers" appreciate that "flavorful steaks won't break the bank" at this "authentic" Argentinean BYO in Lakeview where "huge" servings of "delicious" beef with "flavorful sauces" come at "surprisingly low prices"; some lament "long waits" and "crowded weekends", but service that gets few complaints, a "candlelit" ambiance and outdoor seating help keep it "worth a stop."

Tank Sushi *Japanese*

21 | 17 | 16 | $30

Lincoln Square | 4514 N. Lincoln Ave. (Sunnyside Ave.) | 773-769-2600 | www.tanksushi.com

Fans declare this "happening" Lincoln Square Japanese in simple, modern digs a "destination for sushi and rolls"; though detractors deem it "nothing memorable" and call out "spotty" service, bargain-hunters can't resist the weekday lunch and weekend specials when half-off maki offers "more bang for your buck."

Tanoshii *Japanese*

∇ 28 | 17 | 22 | $40

Andersonville | 5547 N. Clark St. (Gregory St.) | 773-878-6886

Chef-owner Mike Ham "takes pride and joy in his work and it shows" gush Andersonville groupies of the "spectacularly beautiful" sushi and other "custom-made creations" at this midpriced Japanese BYO; if the decor doesn't exactly inspire praise, "congenial, pleas-ant" service does, and most agree "you will not be disappointed."

Tapas Barcelona *Spanish*

20 | 18 | 19 | $28

Evanston | Northshore Hotel Retirement Home | 1615 Chicago Ave. (bet. Church & Davis Sts.) | 847-866-9900 | www.tapasbarcelona.com

"You can almost picture an Almodóvar scene playing out at the next table" at this "festive", "energetic" Evanston Spaniard where diners leave "happy and satisfied" thanks to "high-quality", "share-friendly" tapas (paella, sandwiches and pizza too) at moderate prices; servers are generally "attentive" and seating on the outdoor patio is "a dream."

Tapas Gitana *Spanish*

23 | 16 | 20 | $35

Lakeview | 3445 N. Halsted St. (bet. Cornelia & Newport Aves.) | 773-296-6046 Ⓜ

Northfield | Northfield Village Ctr. | 310 Happ Rd. (Mt. Pleasant St.) | 847-784-9300

www.tapasgitana.com

"Variety" is the name of the game at this Northfield taparia and its newer Lakeview twin where "classic Spanish ingredients" add an "authentic" touch to a "great selection" of "well-prepared" small plates and paellas; decor might be merely "passable" and service veers between "awesome" and "lacking", but "reasonably priced" wines and overall moderate tabs help make up for it.

Taqueria El Ojo de Agua *Mexican*

- | - | - | I

Bucktown | 2235 N. Western Ave. (Lyndale St.) | 773-235-8807

At this ultracasual taqueria in Bucktown, tortillas made with rustic wood presses are used for burritos and quesadillas stuffed with a choice of six meats, accompanied by several tortas and a handful of entree plates and salads; thirst-slaking options include shakes (e.g. oatmeal, pecan and coconut) and fruit drinks, or you can BYO.

Tasting Room 🅱 *American*

∇ 16 | 20 | 20 | $44

West Loop | 1415 W. Randolph St. (Ogden Ave.) | 312-942-1313 | www.thetastingroomchicago.com

"Impressive" skyline views from the upstairs lounge and "endless wine options" are "the stars" at this "tastefully decorated" West

Loop New American in a "warehouse space" complete with brick-work and overhead ducts; though doubters dub the small and large plates merely "decent" and "a tad overpriced", cushy couches and candlelight still make it a "good place to take a date."

NEW Taverna 750 ● *Italian* ▽ 25 | 26 | 20 | $31

Wrigleyville | 750 W. Cornelia Ave. (Halsted St.) | 773-904-7466 | www.taverna750.com

"Interesting, tasty" small plates and "housemade" liqueur cocktails are offered at "downscale" prices despite the "upscale" setting at this Boys Town Italian; "unique tavern" environs, with brick-lined walls and an outdoor dining option, combine with solid service to make it "great for a date or dinner with friends."

Tavern at the Park ⑤ *American* 17 | 18 | 19 | $44

Loop | 130 E. Randolph St. (Michigan Ave.) | 312-552-0070 | www.tavernatthepark.com

A Loop location complete with an "outdoor patio facing Millennium Park" help make this "cozy" bi-level New American "a good option", especially since "many menu options" ensure "everyone will find something"; it's "reasonably priced" and service is "warm", so even those who find it merely "satisfactory" concede it's "convenient" for "happy-hour cocktails", "power lunches" and pre-event dinners.

NEW Tavernita ● *Spanish* - | - | - | M

River North | 151 W. Erie St. (bet. LaSalle Dr. & Wells St.) | 312-274-1111 | www.tavernita.com

A River North Spaniard with scenester appeal, this midpriced hot spot from chef Ryan Poli (ex Perennial) and the Mercadito team offers Latino-influenced share plates and kegged cocktails in a spacious, wood-trimmed dining room with checked tile floors and globes of warm lighting; the companion pintxo bar, Barcito, showcases one-bite noshes and has limited seats.

Tavern on Rush ● *Steak* 21 | 22 | 20 | $48

Gold Coast | 1031 N. Rush St. (Bellevue Pl.) | 312-664-9600 | www.tavernonrush.com

"See and be seen" at this "major" Gold Coast "hot spot" where the "solid" steakhouse fare comes with a side of "prime people-watching"; an "attractive" staff stays "cheerful even amid the chaos" and there's a "gorgeous" horseshoe bar, so despite somewhat "pricey" tabs it's "always crowded"; P.S. "in summer, the outdoor seating is the heartbeat of Chicago."

Taxim *Greek* 26 | 24 | 24 | $42

Wicker Park | 1558 N. Milwaukee Ave. (Damen Ave.) | 773-252-1558 | www.taximchicago.com

Diners who've gone once "daydream" about the "authentic" "carefully prepared" fare at this moderate Wicker Park Greek where the "flavorful" small and large plates are so "inventive", they're "unlike any other"; a "beautiful", "modern" space featuring archways and vaulted ceilings and "delightful" staffers further ensure it earns "must-try" status.

NEW Telegraph Wine Bar ❶ *American*   23 | 22 | 25 | $39

Logan Square | 2601 N. Milwaukee Ave. (Kedzie Ave.) | 773-292-9463 |
www.telegraphwinebar.com

Oenophiles venture "off the beaten track" to this "warm and cozy"
Logan Square wine bar offering "interesting" Euro-centric bottles
backed by "inventive" New American small plates highlighting seasonal ingredients; "knowledgeable servers" elevate the "cool"
rustic-chic space, and with moderate prices it has all the makings
for an "awesome date place."

Tempo ❶⇄ *Diner*   20 | 12 | 17 | $20

Gold Coast | 6 E. Chestnut St. (State St.) | 312-943-4373 |
www.tempocafechicago.com

Eggs "almost as fluffy as the clouds over Lake Michigan" keep "loyal
devotees" coming to this 24/7 Gold Coast diner, a "favorite" for
breakfasts and "late-night" bites; though warnings include "30-
minute waits" on weekends and occasional "drunk, annoying" wee-
hours eaters, the "well-priced", "quality comfort food" wins over
most; P.S. it's cash-only and BYO is allowed until 10 PM, inside only.

Terzo Piano *Italian*   22 | 25 | 22 | $48

Loop | Art Institute of Chicago | 159 E. Monroe St. (bet. Columbus Dr. &
Michigan Ave.) | 312-443-8650 | www.terzopianochicago.com

The "sublime setting" includes an "open", "minimalist" dining room
"bathed in light from huge windows" and a terrace featuring "knockout views" of the city skyline at this Loop Italian in the Modern Wing
of the Art Institute where chef Tony Mantuano (Spiaggia) delivers
"interesting" farm-to-table lunch fare (and dinner on Thursday); if
pickier diners deem it "overpriced" with "precious" portions, fans
point to "attentive" service and find it "reliable in all respects"; P.S.
Piano Terra, an outdoor extension, opened post-Survey.

Texas de Brazil Churrascaria *Brazilian*   23 | 23 | 24 | $53

River North | 51 E. Ohio St. (bet. Rush St. & Wabash Ave.) | 312-670-1006
Schaumburg | Woodfield Mall | 5 Woodfield Mall (Frontage & Golf Rds.) |
847-413-1600
www.texasdebrazil.com

"Bring your appetite" ("and maybe some Lipitor") in preparation for
a "meat overdose" at these all-you-can-eat Brazilians in River North
and Schaumburg where "attentive" gaucho waiters keep the "high-
quality" cuts coming and a "carnival" of flavors" awaits at the "extensive" salad bar; it's not cheap, but those focused on "pricey" tabs
simply "munch until out of steam"; P.S. the city outpost also has
"cool" "flying acrobats" who retrieve bottles from a showy, two-
story wine cellar.

Thai Pastry *Thai*   25 | 14 | 19 | $20

Uptown | 4925 N. Broadway (Rosemont Ave.) | 773-784-5399
Harwood Heights | 7350 W. Lawrence Ave. (Odell Ave.) | 708-867-8840
www.thaipastry.com

"Authentic" Thai "classics", including "wonderful" curries with
"some spice", are a "good value" at this "unpretentious" Uptowner

| | FOOD | DECOR | SERVICE | COST |

with a Harwood Heights sequel; service is "friendly" and, though the neon interior and nothing-special storefront earn middling marks, those who don't want to dine in can get "prompt" delivery.

3rd Coast Cafe & Wine Bar ● *American*

| 19 | 15 | 18 | $20 |

Gold Coast | 1260 N. Dearborn Pkwy. (Goethe St.) | 312-649-0730 | www.3rdcoastcafe.com

A "quirky mix of college students and older couples" populates this "small, cozy" Gold Coast American where "solid", "basic" eats make it a "go-to breakfast spot" and "nice place" for lunch or an "informal dinner"; a "casual atmosphere and helpful staff" lend a "welcoming feel" and tabs are "moderate", so even those who find it merely "ordinary" concede it's "very convenient."

Three Aces ● *Italian*

| ▽ 24 | 19 | 21 | $28 |

Little Italy/University Village | 1321 W. Taylor St. (bet. Loomis & Throop Sts.) | 312-243-1577 | www.threeaceschicago.com

Though it may look like "Keith Richards' basement bar", this mid-priced "rockabilly gastropub" gives culinary nods to its Little Italy neighborhood while swapping out the mixed nuts and such for grub that goes "way beyond normal bar fare"; service can be "varied", but with a "great beer selection" featuring many Midwestern brews, most barely notice.

NEW III Forks *American/Steak*

| 22 | 24 | 24 | $64 |

Loop | Village Market at Lakeshore East | 333 E. Benton Pl. (Park Dr.) | 312-938-4303 | www.3forks.com

A "gorgeous" Loop setting with floor-to-ceiling windows, fire-places and "the coolest ever rooftop bar" complement the menu of "reliable" chops and "classic" American "standouts" at this "contemporary" Dallas-based addition to the "high-end" steak-house scene; service is "professional" and "personable" too, leading even those "against chains" to say it's "a serious contender" (with prices to match).

Three Happiness ● *Chinese*

| 22 | 11 | 17 | $22 |

Chinatown | 209 W. Cermak Rd. (Wentworth Ave.) | 312-842-1964

"One steamed, one fried, one vegetable: eat, repeat" chant champions of this "real-deal" "dim 'yum'" spot in Chinatown, where trolleys ferry midpriced "choices, choices and more choices" of "authentic" Chinese "snack food"; despite decor that's "nothing special" and weekends that are "quite a scene", it "brings customers back for more"; P.S. it's not related to nearby New Three Happiness.

312 Chicago *Italian*

| 21 | 20 | 21 | $41 |

Loop | Hotel Allegro | 136 N. LaSalle St. (Randolph St.) | 312-696-2420 | www.312chicago.com

"The location is key" for this "elegant" "pre-theater hot spot" in a "historic" Loop building that offers "consistently good" Italian fare via "quick", "professional" servers who further ensure it's a "reliable" choice "before a show" and also "perfect for the business lunch crowd"; if a few sniff it's "not the cheapest", regulars rate it "reasonable" for being "so convenient."

Tiffin *Indian*
20 | 18 | 19 | $24

West Rogers Park | 2536 W. Devon Ave. (Maplewood Ave.) | 773-338-2143 | www.tiffinrestaurant.com

The "reliably good" fare at this West Rogers Park Indian "tastes as if it came right from" the subcontinent with its "large portions" of "family favorites" such as chicken tikka masala and "succulent lamb chops" offered at prices "low enough not to complain"; "civilized" service, a "well-kept" setting and a "quite serviceable" lunch buffet round out the package.

Tin Fish *Seafood*
25 | 20 | 21 | $44

Tinley Park | Cornerstone Ctr. | 18201 S. Harlem Ave. (183rd St.) | 708-532-0200 | www.tinfishrestaurant.com

Seafood is the "expected star" at this Tinley Parker where the "well-prepared" fare, including customizable "mix-and-match" options (you choose the preparation and sides), gets a boost from the "well-chosen wine list"; pictures of fish decorate the upscale-casual space, and with "helpful" staffers and "fair prices" don't be surprised if you "have to wait."

Toast *American*
23 | 16 | 18 | $18

Lincoln Park | 746 W. Webster Ave. (Halsted St.) | 773-935-5600
Bucktown | 2046 N. Damen Ave. (bet. Dickens & McLean Aves.) | 773-772-5600
www.toast-chicago.com

Go "healthy" or go "decadent" at these American "perfect little brunch spots" in Lincoln Park and Bucktown dishing out affordable, "inventive", "hangover-curing" breakfast and lunch fare daily; though some grouse about the "cramped" interiors and "long waits on weekends", service is "always competent" (if only "sometimes friendly").

Tocco *Italian*
- | - | - | E

Bucktown | 1266 N. Milwaukee Ave. (bet. Ashland Ave. & Paulina St.) | 773-687-8895 | www.toccochicago.com

Surveyors visit this Bucktown Italian for "incredible pastas" and "Neapolitan-style" pizza with "appropriately blackened" crusts as "wafer-thin" as the upscale clientele; with a "mighty sleek" pink-and-white dining room and an accommodating staff, those in the know dub it "one of Chicago's best-kept secrets."

NEW Todoroki Hibachi & Sushi *Japanese*
- | - | - | M

Evanston | 526 Davis St. (bet. Chicago & Hinman Aves.) | 847-750-6565 | www.mytodoroki.com

Japanese steakhouse showmanship involving knives and flames constitute the 'turf' side of this reasonably priced Evanston BYO, while sushi both classic and creative (including all-you-can-eat options) comprises the 'surf'; the divided dining areas offer hibachi grill seating, a sushi bar, long leather banquettes and bare tables, as well as tatami rooms and modern artwork.

	FOOD	DECOR	SERVICE	COST

NEW Tokio Pub ⑤ *Japanese* — | — | — | M

Schaumburg | 1900 E. Higgins Rd. (Rte. 53) | 847-278-5181 | www.tokiopub.com

"Surprisingly edgy" and "hip" for its Schaumburg setting, this Japanese fusioner offers "inexpensive" small plates and "interesting" cocktails delivered by "helpful" servers; the less-impressed carp about "subpar" sushi, suggesting it "needs a tune up."

NEW Tokyo 21 Asian Pub ● *Asian* — | — | — | M

Old Town | 1400 N. Wells St. (Schiller St.) | 312-664-1900 | www.tokyo21asianpub.com

Set in the former Kamehachi Old Town space, this izakaya-style spot serves Asian pub fare like dumplings and noodles, mixed grill goodies from yakitori to kalbi, and some twists on sliders and tacos, paired with 21 'sake bombs' (including a splurge version with gold leaf); the space now sports a rustic-chic look with distressed wood and metal, leather stools and banquettes, a fireplace and TVs over the concrete bar, and locals will be glad to see the return of a secluded outdoor patio.

Tom & Eddie's *Burgers* 17 | 14 | 17 | $16

NEW Deerfield | 740 Waukegan Road (bet. Deerfield Rd. & Osterman Ave.) | 847-948-5117
NEW Vernon Hills | 1260 S. Milwaukee Ave. (Old Half Day Rd.) | 847-478-1019
Geneva | The Shops at Geneva Commons | 1042 Commons Dr. (bet. Bricher Rd. & Williamsburg Ave.) | 630-208-1351
Lombard | The Shops on Butterfield | 348 Yorktown Ctr. (bet. Butterfield Rd. & Highland Ave.) | 630-705-9850
www.tomandeddies.com

"It's not your typical burger joint" say groupies of this northwest suburbs counter-service mini-chain turning out "inventive" burgers in "a wonderful variety" of options including turkey, ahi tuna and edamame patties, plus loads of topping and sauce choices too; though some deem the offerings "overrated" and "a bit pricey", a Coca-Cola Freestyle machine with some 125 flavor combos is a "cool touch"; P.S. a Naperville location is planned.

Top Notch Beefburger ⑤🍴 *Burgers* ▽ 26 | 13 | 21 | $12

Far South Side | 2116 W. 95th St. (bet. Hamilton & Hoyne Aves.) | 773-445-7218

Since 1942 this "local gem" on the Far South Side has been slinging "mouthwatering" burgers (they grind their own meat daily), beef fat fries and "awesome" chocolate shakes; "prices are great" and service is solid, so surveyors say just "forget about the decor" and focus on the "hearty, homemade food" with a side of "tradition."

Topo Gigio Ristorante *Italian* 26 | 21 | 24 | $38

Old Town | 1516 N. Wells St. (bet. North Ave. & Schiller St.) | 312-266-9355 | www.topogigiochicago.com

Diners "keep going back" to this "casual" Old Town "standout" for "pasta done perfectly" and other "authentic" "Italian favorites" at "moderate prices"; "charming" service also helps keep it a "popular" local hangout", especially in summer when the "lively" patio provides ample "people-watching."

Z Topolobampo 🔲🅼 *Mexican* — 28 | 24 | 26 | $70

River North | 445 N. Clark St. (Illinois St.) | 312-661-1434 | www.rickbayless.com

Celeb chef Rick Bayless "wrote the book on fine Mexican cuisine" (literally and figuratively) and he "keeps rewriting it" by "setting new standards" at his "upscale" River North "institution" where "inventive", "refined interpretations" result in "sublime", "mind-melting" moles and other "subtle" yet "complex" dishes served alongside "gold standard margaritas"; "kind", "informative" servers are "as comforting as family" in the "elegant", art-enhanced dining room, so "if you win the fight to land a reservation, you will be a very happy camper"; P.S. for a "cheaper" experience try the adjoining Frontera Grill.

NEW Topper's Pizza ➊ *Pizza/Sandwiches* — | - | - | I

Greektown | 120 S. Halsted St. (bet. Adams & Monroe Sts.) | 312-226-6664 | www.toppers.com

This 20-year-old Wisconsin chain has put down roots in Greektown, offering crispy, hand-tossed pies (or you can opt for a breadstick-crust variation) with whimsical toppings like mac 'n' cheese, potato skins and gyro ingredients, plus other budget-friendly fare including wings and grinders; the funky, bright storefront is mostly geared toward delivery and takeout, although there are about 10 seats.

Toro Sushi 🅼 *Japanese* — ▽ 28 | 14 | 22 | $26

Lincoln Park | 2546 N. Clark St. (bet. Deming Pl. & Wrightwood Ave.) | 773-348-4877 | www.torosushi.biz

A "cult following" clamors for "talented" chef-owner Mitch Kim's "fresh", "imaginative" sushi at this "tiny", affordable Lincoln Park BYO; "you don't come for the ease of getting a table, the prompt service or the decor" but it's still a "favorite" of many, though it "pains" them to say so since "the wait is long enough already."

NEW Township ⇧ *Eclectic/Coffeehouse* — | - | - | I

Logan Square | 2200 N. California Ave. (Palmer St.) | 773-384-1865 | www.townshipchicago.com

A funky fusion of restaurant, stage venue and coffee shop, this cash-only Logan Square lair serves Eclectic eats from Indian-accented and veggie options to a caprese panini and beer-battered cod sandwich, with brunch bites including bagels, various Benedicts and pakora pancakes; beverages range from coffee drinks to 60 craft beers and specialty cocktails, which help the back stage room rock late with live music.

Tozi *Korean* — | - | - | M

Wicker Park | 1265 N. Milwaukee Ave. (bet. N. Ashland Ave. & N. Paulina St.) | 773-252-2020 | www.tozirestaurant.com

Tabletop grilling of multiple meats and offal woos Wicker Parkers to this moderately priced Korean arrival, which also serves a menu of kitchen-cooked fare like pancakes and dumplings, noodles and rice bowls, stews and hot pots (plus bargain lunches) and full bar service highlighted by soju and specialty martinis; the warmly lit modern space features calligraphy panels, wood booths, walls of windows, a bar with space-age stools and (whew!) effective ventilation.

Tramonto's Steak & Seafood *Seafood/Steak*

21 | 23 | 21 | $60

Wheeling | Westin Chicago North Shore | 601 N. Milwaukee Ave. (Lake Cook Rd.) | 847-777-6575 | www.westinnorthshore.com
Though namesake chef Rick Tramonto is no longer in-house, patrons promise this "haute" surf 'n' turfer at the Wheeling Westin remains "worth" the trek with its "gorgeous" waterfall wall-enhanced setting, "well-prepared steaks" and "sure-bet" fish dishes; though specials at "reasonable" prices have their fans, detractors deem it "overpriced" and the service "inconsistent" (sometimes "incredible", sometimes "spotty"), saying the experience "has declined in quality."

Trattoria D.O.C. *Italian*

20 | 17 | 21 | $32

Evanston | 706 Main St. (Custer Ave.) | 847-475-1111 | www.trattoria-doc.com
Despite being "hidden" on a "quiet" street in Evanston, this "homey" Italian is "always busy" thanks to "reliable all-day dining" and a "friendly" staff; pasta fans praise the "fresh ingredients" and "inventive variations on familiar themes" while "moderate prices" and roomy digs make it a "great option for families" and other locals.

Trattoria Gianni Ⓜ *Italian*

20 | 18 | 22 | $38

Lincoln Park | 1711 N. Halsted St. (bet. North Ave. & Willow St.) | 312-266-1976 | www.trattoriagianni.com
Located across the street from Lincoln Park's Steppenwolf theater, this midpriced Italian is a "good choice for pre- or post-theater dining" on "tasty, traditional" fare; service is "without pretension", but dissenters say that the atmosphere is "plain" and the menu "needs an overhaul" to compete with culinary "greats up the street."

Trattoria No. 10 Ⓢ *Italian*

25 | 21 | 24 | $47

Loop | 10 N. Dearborn St. (bet. Madison & Washington Sts.) | 312-984-1718 | www.trattoriaten.com
"Excellent" risotto, "dreamy" homemade ravioli and other "fantastico" Italian dishes crafted with "quality ingredients" are "not crazily priced" at this "charming" Loop lair whose "underground location helps keep down outside noise"; "capable", "speedy" service suits it to business lunches or "pre- or post-theater" meals, while early birds "go at 5 and graze" the lavish bar buffet.

Trattoria Roma *Italian*

23 | 21 | 22 | $36

Old Town | 1535 N. Wells St. (bet. North Ave. & Schiller St.) | 312-664-7907 | www.trattoriaroma.com
"Fresh, homemade pastas" and other "simple and delicious" Italian fare is served in a "charming, old-world club atmosphere" at this Old Town trattoria; with "attentive" service and "affordable" prices it's clear why "lots of locals" call it their "favorite haunt."

	FOOD	DECOR	SERVICE	COST

Tre Kronor *Scandinavian* | 25 | 20 | 23 | $20

Albany Park | 3258 W. Foster Ave. (bet. Sawyer & Spaulding Aves.) | 773-267-9888 | www.trekronorrestaurant.com

"Herring worshipers" who "long for the old country" feast on "lovingly prepared" Scandinavian fare (breakfast is a particular "favorite") at this "value" Albany Park BYO; "elves dancing on the walls" and a "lovely patio" add to the "rustic charm", while service "makes you feel like family" – no wonder locals feel so "lucky."

NEW Troquet ● *French* | - | - | - | I

Ravenswood | 1834 W. Montrose Ave. (Wolcott St.) | 773-334-5664 | www.troquetchicago.com

The LM group's quaint corner tavern with a French accent takes over the Ravenswood residence of Wolcott's with a budget-friendly menu of small plates (moules frites, quiche, fromage and charcuterie), sandwiches and entrees (pork belly, duck confit) paired with a handful of wines, Gallic cocktails and craft brews on tap; the welcoming, wood-on-wood room includes an open kitchen, a long bar with TVs and evocative black-and-white photography.

Z Tru Ⓢ *French* | 28 | 27 | 28 | $129

Streeterville | 676 N. St. Clair St. (bet. Erie & Huron Sts.) | 312-202-0001 | www.trurestaurant.com

A "true pampering experience" awaits at this Streeterville "bastion of epicurean splendor" where Anthony Martin's "creative, sometimes daring" New French tasting menus are "beautifully presented" and offered alongside "excellent wine recommendations"; "world-class" servers manage to be "both ballerinas and ninjas at the same time" and the "minimalist yet elegant" "art-filled room" is "serene", so admirers attest it's "excellent in every respect" – just "plan to stay awhile and spend a lot"; P.S. jackets required.

Tsukasa of Tokyo *Japanese* | 24 | 23 | 24 | $39

Vernon Hills | 561 N. Milwaukee Ave. (E. Townline Rd) | 847-816-8770 | www.tsukasaoftokyo.com

Kids and adults "have a ball" watching the "friendly" chefs "flip their food" at this "top-notch" Vernon Hills teppanyaki that's an "entertaining" alternative to Japanese chain counterparts; while the hibachi fare "hits the spot", it can also "hit the pocketbook", though surveyors shrug it off as the price of "the show."

Tufano's Vernon Park Tap Ⓜ🍴 *Italian* | 24 | 16 | 21 | $26

Little Italy/University Village | 1073 W. Vernon Park Pl. (Carpenter St.) | 312-733-3393 | www.tufanosrestaurant.com

Open since 1930, this "fourth-generation family place" in University Village is a "casual" "Chicago classic", "attracting a loyal following" with "authentic Italian home cooking" delivered by servers with "gruff charm"; "checkered tablecloths" and a *Godfather* feel further make it a "true character place", just be warned it's cash-only and doesn't accept reservations.

	FOOD	DECOR	SERVICE	COST

NEW Tuman's Tap & Grill *American*

-	-	-	I

Ukrainian Village | 2159 W. Chicago Ave. (Leavitt St.) | 773-782-1400

The former Tuman's Tavern (once notorious for its Alcohol Abuse Center sign, now hanging inside) has been revamped into this casual Ukrainian Village respite serving seasonal, chef-driven American pub food accompanied by 28 rotating brews on tap; the vintage tavern setting with outdoor seating makes room for some modern touches like black leather booths, TVs screening sporting events, free WiFi and an on-site ATM.

Turquoise *Turkish*

25	19	22	$34

Roscoe Village | 2147 W. Roscoe St. (bet. Hamilton Ave. & Leavitt St.) | 773-549-3523 | www.turquoisedining.com

A "Turkish delight" laud loyalists of the "flavorful", "exquisitely prepared" plates at this "value" Roscoe Villager with casual, white-tablecloth environs and a "low noise level" fit for "big groups" and "first dates" alike; there's also "pleasant sidewalk seating", so though service can be "slow" when it's "packed", it remains a "favorite local spot."

Tuscany *Italian*

23	20	22	$41

Little Italy/University Village | 1014 W. Taylor St. (Morgan St.) | 312-829-1990

Wheeling | 550 S. Milwaukee Ave. (Manchester Dr.) | 847-465-9988

Oak Brook | 1415 W. 22nd St. (Rte. 83) | 630-990-1993 ⓢ

Stefani's Tuscany Cafe ⓢⓂ *Italian*

Loop | United Bldg. | 77 W. Wacker Dr. (N. Clark St.) | 312-252-0863

O'Hare Area | O'Hare Int'l Airport | Terminal 1, Concourse B (I-190)

O'Hare Area | O'Hare Int'l Airport | Terminal 1, Concourse C (60666)

www.tuscanychicago.com

"Authentic" "homestyle" Italian fare comes in "big portions" and is ferried by "experienced" servers at this trio from Phil Stefani (Riva, Tavern on Rush); regulars "love" the trattoria setting, saying it's as suitable for a "special occasion" as for "more frequent dining", considering the "fair" prices; P.S. the cafes at the United Building and the airport are quick-serve spots.

Tweet ⌷ *American*

26	20	23	$19

Uptown | 5020 N. Sheridan Rd. (Argyle St.) | 773-728-5576 | www.tweet.biz

A local "favorite", this cash-only Uptown American is known for its "incredible variety" of "uniformly excellent" breakfast and lunch dishes (including "standout specials"); a "helpful" staff brightens the small art-enhanced space, and savvy types say "get there early because waits can be long" – or just "sit at the bar, grab a mimosa or Bloody Mary and relax before you're called."

NEW 25 Degrees *Burgers*

∇ 22	20	21	$23

River North | 736 N. Clark St. (bet. Grand Ave. & Ohio St.) | 312-943-9700 | www.25degreesrestaurant.com

"Imaginative burgers", including a "build-your-own" option, are joined by sandwiches, sides, "adult milkshakes" and "refreshing" cocktails at this "casual", "modernistic" River North chain link; it may be "a little pricey" for what's on offer, but loyalists "love the atmosphere" and "bar scene" ("no place for old men"); P.S. outdoor tables are "lovely during the warm months."

Twin Anchors *BBQ* | 22 | 15 | 19 | $29 |

Old Town | 1655 N. Sedgwick St. (bet. Eugenie St. & North Ave.) | 312-266-1616 | www.twinanchorsribs.com

"Steeped in history", this midpriced Old Town barbecue "benchmark" and Sinatra favorite owes its long-standing popularity to "fall-off-the-bone" ribs and "lively" servers; the setting is either "dated or classic – depending on your POV", and while waits can be "brutally long", regulars insist it's "worth every minute"; P.S. no reservations.

Twisted Spoke ● *Pub Food* | 20 | 16 | 18 | $21 |

Noble Square | 501 N. Ogden Ave. (Grand Ave.) | 312-666-1500 | www.twistedspoke.com

Your "basic neighborhood biker bar", this Noble Square stop slings solid burgers and other "quite filling" midpriced pub grub while pouring "slammin' Bloody Marys"; the staff provides "service with an edge" (while on some nights "X-rated TV screens" play), and whether patrons call it "funky" and "casual" or just " a dump", most agree "it's fun to try at least once."

NEW 2 Sparrows *American* | 20 | 19 | 19 | $23 |

Lincoln Park | 553 W. Diversey Pkwy. (bet. Hampden & Lehmann Cts.) | 773-234-2320 | www.2sparrowschicago.com

Fans of this "charming" Lincoln Park "'in' spot" from Trotter's alums nestle in for "creative" and "indulgent" New American breakfast, brunch and lunch fare ("foie gras pop tarts, bacon donuts"), plus a "fantastic drink selection" served in "cool", "easy surroundings" with "brilliant natural lighting"; if a few aren't "impressed", citing service "kinks" and "long waits", those who see "tons of potential" would "try it again."

NEW Umami *Asian* | - | - | - | M |

Little Italy/University Village | 1311 W. Taylor St. (Throop St.) | 312-226-8117 | www.umamichicago.com

In a nod to the elusive fifth flavor, this Little Italy BYO brings assorted Asian eats (Japanese, Thai, Chinese), including lots of signature sushi rolls and a luscious variety of smoothies and bubble teas, though note that there's no alcohol; the casually hip setting has wood bench and table seating with golden walls, tile floors and glowing pendant lights; P.S. with its proximity to UIC campus, students get a 15% discount.

Uncle Bub's *BBQ* | 24 | 16 | 20 | $19 |

Westmont | 132 S. Cass Ave. (bet. Dallas & Richmond Sts.) | 630-493-9000 | www.unclebubs.com

"Tie on a bib and dig in" coach fans of this wallet-friendly "Southern rib joint" in Westmont, where you order "awesome" "smoky BBQ" from "efficient" servers at the counter before chowing down in a "comfortably rustic setting"; it's all ultra-"casual" – so "when you spill the sauce on yourself it won't matter."

	FOOD	DECOR	SERVICE	COST

Uncle Julio's Hacienda ● *Tex-Mex* | 19 | 17 | 18 | $29 |

Old Town | 855 W. North Ave. (Clybourn Ave.) | 312-266-4222
Lombard | 2360 Fountain Square Dr. (Butterfield Rd.) |
630-705-9260
www.unclejulios.com

"Best enjoyed with a group", this "lively" midpriced national Tex-Mex chain link Downtown (with a Lombard twin) lures the masses with just-made tortillas and "signature swirl" margaritas; service is decent in the "cavernous, noisy" space, and though even fans agree its "food lacks imagination", it remains "popular" – and "kid-friendly" too.

Uncommon Ground *Coffeehouse/Eclectic* | 23 | 21 | 20 | $28 |

Edgewater | 1401 W. Devon Ave. (Glenwood Ave.) |
773-465-9801
Lakeview | 3800 N. Clark St. (Grace St.) | 773-929-3680
www.uncommonground.com

With a "delicious" menu so local some produce comes from "their own rooftop garden", these Eclectic "green" coffeehouses in Edgewater and Lakeview only seem "overpriced" "until you experience the quality of the ingredients"; while service varies, a "stellar beer selection" and "laid-back" ambiance are pluses – and "don't forget to check out the bands" (nightly at both locales).

Union Pizzeria *Pizza* | 21 | 18 | 18 | $28 |

Evanston | 1245 Chicago Ave. (bet. Dempster & Hamilton Sts.) |
847-475-2400 | www.unionevanston.com

"Lovely" wood-fired pizzas and "interesting" small plates "perfect for sharing" provide "good value" at this "hip" Evanston pizzeria with solid service and an "airy, funky atmosphere"; what some call "loud and crowded" others dub "happy noise", but it's indisputably convenient before a show at Space, the "thriving" music venue that shares the building.

🆕 Union Sushi + Barbeque Bar *Japanese* | 22 | 25 | 21 | $40 |

River North | 230 W. Erie St. (Franklin St.) | 312-662-4888 |
www.eatatunion.com

"Clever ingredients", "unique rolls" and "creative items" from the robata grill set this midpriced River North Japanese "apart from the competition" while its "casual" but "upscale" "open space" bedecked with grafiitti and other urban stylings make it "very cool and trendy"; service rates highly too and tabs are moderate, so even if sushi purists complain that "raw ingredients are hard to find", it remains a "popular" pick.

Urbanbelly Ⓜ *Asian/Noodle Shop* | 25 | 16 | 17 | $21 |

Logan Square | 3053 N. California Ave. (bet. Barry Ave. & Nelson St.) |
773-583-0500 | www.urbanbellychicago.com

"Interesting", "addictive" Asian fusion fare like "satisfying, belly-warming noodles" and "divine dumplings" are "elevated to a high level with quality, flavor and care" at "genius" chef-owner Bill Kim's counter-service Logan Square BYO; given "efficient" staffers and tabs "priced right" most "don't mind sitting at community tables" in the "unassuming", "hipster"-ish digs – and those who do simply "take it to go."

NEW Urban Union American

`-` | `-` | `-` | M

Little Italy/University Village | 1421 W. Taylor St. (bet. Laflin & Loomis Sts.) | 312-929-4302 | www.urbanunionchicago.com
Chef Michael Shrader (ex N9ne, Epic) prepares New American small plates (with seafood and vegetables outnumbering meats) offered alongside craft cocktails and a few dozen by-the-glass wines (including six on tap) at this midpriced Little Italy respite; rustic-chic design highlights include industrial light fixtures, a wood-burning oven in the open kitchen and a repurposed antique welding table where a 'chef's whim' tasting menu is served communally.

NEW Vapiano ● Italian/Pizza

▽ 17 | 21 | 14 | $21

Lincoln Park | 2577 N. Clark St. (Wrightwood Ave.) | 773-904-7984 | www.vapianointernational.com
Boutique hotel atmosphere meets modern food court at this Lincoln Park link of the "semi-self-service" chain where multiple Italian-focused stations (pastas, pizzas, panini) give guests "lots of choices"; seating options include a plush red lounge and two modern dining areas, and while detractors dub it "just ok", others find it "reasonable, tasty and quick."

NEW Vera ●M Spanish

▽ 24 | 21 | 25 | $63

West Loop | 1023 W. Lake St. (bet. Carpenter & Morgan Sts.) | 312-243-9770 | www.verachicago.com
"High-quality" Spanish small plates form a "festival of flavor" at this spendy West Loop wine bar from ex-Carnivale employees, where a "lively" yet intimate space with exposed brick and Edison bulb lighting helps create an appealing "environment for a night out"; "superb" staffers are a big plus, as is an ambitious sherry and global vino list (including some poured by tap); P.S. no reservations.

Vermilion Indian/Nuevo Latino

23 | 22 | 20 | $52

River North | 10 W. Hubbard St. (bet. Dearborn & State Sts.) | 312-527-4060 | www.thevermilionrestaurant.com
Indian and Latin flavors "pop" at this pricey River North "fusion concept" (with an NYC sib), where artfully presented "eclectic", "spicy" fare, "sophisticated" decor featuring fashion photography and "courteous" service combine; though a few find the "innovative" model to be "ill-conceived", most say it's an "appealing" food adventure."

Via Carducci Italian

21 | 18 | 21 | $35

Lincoln Park | 1419 W. Fullerton Ave. (bet. Janssen & Southport Aves.) | 773-665-1981

Via Carducci La Sorella Italian
Wicker Park | 1928 W. Division St. (Winchester Ave.) | 773-252-2246
www.viacarducci-lasorella.com
Wicker Park and Lincoln Park locals swing by these midpriced "family places" for "authentic" Southern Italian standards including thin-

crust pizza and rotini Santa Lucia (with sausage and tomato-cream sauce); unassuming "neighborhood" settings and "attentive, pleasant" service further prompt patrons to "recommend and return."

Viaggio 🗷🅜 *Italian* ▽ 26 | 20 | 23 | $42

Near West | 1330 W. Madison St. (Odgen Ave.) | 312-829-3333 | www.viaggiochicago.com

Even mama "would have loved" this slightly spendy Near West Italian say loyalists who crave the "wonderful selection" of dishes including the signature pork chop Parmesan and "go-to" meatball salad ("yeah, you read right"); warm wood details and white tablecloths create a classy vibe, and "great service" helps it "feel like the place where everyone knows you."

🖾 Vie *American* 29 | 26 | 28 | $68

Western Springs | 4471 Lawn Ave. (Burlington Ave.) | 708-246-2082 | www.vierestaurant.com

For a "gourmet experience miles from the Loop", foodies head to this "exceptional" Western Springs New American, a "culinary jewel" from Paul Virant (Perennial Virant) who "treats the freshest ingredients with great respect" while crafting "outstanding, inventive" plates highlighting "subtle spices and textures"; "thoughtful", "well-timed" service and a "beautiful" dining room featuring "mostly black and white decor" further make for an "incomparable" experience, especially since it's "reasonably priced" given its caliber.

The Village ● *Italian* 22 | 24 | 22 | $33

Loop | Italian Vill. | 71 W. Monroe St., 2nd fl. (bet. Clark & Dearborn Sts.) | 312-332-7005 | www.italianvillage-chicago.com

"Twinkling lights" and "hidden booths" await at this "charming" "old-world" "standby", a part of the Capitanini family's "red-sauce Italian" trio in the Loop that's been "around forever" thanks to "dependable" "homestyle" food at affordable prices, a "mammoth" wine list and waiters who are "pros"; even those who find it "boring" concede it often "hits the spot."

Vincent 🅜 *European* 21 | 20 | 23 | $40

Andersonville | 1475 W. Balmoral Ave. (bet. Clark St. & Glenwood Ave.) | 773-334-7168 | www.vincentchicago.com

Some "crazy, Amsterdam-good" Dutch dishes still remain on the new Northern European menu offered at this "upscale yet casual" Andersonville bistro with a "local feel"; moderate prices coupled with admirable service in cozy confines with a zinc bar make patrons want to "stay all night"; P.S. a post–Survey chef change is not reflected in the Food score.

Vinci 🅜 *Italian* 22 | 19 | 22 | $41

Lincoln Park | 1732 N. Halsted St. (Willow St.) | 312-266-1199 | www.vincichicago.com

Theatergoers choose this "low-key", "fairly priced" Lincoln Park trattoria "near the Steppenwolf" for its "consistently well-prepared" "classic" Italian dishes delivered with "attentive, warm" service;

regulars add the "pleasantness" of the villa-like surroundings as another reason it's an "old reliable favorite."

Vito & Nick's ⊘ *Pizza*   26 | 13 | 19 | $22

Far South Side | 8433 S. Pulaski Rd. (84th Pl.) | 773-735-2050 | www.vitoandnick.com

"Thin crust rules" at this South Side pizza "icon" dishing out "awesome" pies that groupies grade some of the "best in Chicago"; "carpet on the walls" and "funky" decor "reminiscent of a grandmother's basement in the 1960s" is "so bad that it's good", and with "decent prices" and generally solid service, it's "packed every night of the week" (insiders keep it on "speed dial" for takeout too).

Vivere ☒ *Italian*   24 | 24 | 24 | $50

Loop | Italian Vill. | 71 W. Monroe St. (bet. Clark & Dearborn Sts.) | 312-332-4040 | www.vivere-chicago.com

Deemed the Italian Village's "fanciest" option, this Loop entry offers a "festive" baroque gold and velvet-trimmed dining room as a backdrop for "upscale", "quality" fare and a "comprehensive" wine list delivered by an "excellent" staff; true, it's "a little expensive", but then that's the price of "the good life."

Vivo *Italian*   23 | 22 | 20 | $42

West Loop | 838 W. Randolph St. (bet. Green & Peoria Sts.) | 312-733-3379 | www.vivo-chicago.com

"Still chic" after some 20 years, this "upscale" West Loop Italian housed in a "loft-ish, industrial" space offers "delicious" classics in environs that are "a bit more exciting" than usual ("request the elevator shaft table" above the main floor for special occasions); add in "polite and prompt" service and regulars insist it "will never go out of style."

Volare *Italian*   24 | 19 | 22 | $39

Streeterville | 201 E. Grand Ave. (St. Clair St.) | 312-410-9900
Oakbrook Terrace | 1919 S. Meyers Rd. (22nd St.) | 630-495-0200
www.volarerestaurant.com

"It's always crowded, so come early" to these "red-gravy" Italians in Streeterville and Oakbrook Terrace dishing out "overall excellent" heaps of "moderately priced" "homestyle cooking" with "accommodating", "family-friendly" service; "close-together" tables, "noise" and all, supporters "keep coming back"; P.S. outdoor seating is "perfect in summer."

The Walnut Room *American*   18 | 24 | 20 | $31

Loop | Macy's | 111 N. State St. (bet. Randolph & Washington Sts.) | 312-781-3125 | www.visitmacyschicago.com

A "longtime Loop staple" set in Macy's, this American decked out in Russian Circassian walnut paneling and Austrian chandeliers vends "basic" fare that "doesn't quite match the elegant surroundings" (though you can still order the storied chicken pot pie); nostalgics note "it's not the same" as it once was, but many concur it's a "must-go" during the holidays when it's a "Christmas tradition" and "the stuff family memories are made of."

	FOOD	DECOR	SERVICE	COST

NEW Wasabi Cafe *Japanese*

| - | - | - | M |

North Center/St. Ben's | 3908 N. Lincoln Ave. (bet. Byron St. & Larchmont Ave.) | 773-698-6252 | www.wasabicafe.com

This moderately priced North Center Japanese serves a full complement of raw and cooked cuisine, accompanied by a thoughtful sake selection; the low-lit space with a sushi bar features glass-block dividers, acid-green walls and black lacquered tables.

Weber Grill *BBQ*

| 21 | 18 | 20 | $36 |

River North | Hilton Garden Inn | 10 E. Grand Ave. (State St.) | 312-467-9696

Schaumburg | 1010 N. Meacham Rd. (American Ln.) | 847-413-0800

Lombard | 2331 Fountain Square Dr. (bet. Butterfield & Meyers Rds.) | 630-953-8880

www.webergrillrestaurant.com

"A step up from the backyard barbecue", this midpriced all-American trio features an "exhibition kitchen" concept where grill masters flip "reliably good" steaks, patties, pork ribs and more on giant Weber kettles; service is "friendly", and though eager eaters claim it's "always clogged with people", it's still "worth the trip."

Webster's Wine Bar ● *Eclectic*

| 19 | 20 | 20 | $35 |

Lincoln Park | 1480 W. Webster Ave. (bet. Ashland Ave. & Clybourn St.) | 773-868-0608 | www.websterwinebar.com

Oenophiles may come to this "cozy, romantic" Lincoln Park wine bar for the "killer" 500-bottle list (some 40 by the glass) and frequent tasting events tended by knowledgeable servers; the moderately priced menu of Eclectic small plates "is a pleasant surprise" too, further making it a "nice date place."

NEW Wellfleet ⊠ *Seafood*

| - | - | - | M |

Albany Park | 4423 N. Elston Ave. (Montrose Ave.) | 773-283-7400 | www.fishguy.com

Longtime Albany Park seafood purveyor Bill Dugan has expanded his former temporary in-house restaurant to this petite BYO inside the Fish Guy Market serving a rotating menu of simply prepared fin-focused offerings plus New Haven–style pizzas; the rehabbed store features a stainless-steel dining counter set amid display cases and mounted game fish; P.S. dinner's in the works, as is a liquor license.

West Egg Cafe *Diner*

| 19 | 10 | 15 | $18 |

Near North | 620 N. Fairbanks Ct. (bet. Ohio & Ontario Sts.) | 312-280-8366

Bright and "bustling", this casual, "always crowded" Near North American diner offers egg creations, sandwiches and ultra-early eats that are a "must-have after a long night out"; "potentially long waits" come with the territory on weekends; P.S. closes at 6 PM.

NEW Westminster Hot Dog ⊠ *Hot Dogs*

| ▽ 18 | 6 | 12 | $10 |

Loop | 11 N. Wells St. (bet. Calhoun Pl. & Madison St.) | 312-445-9514 | www.westminsterhotdog.com

"High-end" hot dogs and specialty sausages (bison, anyone?) are "made fresh on the premises", and topped with "creative" extras like avocado ranch dressing and sundried-tomato pesto at this counter-service Loop lunch spot; though the cheap prices come with a "hole-in-the-wall" setting, the "deliciousness-to-convenience factor is a plus."

ⲚⲈⲰ West on North *American*   – | – | – | I

Humboldt Park | 2509 W. North Ave. (bet. Campbell & Maplewood Aves.) | 773-278-7710

Hearty, budget-friendly American comfort food (flatbreads, burgers, mac 'n' cheese) with some tongue-in-cheek twists – think deep-fried pickles and Twinkies, bacon pretzel sticks and cheesecake chimichangas – is the draw at this casual, family-friendly Humboldt Park haunt serving lunch, dinner and weekend brunch; the casual, family-friendly setting includes compass-topped tables, black booths, multiple TVs and retro barstools, and there's also fenced patio seating.

West Town Tavern ⊠ *American*   26 | 23 | 24 | $43

Noble Square | 1329 W. Chicago Ave. (Throop St.) | 312-666-6175 | www.westtowntavern.com

Situated in "up-and-coming" Noble Square, this "reliably splendid" American offers chef Susan Goss' "well-thought-out" "gourmet comfort food" "with a contemporary spin" in "welcoming" wood and brick-lined environs; with "value" tabs and a staff that "makes you feel like you're part of the family", it's "the rare place that can be both everyday and special occasion."

ⲚⲈⲰ Wheel House ● *Burgers/Pub Food*   – | – | – | I

Wrigleyville | 3553 N. Southport Ave. (bet. Addison & Eddy Sts.) | 773-325-0123 | www.messnerschicago.com

Baseball-themed burgers, bar starters and build-your-own mac 'n' cheese go well with a big list of craft brews, signature cocktails and whiskey flights at this casual, budget-friendly Wrigleyville way-station; the cozy, warm tavern vibe is set by a long wood bar, rustic brick walls and vintage black-and-white photos and film reels.

White Fence Farm Ⓜ *American*   24 | 18 | 21 | $23

Romeoville | 1376 Joliet Rd. (Bolingbrook Dr.) | 630-739-1720 | www.whitefencefarm-il.com

Since the 1950s, "old-time customers" and their broods have been flocking to this affordable American comfort-fooder in Romeoville, where fried chicken "way better than mom's" can be smelled even "from the parking lot"; "quick" service and a "throwback" setting add to the "family-friendly" vibe, as do the on-site petting zoo and auto museum.

White Palace Grill ●⊠Ⓜ *Diner*   21 | 16 | 20 | $15

South Loop | 1159 S. Canal St. (Roosevelt Rd.) | 312-939-7167 | www.whitepalacegrill.com

Ideal for "late-night grease" and "enormous portions" of breakfast eats from a "never-ending" menu, this 24/7 South Loop diner also offers "fast" service and palatable prices; despite decor that's almost "nonexistent", surveyors say "you'll be back" to visit.

	FOOD	DECOR	SERVICE	COST

⛫ Wholly Frijoles ⊠ *Mexican*   27 | 16 | 21 | $22

Lincolnwood | 3908 W. Touhy Ave. (Prairie Rd.) | 847-329-9810 |
www.whollyfrijoles.net

It may have the "worst name in greater Chicago", but this "bargain"-
priced Lincolnwood BYO "deserves the crowds" for its *magnifico*
"mouthwatering" Mexican fare "prepared and presented with a
gourmet hand"; service gets high marks too, so the only complaint
is that its "small, tight" space means "getting in isn't easy."

Wiener's Circle ●⇄ *Hot Dogs*   19 | 5 | 12 | $10

Lincoln Park | 2622 N. Clark St. (Wrightwood Ave.) | 773-477-7444 |
www.wienercircle.net

In the wee hours, "manners get tossed out the window" at this cheap
Lincoln Park hot dog "dive", where late-nighters line up for the leg-
endarily "crude" "humor and abuse" dealt by "obscenity-screaming"
cashiers when ordering the "satisfying" char-dogs and "sinfully
crispy" fries; sober sorts may find the "sass" "an acquired taste."

Wildberry Pancakes & Cafe *American*   22 | 19 | 22 | $18

NEW **Loop** | 130 E. Randolph St. (bet. Beaubien Ct. & Stetson Ave.) |
312-938-9777
Libertyville | 1783 N. Milwaukee Ave. (Buckley Rd.) | 847-247-7777
Schaumburg | 1383 N. Meacham Rd. (McConnor Pkwy.) | 847-517-4000
www.wildberrycafe.com

"Get your day off to a great start" at this "slightly upscale" breakfast-
and lunch-only pancake emporium with locations in the Loop and
suburbs, where "solid" servers send out "huge", "reasonably priced"
portions from an "amazingly big" American menu that has "more flair"
than expected; it's "mobbed" on weekends, so "be prepared to wait."

NEW Wilde & Greene Restaurant +   ▽ 18 | 17 | 11 | $19
Natural Market *Eclectic*

Skokie | 4999 Old Orchard Ctr. (bet. Golf Rd. & Skokie Blvd.) |
847-679-2019 | www.wildeandgreene.com

Mallgoers agree the options at the multiple food and beverage stations are "much better than typical food court fare" at this midpriced Eclectic in the Skokie Old Orchard Center providing "natural
and sometimes healthier options" plus "everything from steak to sushi" in a "shopping-center-chic" format that also includes a market
and rooftop bar; though the service is middling and it appears to still
be "working the bugs out", "the idea has potential."

⛫ Wildfire *Steak*   24 | 21 | 22 | $43

River North | 159 W. Erie St. (bet. LaSalle Blvd. & Wells St.) |
312-787-9000
Lincolnshire | 235 Parkway Dr. (Milwaukee Ave.) | 847-279-7900
Glenview | 1300 Patriot Blvd. (Lake Ave.) | 847-657-6363
Schaumburg | 1250 E. Higgins Rd. (National Pkwy.) | 847-995-0100
Oak Brook | Oakbrook Center Mall | 232 Oakbrook Ctr. (Rte. 83) |
630-586-9000
www.wildfirerestaurant.com

You'll get "a good meal every time" assure fans of this masculine
River North and suburban steakhouse "staple", where a "gracious"

staff serves "insane" martinis and "outstanding", "huge" cuts of beef in a "noisy and vibrant" setting recalling a 1940s supper club; some call it "predictable", but those who find it an "excellent value" say there's a reason it's "always busy."

Wildfish *Japanese*   20 | 19 | 19 | $38

Deerfield | Deerfield Commons Shopping Ctr. | 730 Waukegan Rd. (bet. Deerfield Rd. & Osterman Ave.) | 847-317-9453
Arlington Heights | Arlington Town Sq. | 60 S. Arlington Heights Rd. (bet. Northwest Hwy. & Sigwalt St.) | 847-870-8260
www.wildfishsushi.com

"Fresh" specialty rolls in "creative" combinations please both sushi lovers and more "occidental palates" at this midpriced Japanese duo in Arlington Heights and Deerfield; service can be "pleasant" or just "adequate" in the modern setting, but friends say it's "worth a drop in."

NEW Wild Monk 🌑 *American*   - | - | - | M

La Grange | 88 S. La Grange Rd. (Cossitt Ave.) | 708-255-2337 | www.wildmonkbar.com

At this La Grange gastropub, fuel for wild nights includes an impressive whiskey selection and a dizzying array of micro-taps and bottles, plus a moderately priced menu that incorporates game and creative, house-hewn garnishes; flooded with light, the modern digs have a science-lab-chic vibe, with warm wood details and metal seating.

Wishbone *Southern*   20 | 17 | 19 | $21

Roscoe Village | 3300 N. Lincoln Ave. (School St.) | 773-549-2663
West Loop | 1001 W. Washington Blvd. (Morgan St.) | 312-850-2663
www.wishbonechicago.com

Serving "Southern vittles" "with a smile", this "affordable" "down-home" duo also puts a Cajun "spin on breakfast" with the likes of andouille hash; the settings are "relaxed" and feature a "spacious patio" in the West Loop and an art-filled interior in Roscoe Village, and though the service can sometimes seem "harried" due to "noisy kids" and "hideous lines for Sunday brunch", it remains a "longtime favorite."

Wow Bao *Chinese*   19 | 13 | 17 | $11

Loop | 1 W. Wacker Dr. (State St.) | 312-658-0305
Loop | 175 W. Jackson Blvd. (bet. State St. & Wacker Dr.) | 312-334-6395 🛇
NEW Loop | 225 N. Michigan Ave. (bet. Randolph St. & Wacker Dr.) | 312-226-2299 🛇
Streeterville | Water Tower | 835 N. Michigan Ave. (bet. Chestnut & Pearson Sts.) | 312-642-5888
Far South Side | US Cellular Field | 333 W. 35th St. (Wentworth Ave.) | no phone 🛇 Ⓜ
www.wowbao.com

"On-the-go" locals fill up at this "funky" citywide Chinese chain, where the "inventive riffs on buns" are chased down with "fabulous homemade ginger ale" and served "fast-food" style with orders placed by touch-screen; though "Chinatown is much cheaper" and

	FOOD	DECOR	SERVICE	COST

the eats can be "hit-or-miss", it's still "a nice change of pace from sandwiches"; P.S. there's also a mobile food truck.

Xni-Pec 🆔 *Mexican*

−	−	−	M

Brookfield | 3755 Grand Blvd. (Ogden Prarie Rd.) | 708-290-0082 | www.xnipec.us

This midpriced Brookfielder offers "authentic" Mayan cuisine that's "just like mom used to make – if mom were from the Yucatán peninsula"; fans find the fare "interesting" and the "homey, casual" setting "great for families."

🔢 Xoco 🆘🆔 *Mexican*

26	16	18	$19

River North | 449 N. Clark St. (Illinois St.) | 312-334-3688 | www.rickbayless.com

Fans go "loco for Xoco" at this "freaking amazing" River North counterserve delivering "master" chef Rick Bayless' "take on Mexican street food", like "rich", "inventive" tortas, "delicious" caldos and "well-seasoned guac", topped off by "don't-miss" churros and "thick, creamy" hot chocolate, all at a "fraction of the price" of his other places; the ordering process may be "bewildering", the "small" space "crowded" and the lines "nightclub-style" long, so either "go off-times or just suck it up and think about all the great flavors that await you."

Yard House *American*

18	18	19	$29

Glenview | The Glen | 1880 Tower Dr. (Patriot Blvd.) | 847-729-9273 | www.yardhouse.com

"More beer taps than one can count" bring hop hounds to this midpriced Glenview chain link, an American grill offering a "vast" menu of over 130 draft brews, "above-average bar food" and "sporty" surroundings; tons of TVs and a "reliably friendly" staff make it a destination to "hang and watch the game", but only "if you can stand the noise."

Yolk *Diner*

22	17	19	$17

River North | 747 N. Wells St. (bet. Chicago Ave. & Superior St.) | 312-787-2277
Streeterville | 355 E. Ohio St. (bet. Fairbanks & McClurg Cts.) | 312-822-9655
South Loop | 1120 S. Michigan Ave. (11th St.) | 312-789-9655
www.yolk-online.com

"Enormous portions" of "gorgeous" pancakes and "perfectly done" eggs make for a "filling breakfast" or "outstanding brunch" (they also serve lunch) at this "bright and sunny" daytime diner trio; even "efficient and friendly" service can't tame lengthy "weekend waits", but fans assure "people are waiting for a reason."

Yoshi's Café 🆔 *French/Japanese*

26	21	25	$53

Lakeview | 3257 N. Halsted St. (Aldine Ave.) | 773-248-6160 | www.yoshiscafe.com

"Regulars abound" at chef-owner Yoshi Katsumura's Lakeview "fixture" that's "still a wonderful foodie experience" after 30 years thanks to a "frequently updated menu" of "consistently creative", "well-crafted" cuisine with a French-Japanese "fusion twist"; its "casual" exterior gives way to an "elegant" yet "comfortable" space helmed by "professional", "knowledgeable" servers, and though not cheap, most find tabs "reasonable, especially considering the quality of the ingredients."

NEW Yusho *Japanese*   — | — | — | M

Avondale | 2853 N. Kedzie Ave. (bet. Diversey Ave. & George St.) | 773-904-8558 | www.yusho-chicago.com

Chef Matthias Merges (ex Charlie Trotter's) helms this midpriced Avondale Japanese with a focus on "imaginative" yakitori-driven street food offered in "flavorful", "gorgeously" presented "petite" plates; a "comfortable" storefront setting featuring exposed brick and booths contributes to the "overall nice experience."

Yu's Mandarin Restaurant *Chinese*   23 | 14 | 19 | $25

Schaumburg | 200 E. Golf Rd. (Wilkening Rd.) | 847-882-5340 | www.yusrestaurant.com

"Take a tour" of China through cuisine (with a side trip to Korea) at this affordable Schaumburg stop, where noodle-pulling shows (Friday–Saturday at 8 PM) and "wok flare-ups" in the open kitchen add entertainment value; service varies between "attentive" and "too slow", as it's "always crowded" at peak times, but fans attest the "quality" "can't be beat."

NEW Yuzu Sushi &   — | — | — | I
Robata Grill *Japanese*

East Village | 1715 W. Chicago Ave. (bet. Hermitage Ave. & Paulina St.) | 312-666-4100 | www.yuzuchicago.com

Sushi, small plates and robata-grilled items are "fresh" and affordable at this "awesome" BYO East Villager from a Sushi Wabi vet; 100-year-old reclaimed wood and walls lined with *manga* (Japanese comic-strip art) warm up the industrial decor, and if it "takes awhile" for the "friendly" staff to deliver the goods, fans attest it's "worth the wait."

Zak's Place 🅱 *American*   22 | 21 | 20 | $44

Hinsdale | 112 S. Washington St. (bet. 1st & 2nd Sts.) | 630-323-9257 | www.zaksplace.com

"Quality seasonal menu items" keep regulars coming to this New American "hidden" in Hinsdale, where "savory", "well-prepared" dishes might be a bit "pricey", but come with "polite, professional" service; an "eclectic" upscale atmosphere featuring exposed brick and mirrors and a "great wine list" are additional reasons "everyone is happy."

Zaleski & Horvath MarketCafe *Deli*   ▽ 23 | 13 | 19 | $12

Hyde Park | 1323 E. 57th St. (bet. Kenwood & Kimbark Aves.) | 773-538-7372
Kenwood | 1126 E. 47th St. (bet. Greenlawn & Woodlawn Aves.) | 773-538-7372
www.zhmarketcafe.com

Fans find an "oasis of deliciousness" at these "feel-good" counter-service delis in Kenwood and Hyde Park offering up "fabulous sandwiches" and more from a chalkboard menu; "local ownership that

	FOOD	DECOR	SERVICE	COST

supports the neighborhood" is a further draw, and noshers can also peruse the "interesting, eclectic" products including "locally sourced, artisanal discoveries" in the adjoining "specialty markets."

Zapatista *Mexican*
18 | 19 | 19 | $28

Lincoln Park | 444 W. Fullerton Pkwy. (Clark St.) | 773-525-4100
South Loop | 1307 S. Wabash Ave. (13th St.) | 312-435-1307
Northbrook | 992 Willow Rd. (Three Lakes Dr.) | 847-559-0939
www.zapatistamexicangrill.com

"Tableside guac" has fans declaring "they really bust the piñata" at this midpriced Mexican trio in South Loop, Lincoln Park and Northbrook where the fajitas are "sizzling" and "the tequilas are many"; the "big", colorfully rustic settings have optional patio dining, and though sticklers call out "forgettable" fare, "extreme" noise and spotty service, the majority applauds the "upscale approach."

Zealous 🛇Ⓜ *American*
24 | 23 | 23 | $65

River North | 419 W. Superior St. (bet. Hudson Ave. & Sedgewick St.) | 312-475-9112 | www.zealousrestaurant.com

Chef-owner Michael Taus delivers "delicious", "well-prepared" New American cuisine at this River North "gem", where an "interesting menu" sporting global influences combines with "pleasant" service in a lofty, "modern" setting; a "tranquil" vibe enhances the "tasteful" "wine and dine experience" that's "highly romantic", and "price puts it in a special-occasion category" for some.

NEW Zebra's Gourmet Hot Dogs 🛇 *Hot Dogs*
- | - | - | I

Bridgeport | 3351 S. Halsted St. (bet. 33rd Pl. & 34th St.) | 773-940-1526

Cheap, quarter-pound red hots heaped with iconic, city-themed ingredients are top dog at this petite, counter-service BYO in Bridgeport, a U.S. Cellular alternative with zebra-striped walls and an unassuming neighborhood clientele; should takes from Cincy to El Paso fail to inspire, a handful of other edibles (shaved ham-off-the-bone and fillet sandwiches, tamales), fresh-cut fries and fluffy, kernel-flecked corn fritters goad cost-conscious gourmets.

Zed 451 *Eclectic/Steak*
23 | 24 | 22 | $51

River North | 739 N. Clark St. (Superior St.) | 312-266-6691 | www.zed451.com

"Wowza" say fans partaking in the all-you-can-eat "food-a-palooza" at this "chichi" Eclectic Steakhouse in River North offering a "huge selection of appetizers" and "endless swords" of "mouthwatering" meat and seafood (à la carte is also an option) via "attentive" staffers; the "stunning", airy space also has an "awesome" rooftop bar for a "perfect summer hideaway."

Zia's Trattoria *Italian*
23 | 19 | 21 | $37

Edison Park | 6699 N. Northwest Hwy. (Oliphant Ave.) | 773-775-0808 | www.ziaschicago.com

"Solid", "pretty authentic" Italian dishes, "warm" service and a "cozy", "relaxed" atmosphere keep people coming to this "*bellissimo*" Edison

Park "find"; the environs are "nothing fancy" but it is "kid-friendly", and even those who grouse about "crowded" tables and "noisy" patrons call it a "good value."

Zocalo *Mexican*

22 | 22 | 21 | $35

River North | 358 W. Ontario St. (Orleans St.) | 312-302-9977 | www.zocalochicago.com

A "sophisticated" "modern flair" takes the "traditional" Mexican cooking "up a notch" at this "affordable" River Norther also winning fans with a "wonderful tequila selection" and the "best" margaritas; "friendly" service contributes to a "lively", "unpretentious" vibe in the warm, wood-accented space so it's a "reliable favorite."

CHICAGO
INDEXES

LOCATION MAPS

Cuisines

Includes names, locations and Food ratings.

AMERICAN

Abigail's | **Highland Pk**	25
NEW Acadia | **S Loop**	-
Acre | **Andersonville**	20
NEW Ada St. | **Bucktown**	-
Z Adelle's | **Wheaton**	27
NEW Al Dente | **NW Side**	-
Z Alinea | **Lincoln Pk**	29
Allgauer's | **Lisle**	21
NEW Allium | **Gold Coast**	-
American Girl | **Streeterville**	14
NEW Amuse | **Loop**	-
Ann Sather | **multi.**	22
NEW Anthem | **Ukrainian Vill**	-
Aquitaine | **Lincoln Pk**	21
NEW Argent | **River N**	-
Athenian Room | **Lincoln Pk**	22
Atwood Cafe | **Loop**	22
NEW Au Cheval | **W Loop**	-
NEW Bakersfield | **Westmont**	-
Bakin' & Eggs | **Lakeview**	21
Bandera | **Streeterville**	23
Bangers/Lace | **Wicker Pk**	20
Bank Lane | **Lake Forest**	22
Bar Louie | **multi.**	17
NEW Barrelhouse Flat | **Lincoln Pk**	-
Z Bedford | **Wicker Pk**	17
NEW Benjamin | **Highland Pk**	16
Bijan's | **River N**	19
Billy Goat | **multi.**	16
Bin | **River N**	22
Bin | **Wicker Pk**	20
Bite | **Ukrainian Vill**	22
Z Blackbird | **W Loop**	27
Blackie's | **Loop**	20
Bluebird | **Bucktown**	23
Bluegrass | **Highland Pk**	23
Boka | **Lincoln Pk**	26
Bongo Room | **multi.**	24
Z Bonsoirée | **Logan Sq**	27
Boston Blackie's | **multi.**	17
Branch 27 | **Noble Sq**	20
Bridge Bar Chicago | **River N**	-
NEW Bridge House | **River N**	18
Bristol | **Bucktown**	25
Broadway Cellars | **Edgewater**	24
Browntrout | **North Ctr/St. Ben's**	24
NEW Brunch | **River N**	15
Butch McGuire's | **Near North**	20
Café Absinthe | **Bucktown**	23
Café Selmarie | **Lincoln Sq**	22

Ceres' Table | **Uptown**	24
Chalkboard | **Lakeview**	21
Z Charlie Trotter's | **Lincoln Pk**	28
Cheesecake Factory | **multi.**	20
Chef's Station | **Evanston**	25
Chicago Firehouse | **S Loop**	22
Cité | **Streeterville**	19
NEW City Farms Mkt. | **Lakeview**	-
City Provisions | **Ravenswood**	25
Clubhouse | **Oak Brook**	23
Cooper's Hawk | **multi.**	21
Z Courtright's | **Willow Spgs**	28
Custom House | **Printer's Row**	26
Dan McGee | **Frankfort**	-
David Burke Prime | **River N**	25
Deleece Grill | **Lakeview**	18
Depot/Diner | **Far W**	25
NEW Derby | **Lincoln Pk**	-
NEW Deuce's/Diamond | **Wrigleyville**	-
Ditka's | **multi.**	22
DMK Burger Bar | **Lakeview**	21
Ed Debevic's | **River N**	16
NEW Eduardo's Enoteca | **Gold Coast**	-
Egg Harbor | **multi.**	22
Eggsperience | **multi.**	19
NEW Eggy's | **Streeterville**	-
Elate | **River N**	23
NEW EL Ideas | **Pilsen**	29
Elly's Pancake House | **multi.**	19
Epic Burger | **Lincoln Pk**	19
Epic Restaurant | **River N**	-
Erwin | **Lakeview**	23
NEW Estate Ultra Bar | **River W**	-
Exchequer | **Loop**	20
NEW Farmhouse | **Near North**	22
FatDuck Tavern | **Forest Pk**	19
Feast | **multi.**	20
Fifty/50 | **Wicker Pk**	19
Fireside | **Andersonville**	22
NEW Flight 1551 | **Old Town**	-
Fox & Obel | **Near North**	20
Fred's | **Gold Coast**	20
Freshii | **multi.**	18
NEW Frog n Snail | **Lakeview**	-
Frontier | **Noble Sq**	23
Gage | **Loop**	24
Gale St. Inn | **Jefferson Pk**	22
Gemini | **Lincoln Pk**	22
Gilt Bar | **River N**	26
Z Girl/The Goat | **W Loop**	27

Glenn's Diner | **Ravenswood**	25
NEW Glenview House | **Glenview**	19
NEW Goosefoot | **Lincoln Sq**	-
Goose Island | **multi.**	17
Gordon Biersch | **Bolingbrook**	17
Graham Elliot | **River N**	25
NEW Grange Hall | **W Loop**	-
Grill on the Alley | **Streeterville**	21
Hackney's | **multi.**	19
Hamburger Mary's | **Andersonville**	19
Happ Inn | **Northfield**	17
Hard Rock | **River N**	14
Harry Caray's Tavern | **River N**	19
HB Home Bistro | **Lakeview**	25
Hearty | **Lakeview**	23
Z Henri | **Loop**	27
Hot Chocolate | **Bucktown**	24
Hubbard Inn | **River N**	21
Hub 51 | **River N**	21
Ina's | **W Loop**	23
Ing | **W Loop**	23
Inovasi | **Lake Bluff**	26
Jack's/Halsted | **Lakeview**	16
Jake Melnick's | **Gold Coast**	19
J. Alexander's | **multi.**	21
NEW Jam | **Logan Sq**	28
Jane's | **Bucktown**	24
Jerry's Restaurant | **Winnetka**	23
Jilly's | **Evanston**	21
Joe's Crab Shack | **Schaumburg**	20
John Barleycorn | **multi.**	17
John's Pl. | **multi.**	18
Karyn's/Green | **Greektown**	23
Keefer's | **River N**	25
NEW Lady Gregory's | **Andersonville**	19
Lawry's | **River N**	26
Lloyd's Chicago | **Loop**	16
Lockwood | **Loop**	22
Z Longman/Eagle | **Logan Sq**	27
Lou Mitchell's | **multi.**	24
Lovells | **Lake Forest**	22
Luxbar | **Gold Coast**	19
L. Woods Tap | **Lincolnwood**	20
NEW M | **Highland Pk**	-
Magnolia Cafe | **Uptown**	23
Margie's Candies | **multi.**	23
NEW Marmalade | **North Ctr/St. Ben's**	26
Medici/57th | **Hyde Pk**	19
NEW Melt Sandwich | **Bucktown**	-
M Henry/Henrietta | **multi.**	25
Milk/Honey | **Wicker Pk**	23
Miller's Pub | **multi.**	18
Mity Nice | **Streeterville**	19

Z MK | **Near North**	28
Montarra | **Algonquin**	-
Moody's Pub | **Edgewater**	20
NEW Morso | **Lincoln Pk**	-
Z Naha | **River N**	27
NEW Nellcôte | **W Loop**	-
Next Door | **Northbrook**	21
Niche | **Geneva**	27
NEW Nieto's | **Highland Pk**	-
Z Nightwood | **Pilsen**	27
Z NEW NoMI Kitchen | **Gold Coast**	26
Nookies | **multi.**	21
Z North Pond | **Lincoln Pk**	26
Norton's | **Highland Pk**	19
Oak Tree Bakery | **Gold Coast**	16
NEW Ogden | **W Loop**	-
NEW Old Town Pour Hse. | **Old Town**	-
Old Town Social | **Old Town**	24
One North | **Loop**	16
Original/Walker Pancake | **multi.**	24
Over Easy | **Ravenswood**	27
Park Grill | **Loop**	19
NEW Perennial Virant | **Lincoln Pk**	26
Petterino's | **Loop**	19
Pinstripes | **multi.**	17
P.J. Clarke's | **multi.**	18
NEW Point | **W Loop**	-
Portillo's Hot Dogs | **Near North**	23
Prairie Grass | **Northbrook**	22
Prasino | **multi.**	23
NEW Premise | **Andersonville**	-
Province | **W Loop**	25
Z Publican | **W Loop**	26
NEW Publican Meats | **W Loop**	-
Public House | **River N**	19
Z NEW Pump Room | **Gold Coast**	21
NEW Quay | **Streeterville**	19
Quince | **Evanston**	25
NEW Red Door | **Bucktown**	-
Revolution Brewing | **Logan Sq**	23
Rhapsody | **Loop**	21
Z Ria | **Gold Coast**	27
R.J. Grunts | **Lincoln Pk**	20
RL | **Gold Coast**	24
Rock Bottom | **multi.**	19
Rockit | **multi.**	19
NEW Roots Pizza | **W Town**	23
Rootstock | **Humboldt Pk**	24
NEW Rustic Hse. | **Lincoln Pk**	22
Sable | **River N**	24
Z Schwa | **Wicker Pk**	28
NEW Scofflaw | **Logan Sq**	-
NEW Scout Waterhouse | **S Loop**	-

Seasons 52 | **Schaumburg** 26
NEW 2nd Street Bistro | **Highland Pk** 21
Sepia | **W Loop** 26
1776 | **Crystal Lake** 26
NEW 720 South B&G | **S Loop** -
Signature Room | **Streeterville** 17
Z Sixteen | **River N** 25
Small Bar | **multi.** 20
Smashburger | **Batavia** 19
Sola | **Lakeview** 24
South Branch | **Loop** 22
South Gate | **Lake Forest** 18
NEW Southport & Irving | **North Ctr/St. Ben's** -
Southport | **Lakeview** 24
South Water | **Loop** 15
Z Sprout | **Lincoln Pk** 28
Stained Glass | **Evanston** 25
NEW Standard Grill | **Westmont** -
Stanley's | **Lincoln Pk** 19
State/Lake | **Loop** 17
NEW Storefront Co. | **Wicker Pk** -
NEW Sutherlands | **NW Side** -
Sweet Maple | **Little Italy/University Vill** 25
Table Fifty-two | **Gold Coast** 25
Z Takashi | **Bucktown** 28
Tasting Room | **W Loop** 16
Tavern/Park | **Loop** 17
Tavern/Rush | **Gold Coast** 21
NEW Telegraph Wine Bar | **Logan Sq** 23
3rd Coast Cafe | **Gold Coast** 19
NEW III Forks | **Loop** 22
Toast | **multi.** 23
NEW Tuman's Tap & Grill | **Ukrainian Vill** -
Tweet | **Uptown** 26
Twisted Spoke | **Noble Sq** 20
NEW 2 Sparrows | **Lincoln Pk** 20
NEW Urban Union | **Little Italy/University Vill** -
Z Vie | **W Springs** 29
Walnut Room | **Loop** 18
Weber Grill | **multi.** 21
NEW West on North | **Humboldt Pk** -
West Town | **Noble Sq** 26
White Fence | **Romeoville** 24
Wildberry Pancakes | **multi.** 22
Z Wildfire | **multi.** 24
NEW Wild Monk | **La Grange** -
Yard House | **Glenview** 18
Zak's Place | **Hinsdale** 22

Zaleski/Horvath | **Hyde Pk** 23
Zealous | **River N** 24

ARGENTINEAN

Tango Sur | **Lakeview** 24

ARMENIAN

Sayat Nova | **Streeterville** 23

ASIAN

NEW Anna's Asian | **W Loop** -
Belly Shack | **Humboldt Pk** 25
Bento Box | **Bucktown** -
Big Bowl | **multi.** 20
Flat Top | **multi.** 19
Han 202 | **Bridgeport** 25
Hot Woks | **multi.** 19
NEW Hutong | **Oak Pk** -
Joy Yee | **multi.** 21
Karma | **Mundelein** 23
Koi | **Evanston** 18
Niu | **Streeterville** 23
NEW Seven Ocean | **Oak Pk** -
NEW Soulwich | **Evanston** -
Stir Crazy | **multi.** 20
Sunda | **River N** 24
NEW Tokyo 21 | **Old Town** -
NEW Township | **Logan Sq** -
NEW Umami | **Little Italy/University Vill** -

AUSTRIAN

Julius Meinl | **multi.** 21

BAKERIES

NEW Baker & Nosh | **Uptown** -

BARBECUE

Aloha Eats | **Lincoln Pk** 19
Bricks | **North Ctr/St. Ben's** 25
Carson's | **multi.** 22
Chicago Q | **Gold Coast** 22
Fat Willy's | **Logan Sq** 20
Hecky's | **Evanston** 22
Honey 1 BBQ | **Bucktown** 21
Jake Melnick's | **Gold Coast** 19
Lillie's Q | **Bucktown** 22
L. Woods Tap | **Lincolnwood** 20
Piggery | **Lakeview** 19
Pork Shoppe | **Avondale** 19
Real Urban BBQ | **Highland Pk** 21
Robinson's Ribs | **multi.** 20
Russell's BBQ | **Elmwood Pk** 19
Smoke Daddy | **Wicker Pk** 22
Z Smoque BBQ | **Old Irving Pk** 26
Twin Anchors | **Old Town** 22
Uncle Bub's | **Westmont** 24
Weber Grill | **multi.** 21

BELGIAN

Hopleaf | **Andersonville**	24
Leopold | **Noble Sq**	23

BRAZILIAN

Brazzaz | **River N**	21
Fogo de Chão | **River N**	25
Texas de Brazil | **multi.**	23

BRITISH

Blokes/Birds | **Lakeview**	18
Elephant & Castle | **Loop**	15
Owen/Engine | **Logan Sq**	23

BURGERS

NEW Au Cheval | **W Loop**	-
Billy Goat | **multi.**	16
Boston Blackie's | **multi.**	17
Burger Bar | **Lincoln Pk**	23
NEW Burger Joint | **River N**	-
NEW Burger Point | **S Loop**	-
NEW Butcher/The Burger | **Lincoln Pk**	26
Claim Company | **Northbrook**	17
Counter | **Lincoln Pk**	20
DMK Burger Bar | **multi.**	21
Z Edzo's | **Evanston**	27
Epic Burger | **multi.**	19
Five Guys | **multi.**	20
NEW Grange Hall | **W Loop**	-
Hackney's | **multi.**	19
Hamburger Mary's | **Andersonville**	19
Hop Häus | **multi.**	19
Jury's | **North Ctr/St. Ben's**	18
Z Kuma's | **Avondale**	27
NEW Linkin House | **Lincoln Pk**	-
M Burger | **multi.**	17
NEW Mo Dailey's Pub | **NW Side**	-
NEW Phil's Last Stand | **Ukrainian Vill**	-
P.J. Clarke's | **multi.**	18
Smashburger | **multi.**	19
NEW Sutherlands | **NW Side**	-
Tom & Eddie's | **multi.**	17
Top Notch | **Far S Side**	26
NEW 25 Degrees | **River N**	22
Twisted Spoke | **Noble Sq**	20
NEW Wheel House | **Wrigleyville**	-
Wiener's Circle | **Lincoln Pk**	19

CAJUN

NEW Big Easy | **Loop**	-
Dixie Kitchen | **multi.**	19
NEW French Quarter | **Lombard**	-
Heaven/Seven | **multi.**	21
Pappadeaux | **Westmont**	23
Wishbone | **multi.**	20

CHINESE

(* dim sum specialist)

Chens | **Wrigleyville**	21
Dee's | **Lincoln Pk**	19
Emperor's Choice | **Chinatown**	22
Hai Yen | **multi.**	22
Lao | **multi.**	24
NEW Lao Hunan | **Chinatown**	28
LuLu's* | **Evanston**	22
P.F. Chang's | **multi.**	20
Phoenix* | **Chinatown**	24
Pine Yard | **Evanston**	17
NEW Red Violet | **River N**	-
Z Shanghai Terrace | **River N**	27
Silver Seafood | **Uptown**	27
Sun Wah BBQ | **Uptown**	25
Three Happiness* | **Chinatown**	22
Wow Bao | **multi.**	19
Yu's Mandarin | **Schaumburg**	23

COFFEEHOUSES

Bourgeois Pig | **Lincoln Pk**	21
Cafecito | **Loop**	23
Café Selmarie | **Lincoln Sq**	22
Caffe Rom | **Loop**	24
Egg Harbor | **multi.**	22
Intelligentsia | **multi.**	23
Julius Meinl | **multi.**	21
NEW Township | **Logan Sq**	-
Uncommon Ground | **multi.**	23

COLOMBIAN

NEW La Parrilla | **NW Side**	-
Las Tablas | **multi.**	23

COSTA RICAN

Irazu | **Bucktown**	23

CREOLE

NEW Big Easy | **Loop**	-
NEW French Quarter | **Lombard**	-
Heaven/Seven | **multi.**	21
Pappadeaux | **Westmont**	23

CUBAN

Cafecito | **Loop**	23
Cafe Laguardia | **Bucktown**	22
Cafe 28 | **North Ctr/St. Ben's**	25
90 Miles | **multi.**	23

DELIS

Ashkenaz Deli | **Gold Coast**	19
Bagel | **multi.**	20
Chicago Bagel | **Lincoln Pk**	25
City Provisions | **Ravenswood**	25
Conte Di Savoia | **multi.**	24
Eleven City | **S Loop**	19
Goddess & Grocer | **multi.**	21

Manny's | **multi.**	24
Steve's Deli | **River N**	21
Zaleski/Horvath | **multi.**	23

DINER

Bakin' & Eggs | **Lakeview**	21
Chicago Diner | **Lakeview**	23
Depot/Diner | **Far W**	25
Ed Debevic's | **River N**	16
NEW Eggy's | **Streeterville**	–
Eleven City | **S Loop**	19
Glenn's Diner | **Ravenswood**	25
Lou Mitchell's | **multi.**	24
Manny's | **multi.**	24
Milk/Honey | **Wicker Pk**	23
Nookies | **multi.**	21
Orange | **multi.**	20
Original/Walker Pancake | **multi.**	24
Tempo | **Gold Coast**	20
West Egg | **Near North**	19
White Palace | **S Loop**	21
Yolk | **multi.**	22

ECLECTIC

NEW Al Dente | **NW Side**	–
Z Aviary | **W Loop**	27
NEW BadHappy Poutine | **River N**	–
Cellar/Stained Glass | **Evanston**	22
Cooper's Hawk | **Orland Pk**	21
Deleece | **Lakeview**	22
Flight | **Glenview**	23
Foodlife/Foodease | **Streeterville**	19
Fox & Obel | **Near North**	20
Freshii | **Loop**	18
Grand Lux | **River N**	21
Han 202 | **Bridgeport**	25
Heartland Cafe | **Rogers Pk**	17
Hub 51 | **River N**	21
Jane's | **Bucktown**	24
Kitsch'n on Roscoe | **Roscoe Vill**	21
Z Lula | **Logan Sq**	27
Mana | **Wicker Pk**	26
Z Moto | **W Loop**	27
Mundial | **Pilsen**	26
Z Next | **W Loop**	29
Orange | **multi.**	20
NEW Red Door | **Bucktown**	–
Z Ruxbin | **Noble Sq**	28
Z Sixteen | **River N**	25
NEW Tavernita | **River N**	–
NEW Township | **Logan Sq**	–
Uncommon Ground | **Lakeview**	23
Webster's Wine Bar | **Lincoln Pk**	19
NEW Wilde & Greene | **Skokie**	18
Zed 451 | **River N**	23

ETHIOPIAN

Demera | **Uptown**	20
Ethiopian Diamond | **multi.**	22
Ras Dashen | **Edgewater**	27

EUROPEAN

NEW Autre Monde | **Berwyn**	25
Balsan | **Gold Coast**	24
NEW Goosefoot | **Lincoln Sq**	–
Lobby | **River N**	24
Vincent | **Andersonville**	21

FILIPINO

Coobah | **Lakeview**	22

FONDUE

Geja's | **Lincoln Pk**	22
Melting Pot | **multi.**	19

FRENCH

Aquitaine | **Lincoln Pk**	21
Bistronomic | **Gold Coast**	23
Z Bonsoirée | **Logan Sq**	27
NEW Brasserie by LM | **S Loop**	–
Café Absinthe | **Bucktown**	23
Café/Architectes | **Gold Coast**	24
Convito | **Wilmette**	20
NEW Crêperie Saint-Germain | **Evanston**	–
NEW Cyrano's | **River N**	–
Deca | **Streeterville**	22
Dining Room/Kendall | **Near W**	23
Dorado | **Lincoln Sq**	25
Z Everest | **Loop**	27
Froggy's | **Highwood**	25
NEW Frog n Snail | **Lakeview**	–
Gabriel's | **Highwood**	25
Jilly's | **Evanston**	21
La Petite Folie | **Hyde Pk**	26
Z Les Nomades | **Streeterville**	28
Z Le Titi/Paris | **Arlington Hts**	27
Le Vichyssois | **Lakemoor**	26
LM | **Lincoln Sq**	25
Maude's Liquor | **W Loop**	25
MC | **Wicker Pk**	–
Mexique | **Noble Sq**	24
Z Michael | **Winnetka**	27
Oceanique | **Evanston**	25
Paris Club | **River N**	21
Pasteur | **Edgewater**	–
Pret A Manger | **Loop**	19
Sabor Saveur | **Ukrainian Vill**	21
Z Takashi | **Bucktown**	28
Z Tallgrass | **Lockport**	27
NEW Troquet | **Ravenswood**	–
Z Tru | **Streeterville**	28
Yoshi's Café | **Lakeview**	26

FRENCH (BISTRO)

Barrington Country | **Barrington** 25
Bistro Bordeaux | **Evanston** 24
Bistro Campagne | **Lincoln Sq** 25
Bistrot Margot | **Old Town** 22
Bistrot Zinc | **Gold Coast** 21
NEW Bistro Voltaire | **Near North** 23
Cafe Central | **Highland Pk** 23
Café Touché | **Edison Pk** 24
Chez Joël |
   Little Italy/University Vill 26
D & J Bistro | **Lake Zurich** 25
Kiki's | **Near North** 25
Koda | **Far S Side** 23
La Crêperie | **Lakeview** 21
La Sardine | **W Loop** 25
Le Bouchon | **Bucktown** 23
Maijean | **Clarendon Hills** 26
Miramar | **Highwood** 17
Mon Ami Gabi | **multi.** 24
Pierrot Gourmet | **River N** 24
Retro Bistro | **Mt. Prospect** 25
Socca | **Lakeview** 23

GASTROPUB

Bangers/Lace | Amer. | **Wicker Pk** 20
Blokes/Birds | British | **Lakeview** 18
Branch 27 | Amer. | **Noble Sq** 20
NEW Bridge House | Amer. |
   River N 18
Bristol | Amer. | **Bucktown** 25
Chizakaya | Japanese |
   Lakeview 24
NEW Derby | Amer. | **Lincoln Pk** –
NEW Forza | Italian | **Lincoln Pk** –
Fountainhead | Japanese |
   Ravenswood 21
Frontier | Amer. | **Noble Sq** 23
Gage | Amer. | **Loop** 24
Gilt Bar | Amer. | **River N** 26
Hopleaf | Belgian | **Andersonville** 24
Leopold | Belgian | **Noble Sq** 23
Z Longman/Eagle | Amer. |
   Logan Sq 27
NEW Old Town Pour Hse. |
   Amer. | **Old Town** –
Old Town Social | Amer. |
   Old Town 24
Owen/Engine | British | **Logan Sq** 23
Z Publican | Amer. | **W Loop** 26
Public House | Amer. | **River N** 19
Z Purple Pig | Med. | **River N** 26
NEW Red Door | Eclectic |
   Bucktown –
Revolution Brewing | Amer. |
   Logan Sq 23
Small Bar | Amer. | **multi.** 20

Three Aces | Italian |
   Little Italy/University Vill 24
NEW Troquet | French |
   Ravenswood –
NEW Tuman's Tap & Grill |
   Amer. | **Ukrainian Vill** –
NEW Wild Monk | Amer. |
   La Grange –

GERMAN

Berghoff | **multi.** 20
Edelweiss | **Norridge** 22

GREEK

Artopolis | **Greektown** 21
Athena | **Greektown** 21
Athenian Room | **Lincoln Pk** 22
Avli | **Winnetka** 22
Greek Islands | **multi.** 22
NEW Gyro-Ména | **Lakeview** –
Opa! Estiatorio | **Vernon Hills** 23
Parthenon | **Greektown** 21
Pegasus | **multi.** 21
Roditys | **Greektown** 22
Santorini | **Greektown** 22
Taxim | **Wicker Pk** 26

HAWAIIAN

Aloha Eats | **Lincoln Pk** 19
Roy's | **River N** 25

HOT DOGS

Al's Beef | **multi.** 23
Byron's Hot Dog | **multi.** 21
Franks 'N' Dawgs | **Lincoln Pk** 26
Gene & Jude's | **O'Hare Area** 24
Gold Coast | **multi.** 17
Z Hot Doug's | **Avondale** 26
NEW Jimbo's Top Gun |
   Wrigleyville –
NEW Phil's Last Stand |
   Ukrainian Vill –
Portillo's Hot Dogs | **multi.** 23
Superdawg | **multi.** 21
NEW Westminster Hot Dog |
   Loop 18
Wiener's Circle | **Lincoln Pk** 19
NEW Zebra's | **Bridgeport** –

ICE CREAM PARLORS

Z Black Dog Gelato |
   Ukrainian Vill 26
Margie's Candies | **multi.** 23

INDIAN

NEW Bombay Spice | **River N** 21
Chicago Curry | **S Loop** 20
Cumin | **Wicker Pk** 24

Curry Hut | **Highwood**	19
Gaylord Indian | **multi.**	22
Hema's | **multi.**	22
India House | **multi.**	22
Indian Garden | **Streeterville**	20
Klay Oven | **multi.**	19
Marigold | **Uptown**	23
Mt. Everest | **Evanston**	22
NEW Tandoor Char House | **Lincoln Pk**	-
Tiffin | **W Rogers Pk**	20
Vermilion | **River N**	23

IRISH

Abbey | **NW Side**	18
Chief O'Neill's | **NW Side**	17
Grafton Pub & Grill | **Lincoln Sq**	23
NEW Lady Gregory's | **Andersonville**	19

ITALIAN

(N=Northern; S=Southern)

NEW Amoremia | **Old Irving Pk**	-
Angelina | S | **Lakeview**	24
Anna Maria | **Ravenswood**	21
Anteprima | **Andersonville**	26
Antico Posto | **Oak Brook**	24
A Tavola | N | **Ukrainian Vill**	26
Aurelio's Pizza | **multi.**	23
Bacchanalia | **SW Side**	24
Bacino's | **multi.**	22
NEW Balena | **Lincoln Pk**	-
NEW Bar Toma | **Gold Coast**	17
Basil Leaf | N | **Lincoln Pk**	20
Bella Notte | S | **Noble Sq**	24
Bella Via | **Highland Pk**	21
NEW Bongiorno's | **River N**	-
Brio | **Lombard**	20
Bruna's | **SW Side**	24
Cafe Lucci | **Glenview**	25
Café Spiaggia | **Gold Coast**	25
NEW Caffè Italia | **Elmwood Pk**	-
Caffe Rom | **Loop**	24
Calo Ristorante | **Andersonville**	22
Campagnola | **Evanston**	24
NEW Carlos & Carlos | N | **Arlington Hts**	-
Carlucci | N | **Rosemont**	22
Carlucci | N | **Downers Grove**	20
Carmine's | **Gold Coast**	21
Club Lucky | S | **Bucktown**	22
Coco Pazzo | N | **River N**	25
Coco Pazzo | N | **Streeterville**	23
Conte Di Savoia | **multi.**	24
Convito | **Wilmette**	20
Z Davanti | **Little Italy/University Vill**	27

Dave's Italian | S | **Evanston**	18
Del Rio | **Highwood**	21
Dinotto | **Old Town**	21
Di Pescara | **Northbrook**	20
DiSotto | **Streeterville**	25
Due Lire | **Lincoln Sq**	23
NEW Eduardo's Enoteca | **Gold Coast**	-
Edwardo's Pizza | **multi.**	20
EJ's Pl. | N | **Skokie**	22
Erie Cafe | **River N**	22
NEW Filini | **Loop**	24
Florentine | **Loop**	22
NEW Forza | **Lincoln Pk**	-
Z Francesca's | **multi.**	22
Francesco's | **Northbrook**	23
Frankie's Scaloppine | **Gold Coast**	19
Gabriel's | **Highwood**	25
Gaetano's | **Forest Pk**	28
NEW Gemellato | **Bridgeport**	-
Gioco | N | **S Loop**	22
Harry Caray's | **multi.**	23
Il Mulino | **Gold Coast**	25
La Bocca/Verità | **Lincoln Sq**	22
Labriola Bakery | **Oak Brook**	25
La Gondola | **Lakeview**	20
La Madia | **River N**	24
La Scarola | **River W**	26
Macello | **W Loop**	-
Maggiano's | **multi.**	22
NEW Mama Milano | S | **Old Town**	-
Merlo | N | **multi.**	24
Mia Francesca | **Lakeview**	24
NEW Moderno | **Highland Pk**	-
Next Door | **Northbrook**	21
NEW Ombra | **Andersonville**	-
Osteria/Pizza Metro | **Lakeview**	-
Osteria/Pizzeria Via Stato | **River N**	23
Pane Caldo | N | **Gold Coast**	23
Z Pelago | **Streeterville**	26
Pensiero | **Evanston**	21
Petterino's | **Loop**	19
Philly G's | **Vernon Hills**	21
Phil Stefani's | **River N**	23
Z Piccolo Sogno | **Near W**	26
Pinstripes | **multi.**	17
Pizano's Pizza | **multi.**	21
Pizza D.O.C. | **Lincoln Sq**	24
Pompei Pizza | **multi.**	19
Prosecco | **River N**	24
Quartino | **River N**	22
Z Riccardo | N | **Lincoln Pk**	28
Ricobene's | **multi.**	24

NEW Ripasso | **Bucktown** -
Rosal's | S |
   Little Italy/University Vill 29
Rose Angelis | **Lincoln Pk** 26
Rosebud | **multi.** 22
NEW RPM Italian | **River N** -
Sabatino's | **Old Irving Pk** 25
NEW Sacco Bruno | **Bucktown** -
Salatino's |
   Little Italy/University Vill -
Sapori Trattoria | **Lincoln Pk** 26
NEW Saranello's | **Wheeling** 24
Scoozi! | **River N** 21
Socca | **Lakeview** 23
Spacca Napoli | **Ravenswood** 26
☑ Spiaggia | **Gold Coast** 26
NEW Taverna 750 | **Wrigleyville** 25
Terzo Piano | **Loop** 22
Three Aces |
   Little Italy/University Vill 24
312 Chicago | **Loop** 21
Tocco | **Bucktown** -
Topo Gigio | **Old Town** 26
Trattoria D.O.C. | **Evanston** 20
Trattoria Gianni | **Lincoln Pk** 20
Trattoria No. 10 | **Loop** 25
Trattoria Roma | **Old Town** 23
Tufano's Tap | S |
   Little Italy/University Vill 24
Tuscany | N | **multi.** 23
NEW Vapiano | **Lincoln Pk** 17
Via Carducci | S | **multi.** 21
Viaggio | **Near W** 26
Village | **Loop** 22
Vinci | **Lincoln Pk** 22
Vito & Nick's | **Far S Side** 26
Vivere | **Loop** 24
Vivo | **W Loop** 23
Volare | **multi.** 24
Zia's Trattoria | **Edison Pk** 23

JAPANESE

(* sushi specialist)
Agami* | **Uptown** 23
Ai Sushi* | **River N** 22
Akai Hana* | **Wilmette** 20
☑ Arami* | **W Town** 27
Aria* | **Loop** 24
Benihana | **multi.** 21
Bob San* | **Wicker Pk** 23
Butterfly Sushi/Thai* | **multi.** 21
Chens* | **Wrigleyville** 21
Chizakaya | **Lakeview** 24
Coast Sushi/South Coast* | **multi.** 25
Dee's* | **Lincoln Pk** 19
NEW E wok Café | **NW Side** -

NEW Fuji Sushi | **Lakeview** -
Gyu-Kaku | **Streeterville** 23
Indie Cafe* | **Edgewater** 23
Itto Sushi* | **Lincoln Pk** 24
Japonais* | **River N** 24
Kamehachi* | **multi.** 22
☑ Katsu* | **NW Side** 29
Kuni's* | **Evanston** 26
Macku Sushi* | **Lincoln Pk** 26
☑ Mirai Sushi* | **Wicker Pk** 27
Nabuki | **Hinsdale** 26
Noodles by Yagihashi | **Loop** 23
Nori | **multi.** 24
Oysy* | **multi.** 23
RA Sushi* | **multi.** 18
NEW Roka Akor* | **River N** 24
Ron of Japan* | **multi.** 24
☑ Sai Café* | **Lincoln Pk** 27
NEW Slurping Turtle | **River N** 22
Sushi Naniwa* | **River N** 23
Sushi Para/Sai* | **multi.** 20
Sushisamba Rio* | **River N** 22
Swordfish* | **Batavia** 27
Tank Sushi* | **Lincoln Sq** 21
Tanoshii* | **Andersonville** 28
NEW Todoroki Hibachi | **Evanston** -
NEW Tokio Pub | **Schaumburg** -
Toro Sushi | **Lincoln Pk** 28
NEW Union Sushi + BBQ |
   River N 22
NEW Wasabi Cafe* |
   North Ctr/St. Ben's -
Wildfish* | **multi.** 20
Yoshi's Café | **Lakeview** 26
NEW Yusho | **Avondale** -
NEW Yuzu Sushi | **E Vill** -

JEWISH

Ashkenaz Deli | **Gold Coast** 19
Bagel | **multi.** 20
Manny's | **multi.** 24

KOREAN

(* barbecue specialist)
Crisp | **Lakeview** 24
Del Seoul | **Lakeview** 24
Jin Ju | **Andersonville** 22
San Soo Gab San* | **Lincoln Sq** 26
NEW Tozi* | **Wicker Pk** -

MEDITERRANEAN

NEW Ada St. | **Bucktown** -
Andies | **multi.** 21
Artopolis | **Greektown** 21
NEW Autre Monde | **Berwyn** 25
☑ Avec | **W Loop** 28

NEW Barbari | **Ukrainian Vill** — |
NEW Caravan | **Uptown** — |
Dawali | **multi.** 22 |
Olive Mediterranean | **multi.** — |
Pita Inn | **multi.** 24 |
Z Purple Pig | **River N** 26 |
Reza's | **multi.** 19 |
Roti | **multi.** 22 |

MEXICAN

Adobo | **Old Town** 21 |
NEW Barrio | **Lakeview** — |
Bien Trucha | **Geneva** 29 |
Big Star | **Wicker Pk** 26 |
Birrieria Zaragoza | **multi.** — |
Blue Agave | **Near North** 15 |
NEW Bullhead Cantina | **Humboldt Pk** — |
Cafe Laguardia | **Bucktown** 22 |
Cafe 28 | **North Ctr/St. Ben's** 25 |
NEW Cantina Laredo | **River N** 17 |
Cemitas Puebla | **Humboldt Pk** 24 |
Chilam Balam | **Lakeview** 25 |
NEW Chilapan | **Ravenswood** 24 |
De Cero | **W Loop** 21 |
Don Juan's | **Edison Pk** 19 |
Dorado | **Lincoln Sq** 25 |
El Jardin | **Lakeview** 18 |
Frontera Fresco/Tortas | **multi.** 24 |
Z Frontera Grill | **River N** 27 |
La Casa/Isaac | **multi.** 21 |
La Lagartija | **W Loop** — |
Las Palmas | **Bucktown** 22 |
Los Nopales | **Lincoln Sq** 23 |
Lupita's | **Evanston** 20 |
Mago | **multi.** 25 |
Mercadito | **River N** 22 |
Mexique | **Noble Sq** 24 |
NEW Mitad del Mundo | **Logan Sq** — |
Z Mixteco Grill | **Lakeview** 27 |
Mundial | **Pilsen** 26 |
NEW Patron's Hacienda | **River N** — |
Pequod's Pizza | **Lincoln Pk** 25 |
Sabor Saveur | **Ukrainian Vill** 21 |
Salpicón | **Old Town** 25 |
Salsa 17 | **Arlington Hts** 23 |
Taco Grill | **multi.** — |
Taco Joint | **Lincoln Pk** 24 |
Taqueria El Ojo/Agua | **Bucktown** — |
Z Topolobampo | **River N** 28 |
Z Wholly Frijoles | **Lincolnwood** 27 |
Xni-Pec | **Brookfield** — |
Z Xoco | **River N** 26 |
Zapatista | **multi.** 18 |
Zocalo | **River N** 22 |

MIDDLE EASTERN

Alhambra | **W Loop** 18 |
Andies | **multi.** 21 |
NEW Caravan | **Uptown** — |
Dawali | **multi.** 22 |
Old Jerusalem | **Old Town** 20 |
Pita Inn | **multi.** 24 |
Sultan's Market | **multi.** 21 |

NEPALESE

Chicago Curry | **S Loop** 20 |
Cumin | **Wicker Pk** 24 |
Curry Hut | **Highwood** 19 |
Mt. Everest | **Evanston** 22 |

NOODLE SHOPS

Joy Yee | **multi.** 21 |
Penny's | **multi.** 21 |
NEW Slurping Turtle | **River N** 22 |
Urbanbelly | **Logan Sq** 25 |

NUEVO LATINO

Belly Shack | **Humboldt Pk** 25 |
Carnivale | **W Loop** 22 |
Coobah | **Lakeview** 22 |
Depot Nuevo | **Wilmette** 17 |
NEW Libertad | **Skokie** 24 |
Maya Del Sol | **Oak Pk** 23 |
Nacional 27 | **River N** 22 |
Vermilion | **River N** 23 |

PAKISTANI

NEW Tandoor Char House | **Lincoln Pk** — |

PERSIAN

NEW Barbari | **Ukrainian Vill** — |
Noon-O-Kabab | **Albany Pk** 24 |
Reza's | **multi.** 19 |

PERUVIAN

NEW 4Suyos | **Logan Sq** — |

PIZZA

Apart Pizza | **multi.** 25 |
Art of Pizza | **Lakeview** 23 |
Aurelio's Pizza | **multi.** 23 |
Bacino's | **multi.** 22 |
NEW Barbari | **Ukrainian Vill** — |
NEW Bar Toma | **Gold Coast** 17 |
Bricks | **multi.** 25 |
NEW Bongiorno's | **River N** — |
Chicago Pizza | **Lincoln Pk** 25 |
Chicago's Pizza | **multi.** 16 |
Coalfire Pizza | **Noble Sq** 24 |
Dimo's Pizza | **Lakeview** 23 |
Edwardo's Pizza | **multi.** 20 |

NEW Eshticken Pizza | Hoffman Est	-|
Exchequer | Loop	20|
NEW Felice's Pizza | Rogers Pk	-|
Frankie's Scaloppine | Gold Coast	19|
Giordano's | multi.	22|
NEW Gratto Pizza | Wicker Pk	-|
Z Great Lake | Andersonville	27|
Home Run Inn | multi.	25|
NEW Jimbo's Top Gun | Wrigleyville	-|
La Gondola | Lakeview	20|
La Madia | River N	24|
Z Lou Malnati's | multi.	25|
NEW Mama Milano | Old Town	-|
Original Gino's | multi.	21|
Osteria/Pizza Metro | Lakeview	-|
Osteria/Pizzeria Via Stato | River N	23|
Pequod's Pizza | Lincoln Pk	25|
Piece | Wicker Pk	25|
Pizano's Pizza | multi.	21|
Pizza D.O.C. | Lincoln Sq	24|
Pizzeria Uno/Due | River N	23|
Pompei Pizza | multi.	19|
NEW Roots Pizza | W Town	23|
Salatino's | Little Italy/University Vill	-|
Spacca Napoli | Ravenswood	26|
NEW Topper's Pizza | Greektown	-|
Union Pizza | Evanston	21|
NEW Vapiano | Lincoln Pk	17|
Vito & Nick's | Far S Side	26|

PUB FOOD

Abbey | NW Side	18|
NEW Anthem | Ukrainian Vill	-|
Bar Louie | multi.	17|
Billy Goat | multi.	16|
Boston Blackie's | multi.	17|
Chief O'Neill's | NW Side	17|
City Park Grill | Highland Pk	17|
Duke/Perth | Lakeview	20|
Elephant & Castle | multi.	15|
Goose Island | multi.	17|
Gordon Biersch | Bolingbrook	17|
Haymarket Pub | W Loop	18|
John Barleycorn | multi.	17|
Jury's | North Ctr/St. Ben's	18|
NEW Linkin House | Lincoln Pk	-|
Moody's Pub | Edgewater	20|
Norton's | Highland Pk	19|
NEW Wheel House | Wrigleyville	-|

RUSSIAN

Russian Tea | Loop	22|

SANDWICHES

(See also Delis)

Al's Beef | multi.	23|
Bagel | Skokie	20|
NEW Baker & Nosh | Uptown	-|
Ba Le Sandwich | multi.	23|
NEW Banh Mi & Co. | Lakeview	-|
Berghoff | multi.	20|
Big & Little's | River N	25|
Birchwood | Wicker Pk	24|
Bourgeois Pig | Lincoln Pk	21|
NEW Brunch | River N	15|
Chicago Bagel | multi.	25|
Del Seoul | Lakeview	24|
Z Fontano's Subs | multi.	28|
Frontera Fresco/Tortas | Loop	24|
Goddess & Grocer | multi.	21|
Grahamwich | River N	19|
NEW Gratto Pizza | Wicker Pk	-|
Hannah's Bretzel | multi.	23|
Jerry's | Wicker Pk	21|
NEW Melt Sandwich | Bucktown	-|
Mr. Beef | River N	24|
Pockets | multi.	18|
Potbelly Sandwich | multi.	18|
Pret A Manger | Loop	19|
NEW Publican Meats | W Loop	-|
Ricobene's | multi.	24|
NEW Sacco Bruno | Bucktown	-|
NEW Soulwich | Evanston	-|
Southport | Lakeview	24|

SCANDINAVIAN

Tre Kronor | Albany Pk	25|

SCOTTISH

Duke/Perth | Lakeview	20|

SEAFOOD

NEW Acadia | S Loop	-|
Big & Little's | River N	25|
Bob Chinn's | Wheeling	24|
Cape Cod | Streeterville	22|
Catch 35 | multi.	24|
C-House | Streeterville	21|
Davis St. Fish | Evanston	20|
Devon Seafood | River N	21|
Di Pescara | Northbrook	20|
Emperor's Choice | Chinatown	22|
Fireside | Andersonville	22|
Fish Bar | Lakeview	24|
Fulton's | River N	19|
Glenn's Diner | Ravenswood	25|
GT Fish/Oyster | River N	26|
Half Shell | Lakeview	24|
Z Hugo's | multi.	25|

Joe's Crab Shack	**multi.**	20
Z Joe's Sea/Steak	**River N**	27
Keefer's	**River N**	25
Z L2O	**Lincoln Pk**	25
McCormick/Schmick	**multi.**	20
NEW New England Sea	**Lakeview**	-
Nick's Fish	**multi.**	25
N9ne Steak	**Loop**	22
Oceanique	**Evanston**	25
Pappadeaux	**Westmont**	23
Z Pelago	**Streeterville**	26
Pete Miller	**multi.**	22
Reel Club	**Oak Brook**	23
Riva	**Streeterville**	20
Santorini	**Greektown**	22
Z Shaw's Crab	**multi.**	25
Silver Seafood	**Uptown**	27
Tin Fish	**Tinley Park**	25
Tramonto's Steak/Sea	**Wheeling**	21
NEW Wellfleet	**Albany Pk**	-

SMALL PLATES

(See also Spanish tapas specialist)

NEW Ada St.	Amer./Med.	**Bucktown**	-
Z Avec	Med.	**W Loop**	28
Z Aviary	Eclectic	**W Loop**	27
NEW Barrelhouse Flat	Amer.	**Lincoln Pk**	-
NEW Bar Toma	Italian/Pizza	**Gold Coast**	17
Bluebird	Amer.	**Bucktown**	23
Boka	Amer.	**Lincoln Pk**	26
Browntrout	Amer.	**North Ctr/St. Ben's**	24
Cellar/Stained Glass	Eclectic	**Evanston**	22
C-House	Seafood	**Streeterville**	21
NEW Cyrano's	French	**River N**	-
Z Davanti	Italian	**Little Italy/University Vill**	27
DiSotto	Italian	**Streeterville**	25
Flight	Eclectic	**Glenview**	23
Z Girl/The Goat	Amer.	**W Loop**	27
Z Green Zebra	Veg.	**Noble Sq**	28
Lao	Chinese	**Chinatown**	24
NEW Libertad	Nuevo Latino	**Skokie**	24
NEW Morso	Amer.	**Lincoln Pk**	-
NEW Ombra	Italian	**Andersonville**	-
Z Purple Pig	Med.	**River N**	26
Quartino	Italian	**River N**	22
Rootstock	Amer.	**Humboldt Pk**	24
Sable	Amer.	**River N**	24
NEW Tavernita	Latin	**River N**	-

Taxim	Greek	**Wicker Pk**	26
NEW Telegraph Wine Bar	Amer.	**Logan Sq**	23
NEW Urban Union	Amer.	**Little Italy/University Vill**	-
NEW Vera	Spanish	**W Loop**	24
Webster's Wine Bar	Eclectic	**Lincoln Pk**	19
NEW Yusho	Japanese	**Avondale**	-

SOUTH AMERICAN

Sushisamba Rio	**River N**	22

SOUTHERN

Big Jones	**Andersonville**	25
Dixie Kitchen	**multi.**	19
Fat Willy's	**Logan Sq**	20
Lillie's Q	**Bucktown**	22
NEW My Mother's Kitchen	**Elmwood Pk**	-
Southern Mac	**multi.**	18
Southern	**Wicker Pk**	21
Table Fifty-two	**Gold Coast**	25
Wishbone	**multi.**	20

SOUTHWESTERN

Bandera	**Streeterville**	23
Flo	**Noble Sq**	22
NEW Masa Azul	**Logan Sq**	-

SPANISH

(* tapas specialist)

Cafe Ba-Ba-Reeba!*	**Lincoln Pk**	23
Café Iberico*	**River N**	22
Emilio's Tapas*	**multi.**	24
NEW Hota	**Evanston**	-
La Tasca*	**Arlington Hts**	22
Mercat	**S Loop**	26
Mesón Sabika*	**multi.**	25
Tapas Barcelona*	**Evanston**	20
Tapas Gitana*	**multi.**	23
NEW Tavernita*	**River N**	-
NEW Vera	**W Loop**	24

STEAKHOUSES

Benihana	**multi.**	21
Benny's Chop	**River N**	26
Brazzaz	**River N**	21
Z Capital Grille	**multi.**	26
Carmichael's	**W Loop**	20
Chicago Chop	**River N**	24
Chicago Cut	**River N**	26
Chicago Prime Steak	**Schaumburg**	-
David Burke Prime	**River N**	25
Deleece Grill	**Lakeview**	18
Ditka's	**multi.**	22
EJ's Pl.	**Skokie**	22

Erie Cafe	**River N**	22
Fleming's	**multi.**	24
Fogo de Chão	**River N**	25
Fulton's	**River N**	19
☑ Gene/Georgetti	**River N**	25
☑ Gibsons	**multi.**	26
Grill on the Alley	**Streeterville**	21
Harry Caray's	**multi.**	23
☑ Hugo's	**multi.**	25
☑ Joe's Sea/Steak	**River N**	27
Keefer's	**River N**	25
Kinzie Chop	**River N**	23
NEW La Parrilla	**NW Side**	-
Las Tablas	**multi.**	23
Lawry's	**River N**	26
Mastro's Steak	**River N**	26
NEW Michael Jordan's	**Streeterville**	23
☑ Morton's	**multi.**	26
Myron/Phil Steak	**Lincolnwood**	20
N9ne Steak	**Loop**	22
Palm	**Loop**	24
NEW Patron's Hacienda	**River N**	-
Pete Miller	**multi.**	22
Phil Stefani's	**River N**	23
NEW Roka Akor	**River N**	24
Ron of Japan	**multi.**	24
Rosebud Prime/Steak	**multi.**	24
Rosewood	**Rosemont**	26
Ruth's Chris	**multi.**	26
Saloon Steak	**Streeterville**	23
Shula's Steak	**multi.**	21
Smith/Wollensky	**River N**	23
Sullivan's Steak	**multi.**	24
Tango Sur	**Lakeview**	24
Tavern/Rush	**Gold Coast**	21
Texas de Brazil	**Schaumburg**	23
NEW III Forks	**Loop**	22
Tramonto's Steak/Sea	**Wheeling**	21
☑ Wildfire	**multi.**	24
Zed 451	**River N**	23

SWEDISH

Ann Sather	**multi.**	22

TEX-MEX

Uncle Julio's	**multi.**	19

THAI

☑ Arun's	**NW Side**	27
Butterfly Sushi/Thai	**multi.**	21
Chens	**Wrigleyville**	21
Cozy Noodles & Rice	**Lakeview**	23
Indie Cafe	**Edgewater**	23
NEW Jin Thai	**Edgewater**	-
Joy's Noodles	**Lakeview**	22
Opart Thai	**multi.**	24
Ruby/Siam	**multi.**	22
Star/Siam	**River N**	22
☑ TAC Quick	**Wrigleyville**	27
Thai Pastry	**multi.**	25

TURKISH

Turquoise	**Roscoe Vill**	25

VEGETARIAN

(* vegan)

Andies	**multi.**	21
Blind Faith*	**Evanston**	20
Chicago Diner	**Lakeview**	23
Ethiopian Diamond	**multi.**	22
☑ Green Zebra	**Noble Sq**	28
Heartland Cafe	**Rogers Pk**	17
Hema's	**multi.**	22
Karyn's*	**multi.**	21
Karyn's/Green*	**Greektown**	23
Mana	**Wicker Pk**	26
NEW Native Foods*	**multi.**	23
Tiffin	**W Rogers Pk**	20

VIETNAMESE

Ba Le Sandwich	**multi.**	23
NEW Banh Mi & Co.	**Lakeview**	-
Hai Yen	**multi.**	22
Le Colonial	**Gold Coast**	23
MC	**Wicker Pk**	-
Pasteur	**Edgewater**	-
Pho 777	**Uptown**	23
Phò Xe Tång	**Uptown**	26
Saigon Sisters	**W Loop**	24
Simply It	**Lincoln Pk**	22

Locations

Includes names, cuisines and Food ratings.

City North

ANDERSONVILLE/ EDGEWATER

Acre	*Amer.*	20
Andies	*Med./Mideast*	21
Ann Sather	*Amer./Swedish*	22
Anteprima	*Italian*	26
Apart Pizza	*Pizza*	25
Big Jones	*Southern*	25
Bongo Room	*Amer.*	24
Broadway Cellars	*Amer.*	24
Calo Ristorante	*Italian*	22
Ethiopian Diamond	*Ethiopian*	22
Fireside	*Amer./Seafood*	22
❷ Francesca's	*Italian*	22
❷ Great Lake	*Pizza*	27
Hamburger Mary's	*Burgers*	19
Hopleaf	*Belgian*	24
Indie Cafe	*Japanese/Thai*	23
Jin Ju	*Korean*	22
NEW Jin Thai	*Thai*	-
NEW Lady Gregory's	*Amer./Irish*	19
M Henry/Henrietta	*Amer.*	25
Moody's Pub	*Pub*	20
Nookies	*Diner*	21
NEW Ombra	*Italian*	-
Pasteur	*French/Viet.*	-
NEW Premise	*Amer.*	-
Ras Dashen	*Ethiopian*	27
Reza's	*Med./Mideast.*	19
Tanoshii	*Japanese*	28
Uncommon Ground	*Coffee/Eclectic*	23
Vincent	*Euro.*	21

GOLD COAST

NEW Allium	*Amer.*	-
Ashkenaz Deli	*Deli*	19
Balsan	*Euro.*	24
NEW Bar Toma	*Italian/Pizza*	17
Big Bowl	*Asian*	20
Bistronomic	*French*	23
Bistrot Zinc	*French*	21
Café/Architectes	*French*	24
Café Spiaggia	*Italian*	25
Carmine's	*Italian*	21
Chicago Q	*BBQ*	22
Ditka's	*Steak*	22
NEW Eduardo's Enoteca	*Italian*	-
Edwardo's Pizza	*Pizza*	20

Epic Burger	*Burgers*	19
Feast	*Amer.*	20
Frankie's Scaloppine	*Italian/Pizza*	19
Fred's	*Amer.*	20
Gaylord Indian	*Indian*	22
❷ Gibsons	*Steak*	26
Goddess & Grocer	*Sandwiches/Deli*	21
❷ Hugo's	*Seafood/Steak*	25
Il Mulino	*Italian*	25
Jake Melnick's	*Pub*	19
Le Colonial	*Viet.*	23
Luxbar	*Amer.*	19
M Burger	*Burgers*	17
McCormick/Schmick	*Seafood*	20
Merlo	*Italian*	24
❷ Morton's	*Steak*	26
❷ NEW NoMI Kitchen	*Amer.*	26
Oak Tree Bakery	*Amer.*	16
Original/Walker Pancake	*Diner*	24
Pane Caldo	*Italian*	23
Pizano's Pizza	*Italian/Pizza*	21
P.J. Clarke's	*Amer.*	18
❷ NEW Pump Room	*Amer.*	21
RA Sushi	*Japanese*	18
❷ Ria	*Amer.*	27
RL	*Amer.*	24
❷ Spiaggia	*Italian*	26
Table Fifty-two	*Amer./Southern*	25
Tavern/Rush	*Steak*	21
Tempo	*Diner*	20
3rd Coast Cafe	*Amer.*	19

LAKEVIEW/ WRIGLEYVILLE

Al's Beef	*Sandwiches*	23
Andies	*Med./Mideast*	21
Angelina	*Italian*	24
Ann Sather	*Amer./Swedish*	22
Art of Pizza	*Pizza*	23
Bagel	*Deli*	20
Bakin' & Eggs	*Amer.*	21
NEW Banh Mi & Co.	*Sandwiches/Viet.*	-
NEW Barrio	*Mex.*	-
Blokes/Birds	*British*	18
Byron's Hot Dog	*Hot Dogs*	21
Chalkboard	*Amer.*	21
Chens	*Asian*	21
Chicago Bagel	*Bakery/Sandwiches*	25
Chicago Diner	*Diner/Veg.*	23
Chicago's Pizza	*Pizza*	16

Chilam Balam | *Mex.*	25
Chizakaya | *Japanese*	24
NEW City Farms Mkt. | *Amer.*	-
Coobah | *Filipino/Nuevo Latino*	22
Cozy Noodles & Rice | *Thai*	23
Crisp | *Korean*	24
Deleece | *Eclectic*	22
Deleece Grill | *Amer.*	18
Del Seoul | *Korean*	24
NEW Deuce's/Diamond | *Amer.*	-
Dimo's Pizza | *Pizza*	23
DMK Burger Bar | *Burgers*	21
Duke/Perth | *Scottish*	20
El Jardin | *Mex.*	18
Erwin | *Amer.*	23
Fish Bar | *Seafood*	24
Flat Top | *Asian*	19
NEW Frog n Snail | *Amer./French*	-
NEW Fuji Sushi | *Japanese*	-
Giordano's | *Pizza*	22
Goose Island | *Pub*	17
NEW Gyro-Ména | *Greek*	-
Half Shell | *Seafood*	24
HB Home Bistro | *Amer.*	25
Hearty | *Amer.*	23
Intelligentsia | *Coffee*	23
Jack's/Halsted | *Amer.*	16
NEW Jimbo's Top Gun | *Hot Dogs/Pizza*	-
John Barleycorn | *Pub*	17
Joy's Noodles | *Thai*	22
Julius Meinl | *Austrian*	21
La Crêperie | *Crêpes/French*	21
La Gondola | *Italian*	20
Las Tablas | *Colombian/Steak*	23
Mia Francesca | *Italian*	24
☑ Mixteco Grill | *Mex.*	27
NEW Native Foods | *Vegan*	23
NEW New England Sea | *Seafood*	-
90 Miles | *Cuban*	23
Nookies | *Diner*	21
Nori | *Japanese*	24
Osteria/Pizza Metro | *Italian/Pizza*	-
Penny's | *Asian*	21
Piggery | *Amer./BBQ*	19
Pockets | *Sandwiches*	18
Pompei Pizza | *Italian*	19
Potbelly Sandwich | *Sandwiches*	18
Rockit | *Burgers*	19
Socca | *French/Italian*	23
Sola | *Amer.*	24
Southport | *Amer.*	24
☑ TAC Quick | *Thai*	27
Tango Sur | *Argent./Steak*	24
Tapas Gitana | *Spanish*	23

NEW Taverna 750 | *Italian*	25
Uncommon Ground | *Coffee/Eclectic*	23
NEW Wheel House | *Burgers/Pub*	-
Yoshi's Café | *French/Japanese*	26

LINCOLN PARK

☑ Alinea | *Amer.*	29
Aloha Eats | *Hawaiian*	19
Aquitaine | *Amer./French*	21
Athenian Room | *Amer./Greek*	22
Bacino's | *Italian*	22
NEW Balena | *Italian*	-
NEW Barrelhouse Flat | *Amer.*	-
Basil Leaf | *Italian*	20
Boka | *Amer.*	26
Bourgeois Pig | *Coffee/Sandwich*	21
Bricks | *BBQ/Pizza*	25
Burger Bar | *Burgers*	23
NEW Butcher/The Burger | *Burgers*	26
Cafe Ba-Ba-Reeba! | *Spanish*	23
☑ Charlie Trotter's | *Amer.*	28
Chicago Bagel | *Bakery/Sandwiches*	25
Chicago Pizza | *Pizza*	25
Chicago's Pizza | *Pizza*	16
Counter | *Burgers*	20
Dawali | *Med./Mideast.*	22
Dee's | *Asian*	19
NEW Derby | *Amer.*	-
Edwardo's Pizza | *Pizza*	20
Epic Burger | *Burgers*	19
Five Guys | *Burgers*	20
NEW Forza | *Italian*	-
Franks 'N' Dawgs | *Hot Dogs*	26
Geja's | *Fondue*	22
Gemini | *Amer.*	22
Goose Island | *Pub*	17
Hai Yen | *Chinese/Viet.*	22
Hema's | *Indian*	22
Itto Sushi | *Japanese*	24
J. Alexander's | *Amer.*	21
John Barleycorn | *Pub*	17
John's Pl. | *Amer.*	18
Karyn's | *Vegan/Veg.*	21
NEW Linkin House | *Burgers/Pub*	-
☑ Lou Malnati's | *Pizza*	25
☑ L2O | *Seafood*	25
Macku Sushi | *Japanese*	26
Merlo | *Italian*	24
Mon Ami Gabi | *French*	24
NEW Morso | *Amer.*	-
Nookies | *Diner*	21
☑ North Pond | *Amer.*	26
Orange | *Eclectic*	20
Original Gino's | *Pizza*	21

Original/Walker Pancake	*Amer.*	24
Penny's	*Asian*	21
Pequod's Pizza	*Pizza*	25
NEW Perennial Virant	*Amer.*	26
Potbelly Sandwich	*Sandwiches*	18
Reza's	*Med./Mideast.*	19
Z Riccardo	*Italian*	28
R.J. Grunts	*Amer.*	20
Robinson's Ribs	*BBQ*	20
Rose Angelis	*Italian*	26
NEW Rustic Hse.	*Amer.*	22
Z Sai Café	*Japanese*	27
Sapori Trattoria	*Italian*	26
Simply It	*Viet.*	22
Z Sprout	*Amer.*	28
Stanley's	*Amer.*	19
Sultan's Market	*Mideast.*	21
Sushi Para/Sai	*Japanese*	20
Taco Joint	*Mex.*	24
NEW Tandoor Char House	*Indian/Pakistani*	–
Toast	*Amer.*	23
Toro Sushi	*Japanese*	28
Trattoria Gianni	*Italian*	20
NEW 2 Sparrows	*Amer.*	20
NEW Vapiano	*Italian/Pizza*	17
Via Carducci	*Italian*	21
Vinci	*Italian*	22
Webster's Wine Bar	*Eclectic*	19
Wiener's Circle	*Hot Dogs*	19
Zapatista	*Mex.*	18

LINCOLN SQUARE/ UPTOWN

Agami	*Japanese*	23
NEW Baker & Nosh	*Bakery/Sandwiches*	–
Ba Le Sandwich	*Sandwiches/Viet.*	23
Bistro Campagne	*French*	25
Café Selmarie	*Amer.*	22
NEW Caravan	*Med./Mideast.*	–
Ceres' Table	*Amer.*	24
Demera	*Ethiopian*	20
Dorado	*French/Mex.*	25
Due Lire	*Italian*	23
NEW Goosefoot	*Amer.*	–
Grafton Pub & Grill	*Pub*	23
Hai Yen	*Chinese/Viet.*	22
Julius Meinl	*Austrian*	21
La Bocca/Verità	*Italian*	22
LM	*French*	25
Los Nopales	*Mex.*	23
Magnolia Cafe	*Amer.*	23
Marigold	*Indian*	23
NEW Monti's	*Amer./Sandwiches*	–

Opart Thai	*Thai*	24
Pho 777	*Viet.*	23
Phò Xe Tẳng	*Viet.*	26
Pizza D.O.C.	*Italian/Pizza*	24
San Soo Gab San	*Korean*	26
Silver Seafood	*Chinese/Seafood*	27
Sun Wah BBQ	*Chinese*	25
Tank Sushi	*Japanese*	21
Thai Pastry	*Thai*	25
Tweet	*Amer.*	26

NEAR NORTH

NEW Bistro Voltaire	*French*	23
Blue Agave	*Mex.*	15
Butch McGuire's	*Amer.*	20
Elephant & Castle	*Pub*	15
NEW Farmhouse	*Amer.*	22
Fleming's	*Steak*	24
Fox & Obel	*Eclectic*	20
Freshii	*Amer.*	18
Kiki's	*French*	25
Z MK	*Amer.*	28
Portillo's Hot Dogs	*Hot Dogs*	23
Rock Bottom	*Amer.*	19
Ron of Japan	*Japanese/Steak*	24
West Egg	*Diner*	19

NORTH CENTER/ ST. BEN'S

Bricks	*BBQ/Pizza*	25
Browntrout	*Amer.*	24
Cafe 28	*Cuban/Mex.*	25
Jury's	*Pub*	18
NEW Marmalade	*Amer.*	26
NEW Southport & Irving	*Amer.*	–
NEW Wasabi Cafe	*Japanese*	–

OLD TOWN

Adobo	*Mex.*	21
Bistrot Margot	*French*	22
Dinotto	*Italian*	21
Elly's Pancake House	*Amer.*	19
Flat Top	*Asian*	19
NEW Flight 1551	*Amer.*	–
Kamehachi	*Japanese*	22
NEW Mama Milano	*Italian/Pizza*	–
Nookies	*Diner*	21
Old Jerusalem	*Mideast.*	20
NEW Old Town Pour Hse.	*Amer.*	–
Old Town Social	*Amer.*	24
Olive Mediterranean	*Med.*	–
Salpicón	*Mex.*	25
NEW Tokyo 21	*Asian*	–
Topo Gigio	*Italian*	26
Trattoria Roma	*Italian*	23
Twin Anchors	*BBQ*	22
Uncle Julio's	*Tex-Mex*	19

ROGERS PARK/ WEST ROGERS PARK

Ethiopian Diamond	*Ethiopian*	22
NEW Felice's Pizza	*Pizza*	-
Five Guys	*Burgers*	20
Heartland Cafe	*Eclectic/Veg.*	17
Hema's	*Indian*	22
Hop Häus	*Burgers*	19
Nori	*Japanese*	24
Tiffin	*Indian*	20

Downtown

LOOP

Al's Beef	*Sandwiches*	23
NEW Amuse	*Amer.*	-
Aria	*Asian*	24
Atwood Cafe	*Amer.*	22
Aurelio's Pizza	*Pizza*	23
Bacino's	*Italian*	22
Berghoff	*German*	20
NEW Big Easy	*Cajun/Creole*	-
Billy Goat	*Amer.*	16
Blackie's	*Amer.*	20
Boston Blackie's	*Burgers*	17
Cafecito	*Coffee/Cuban*	23
Caffe Rom	*Coffee*	24
Catch 35	*Seafood*	24
Elephant & Castle	*Pub*	15
Epic Burger	*Burgers*	19
Z Everest	*French*	27
Exchequer	*Amer./Pizza*	20
NEW Filini	*Italian*	24
Flat Top	*Asian*	19
Florentine	*Italian*	22
Z Fontano's Subs	*Sandwiches*	28
Freshii	*Amer.*	18
Frontera Fresco/Tortas	*Mex.*	24
Gage	*Amer.*	24
Giordano's	*Pizza*	22
Gold Coast	*Hot Dogs*	17
Hannah's Bretzel	*Sandwiches*	23
Heaven/Seven	*Cajun/Creole*	21
Z Henri	*Amer.*	27
Hot Woks	*Asian*	19
Intelligentsia	*Coffee*	23
Kamehachi	*Japanese*	22
Lloyd's Chicago	*Amer.*	16
Lockwood	*Amer.*	22
Lou Mitchell's	*Diner*	24
M Burger	*Burgers*	17
McCormick/Schmick	*Seafood*	20
Miller's Pub	*Amer.*	18
Z Morton's	*Steak*	26
NEW Native Foods	*Vegan*	23

N9ne Steak	*Seafood/Steak*	22
Noodles by Yagihashi	*Japanese*	23
Olive Mediterranean	*Med.*	-
One North	*Amer.*	16
Palm	*Steak*	24
Park Grill	*Amer.*	19
Petterino's	*Amer.*	19
Pizano's Pizza	*Italian/Pizza*	21
Pockets	*Sandwiches*	18
Potbelly Sandwich	*Sandwiches*	18
Pret A Manger	*Sandwiches*	19
Rhapsody	*Amer.*	21
Robinson's Ribs	*BBQ*	20
Rosebud	*Italian*	22
Rosebud Prime/Steak	*Steak*	24
Roti	*Med.*	22
Ruby/Siam	*Thai*	22
Russian Tea	*Russian*	22
South Branch	*Pub*	22
Southern Mac	*Southern*	18
South Water	*Amer.*	15
State/Lake	*Amer.*	17
Stefani's Tuscany Cafe		-
Sushi Para/Sai	*Japanese*	20
Tavern/Park	*Amer.*	17
Terzo Piano	*Italian*	22
NEW III Forks	*Amer./Steak*	22
312 Chicago	*Italian*	21
Trattoria No. 10	*Italian*	25
Village	*Italian*	22
Vivere	*Italian*	24
Walnut Room	*Amer.*	18
NEW Westminster Hot Dog	*Hot Dogs*	18
Wildberry Pancakes	*Amer.*	22
Wow Bao	*Chinese*	19

RIVER NORTH

Ai Sushi	*Japanese*	22
Al's Beef	*Sandwiches*	23
NEW Argent	*Amer.*	-
NEW BadHappy Poutine	*Eclectic*	-
Benny's Chop	*Steak*	26
Big & Little's	*Seafood*	25
Big Bowl	*Asian*	20
Bijan's	*Amer.*	19
Billy Goat	*Amer.*	16
Bin	*Amer.*	22
NEW Bombay Spice	*Indian*	21
NEW Bongiorno's	*Italian/Pizza*	-
Brazzaz	*Brazilian/Steak*	21
Bridge Bar Chicago	*Amer.*	-
NEW Bridge House	*Amer.*	18
NEW Brunch	*Amer./Sandwiches*	15
NEW Burger Joint	*Burgers*	-

Café Iberico	*Spanish*	22
NEW Cantina Laredo	*Mex.*	17
Carson's	*BBQ*	22
Chicago Chop	*Steak*	24
Chicago Cut	*Steak*	26
Coco Pazzo	*Italian*	25
NEW Cyrano's	*French*	-
David Burke Prime	*Steak*	25
Devon Seafood	*Seafood*	21
Ed Debevic's	*Diner*	16
Eggsperience	*Amer.*	19
Elate	*Amer.*	23
Epic Restaurant	*Amer.*	-
Erie Cafe	*Italian/Steak*	22
Fogo de Chão	*Brazilian/Steak*	25
Z Frontera Grill	*Mex.*	27
Fulton's	*Seafood/Steak*	19
Z Gene/Georgetti	*Steak*	25
Gilt Bar	*Amer.*	26
Giordano's	*Pizza*	22
Graham Elliot	*Amer.*	25
Grahamwich	*Sandwiches*	19
Grand Lux	*Eclectic*	21
GT Fish/Oyster	*Seafood*	26
Hannah's Bretzel	*Sandwiches*	23
Hard Rock	*Amer.*	14
Harry Caray's	*Italian/Steak*	23
Harry Caray's Tavern	*Amer.*	19
Heaven/Seven	*Cajun/Creole*	21
Hop Häus	*Burgers*	19
Hubbard Inn	*Amer.*	21
Hub 51	*Amer./Eclectic*	21
India House	*Indian*	22
Intelligentsia	*Coffee*	23
Japonais	*Japanese*	24
Z Joe's Sea/Steak	*Seafood/Steak*	27
Kamehachi	*Japanese*	22
Karyn's	*Vegan/Veg.*	21
Keefer's	*Amer.*	25
Kinzie Chop	*Steak*	23
Klay Oven	*Indian*	19
La Madia	*Italian/Pizza*	24
Lawry's	*Amer./Steak*	26
Lobby	*Euro./Seafood*	24
Z Lou Malnati's	*Pizza*	25
Maggiano's	*Italian*	22
Mastro's Steak	*Steak*	26
M Burger	*Burgers*	17
Melting Pot	*Fondue*	19
Mercadito	*Mex.*	22
Mr. Beef	*Sandwiches*	24
Nacional 27	*Nuevo Latino*	22
Z Naha	*Amer.*	27
Nick's Fish	*Seafood*	25
Orange	*Eclectic*	20

Original Gino's	*Pizza*	21
Osteria/Pizzeria Via Stato	*Italian/Pizza*	23
Oysy	*Japanese*	23
Paris Club	*French*	21
NEW Patron's Hacienda	*Mex./Steak*	-
P.F. Chang's	*Chinese*	20
Phil Stefani's	*Italian/Steak*	23
Pierrot Gourmet	*French*	24
Pizano's Pizza	*Italian/Pizza*	21
Pizzeria Uno/Due	*Pizza*	23
Potbelly Sandwich	*Sandwiches*	18
Prosecco	*Italian*	24
Public House	*Amer.*	19
Z Purple Pig	*Med.*	26
Quartino	*Italian*	22
NEW Red Violet	*Chinese*	-
Reza's	*Med./Mideast.*	19
Rockit	*Amer.*	19
NEW Roka Akor	*Japanese/Steak*	24
Rosebud	*Italian*	22
Roy's	*Hawaiian*	25
NEW RPM Italian	*Italian*	-
Ruth's Chris	*Steak*	26
Sable	*Amer.*	24
Scoozi!	*Italian*	21
Z Shanghai Terrace	*Chinese*	27
Z Shaw's Crab	*Seafood*	25
Z Sixteen	*Amer.*	25
NEW Slurping Turtle	*Japanese/Noodles*	22
Smith/Wollensky	*Steak*	23
Star/Siam	*Thai*	22
Steve's Deli	*Deli*	21
Sullivan's Steak	*Steak*	24
Sunda	*Asian*	24
Sushi Naniwa	*Japanese*	23
Sushisamba Rio	*Japanese/S Amer.*	22
NEW Tavernita	*Spanish*	-
Texas de Brazil	*Brazilian*	23
Z Topolobampo	*Mex.*	28
NEW 25 Degrees	*Burgers*	22
NEW Union Sushi + BBQ	*Japanese*	22
Vermilion	*Indian/Nuevo Latino*	23
Weber Grill	*BBQ*	21
Z Wildfire	*Steak*	24
Z Xoco	*Mex.*	26
Yolk	*Diner*	22
Zealous	*Amer.*	24
Zed 451	*Eclectic/Steak*	23
Zocalo	*Mex.*	22

STREETERVILLE

American Girl	*Amer.*	14
Bandera	*Amer.*	23

Billy Goat	*Amer.*	16
Cape Cod	*Seafood*	22
Z Capital Grille	*Steak*	26
Cheesecake Factory	*Amer.*	20
C-House	*Seafood*	21
Cité	*Amer.*	19
Coco Pazzo	*Italian*	23
Deca	*French*	22
DiSotto	*Italian*	25
NEW Eggy's	*Diner*	–
Emilio's Tapas	*Spanish*	24
Epic Burger	*Burgers*	19
Foodlife/Foodease	*Eclectic*	19
Z Francesca's	*Italian*	22
Grill on the Alley	*Amer.*	21
Gyu-Kaku	*Japanese*	23
Indian Garden	*Indian*	20
Z Les Nomades	*French*	28
M Burger	*Burgers*	17
NEW Michael Jordan's	*Steak*	23
Mity Nice	*Amer.*	19
Niu	*Asian*	23
Original Gino's	*Pizza*	21
Z Pelago	*Italian*	26
P.J. Clarke's	*Amer.*	18
Pockets	*Sandwiches*	18
Pompei Pizza	*Italian*	19
NEW Quay	*Amer.*	19
Riva	*Seafood*	20
Rosebud	*Italian*	22
Rosebud Prime/Steak	*Steak*	24
Saloon Steak	*Steak*	23
Sayat Nova	*Armenian*	23
Shula's Steak	*Steak*	21
Signature Room	*Amer.*	17
Z Tru	*French*	28
Volare	*Italian*	24
Wow Bao	*Chinese*	19
Yolk	*Diner*	22

City Northwest

AVONDALE

Z Hot Doug's	*Hot Dogs*	26
Z Kuma's	*Burgers*	27
Pork Shoppe	*BBQ*	19
NEW Yusho	*Japanese*	–

BUCKTOWN

NEW Ada St.	*Amer./Med.*	–
Bento Box	*Asian*	–
Bluebird	*Amer.*	23
Bristol	*Amer.*	25
Café Absinthe	*Amer./French*	23
Cafe Laguardia	*Cuban/Mex.*	22
Club Lucky	*Italian*	22

Coast Sushi/South Coast	*Japanese*	25
Feast	*Amer.*	20
Goddess & Grocer	*Sandwiches/Deli*	21
Honey 1 BBQ	*BBQ*	21
Hot Chocolate	*Amer.*	24
Irazu	*Costa Rican*	23
Jane's	*Amer./Eclectic*	24
Las Palmas	*Mex.*	22
Le Bouchon	*French*	23
Lillie's Q	*BBQ/Southern*	22
Margie's Candies	*Amer.*	23
NEW Melt Sandwich	*Sandwiches*	–
NEW Red Door	*Eclectic*	–
NEW Ripasso	*Italian*	–
NEW Sacco Bruno	*Italian/Sandwiches*	–
Sushi Para/Sai	*Japanese*	20
Z Takashi	*Amer./French*	28
Taqueria El Ojo/Agua	*Mex.*	–
Toast	*Amer.*	23
Tocco	*Italian*	–

EDISON PARK/ O'HARE AREA

Bar Louie	*Pub*	17
Berghoff	*German*	20
Big Bowl	*Asian*	20
Billy Goat	*Amer.*	16
Café Touché	*French*	24
Z Capital Grille	*Steak*	26
Carlucci	*Italian*	22
Cheesecake Factory	*Amer.*	20
Don Juan's	*Mex.*	19
Egg Harbor	*Amer.*	22
Fleming's	*Steak*	24
Frontera Fresco/Tortas	*Mexican*	24
Gene & Jude's	*Hot Dogs*	24
Z Gibsons	*Steak*	26
Gold Coast	*Hot Dogs*	17
Harry Caray's	*Italian/Steak*	23
Z Hugo's	*Seafood/Steak*	25
Lou Mitchell's	*Diner*	24
McCormick/Schmick	*Seafood*	20
Z Morton's	*Steak*	26
Nick's Fish	*Seafood*	25
Original Gino's	*Pizza*	21
Original/Walker Pancake	*Amer.*	24
Rosewood	*Steak*	26
Stefani's Tuscany Cafe		23
Sullivan's Steak	*Steak*	24
Z Wildfire	*Steak*	24
Zia's Trattoria	*Italian*	23

HUMBOLDT PARK

Belly Shack	*Asian*	25
NEW Bullhead Cantina	*Mex.*	–

CHICAGO

LOCATIONS

Cemitas Puebla	Mex.	24
Rootstock	Amer.	24
NEW West on North	Amer.	-

LOGAN SQUARE

Z Bonsoirée	Amer./French	27
Fat Willy's	BBQ/Southern	20
NEW 4Suyos	Peruvian	-
Giordano's	Pizza	22
NEW Jam	Amer.	28
Z Longman/Eagle	Amer.	27
Z Lula	Eclectic	27
Margie's Candies	Amer.	23
NEW Masa Azul	SW	-
NEW Mitad del Mundo	Mex.	-
90 Miles	Cuban	23
Owen/Engine	British	23
Revolution Brewing	Amer.	23
NEW Scofflaw	Pub	-
Small Bar	Amer.	20
NEW Telegraph Wine Bar	Amer.	23
NEW Township	Eclectic/Coffee	-
Urbanbelly	Asian/Noodle Shop	25

NORTHWEST SIDE/RAVENSWOOD

Abbey	Pub	18
NEW Al Dente	Amer./Eclectic	-
Anna Maria	Italian	21
Apart Pizza	Pizza	25
Z Arun's	Thai	27
Byron's Hot Dog	Hot Dogs	21
Chicago's Pizza	Pizza	16
Chief O'Neill's	Irish	17
NEW Chilapan	Mex.	24
City Provisions	Deli	25
Dawali	Med./Mideast.	22
NEW E wok Café	Japanese	-
Fountainhead	Japanese	21
Gale St. Inn	Amer.	22
Giordano's	Pizza	22
Glenn's Diner	Diner	25
Goddess & Grocer	Sandwiches/Deli	21
Julius Meinl	Austrian	21
Z Katsu	Japanese	29
NEW La Parrilla	Colombian/Steak	-
Las Tablas	Colombian/Steak	23
NEW Mo Dailey's Pub	Burgers	-
Noon-O-Kabab	Persian	24
Over Easy	Amer.	27
Pockets	Sandwiches	18
Spacca Napoli	Pizza	26
Superdawg	Hot Dogs	21
NEW Sutherlands	Amer./Burgers	-
Tre Kronor	Scan.	25

| NEW Troquet | French | - |
| NEW Wellfleet | Seafood | - |

OLD IRVING PARK

NEW Amoremia	Italian	-
NEW Bread & Wine	Amer./Eclectic	-
Chicago's Pizza	Pizza	16
Hot Woks	Asian	19
Sabatino's	Italian	25
Z Smoque BBQ	BBQ	26

ROSCOE VILLAGE

Hot Woks	Asian	19
John's Pl.	Amer.	18
Kitsch'n on Roscoe	Eclectic	21
Orange	Eclectic	20
Turquoise	Turkish	25
Wishbone	Southern	20

WICKER PARK

Bangers/Lace	Amer.	20
Z Bedford	Amer.	17
Big Star	Mex.	26
Bin	Amer.	20
Birchwood	Sandwiches	24
Bob San	Japanese	23
Bongo Room	Amer.	24
Cumin	Nepalese	24
Fifty/50	Amer.	19
Z Francesca's	Italian	22
NEW Gratto Pizza	Pizza/Sandwiches	-
Jerry's	Sandwiches	21
Mana	Eclectic/Veg.	26
MC	French/Viet.	-
Milk/Honey	Amer.	23
Z Mirai Sushi	Japanese	27
NEW Native Foods	Vegan	23
Nori	Japanese	24
Penny's	Asian	21
Piece	Pizza	25
Prasino	Amer.	23
Z Schwa	Amer.	28
Smoke Daddy	BBQ	22
Southern	Southern	21
NEW Storefront Co.	Amer.	-
Sultan's Market	Mideast.	21
Taxim	Greek	26
NEW Tozi	Korean	-
Via Carducci	Italian	21

City South

BRIDGEPORT

| NEW Gemellato | Italian | - |
| Han 202 | Asian/Eclectic | 25 |

Ricobene's | *Italian* 24
NEW Zebra's | *Hot Dogs* -

CHINATOWN

Al's Beef | *Sandwiches* 23
Ba Le Sandwich | 23
  Sandwiches/Viet.
Emperor's Choice | *Chinese* 22
Joy Yee | *Asian* 21
Lao | *Chinese* 24
NEW Lao Hunan | *Chinese* 28
Phoenix | *Chinese* 24
Three Happiness | *Chinese* 22

FAR SOUTH SIDE

Koda | *French* 23
Z Lou Malnati's | *Pizza* 25
Original/Walker Pancake | *Amer.* 24
Ricobene's | *Italian* 24
Top Notch | *Burgers* 26
Vito & Nick's | *Pizza* 26
Wow Bao | *Chinese* 19

HYDE PARK/ KENWOOD

Bar Louie | *Pub* 17
Edwardo's Pizza | *Pizza* 20
Giordano's | *Pizza* 22
La Petite Folie | *French* 26
Medici/57th | *Amer.* 19
Original/Walker Pancake | *Amer.* 24
Pockets | *Sandwiches* 18
Zaleski/Horvath | *Deli* 23

NEAR SOUTH SIDE

Epic Burger | *Burgers* 19

PILSEN

NEW EL Ideas | *Amer.* 29
Mundial | *Eclectic/Mex.* 26
Z Nightwood | *Amer.* 27

PRINTER'S ROW

Bar Louie | *Pub* 17
Custom House | *Amer.* 26
Hackney's | *Burgers* 19
Z Lou Malnati's | *Pizza* 25

SOUTH LOOP

NEW Acadia | *Amer./Seafood* -
Bongo Room | *Amer.* 24
NEW Brasserie by LM | *French* -
NEW Burger Point | *Burgers* -
Chicago Curry | *Indian/Nepalese* 20
Chicago Firehouse | *Amer.* 22
Edwardo's Pizza | *Pizza* 20
Eleven City | *Diner* 19

Gioco | *Italian* 22
Joy Yee | *Asian* 21
Manny's | *Deli* 24
Mercat | *Spanish* 26
Mesón Sabika | *Spanish* 25
Opart Thai | *Thai* 24
Oysy | *Japanese* 23
NEW Scout Waterhouse | *Amer.* -
NEW 720 South B&G | *Amer.* -
Coast Sushi/South Coast | 25
  Japanese
White Palace | *Diner* 21
Yolk | *Diner* 22
Zapatista | *Mex.* 18

SOUTHWEST SIDE

Bacchanalia | *Italian* 24
Birrieria Zaragoza | *Mex.* -
Bruna's | *Italian* 24
Giordano's | *Pizza* 22
Harry Caray's | *Italian/Steak* 23
Home Run Inn | *Pizza* 25
Manny's | *Deli* 24
Miller's Pub | *Amer.* 18
Pegasus | *Greek* 21

City West

EAST VILLAGE

NEW Yuzu Sushi | *Japanese* -

FAR WEST

Depot/Diner | *Diner* 25

GREEKTOWN

Artopolis | *Greek/Med.* 21
Athena | *Greek* 21
Giordano's | *Pizza* 22
Greek Islands | *Greek* 22
Karyn's/Green | *Amer./Vegan* 23
Parthenon | *Greek* 21
Pegasus | *Greek* 21
Roditys | *Greek* 22
Santorini | *Greek/Seafood* 22
NEW Topper's Pizza | -
  Pizza/Sandwiches

LITTLE ITALY/ UNIVERSITY VILLAGE

Al's Beef | *Sandwiches* 23
Chez Joël | *French* 26
Conte Di Savoia | *Deli/Italian* 24
Z Davanti | *Italian* 27
Z Francesca's | *Italian* 22
Pompei Pizza | *Italian* 19
Rosal's | *Italian* 29
Rosebud | *Italian* 22

Salatino's	*Italian*	-
Sweet Maple	*Amer.*	25
Three Aces	*Italian*	24
Tufano's Tap	*Italian*	24
Tuscany	*Italian*	23
NEW Umami	*Asian*	-
NEW Urban Union	*Amer.*	-

NEAR WEST

Dining Room/Kendall	*French*	23
Orange	*Eclectic*	20
Z Piccolo Sogno	*Italian*	26
Viaggio	*Italian*	26

NOBLE SQUARE

Bella Notte	*Italian*	24
Branch 27	*Amer.*	20
Butterfly Sushi/Thai	*Japanese/Thai*	21
Coalfire Pizza	*Pizza*	24
Flo	*SW*	22
Frontier	*Amer.*	23
Z Green Zebra	*Veg.*	28
Leopold	*Belgian*	23
Mexique	*Mex.*	24
Z Ruxbin	*Eclectic*	28
Twisted Spoke	*Pub*	20
West Town	*Amer.*	26

RIVER WEST

NEW Estate Ultra Bar	*Amer.*	-
La Scarola	*Italian*	26
Roti	*Med.*	22

UKRAINIAN VILLAGE

NEW Anthem	*Pub*	-
A Tavola	*Italian*	26
NEW Barbari	*Mideast./Pizza*	-
Bite	*Amer.*	22
Z Black Dog Gelato	*Ice Cream*	26
NEW Phil's Last Stand	*Burgers/Hot Dogs*	-
Sabor Saveur	*French/Mex.*	21
Small Bar	*Amer.*	20
NEW Tuman's Tap & Grill	*Amer.*	-

WEST LOOP

Alhambra	*Mideast.*	18
NEW Anna's Asian	*Asian*	-
NEW Au Cheval	*Amer.*	-
Z Avec	*Med.*	28
Z Aviary	*Eclectic*	27
Bacino's	*Italian*	22
Billy Goat	*Amer.*	16
Z Blackbird	*Amer.*	27
Butterfly Sushi/Thai	*Japanese/Thai*	21

Carmichael's	*Steak*	20
Carnivale	*Nuevo Latino*	22
De Cero	*Mex.*	21
Flat Top	*Asian*	19
Freshii	*Amer.*	18
Z Girl/The Goat	*Amer.*	27
NEW Grange Hall	*Amer./Burgers*	-
Haymarket Pub	*Pub*	18
Ina's	*Amer.*	23
Ing	*Amer.*	23
La Lagartija	*Mex.*	-
La Sardine	*French*	25
Macello	*Italian*	-
Maude's Liquor	*French*	25
Z Moto	*Eclectic*	27
NEW Nellcôte	*Amer.*	-
Z Next	*Eclectic*	29
NEW Ogden	*Amer.*	-
Pockets	*Sandwiches*	18
NEW Point	*Amer.*	-
Province	*Amer.*	25
Z Publican	*Amer.*	26
NEW Publican Meats	*Amer.*	-
Saigon Sisters	*Viet.*	24
Sepia	*Amer.*	26
Tasting Room	*Amer.*	16
NEW Vera	*Spanish*	24
Vivo	*Italian*	23
Wishbone	*Southern*	20

WEST SIDE

Conte Di Savoia	*Deli/Italian*	24

WEST TOWN

Z Arami	*Japanese*	27
Butterfly Sushi/Thai	*Japanese/Thai*	21
NEW Roots Pizza	*Amer./Pizza*	23

Suburbs

SUBURBAN NORTH

Abigail's	*Amer.*	25
Akai Hana	*Japanese*	20
Avli	*Greek*	22
Bagel	*Deli*	20
Bank Lane	*Amer.*	22
Bar Louie	*Pub*	17
Bella Via	*Italian*	21
Benihana	*Japanese/Steak*	21
NEW Benjamin	*Amer.*	16
Bistro Bordeaux	*French*	24
Blind Faith	*Veg.*	20
Bluegrass	*Amer.*	23
Bob Chinn's	*Seafood*	24
Boston Blackie's	*Burgers*	17

Cafe Central	*French*	23
Cafe Lucci	*Italian*	25
Campagnola	*Italian*	24
Carson's	*BBQ*	22
Cellar/Stained Glass	*Eclectic*	22
Cheesecake Factory	*Amer.*	20
Chef's Station	*Amer.*	25
City Park Grill	*Pub*	17
Claim Company	*Burgers*	17
Convito	*French/Italian*	20
Cooper's Hawk	*Amer.*	21
NEW Crêperie Saint-Germain	*French*	–
Curry Hut	*Indian/Nepalese*	19
Dave's Italian	*Italian*	18
Davis St. Fish	*Seafood*	20
Del Rio	*Italian*	21
Depot Nuevo	*Nuevo Latino*	17
Di Pescara	*Italian/Seafood*	20
Dixie Kitchen	*Cajun/Southern*	19
Edwardo's Pizza	*Pizza*	20
Z Edzo's	*Burgers*	27
Egg Harbor	*Amer.*	22
Eggsperience	*Amer.*	19
EJ's Pl.	*Italian/Steak*	22
Elly's Pancake House	*Amer.*	19
Epic Burger	*Burgers*	19
Five Guys	*Burgers*	20
Flat Top	*Asian*	19
Flight	*Eclectic*	23
Z Francesca's	*Italian*	22
Francesco's	*Italian*	23
Froggy's	*French*	25
Frontera Fresco/Tortas	*Mex.*	24
Gabriel's	*French/Italian*	25
NEW Glenview House	*Amer.*	19
Hackney's	*Burgers*	19
Happ Inn	*Amer.*	17
Hecky's	*BBQ*	22
NEW Hota	*Spanish*	–
La Casa/Isaac	*Mex.*	21
J. Alexander's	*Amer.*	21
Jerry's Restaurant	*Amer.*	23
Jilly's	*Amer./French*	21
Joe's Crab Shack	*Seafood*	20
Joy Yee	*Asian*	21
Kamehachi	*Japanese*	22
Karma	*Asian*	23
Koi	*Asian*	18
Kuni's	*Japanese*	26
NEW Libertad	*Nuevo Latino*	24
Z Lou Malnati's	*Pizza*	25
Lovells	*Amer.*	22
LuLu's	*Asian*	22
Lupita's	*Mex.*	20
L. Woods Tap	*Amer.*	20
NEW M	*Amer.*	–
Maggiano's	*Italian*	22
McCormick/Schmick	*Seafood*	20
Z Michael	*French*	27
Miramar	*French*	17
NEW Moderno	*Italian*	–
Z Morton's	*Steak*	26
Mt. Everest	*Indian/Nepalese*	22
Myron/Phil Steak	*Steak*	20
Next Door	*Amer./Italian*	21
NEW Nieto's	*Amer.*	–
Norton's	*Amer.*	19
Oceanique	*French/Seafood*	25
Opa! Estiatorio	*Greek*	23
Original Gino's	*Pizza*	21
Original/Walker Pancake	*Amer.*	24
Penny's	*Asian*	21
Pensiero	*Italian*	21
Pete Miller	*Seafood/Steak*	22
P.F. Chang's	*Chinese*	20
Philly G's	*Italian*	21
Pine Yard	*Chinese*	17
Pinstripes	*Amer./Italian*	17
Pita Inn	*Med./Mideast.*	24
Pizano's Pizza	*Italian/Pizza*	21
Prairie Grass	*Amer.*	22
Quince	*Amer.*	25
RA Sushi	*Japanese*	18
Real Urban BBQ	*BBQ*	21
Ron of Japan	*Japanese/Steak*	24
Roti	*Med.*	22
Ruby/Siam	*Thai*	22
Ruth's Chris	*Steak*	26
NEW Saranello's	*Italian*	24
NEW 2nd Street Bistro	*Amer.*	21
NEW Soulwich	*Asian/Sandwiches*	–
South Gate	*Amer.*	18
Stained Glass	*Amer.*	25
Stir Crazy	*Asian*	20
Superdawg	*Hot Dogs*	21
Tapas Barcelona	*Spanish*	20
Tapas Gitana	*Spanish*	23
NEW Todoroki Hibachi	*Japanese*	–
Tom & Eddie's	*Burgers*	17
Tramonto's Steak/Sea	*Seafood/Steak*	21
Trattoria D.O.C.	*Italian*	20
Tsukasa of Tokyo	*Japanese*	24
Tuscany	*Italian*	23
Union Pizza	*Pizza*	21
Z Wholly Frijoles	*Mex.*	27
Wildberry Pancakes	*Amer.*	22
NEW Wilde & Greene	*Eclectic*	18
Z Wildfire	*Steak*	24

Wildfish	*Japanese*	20
Yard House	*Amer.*	18
Zapatista	*Mex.*	18

SUBURBAN NW

Al's Beef	*Sandwiches*	23
Aurelio's Pizza	*Pizza*	23
Bar Louie	*Pub*	17
Barrington Country	*French*	25
Benihana	*Japanese/Steak*	21
Big Bowl	*Asian*	20
NEW Carlos & Carlos	*Italian*	-
Cheesecake Factory	*Amer.*	20
Chicago Prime Steak	*Steak*	-
Cooper's Hawk	*Amer.*	21
D & J Bistro	*French*	25
Edelweiss	*German*	22
Egg Harbor	*Amer.*	22
Eggsperience	*Amer.*	19
Elly's Pancake House	*Amer.*	19
NEW Eshticken Pizza	*Eclectic/Pizza*	-
Gaylord Indian	*Indian*	22
Hackney's	*Burgers*	19
Home Run Inn	*Pizza*	25
India House	*Indian*	22
Inovasi	*Amer.*	26
Joe's Crab Shack	*Seafood*	20
John Barleycorn	*Pub*	17
La Tasca	*Spanish*	22
Z Le Titi/Paris	*French*	27
Le Vichyssois	*French*	26
Z Lou Malnati's	*Pizza*	25
Maggiano's	*Italian*	22
Mago	*Mex.*	25
Melting Pot	*Fondue*	19
Montarra	*Amer.*	-
Z Morton's	*Steak*	26
Original Gino's	*Pizza*	21
Original/Walker Pancake	*Amer.*	24
P.F. Chang's	*Chinese*	20
Pinstripes	*Amer./Italian*	17
Portillo's Hot Dogs	*Hot Dogs*	23
Retro Bistro	*French*	25
Rosebud	*Italian*	22
Ruth's Chris	*Steak*	26
Salsa 17	*Mex.*	23
Seasons 52	*Amer.*	26
1776	*Amer.*	26
Z Shaw's Crab	*Seafood*	25
Shula's Steak	*Steak*	21
Smashburger	*Burgers*	19
Stir Crazy	*Asian*	20
Sushi Para/Sai	*Japanese*	20
Texas de Brazil	*Brazilian*	23
Thai Pastry	*Thai*	25

NEW Tokio Pub	*Japanese*	-
Weber Grill	*BBQ*	21
White Fence	*Amer.*	24
Wildberry Pancakes	*Amer.*	22
Z Wildfire	*Steak*	24
Wildfish	*Japanese*	20
Yu's Mandarin	*Chinese*	23

SUBURBAN SOUTH

Al's Beef	*Sandwiches*	23
Aurelio's Pizza	*Pizza*	23
Dixie Kitchen	*Cajun/Southern*	19
Original/Walker Pancake	*Amer.*	24
Smashburger	*Burgers*	19

SUBURBAN SW

Al's Beef	*Sandwiches*	23
Aurelio's Pizza	*Pizza*	23
Cooper's Hawk	*Amer.*	21
Z Courtright's	*Amer.*	28
Dan McGee	*Amer.*	-
Hackney's	*Burgers*	19
P.F. Chang's	*Chinese*	20
Rock Bottom	*Amer.*	19
Z Tallgrass	*French*	27
Original/Walker Pancake	*Amer.*	24
Tin Fish	*Seafood*	25

SUBURBAN WEST

Z Adelle's	*Amer.*	27
Allgauer's	*Amer.*	21
Antico Posto	*Italian*	24
Aurelio's Pizza	*Pizza*	23
NEW Autre Monde	*Med.*	25
Bacino's	*Italian*	22
NEW Bakersfield	*Amer.*	-
Bar Louie	*Pub*	17
Benihana	*Japanese/Steak*	21
Bien Trucha	*Mex.*	29
Birrieria Zaragoza	*Mex.*	-
Brio	*Italian*	20
NEW Caffè Italia	*Italian*	-
Z Capital Grille	*Steak*	26
Carlucci	*Italian*	20
Catch 35	*Seafood*	24
Cheesecake Factory	*Amer.*	20
Clubhouse	*Amer.*	23
Cooper's Hawk	*Amer.*	21
Ditka's	*Steak*	22
DMK Burger Bar	*Burgers*	21
Edwardo's Pizza	*Pizza*	20
Egg Harbor	*Amer.*	22
Eggsperience	*Amer.*	19
Emilio's Tapas	*Spanish*	24
FatDuck Tavern	*Amer.*	19
Five Guys	*Burgers*	20

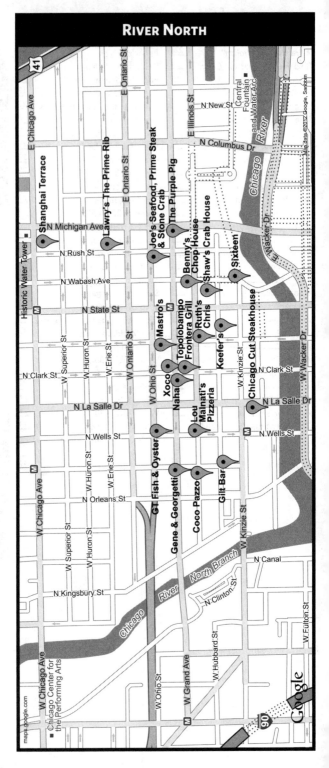

RIVER NORTH

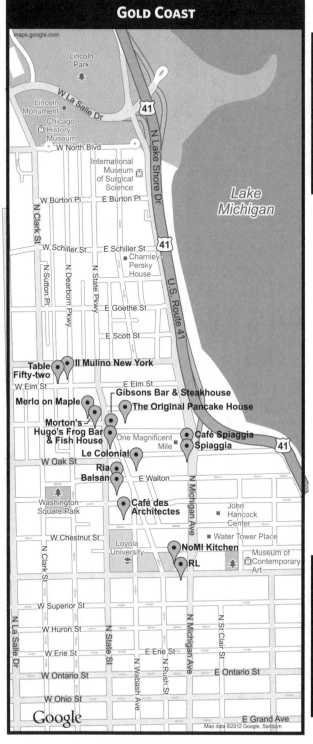

GOLD COAST

maps.google.com

Lincoln Park

W La Salle Dr

Lincoln Monument

Chicago History Museum

W North Blvd

International Museum of Surgical Science

W Burton Pl   E Burton Pl

Lake Michigan

W Schiller St   E Schiller St

Charnley-Persky House

N Clark St
N Sutton Pl
N Dearborn Pkwy
N State Pkwy

E Goethe St

E Scott St

Table Fifty-two   Il Mulino New York

W Elm St   E Elm St

Merlo on Maple   Gibsons Bar & Steakhouse

The Original Pancake House

Morton's
Hugo's Frog Bar & Fish House

One Magnificent Mile   Café Spiaggia
Spiaggia

Le Colonial

W Oak St

Ria
Balsan   E Walton

N Michigan Ave

Washington Square Park   Café des Architectes

John Hancock Center

W Chestnut St   Water Tower Place

Loyola University   Museum of Contemporary Art

NoMI Kitchen

RL

W Superior St

W Huron St
N State St
N Michigan Ave
N St Clair St

N La Salle Dr

W Erie St   E Erie St

W Ontario St
N Wabash Ave
N Rush St
E Ontario St

W Ohio St

Google   E Grand Ave

Map data ©2012 Google, Sanborn

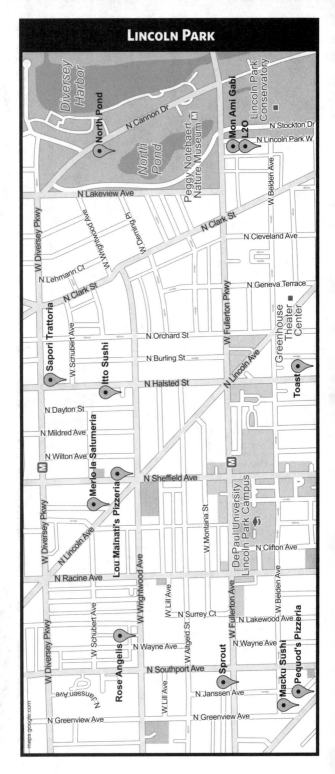

LINCOLN PARK

Diversey Harbor

North Pond

Diversey Harbor

N Cannon Dr

North Pond

Peggy Notebaert Nature Museum

Mon Ami Gabi

L20

Lincoln Park Conservatory

N Stockton Dr

N Lincoln Park W.

N Lakeview Ave

W Belden Ave

W Diversey Pkwy

N Wrightwood Ave

N Deming Pl

N Clark St

N Cleveland Ave

N Lehmann Ct

N Clark St

N Geneva Terrace

Sapori Trattoria

W Schubert Ave

Itto Sushi

N Orchard St

N Burling St

W Fullerton Pkwy

N Lincoln Ave

Greenhouse Theater Center

N Halsted St

Toast

N Dayton St

N Mildred Ave

Merlo la Salumeria

N Wilton Ave

N Sheffield Ave

Lou Malnati's Pizzeria

W Montana St

DePaul University Lincoln Park Campus

N Clifton Ave

W Diversey Pkwy

N Lincoln Ave

N Racine Ave

W Wrightwood Ave

W Fullerton Ave

W Lill Ave

N Surrey Ct

N Lakewood Ave

W Belden Ave

N Schubert Ave

W Altgeld St

N Wayne Ave

Macku Sushi

Pequod's Pizzeria

Rose Angelis

N Wayne Ave

N Southport Ave

Sprout

W Diversey Pkwy

W Lill Ave

N Janssen Ave

N Janssen Ave

N Greenview Ave

N Greenview Ave

maps.google.com

LINCOLN PARK

Map data ©2012 Google, Sanborn

Lincoln Park Zoo

South Pond

Chicago Pizza

Bricks

Perennial Virant

N Clark St

N Wells St

N Stockton Dr

Chicago Academy of Sciences

W Eugenie St

Second City Chicago

Riccardo Trattoria

The Original Pancake House

N Lincoln Ave

N Sedgwick St

N Fern Ct

N Hudson Ave

N Hudson Ave

N Cleveland Ave

N Mohawk St

Urban Taqueria & Cantina

N Larrabee St

Oz Park

N Howe St

N Howe St

N North Ave

Charlie Trotter's

Taco Joint

N Orchard St

N Burling St

W Willow St

Boka

Royal George Theatre

N Halsted St

Alinea

N Dayton St

N Dayton St

Steppenwolf Theatre

Burger Bar

N Fremont St

Sai Café

W Dickens Ave

Chicago Bagel Authority

Franks 'N' Dawgs

N Sheffield Ave

W Webster Ave

N Kenmore Ave

N Maud Ave

N Clybourn Ave

N Kingsbury St

W North Ave

N Clifton Ave

N Marcey St

N Magnolia Ave

W Cortland St

N Ada St

N Wabash Ave

W Willow St

W Willow St

N Besly Ct

Google

90

94

maps.google.com

The Bristol

Toast
Coast Sushi Bar

Le Bouchon
Takashi

Margie's Candies

Bucktown

Irazu

The Bluebird
Hot Chocolate

Birchwood Kitchen

Piece

Taxim

Big Star

Bongo Room

Wicker Park

Mirai Sushi

Holstein Park

Clemente Park

Google

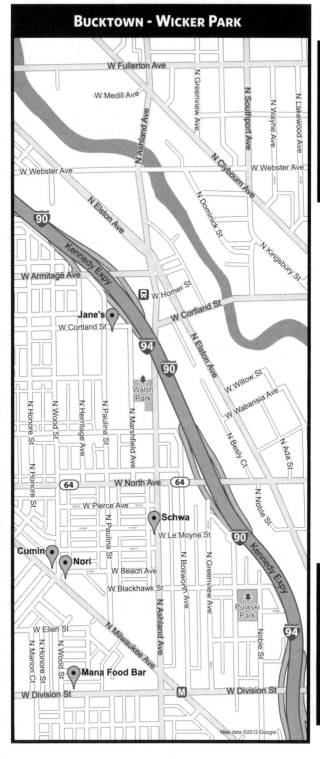

BUCKTOWN - WICKER PARK

Special Features

Listings cover the best in each category and include names, locations and Food ratings. Multi-location restaurants' features may vary by branch.

BREAKFAST

(See also Hotel Dining)

Ann Sather | **multi.**	22
Bagel | **multi.**	20
Bite | **Ukrainian Vill**	22
Bongo Room | **multi.**	24
Café Selmarie | **Lincoln Sq**	22
Chicago Diner | **Lakeview**	23
Depot/Diner | **Far W**	25
Flo | **Noble Sq**	22
Ina's | **W Loop**	23
Julius Meinl | **Lakeview**	21
Kitsch'n on Roscoe | **Roscoe Vill**	21
Lou Mitchell's | **multi.**	24
☑ Lula | **Logan Sq**	27
Manny's | **multi.**	24
M Henry/Henrietta | **Andersonville**	25
Milk/Honey | **Wicker Pk**	23
Nookies | **multi.**	21
Over Easy | **Ravenswood**	27
Phoenix | **Chinatown**	24
Tempo | **Gold Coast**	20
Toast | **multi.**	23
Tre Kronor | **Albany Pk**	25
Uncommon Ground | **Lakeview**	23
Wishbone | **multi.**	20
Yolk | **S Loop**	22

BRUNCH

Ann Sather | **Andersonville**	22
Bakin' & Eggs | **Lakeview**	21
Big Jones | **Andersonville**	25
Bite | **Ukrainian Vill**	22
Bongo Room | **multi.**	24
Bristol | **Bucktown**	25
Cafe 28 | **North Ctr/St. Ben's**	25
Erwin | **Lakeview**	23
Feast | **multi.**	20
Flo | **Noble Sq**	22
☑ Frontera Grill | **River N**	27
Gage | **Loop**	24
Hearty | **Lakeview**	23
Heaven/Seven | **multi.**	21
Hot Chocolate | **Bucktown**	24
Kitsch'n on Roscoe | **Roscoe Vill**	21
Lobby | **River N**	24
Mercadito | **River N**	22
M Henry/Henrietta | **Andersonville**	25
Milk/Honey | **Wicker Pk**	23

☑ Nightwood | **Pilsen**	27
☑ NEW NoMI Kitchen | **Gold Coast**	26
☑ North Pond | **Lincoln Pk**	26
Orange | **multi.**	20
Over Easy | **Ravenswood**	27
Prairie Grass | **Northbrook**	22
☑ Publican | **W Loop**	26
RL | **Gold Coast**	24
Salpicón | **Old Town**	25
☑ Sixteen | **River N**	25
Toast | **multi.**	23
Uncommon Ground | **multi.**	23
Wishbone | **multi.**	20
Yoshi's Café | **Lakeview**	26

BUFFET

(Check availability)

Andies | **Andersonville**	21
Aurelio's Pizza | **multi.**	23
Chicago Curry | **S Loop**	20
Chief O'Neill's | **NW Side**	17
Clubhouse | **Oak Brook**	23
Cumin | **Wicker Pk**	24
Curry Hut | **Highwood**	19
Dining Room/Kendall | **Near W**	23
Edwardo's Pizza | **Oak Pk**	20
Fogo de Chão | **River N**	25
NEW Fuji Sushi | **Lakeview**	-
Gaylord Indian | **multi.**	22
India House | **multi.**	22
Indian Garden | **Streeterville**	20
Karyn's | **Lincoln Pk**	21
Klay Oven | **multi.**	19
Las Tablas | **Lakeview**	23
Lobby | **River N**	24
Mesón Sabika | **Naperville**	25
Mt. Everest | **Evanston**	22
Pinstripes | **Barrington**	17
Pizza D.O.C. | **Lincoln Sq**	24
Reza's | **multi.**	19
R.J. Grunts | **Lincoln Pk**	20
Robinson's Ribs | **Oak Pk**	20
Ruby/Siam | **multi.**	22
☑ Shaw's Crab | **multi.**	25
Signature Room | **Streeterville**	17
☑ Sixteen | **River N**	25
Stanley's | **Lincoln Pk**	19
Tiffin | **W Rogers Pk**	20
Zed 451 | **River N**	23

Vote at zagat.com

BUSINESS DINING

Ai Sushi	**River N**	22
Z Alinea	**Lincoln Pk**	29
NEW Allium	**Gold Coast**	-
NEW Amuse	**Loop**	-
Aria	**Loop**	24
Atwood Cafe	**Loop**	22
Balsan	**Gold Coast**	24
Benihana	**multi.**	21
Benny's Chop	**River N**	26
Z Blackbird	**W Loop**	27
Boka	**Lincoln Pk**	26
NEW Bombay Spice	**River N**	21
NEW Brasserie by LM	**S Loop**	-
Brazzaz	**River N**	21
Café/Architectes	**Gold Coast**	24
Cape Cod	**Streeterville**	22
Z Capital Grille	**multi.**	26
Carlucci	**Rosemont**	22
Carlucci	**Downers Grove**	20
Carmichael's	**W Loop**	20
Catch 35	**multi.**	24
Z Charlie Trotter's	**Lincoln Pk**	28
Chicago Chop	**River N**	24
Chicago Cut	**River N**	26
Chicago Prime Steak	**Schaumburg**	-
C-House	**Streeterville**	21
Clubhouse	**Oak Brook**	23
Coco Pazzo	**River N**	25
Custom House	**Printer's Row**	26
David Burke Prime	**River N**	25
Deca	**Streeterville**	22
Devon Seafood	**River N**	21
Ditka's	**multi.**	22
EJ's Pl.	**Skokie**	22
Elate	**River N**	23
Epic Restaurant	**River N**	-
Erie Cafe	**River N**	22
Z Everest	**Loop**	27
NEW Filini	**Loop**	24
Fleming's	**multi.**	24
Florentine	**Loop**	22
Fogo de Chão	**River N**	25
Fulton's	**River N**	19
Z Gene/Georgetti	**River N**	25
Z Gibsons	**multi.**	26
Grill on the Alley	**Streeterville**	21
Harry Caray's	**multi.**	23
Z Henri	**Loop**	27
NEW Hota	**Evanston**	-
Z Hugo's	**multi.**	25
Il Mulino	**Gold Coast**	25
Inovasi	**Lake Bluff**	26
Japonais	**River N**	24
Z Joe's Sea/Steak	**River N**	27

Karma	**Mundelein**	23
Keefer's	**River N**	25
Kinzie Chop	**River N**	23
Lawry's	**River N**	26
Le Colonial	**Gold Coast**	23
Z Les Nomades	**Streeterville**	28
Lloyd's Chicago	**Loop**	16
Lobby	**River N**	24
Lockwood	**Loop**	22
Z L2O	**Lincoln Pk**	25
Mastro's Steak	**River N**	26
McCormick/Schmick	**multi.**	20
Mercat	**S Loop**	26
Z Michael	**Winnetka**	27
NEW Michael Jordan's	**Streeterville**	23
Z MK	**Near North**	28
Z Morton's	**multi.**	26
Z Naha	**River N**	27
Z Next	**W Loop**	29
Nick's Fish	**multi.**	25
NEW Nieto's	**Highland Pk**	-
N9ne Steak	**Loop**	22
Z NEW NoMI Kitchen	**Gold Coast**	26
Palm	**Loop**	24
Pane Caldo	**Gold Coast**	23
NEW Patron's Hacienda	**River N**	-
Z Pelago	**Streeterville**	26
NEW Perennial Virant	**Lincoln Pk**	26
Phil Stefani's	**River N**	23
Z Piccolo Sogno	**Near W**	26
Prasino	**La Grange**	23
Province	**W Loop**	25
Z NEW Pump Room	**Gold Coast**	21
Quince	**Evanston**	25
Rhapsody	**Loop**	21
Z Ria	**Gold Coast**	27
RL	**Gold Coast**	24
NEW Roka Akor	**River N**	24
Rosewood	**Rosemont**	26
Roy's	**River N**	25
Ruth's Chris	**multi.**	26
Sable	**River N**	24
Saloon Steak	**Streeterville**	23
NEW Saranello's	**Wheeling**	24
Sepia	**W Loop**	26
NEW 720 South B&G	**S Loop**	-
Z Shanghai Terrace	**River N**	27
Z Shaw's Crab	**multi.**	25
Z Sixteen	**River N**	25
Smith/Wollensky	**River N**	23
South Branch	**Loop**	22
Z Spiaggia	**Gold Coast**	26
Sullivan's Steak	**multi.**	24

Z Takashi | **Bucktown** — 28
Z Tallgrass | **Lockport** — 27
NEW III Forks | **Loop** — 22
312 Chicago | **Loop** — 21
Z Topolobampo | **River N** — 28
Trattoria No. 10 | **Loop** — 25
Z Tru | **Streeterville** — 28
Vivere | **Loop** — 24
Weber Grill | **River N** — 21
Zak's Place | **Hinsdale** — 22

BYO

NEW Al Dente | **NW Side** — –
NEW Amoremia | **Old Irving Pk** — –
NEW Anna's Asian | **W Loop** — –
Ann Sather | **multi.** — 22
Apart Pizza | **multi.** — 25
Art of Pizza | **Lakeview** — 23
NEW BadHappy Poutine | **River N** — –
Bagel | **Lakeview** — 20
Bakin' & Eggs | **Lakeview** — 21
NEW Barbari | **Ukrainian Vill** — –
Belly Shack | **Humboldt Pk** — 25
Bento Box | **Bucktown** — –
Birchwood | **Wicker Pk** — 24
Birrieria Zaragoza | **SW Side** — –
Bite | **Ukrainian Vill** — 22
Z Bonsoirée | **Logan Sq** — 27
NEW Brunch | **River N** — 15
NEW Burger Point | **S Loop** — –
NEW Butcher/The Burger | **Lincoln Pk** — 26
Butterfly Sushi/Thai | **multi.** — 21
Cemitas Puebla | **Humboldt Pk** — 24
Chicago Bagel | **Lakeview** — 25
Chicago's Pizza | **multi.** — 16
Chilam Balam | **Lakeview** — 25
NEW Chilapan | **Ravenswood** — 24
NEW City Farms Mkt. | **Lakeview** — –
Coast Sushi/South Coast | **Bucktown** — 25
Cozy Noodles & Rice | **Lakeview** — 23
Crisp | **Lakeview** — 24
Dawali | **Lincoln Pk** — 22
Dimo's Pizza | **Lakeview** — 23
Dorado | **Lincoln Sq** — 25
NEW Eggy's | **Streeterville** — –
NEW EL Ideas | **Pilsen** — 29
Epic Burger | **multi.** — 19
NEW Eshticken Pizza | **Hoffman Est** — –
NEW 4Suyos | **Logan Sq** — –
Franks 'N' Dawgs | **Lincoln Pk** — 26
NEW Fuji Sushi | **Lakeview** — –
Giordano's | **multi.** — 22
NEW Goosefoot | **Lincoln Sq** — –

NEW Gratto Pizza | **Wicker Pk** — –
Z Great Lake | **Andersonville** — 27
Han 202 | **Bridgeport** — 25
HB Home Bistro | **Lakeview** — 25
Hema's | **multi.** — 22
Honey 1 BBQ | **Bucktown** — 21
Hot Woks | **Old Irving Pk** — 19
NEW Hutong | **Oak Pk** — –
Irazu | **Bucktown** — 23
NEW Jam | **Logan Sq** — 28
NEW Jimbo's Top Gun | **Wrigleyville** — –
NEW Jin Thai | **Edgewater** — –
Joy's Noodles | **Lakeview** — 22
Joy Yee | **multi.** — 21
Karyn's | **Lincoln Pk** — 21
La Gondola | **Lakeview** — 20
Los Nopales | **Lincoln Sq** — 23
NEW Marmalade | **North Ctr/St. Ben's** — 26
Medici/57th | **Hyde Pk** — 19
M Henry/Henrietta | **multi.** — 25
Z Mixteco Grill | **Lakeview** — 27
NEW My Mother's Kitchen | **Elmwood Pk** — –
90 Miles | **multi.** — 23
Nookies | **multi.** — 21
Opart Thai | **Lincoln Sq** — 24
Original Gino's | **Lincoln Pk** — 21
Osteria/Pizza Metro | **Lakeview** — –
Over Easy | **Ravenswood** — 27
Penny's | **multi.** — 21
Pho 777 | **Uptown** — 23
Phò Xe Tằng | **Uptown** — 26
NEW Red Violet | **River N** — –
Robinson's Ribs | **multi.** — 20
Ruby/Siam | **multi.** — 22
Z Schwa | **Wicker Pk** — 28
NEW 2nd Street Bistro | **Highland Pk** — 21
Simply It | **Lincoln Pk** — 22
Small Bar | **Logan Sq** — 20
Z Smoque BBQ | **Old Irving Pk** — 26
Sultan's Market | **multi.** — 21
Sushi Para/Sai | **multi.** — 20
Z TAC Quick | **Wrigleyville** — 27
Tango Sur | **Lakeview** — 24
Tanoshii | **Andersonville** — 28
Taqueria El Ojo/Agua | **Bucktown** — –
Tempo | **Gold Coast** — 20
Thai Pastry | **multi.** — 25
NEW Todoroki Hibachi | **Evanston** — –
Toro Sushi | **Lincoln Pk** — 28
Tre Kronor | **Albany Pk** — 25
Urbanbelly | **Logan Sq** — 25
NEW Wellfleet | **Albany Pk** — –

Z Wholly Frijoles | **Lincolnwood**		27
Wildberry Pancakes | **Loop**		22
Wow Bao | **Loop**		19
Yolk | **multi.**		22
NEW Yuzu Sushi | **E Vill**		-
NEW Zebra's | **Bridgeport**		-

CELEBRITY CHEFS

Rodelio Aglibot		
NEW Argent | **River N**		-
Grant Achatz		
Z Alinea | **Lincoln Pk**		29
Z Aviary | **W Loop**		27
Z Next | **W Loop**		29
Jimmy Bannos Jr.		
Z Purple Pig | **River N**		26
Rick Bayless		
Frontera Fresco/Tortas | **multi.**		24
Z Frontera Grill | **River N**		27
Z Topolobampo | **River N**		28
Z Xoco | **River N**		26
Graham Elliot Bowles		
Graham Elliot | **River N**		25
Grahamwich | **River N**		19
George Bumbaris		
Prairie Grass | **Northbrook**		22
David Burke		
David Burke Prime | **River N**		25
Homaro Cantu		
Ing | **W Loop**		23
Z Moto | **W Loop**		27
Michael Carlson		
Z Schwa | **Wicker Pk**		28
Dirk Flanigan		
Gage | **Loop**		24
Z Henri | **Loop**		27
Phillip Foss		
NEW EL Ideas | **Pilsen**		29
Susan Goss		
West Town | **Noble Sq**		26
Danny Grant		
Balsan | **Gold Coast**		24
Z Ria | **Gold Coast**		27
Rick Gresh		
David Burke Prime | **River N**		25
Koren Grieveson		
Z Avec | **W Loop**		28
Sarah Grueneberg		
Z Spiaggia | **Gold Coast**		26
Jason Hammel		
Z Lula | **Logan Sq**		27
Kevin Hickey		
NEW Allium | **Gold Coast**		-
Stephanie Izard		
Z Girl/The Goat | **W Loop**		27

Jean Joho		
Z Everest | **Loop**		27
Paris Club | **River N**		21
Paul Kahan		
Z Avec | **W Loop**		28
Big Star | **Wicker Pk**		26
Z Blackbird | **W Loop**		27
Z Publican | **W Loop**		26
Yoshi Katsumura		
Yoshi's Café | **Lakeview**		26
Bill Kim		
Belly Shack | **Humboldt Pk**		25
Urbanbelly | **Logan Sq**		25
Edward Kim		
Z Ruxbin | **Noble Sq**		28
Michael Kornick		
NEW Ada St. | **Bucktown**		-
DMK Burger Bar | **multi.**		21
Fish Bar | **Lakeview**		24
Z MK | **Near North**		28
Joncarl Lachman		
HB Home Bistro | **Lakeview**		25
Michael Lachowitz		
Z Michael | **Winnetka**		27
Dale Levitski		
NEW Frog n Snail | **Lakeview**		-
Z Sprout | **Lincoln Pk**		28
Roland Liccioni		
Z Les Nomades | **Streeterville**		28
Michael Maddox		
Z Le Titi/Paris | **Arlington Hts**		27
Tony Mantuano		
NEW Bar Toma | **Gold Coast**		17
Café Spiaggia | **Gold Coast**		25
Z Spiaggia | **Gold Coast**		26
Terzo Piano | **Loop**		22
Anthony Martin		
Z Tru | **Streeterville**		28
Ryan McCaskey		
NEW Acadia | **S Loop**		-
Shawn McClain		
Z Green Zebra | **Noble Sq**		28
Matthias Merges		
NEW Yusho | **Avondale**		-
Carrie Nahabedian		
Z Naha | **River N**		27
Martial Noguier		
Bistronomic | **Gold Coast**		23
Chris Nugent		
NEW Goosefoot | **Lincoln Sq**		-
Dan Pancake		
NEW Autre Monde | **Berwyn**		25
Beth Partridge		
NEW Autre Monde | **Berwyn**		25

Chris Pandel
- NEW Balena | **Lincoln Pk** —
- Bristol | **Bucktown** 25

Jason Paskewitz
- Gemini | **Lincoln Pk** 22
- NEW Rustic Hse. | **Lincoln Pk** 22

Ryan Poli
- NEW Tavernita | **River N** —

Tony Priolo
- Ⓩ Piccolo Sogno | **Near W** 26

John des Rosiers
- Inovasi | **Lake Bluff** 26
- NEW Moderno | **Highland Pk** —

Arun Sampanthavivat
- Ⓩ Arun's | **NW Side** 27

Marcus Samuelsson
- C-House | **Streeterville** 21

Priscila Satkoff
- Salpicón | **Old Town** 25

Mindy Segal
- Hot Chocolate | **Bucktown** 24

Jackie Shen
- NEW Argent | **River N** —

Bruce Sherman
- Ⓩ North Pond | **Lincoln Pk** 26

Michael Shrader
- NEW Urban Union | **Little Italy/University Vill** —

Art Smith
- Table Fifty-two | **Gold Coast** 25

Dan Smith
- Hearty | **Lakeview** 23

Brendan Sodikoff
- NEW Au Cheval | **W Loop** —
- Gilt Bar | **River N** 26
- Maude's Liquor | **W Loop** 25

Doug Sohn
- Ⓩ Hot Doug's | **Avondale** 26

Sarah Stegner
- Prairie Grass | **Northbrook** 22

Allen Sternweiler
- NEW Butcher/The Burger | **Lincoln Pk** 26

Michael Taus
- Zealous | **River N** 24

Giuseppe Tentori
- Boka | **Lincoln Pk** 26
- GT Fish/Oyster | **River N** 26

Shin Thompson
- Ⓩ Bonsoirée | **Logan Sq** 27

Charlie Trotter
- Ⓩ Charlie Trotter's | **Lincoln Pk** 28

Amalea Tshilds
- Ⓩ Lula | **Logan Sq** 27

Jared Van Camp
- NEW Nellcôte | **W Loop** —
- Old Town Social | **Old Town** 24

Paul Virant
- NEW Perennial Virant | **Lincoln Pk** 26
- Ⓩ Vie | **W Springs** 29

Jean-Georges Vongerichten
- Ⓩ NEW Pump Room | **Gold Coast** 21

Takashi Yagihashi
- Noodles by Yagihashi | **Loop** 23
- NEW Slurping Turtle | **River N** 22
- Ⓩ Takashi | **Bucktown** 28

Andrew Zimmerman
- Sepia | **W Loop** 26

Randy Zweiban
- Province | **W Loop** 25

CHILD-FRIENDLY

(Alternatives to the usual fast-food places; * children's menu available)

Aloha Eats	**Lincoln Pk**	19
American Girl	**Streeterville**	14
Ann Sather*	**multi.**	22
Antico Posto*	**Oak Brook**	24
Artopolis	**Greektown**	21
Bandera*	**Streeterville**	23
Benihana*	**multi.**	21
Berghoff	**O'Hare Area**	20
Big Bowl*	**multi.**	20
Bob Chinn's*	**Wheeling**	24
Café Selmarie*	**Lincoln Sq**	22
Carson's*	**River N**	22
Cheesecake Factory*	**multi.**	20
Chicago Pizza	**Lincoln Pk**	25
Claim Company*	**Northbrook**	17
Dave's Italian	**Evanston**	18
Davis St. Fish*	**Evanston**	20
Depot/Diner	**Far W**	25
Ed Debevic's*	**River N**	16
Edwardo's Pizza*	**multi.**	20
Five Guys*	**multi.**	20
Flat Top	**multi.**	19
Foodlife/Foodease	**Streeterville**	19
Hackney's*	**multi.**	19
Hard Rock*	**River N**	14
Harry Caray's*	**multi.**	23
Heaven/Seven*	**multi.**	21
Ⓩ Hot Doug's	**Avondale**	26
Ina's	**W Loop**	23
Jake Melnick's*	**Gold Coast**	19
John's Pl.*	**Lincoln Pk**	18
Joy Yee	**Chinatown**	21
Kitsch'n on Roscoe*	**Roscoe Vill**	21

Lawry's* | **River N** 26

Z Lou Malnati's* | **multi.** 25

Lou Mitchell's* | **multi.** 24

LuLu's | **Evanston** 22

Maggiano's* | **multi.** 22

Manny's* | **SW Side** 24

Margie's Candies | **Bucktown** 23

Mity Nice* | **Streeterville** 19

Oak Tree Bakery | **Gold Coast** 16

Opa! Estiatorio* | **Vernon Hills** 23

Original Gino's* | **multi.** 21

Original/Walker Pancake* | **multi.** 24

Pegasus | **SW Side** 21

P.F. Chang's | **River N** 20

Pizza D.O.C. | **Lincoln Sq** 24

Pizzeria Uno/Due* | **River N** 23

Potbelly Sandwich | **multi.** 18

R.J. Grunts* | **Lincoln Pk** 20

Robinson's Ribs* | **multi.** 20

Rock Bottom* | **multi.** 19

Ron of Japan* | **multi.** 24

Russell's BBQ* | **Elmwood Pk** 19

Sapori Trattoria | **Lincoln Pk** 26

Scoozi!* | **River N** 21

Z Smoque BBQ* | **Old Irving Pk** 26

Stanley's* | **Lincoln Pk** 19

Stir Crazy* | **multi.** 20

Tempo | **Gold Coast** 20

Toast* | **multi.** 23

Trattoria D.O.C. | **Evanston** 20

Tufano's Tap | **Little Italy/University Vill** 24

Twin Anchors* | **Old Town** 22

Uncle Julio's* | **Old Town** 19

Uncommon Ground* | **Lakeview** 23

White Fence* | **Romeoville** 24

Wishbone* | **multi.** 20

DINING ALONE

(Other than hotels and places
with counter service)

Ann Sather | **multi.** 22

Artopolis | **Greektown** 21

Z Avec | **W Loop** 28

Bagel | **multi.** 20

Ba Le Sandwich | **multi.** 23

NEW Banh Mi & Co. | **Lakeview** –

Bar Louie | **multi.** 17

NEW Bar Toma | **Gold Coast** 17

Big & Little's | **River N** 25

Big Bowl | **multi.** 20

Bin | **River N** 22

Bistrot Zinc | **Gold Coast** 21

Bite | **Ukrainian Vill** 22

Blind Faith | **Evanston** 20

Bourgeois Pig | **Lincoln Pk** 21

Bridge Bar Chicago | **River N** –

Café Selmarie | **Lincoln Sq** 22

Chicago Chop | **River N** 24

Chicago Diner | **Lakeview** 23

Chief O'Neill's | **NW Side** 17

Davis St. Fish | **Evanston** 20

Depot/Diner | **Far W** 25

DMK Burger Bar | **multi.** 21

Z Edzo's | **Evanston** 27

Eleven City | **S Loop** 19

Epic Burger | **multi.** 19

Exchequer | **Loop** 20

Foodlife/Foodease | **Streeterville** 19

Fox & Obel | **Near North** 20

Franks 'N' Dawgs | **Lincoln Pk** 26

Fred's | **Gold Coast** 20

Gold Coast | **multi.** 17

Goose Island | **multi.** 17

Grafton Pub & Grill | **Lincoln Sq** 23

Grahamwich | **River N** 19

GT Fish/Oyster | **River N** 26

Half Shell | **Lakeview** 24

Harry Caray's | **multi.** 23

Heaven/Seven | **multi.** 21

Honey 1 BBQ | **Bucktown** 21

Hopleaf | **Andersonville** 24

Hubbard Inn | **River N** 21

Joy Yee | **multi.** 21

Julius Meinl | **multi.** 21

Kinzie Chop | **River N** 23

Koi | **Evanston** 18

Lou Mitchell's | **Loop** 24

Z Lula | **Logan Sq** 27

McCormick/Schmick | **multi.** 20

Z Mirai Sushi | **Wicker Pk** 27

Mr. Beef | **River N** 24

Oak Tree Bakery | **Gold Coast** 16

Old Jerusalem | **Old Town** 20

Oysy | **multi.** 23

Reza's | **multi.** 19

Z Shaw's Crab | **multi.** 25

Tanoshii | **Andersonville** 28

Toast | **multi.** 23

Toro Sushi | **Lincoln Pk** 28

ENTERTAINMENT

(Call for days and times
of performances)

Abbey | Irish/rock | **NW Side** 18

Catch 35 | piano | **Loop** 24

Chicago Chop | piano | **River N** 24

Chicago Prime Steak | varies | **Schaumburg** –

Chief O'Neill's | Irish | **NW Side** 17

Edelweiss | German | **Norridge** 22

Geja's | flamenco/guitar | **Lincoln Pk** 22

Lobby | jazz | **River N** 24

Mesón Sabika | flamenco | **Naperville** 25

Myron/Phil Steak | karaoke/piano | **Lincolnwood** 20

Nacional 27 | varies | **River N** 22

Philly G's | piano | **Vernon Hills** 21

Rock Bottom | karaoke | **Warrenville** 19

Sabatino's | piano | **Old Irving Pk** 25

Sayat Nova | DJ | **Streeterville** 23

Z Shaw's Crab | blues/jazz | **River N** 25

Signature Room | jazz | **Streeterville** 17

Smoke Daddy | blues/jazz | **Wicker Pk** 22

Sullivan's Steak | jazz | **multi.** 24

Tapas Gitana | guitar | **Northfield** 23

Uncommon Ground | varies | **Lakeview** 23

FIREPLACES

Acre | **Andersonville** 20

Z Adelle's | **Wheaton** 27

Ai Sushi | **River N** 22

Andies | **Andersonville** 21

Ann Sather | **Lakeview** 22

NEW Argent | **River N** -

Athena | **Greektown** 21

Bacino's | **Loop** 22

Bistrot Margot | **Old Town** 22

Blokes/Birds | **Lakeview** 18

Bluebird | **Bucktown** 23

Bourgeois Pig | **Lincoln Pk** 21

Brio | **Lombard** 20

Cafe Laguardia | **Bucktown** 22

Carlucci | **Downers Grove** 20

Carson's | **Deerfield** 22

Chens | **Wrigleyville** 21

Chicago Firehouse | **S Loop** 22

Chicago Prime Steak | **Schaumburg** -

Chief O'Neill's | **NW Side** 17

Clubhouse | **Oak Brook** 23

Convito | **Wilmette** 20

Z Courtright's | **Willow Spgs** 28

Dee's | **Lincoln Pk** 19

Deleece Grill | **Lakeview** 18

Devon Seafood | **River N** 21

Edelweiss | **Norridge** 22

EJ's Pl. | **Skokie** 22

Elephant & Castle | **multi.** 15

Erie Cafe | **River N** 22

NEW Estate Ultra Bar | **River W** -

Feast | **Bucktown** 20

Z Francesca's | **multi.** 22

Froggy's | **Highwood** 25

Frontier | **Noble Sq** 23

Gage | **Loop** 24

Z Gene/Georgetti | **River N** 25

Grafton Pub & Grill | **Lincoln Sq** 23

Half Shell | **Lakeview** 24

Il Mulino | **Gold Coast** 25

Inovasi | **Lake Bluff** 26

Japonais | **River N** 24

Jerry's | **Wicker Pk** 21

John's Pl. | **Lincoln Pk** 18

Keefer's | **River N** 25

Koi | **Evanston** 18

La Madia | **River N** 24

Z Les Nomades | **Streeterville** 28

Le Vichyssois | **Lakemoor** 26

Lovells | **Lake Forest** 22

Maijean | **Clarendon Hills** 26

Milk/Honey | **Wicker Pk** 23

NEW Mo Dailey's Pub | **NW Side** -

Z North Pond | **Lincoln Pk** 26

Original/Walker Pancake | **Lake Zurich** 24

Owen/Engine | **Logan Sq** 23

Oysy | **S Loop** 23

Park Grill | **Loop** 19

Z Pelago | **Streeterville** 26

Penny's | **multi.** 21

Pensiero | **Evanston** 21

Prairie Grass | **Northbrook** 22

Prasino | **Wicker Pk** 23

Quartino | **River N** 22

Quince | **Evanston** 25

Revolution Brewing | **Logan Sq** 23

Reza's | **River N** 19

RL | **Gold Coast** 24

Robinson's Ribs | **Lincoln Pk** 20

Rockit | **Wrigleyville** 19

NEW Rustic Hse. | **Lincoln Pk** 22

Ruth's Chris | **Northbrook** 26

Z Sai Café | **Lincoln Pk** 27

Santorini | **Greektown** 22

Sola | **Lakeview** 24

Sullivan's Steak | **Lincolnshire** 24

Sunda | **River N** 24

Swordfish | **Batavia** 27

Z Tallgrass | **Lockport** 27

Tavern/Park | **Loop** 17

NEW III Forks | **Loop** 22

Trattoria Gianni | **Lincoln Pk** 20

Uncommon Ground | **multi.** 23

Z Vie | **W Springs** 29

Weber Grill | **multi.** 21

Webster's Wine Bar | **Lincoln Pk** 19

HISTORIC PLACES

(Year opened; * building)

1800 | Chief O'Neill's* | **NW Side** 17
1847 | Mesón Sabika* | **Naperville** 25
1870 | Depot Nuevo* | **Wilmette** 17
1874 | Il Mulino* | **Gold Coast** 25
1880 | Bourgeois Pig* | **Lincoln Pk** 21
1880 | Leopold* | **Noble Sq** 23
1880 | West Town* | **Noble Sq** 26
1881 | Twin Anchors* | **Old Town** 22
1887 | Merlo* | **Gold Coast** 24
1890 | John Barleycorn* | **Lincoln Pk** 17
1890 | Lawry's* | **River N** 26
1890 | Pizzeria Uno/Due* | **River N** 23
1890 | Sapori Trattoria* | **Lincoln Pk** 26
1890 | Sepia* | **W Loop** 26
1890 | Webster's Wine Bar* | **Lincoln Pk** 19
1892 | Francesca's* | **Naperville** 22
1897 | Tallgrass* | **Lockport** 27
1898 | Berghoff | **Loop** 20
1900 | Vivo* | **W Loop** 23
1901 | Bank Lane* | **Lake Forest** 22
1901 | South Gate* | **Lake Forest** 18
1905 | Carnivale* | **W Loop** 22
1905 | Chicago Firehouse* | **S Loop** 22
1906 | Masa Azul* | **Logan Sq** –
1907 | Bistro Voltaire* | **Near North** 23
1910 | Hackney's* | **Printer's Row** 19
1911 | Haymarket Pub* | **W Loop** 18
1912 | Eleven City* | **S Loop** 19
1920 | Chef's Station* | **Evanston** 25
1920 | Dining Room/Kendall* | **Near W** 23
1920 | 3rd Coast Cafe* | **Gold Coast** 19
1921 | Margie's Candies | **Bucktown** 23
1922 | Del Rio* | **Highwood** 21
1923 | Lou Mitchell's | **Loop** 24
1927 | David Burke Prime* | **River N** 25
1927 | Village* | **Loop** 22
1927 | Vivere* | **Loop** 24
1930 | Russell's BBQ | **Elmwood Pk** 19
1930 | Tufano's Tap* | **Little Italy/University Vill** 24
1933 | Bruna's | **SW Side** 24
1933 | Cape Cod | **Streeterville** 22
1934 | Billy Goat | **multi.** 16
1935 | FatDuck Tavern* | **Forest Pk** 19
1938 | Al's Beef | **multi.** 23
1939 | Hackney's | **Glenview** 19
1940 | Due Lire* | **Lincoln Sq** 23
1940 | Township* | **Logan Sq** –
1941 | Gene/Georgetti | **River N** 25
1946 | Ricobene's | **Bridgeport** 24
1948 | Superdawg | **NW Side** 21
1950 | Ashkenaz Deli | **Gold Coast** 19
1950 | Gene & Jude's | **O'Hare Area** 24
1950 | Miller's Pub | **Loop** 18
1954 | White Fence | **Romeoville** 24
1955 | Pizzeria Uno/Due | **River N** 23
1959 | Aurelio's Pizza | **multi.** 23
1959 | Moody's Pub | **Edgewater** 20
1960 | Original/Walker Pancake | **Wilmette** 24

HOTEL DINING

Affinia Chicago Hotel
  C-House | **Streeterville** 21
Belden-Stratford Hotel
  🎽 L2O | **Lincoln Pk** 25
  Mon Ami Gabi | **Lincoln Pk** 24
Blackstone Hotel
  Mercat | **S Loop** 26
Dana Hotel & Spa
  NEW Argent | **River N** –
Doubletree Libertyville
  Karma | **Mundelein** 23
Doubletree O'Hare
  🎽 Gibsons | **Rosemont** 26
Drake Hotel
  Cape Cod | **Streeterville** 22
Embassy Suites Hotel
  Original Gino's | **Deerfield** 21
  P.J. Clarke's | **Streeterville** 18
Essex Inn
  NEW Brasserie by LM | **S Loop** –
Fairmont Chicago Hotel
  Aria | **Loop** 24
Four Seasons Hotel Chicago
  NEW Allium | **Gold Coast** –
Hilton Chicago
  NEW 720 South B&G | **S Loop** –
Hilton Garden Inn
  Weber Grill | **River N** 21
Hilton Lisle/Naperville
  Allgauer's | **Lisle** 21
Holiday Inn Chicago Downtown
  Aurelio's Pizza | **Loop** 23
Holiday Inn Chicago O'Hare
  Bar Louie | **O'Hare Area** 17
Holiday Inn Mount Prospect
  Bar Louie | **Mt. Prospect** 17

Holiday Inn North Shore
Bar Louie | **Skokie** ____17__

Homestead Hotel
Quince | **Evanston** ____25__

Hotel Allegro
312 Chicago | **Loop** ____21__

Hotel Burnham
Atwood Cafe | **Loop** ____22__

Hotel Felix
Elate | **River N** ____23__

Hotel Lincoln
🆕 Perennial Virant | ____26__
Lincoln Pk

Hotel Monaco
South Water | **Loop** ____15__

Hotel Palomar
Sable | **River N** ____24__

InterContinental Chicago
🆕 Michael Jordan's | ____23__
Streeterville

James Chicago Hotel
David Burke Prime | **River N** ____25__

JW Marriott Chicago
Florentine | **Loop** ____22__

Margarita European Inn
Pensiero | **Evanston** ____21__

Palmer House Hilton
Lockwood | **Loop** ____22__

Park Hyatt Chicago
🗷🆕 NoMI Kitchen | ____26__
Gold Coast

Peninsula Chicago
Lobby | **River N** ____24__
Pierrot Gourmet | **River N** ____24__
🗷 Shanghai Terrace | ____27__
River N

Public Hotel
🗷🆕 Pump Room | ____21__
Gold Coast

Radisson Blu Aqua Hotel
🆕 Filini | **Loop** ____24__

Raffaello Hotel
🗷 Pelago | **Streeterville** ____26__

Red Roof Inn
Coco Pazzo | **Streeterville** ____23__

Renaissance North Shore Hotel
Ruth's Chris | **Northbrook** ____26__

Ritz-Carlton Chicago
Deca | **Streeterville** ____22__

Rivers Casino
🗷 Hugo's | **Des Plaines** ____25__

Seneca Hotel
🗷 Francesca's | **Streeterville** ____22__
Saloon Steak | **Streeterville** ____23__

Sheraton Chicago Hotel
Shula's Steak | **Streeterville** ____21__

The Shoreham
Caffe Rom | **Loop** ____24__

Sofitel Chicago Water Tower
Café/Architectes | **Gold Coast** ____24__

Swissôtel Chicago
🆕 Amuse | **Loop** ___-__
Palm | **Loop** ____24__

Tremont Hotel
Ditka's | **Gold Coast** ____22__

Trump Int'l Hotel
🗷 Sixteen | **River N** ____25__

Waldorf-Astoria Chicago
Balsan | **Gold Coast** ____24__
🗷 Ria | **Gold Coast** ____27__

Westin Chicago North Shore
Tramonto's Steak/Sea | ____21__
Wheeling

Westin Chicago NW
Shula's Steak | **Itasca** ____21__

Westin Lombard
Harry Caray's | **Lombard** ____23__

Westin Michigan Ave.
Grill on the Alley | **Streeterville** ____21__

Westin River North
Kamehachi | **River N** ____22__

theWit Hotel
State/Lake | **Loop** ____17__

Wyndham Blake
Custom House | **Printer's Row** ____26__

JACKET REQUIRED

🗷 Les Nomades | **Streeterville** ____28__
🗷 Spiaggia | **Gold Coast** ____26__
🗷 Tru | **Streeterville** ____28__

LATE DINING

(Weekday closing hour)

Abbey | 12:00 AM | **NW Side** ____18__
Al's Beef | varies | **multi.** ____23__
🆕 Anthem | varies | ___-__
Ukrainian Vill
🆕 Argent | 2 AM | **River N** ___-__
Artopolis | 12 AM | **Greektown** ____21__
🆕 Au Cheval | 1:30 AM | ___-__
W Loop
🗷 Avec | 12 AM | **W Loop** ____28__
Bangers/Lace | 2 AM | ____20__
Wicker Pk
Bar Louie | varies | **multi.** ____17__
🆕 Barrelhouse Flat | varies | ___-__
Lincoln Pk
🆕 Bar Toma | varies | ____17__
Gold Coast
🗷 Bedford | varies | **Wicker Pk** ____17__
Bricks | varies | **North Ctr/St. Ben's** ____25__
Big Star | 2 AM | **Wicker Pk** ____26__
Bijan's | 3:30 AM | **River N** ____19__

Billy Goat | varies | **River N** 16

Bite | varies | **Ukrainian Vill** 22

Blokes/Birds | 2 AM | **Lakeview** 18

Blue Agave | 12 AM | **Near North** 15

Bluebird | varies | **Bucktown** 23

NEW Bullhead Cantina | varies | —
  Humboldt Pk

Butch McGuire's | varies | 20
  Near North

Café Iberico | 11:30 PM | **River N** 22

Chicago Cut | 2 AM | **River N** 26

Chicago's Pizza | varies | **multi.** 16

Coast Sushi/South Coast | 12 25
  AM | **Bucktown**

Dimo's Pizza | varies | **Lakeview** 23

DiSotto | varies | **Streeterville** 25

DMK Burger Bar | 12 AM | 21
  Lakeview

Elephant & Castle | varies | **Loop** 15

Elly's Pancake House | 24 hrs. | 19
  Old Town

NEW Estate Ultra Bar | varies | —
  River W

Fifty/50 | 1 AM | **Wicker Pk** 19

Fireside | varies | **Andersonville** 22

NEW Flight 1551 | varies | —
  Old Town

NEW Forza | varies | **Lincoln Pk** —

NEW French Quarter | varies | —
  Lombard

Frontier | varies | **Noble Sq** 23

Gage | varies | **Loop** 24

Gene & Jude's | varies | 24
  O'Hare Area

Z Gibsons | varies | **multi.** 26

Gilt Bar | 12 AM | **River N** 26

Giordano's | varies | **multi.** 22

NEW Glenview House | varies | 19
  Glenview

Greek Islands | varies | **Greektown** 22

NEW Gyro-Ména | varies | —
  Lakeview

Half Shell | 12 AM | **Lakeview** 24

Hard Rock | 12 AM | **River N** 14

Haymarket Pub | varies | 18
  W Loop

Hop Häus | varies | **multi.** 19

Hub 51 | 12 AM | **River N** 21

Z Hugo's | varies | **multi.** 25

Itto Sushi | 12 AM | **Lincoln Pk** 24

Jack's/Halsted | varies | **Lakeview** 16

Jake Melnick's | 1 AM | **Gold Coast** 19

NEW Jimbo's Top Gun | 24 hrs. | —
  Wrigleyville

Joe's Crab Shack | 12 AM | **multi.** 20

John Barleycorn | varies | 17
  Schaumburg

Kamehachi | varies | **Old Town** 22

Z Kuma's | 1 AM | **Avondale** 27

Lao | varies | **Chinatown** 24

NEW La Z De Oro | varies | —
  Berwyn

NEW Linkin House | 12 AM | —
  Lincoln Pk

Z Longman/Eagle | 1 AM | 27
  Logan Sq

Lou Mitchell's | varies | 24
  O'Hare Area

Luxbar | 1:30 AM | **Gold Coast** 19

Margie's Candies | varies | 23
  Bucktown

Mastro's Steak | varies | **River N** 26

Maude's Liquor | 2 AM | **W Loop** 25

Melting Pot | varies | **River N** 19

Mercadito | varies | **River N** 22

Miller's Pub | 2 AM | **Loop** 18

NEW Mitad del Mundo | —
  varies | **Logan Sq**

NEW Mo Dailey's Pub | varies | —
  NW Side

Moody's Pub | 1 AM | **Edgewater** 20

Mr. Beef | 5 AM | **River N** 24

NEW Nellcôte | varies | **W Loop** —

Noodles by Yagihashi | 3 AM | 23
  Loop

NEW Old Town Pour Hse. | —
  2 AM | **Old Town**

Old Town Social | 1:30 AM | 24
  Old Town

Paris Club | varies | **River N** 21

Parthenon | 12 AM | **Greektown** 21

NEW Patron's Hacienda | —
  varies | **River N**

Pegasus | varies | **multi.** 21

Pequod's Pizza | varies | **Lincoln Pk** 25

Pete Miller | varies | **Evanston** 22

NEW Phil's Last Stand | varies | —
  Ukrainian Vill

Pizano's Pizza | varies | **multi.** 21

Pizzeria Uno/Due | varies | 23
  River N

NEW Point | varies | **W Loop** —

Public House | 1 AM | **River N** 19

Z Purple Pig | 12 AM | **River N** 26

Quartino | 1 AM | **River N** 22

NEW Red Door | 12 AM | —
  Bucktown

Revolution Brewing | 12 AM | 23
  Logan Sq

Reza's | varies | **Andersonville** 19

Ricobene's | varies | **multi.** 24

Rockit | 1:30 AM | **River N** 19

Roditys | 12 AM | **Greektown** 22

NEW Roots Pizza | 2 AM | 23
  W Town

Rootstock | 1 AM | **Humboldt Pk** 24

NEW RPM Italian	varies	River N	-
Sable	varies	River N	24
San Soo Gab San	24 hrs.	Lincoln Sq	26
Santorini	12 AM	Greektown	22
NEW Scofflaw	varies	Logan Sq	-
NEW Scout Waterhouse	varies	S Loop	-
Silver Seafood	1 AM	Uptown	27
NEW Slurping Turtle	varies	River N	22
Small Bar	varies	multi.	20
Southern	varies	Wicker Pk	21
NEW Storefront Co.	2 AM	Wicker Pk	-
Superdawg	varies	NW Side	21
Sushisamba Rio	1 AM	River N	22
NEW Sutherlands	12 AM	NW Side	-
Taco Grill	2 AM	Westmont	-
NEW Taverna 750	varies	Wrigleyville	25
NEW Tavernita	varies	River N	-
Tavern/Rush	12 AM	Gold Coast	21
NEW Telegraph Wine Bar	varies	Logan Sq	23
Tempo	24 hrs.	Gold Coast	20
3rd Coast Cafe	12 AM	Gold Coast	19
Three Aces	varies	Little Italy/University Vill	24
Three Happiness	6 AM	Chinatown	22
NEW Tokyo 21	varies	Old Town	-
NEW Topper's Pizza	3 AM	Greektown	-
NEW Township	2 AM	Logan Sq	-
NEW Troquet	varies	Ravenswood	-
Twisted Spoke	1 AM	Noble Sq	20
NEW Vapiano	12 AM	Lincoln Pk	17
NEW Vera	varies	W Loop	24
Village	11:30 PM	Loop	22
Webster's Wine Bar	12:30 AM	Lincoln Pk	19
NEW Wheel House	varies	Wrigleyville	-
White Palace	24 hrs.	S Loop	21
Wiener's Circle	4 AM	Lincoln Pk	19
NEW Wild Monk	varies	La Grange	-

MEET FOR A DRINK

(Most top hotels and the following standouts)

Acre	Andersonville	20
NEW Ada St.	Bucktown	-
Adobo	Old Town	21
NEW Argent	River N	-
NEW Au Cheval	W Loop	-
NEW Balena	Lincoln Pk	-
Balsan	Gold Coast	24
Bandera	Streeterville	23
Bangers/Lace	Wicker Pk	20
NEW Barrelhouse Flat	Lincoln Pk	-
NEW Bar Toma	Gold Coast	17
Z Bedford	Wicker Pk	17
Benny's Chop	River N	26
Blokes/Birds	Lakeview	18
Bluebird	Bucktown	23
Boka	Lincoln Pk	26
NEW Brasserie by LM	S Loop	-
Bridge Bar Chicago	River N	-
NEW Bridge House	River N	18
Bristol	Bucktown	25
Café/Architectes	Gold Coast	24
NEW Caravan	Uptown	-
Carnivale	W Loop	22
Catch 35	multi.	24
Cellar/Stained Glass	Evanston	22
Chicago Cut	River N	26
Chizakaya	Lakeview	24
Cité	Streeterville	19
Clubhouse	Oak Brook	23
Club Lucky	Bucktown	22
Coobah	Lakeview	22
Z Davanti	Little Italy/University Vill	27
NEW Derby	Lincoln Pk	-
NEW Deuce's/Diamond	Wrigleyville	-
DiSotto	Streeterville	25
Ditka's	multi.	22
Duke/Perth	Lakeview	20
Epic Restaurant	River N	-
NEW Estate Ultra Bar	River W	-
NEW Filini	Loop	24
Flight	Glenview	23
NEW Flight 1551	Old Town	-
NEW Forza	Lincoln Pk	-
Fountainhead	Ravenswood	21
Fred's	Gold Coast	20
Fulton's	River N	19
Gage	Loop	24
Z Gibsons	multi.	26
Gilt Bar	River N	26
Z Girl/The Goat	W Loop	27
Goose Island	multi.	17
Gordon Biersch	Bolingbrook	17
Grafton Pub & Grill	Lincoln Sq	23
Graham Elliot	River N	25
Harry Caray's	multi.	23

Henri | **Loop**	27
Hopleaf | **Andersonville**	24
Hubbard Inn | **River N**	21
Hub 51 | **River N**	21
Hugo's | **multi.**	25
Japonais | **River N**	24
Joe's Sea/Steak | **River N**	27
Keefer's | **River N**	25
NEW Lady Gregory's | **Andersonville**	19
Le Colonial | **Gold Coast**	23
Leopold | **Noble Sq**	23
Lockwood | **Loop**	22
Longman/Eagle | **Logan Sq**	27
Lula | **Logan Sq**	27
Luxbar | **Gold Coast**	19
NEW Masa Azul | **Logan Sq**	-
Mastro's Steak | **River N**	26
Maude's Liquor | **W Loop**	25
Mercadito | **River N**	22
NEW Michael Jordan's | **Streeterville**	23
MK | **Near North**	28
NEW Moderno | **Highland Pk**	-
Nacional 27 | **River N**	22
NEW Nellcôte | **W Loop**	-
N9ne Steak | **Loop**	22
NEW NoMI Kitchen | **Gold Coast**	26
NEW Ogden | **W Loop**	-
NEW Old Town Pour Hse. | **Old Town**	-
Old Town Social | **Old Town**	24
Owen/Engine | **Logan Sq**	23
Paris Club | **River N**	21
NEW Patron's Hacienda | **River N**	-
NEW Perennial Virant | **Lincoln Pk**	26
NEW Point | **W Loop**	-
Prosecco | **River N**	24
Publican | **W Loop**	26
Public House | **River N**	19
NEW Pump Room | **Gold Coast**	21
Quartino | **River N**	22
NEW Quay | **Streeterville**	19
Revolution Brewing | **Logan Sq**	23
Rhapsody | **Loop**	21
RL | **Gold Coast**	24
NEW Roka Akor | **River N**	24
Rosebud Prime/Steak | **Streeterville**	24
Rosebud | **River N**	22
Sable | **River N**	24
NEW Saranello's | **Wheeling**	24
NEW Scofflaw | **Logan Sq**	-
Scoozi! | **River N**	21

NEW Scout Waterhouse | **S Loop**	-
Sepia | **W Loop**	26
Shaw's Crab | **multi.**	25
Signature Room | **Streeterville**	17
Sixteen | **River N**	25
Smith/Wollensky | **River N**	23
South Branch | **Loop**	22
Southern | **Wicker Pk**	21
Stained Glass | **Evanston**	25
NEW Standard Grill | **Westmont**	-
State/Lake | **Loop**	17
NEW Storefront Co. | **Wicker Pk**	-
Sullivan's Steak | **River N**	24
Sunda | **River N**	24
Sushisamba Rio | **River N**	22
Tasting Room | **W Loop**	16
NEW Taverna 750 | **Wrigleyville**	25
Tavern/Park | **Loop**	17
NEW Tavernita | **River N**	-
Tavern/Rush | **Gold Coast**	21
NEW Telegraph Wine Bar | **Logan Sq**	23
Three Aces | **Little Italy/University Vill**	24
NEW III Forks | **Loop**	22
312 Chicago | **Loop**	21
NEW Tokyo 21 | **Old Town**	-
Tramonto's Steak/Sea | **Wheeling**	21
Trattoria No. 10 | **Loop**	25
NEW Troquet | **Ravenswood**	-
NEW Union Sushi + BBQ | **River N**	22
NEW Urban Union | **Little Italy/University Vill**	-
NEW Vera | **W Loop**	24
Webster's Wine Bar | **Lincoln Pk**	19
NEW Wild Monk | **La Grange**	-
Zak's Place | **Hinsdale**	22
Zapatista | **S Loop**	18
Zocalo | **River N**	22

MICROBREWERIES

Goose Island | **multi.**	17
Gordon Biersch | **Bolingbrook**	17
Haymarket Pub | **W Loop**	18
Piece | **Wicker Pk**	25
Revolution Brewing | **Logan Sq**	23
Rock Bottom | **multi.**	19
Small Bar | **Ukrainian Vill**	20

NEWCOMERS

Acadia | **S Loop**	-
Ada St. | **Bucktown**	-
Al Dente | **NW Side**	-
Allium | **Gold Coast**	-

Amoremia | **Old Irving Pk**	-
Amuse | **Loop**	-
Anna's Asian | **W Loop**	-
Anthem | **Ukrainian Vill**	-
Argent | **River N**	-
Au Cheval | **W Loop**	-
Autre Monde | **Berwyn**	25
BadHappy Poutine | **River N**	-
Baker & Nosh | **Uptown**	-
Bakersfield | **Westmont**	-
Balena | **Lincoln Pk**	-
Banh Mi & Co. | **Lakeview**	-
Barbari | **Ukrainian Vill**	-
Barrelhouse Flat | **Lincoln Pk**	-
Barrio | **Lakeview**	-
Bar Toma | **Gold Coast**	17
Benjamin | **Highland Pk**	16
Big Easy | **Loop**	-
Bistro Voltaire | **Near North**	23
Bombay Spice | **River N**	21
Bongiorno's | **River N**	-
Brasserie by LM | **S Loop**	-
Bread & Wine | **Old Irving Pk**	-
Bridge House | **River N**	18
Brunch | **River N**	15
Bullhead Cantina | **Humboldt Pk**	-
Burger Joint | **River N**	-
Burger Point | **S Loop**	-
Butcher/The Burger | **Lincoln Pk**	26
Caffè Italia | **Elmwood Pk**	-
Cantina Laredo | **River N**	17
Caravan | **Uptown**	-
Carlos & Carlos | **Arlington Hts**	-
Chilapan | **Ravenswood**	24
City Farms Mkt. | **Lakeview**	-
Crêperie Saint-Germain | **Evanston**	-
Cyrano's | **River N**	-
Derby | **Lincoln Pk**	-
Deuce's/Diamond | **Wrigleyville**	-
Eduardo's Enoteca | **Gold Coast**	-
Eggy's | **Streeterville**	-
EL Ideas | **Pilsen**	29
Eshticken Pizza | **Hoffman Est**	-
Estate Ultra Bar | **River W**	-
E wok Café | **NW Side**	-
Farmhouse | **Near North**	22
Felice's Pizza | **Rogers Pk**	-
Filini | **Loop**	24
Flight 1551 | **Old Town**	-
Forza | **Lincoln Pk**	-
4Suyos | **Logan Sq**	-
French Quarter | **Lombard**	-
Frog n Snail | **Lakeview**	-
Fuji Sushi | **Lakeview**	-
Gemellato | **Bridgeport**	-

Glenview House | **Glenview**	19
Goosefoot | **Lincoln Sq**	-
Grange Hall | **W Loop**	-
Gratto Pizza | **Wicker Pk**	-
Gyro-Ména | **Lakeview**	-
Hota | **Evanston**	-
Hutong | **Oak Pk**	-
Jimbo's Top Gun | **Wrigleyville**	-
Jin Thai | **Edgewater**	-
Lady Gregory's | **Andersonville**	19
Lao Hunan | **Chinatown**	28
La Parrilla | **NW Side**	-
La Z De Oro | **Berwyn**	-
Libertad | **Skokie**	24
Linkin House | **Lincoln Pk**	-
M | **Highland Pk**	-
Mama Milano | **Old Town**	-
Marmalade | **North Ctr/St. Ben's**	26
Masa Azul | **Logan Sq**	-
Melt Sandwich | **Bucktown**	-
Michael Jordan's | **Streeterville**	23
Mitad del Mundo | **Logan Sq**	-
Mo Dailey's Pub | **NW Side**	-
Moderno | **Highland Pk**	-
Monti's | **Lincoln Sq**	-
Morso | **Lincoln Pk**	-
My Mother's Kitchen | **Elmwood Pk**	-
Native Foods | **multi.**	23
Nellcôte | **W Loop**	-
New England Sea | **Lakeview**	-
Nieto's | **Highland Pk**	-
✍ NoMI Kitchen | **Gold Coast**	26
Ogden | **W Loop**	-
Old Town Pour Hse. | **Old Town**	-
Ombra | **Andersonville**	-
Osteria/Pizza Metro | **Lakeview**	-
Pasteur | **Edgewater**	-
Patron's Hacienda | **River N**	-
Perennial Virant | **Lincoln Pk**	26
Phil's Last Stand | **Ukrainian Vill**	-
Point | **W Loop**	-
Premise | **Andersonville**	-
Publican Meats | **W Loop**	-
✍ Pump Room | **Gold Coast**	21
Quay | **Streeterville**	19
Red Door | **Bucktown**	-
Red Violet | **River N**	-
Ripasso | **Bucktown**	-
Roka Akor | **River N**	24
Roots Pizza | **W Town**	23
RPM Italian | **River N**	-
Rustic Hse. | **Lincoln Pk**	22
Sacco Bruno | **Bucktown**	-

Saranello's | **Wheeling**	24
Scofflaw | **Logan Sq**	–
Scout Waterhouse | **S Loop**	–
2nd Street Bistro | **Highland Pk**	21
Seven Ocean | **Oak Pk**	–
720 South B&G | **S Loop**	–
Slurping Turtle | **River N**	22
Soulwich | **Evanston**	–
Southport & Irving | **North Ctr/St. Ben's**	–
Standard Grill | **Westmont**	–
Storefront Co. | **Wicker Pk**	–
Sutherlands | **NW Side**	–
Tandoor Char House | **Lincoln Pk**	–
Taverna 750 | **Wrigleyville**	25
Tavernita | **River N**	–
Telegraph Wine Bar | **Logan Sq**	23
III Forks | **Loop**	22
Todoroki Hibachi | **Evanston**	–
Tokio Pub | **Schaumburg**	–
Tokyo 21 | **Old Town**	–
Topper's Pizza | **Greektown**	–
Township | **Logan Sq**	–
Tozi | **Wicker Pk**	–
Troquet | **Ravenswood**	–
Tuman's Tap & Grill | **Ukrainian Vill**	–
25 Degrees | **River N**	22
2 Sparrows | **Lincoln Pk**	20
Umami | **Little Italy/University Vill**	–
Union Sushi + BBQ | **River N**	22
Urban Union | **Little Italy/University Vill**	–
Vapiano | **Lincoln Pk**	17
Vera | **W Loop**	24
Wasabi Cafe | **North Ctr/St. Ben's**	–
Wellfleet | **Albany Pk**	–
Westminster Hot Dog | **Loop**	18
West on North | **Humboldt Pk**	–
Wheel House | **Wrigleyville**	–
Wilde & Greene | **Skokie**	18
Wild Monk | **La Grange**	–
Yusho | **Avondale**	–
Yuzu Sushi | **E Vill**	–
Zebra's | **Bridgeport**	–

OUTDOOR DINING

Athena | **Greektown**	21
Big Jones | **Andersonville**	25
Big Star | **Wicker Pk**	26
Bistro Campagne | **Lincoln Sq**	25
❷ Blackbird | **W Loop**	27
Boka | **Lincoln Pk**	26
Cafe Ba-Ba-Reeba! | **Lincoln Pk**	23
Carmine's | **Gold Coast**	21
Chez Joël | **Little Italy/University Vill**	26

Chicago Firehouse | **S Loop**	22
Coco Pazzo | **Streeterville**	23
David Burke Prime | **River N**	25
NEW Deuce's/Diamond | **Wrigleyville**	–
Dinotto | **Old Town**	21
Elate | **River N**	23
El Jardin | **Lakeview**	18
Erie Cafe | **River N**	22
NEW Estate Ultra Bar | **River W**	–
Feast | **multi.**	20
Fred's | **Gold Coast**	20
Fulton's | **River N**	19
Gage | **Loop**	24
Hackney's | **multi.**	19
❷ Henri | **Loop**	27
Japonais | **River N**	24
Keefer's | **River N**	25
Le Colonial | **Gold Coast**	23
❷ Longman/Eagle | **Logan Sq**	27
❷ Lula | **Logan Sq**	27
Mercadito | **River N**	22
Mercat | **S Loop**	26
Mesón Sabika | **multi.**	25
Mia Francesca | **Lakeview**	24
Miramar | **Highwood**	17
Moody's Pub | **Edgewater**	20
❷ Naha | **River N**	27
❷ Nightwood | **Pilsen**	27
❷ **NEW** NoMI Kitchen | **Gold Coast**	26
Oceanique | **Evanston**	25
Opa! Estiatorio | **Vernon Hills**	23
Paris Club | **River N**	21
Park Grill | **Loop**	19
Pegasus | **Greektown**	21
❷ Pelago | **Streeterville**	26
Pensiero | **Evanston**	21
❷ Piccolo Sogno | **Near W**	26
Pizzeria Uno/Due | **River N**	23
❷ Purple Pig | **River N**	26
Rhapsody | **Loop**	21
Riva | **Streeterville**	20
RL | **Gold Coast**	24
Rock Bottom | **multi.**	19
Rosebud | **Streeterville**	22
Salpicón | **Old Town**	25
❷ Shanghai Terrace | **River N**	27
❷ Sixteen | **River N**	25
Smith/Wollensky | **River N**	23
South Branch | **Loop**	22
Sushisamba Rio | **River N**	22
Tavern/Park | **Loop**	17
Tavern/Rush | **Gold Coast**	21
Terzo Piano | **Loop**	22

NEW III Forks | **Loop**		22
NEW Tokyo 21 | **Old Town**		-
Topo Gigio | **Old Town**		26
Zed 451 | **River N**		23

PEOPLE-WATCHING

NEW Ada St. | **Bucktown**		-
Adobo | **Old Town**		21
NEW Allium | **Gold Coast**		-
NEW Argent | **River N**		-
NEW Au Cheval | **W Loop**		-
Z Avec | **W Loop**		28
NEW BadHappy Poutine | **River N**		-
NEW Bakersfield | **Westmont**		-
NEW Balena | **Lincoln Pk**		-
Balsan | **Gold Coast**		24
Bangers/Lace | **Wicker Pk**		20
NEW Barrelhouse Flat | **Lincoln Pk**		-
NEW Bar Toma | **Gold Coast**		17
Z Bedford | **Wicker Pk**		17
Benny's Chop | **River N**		26
Big Star | **Wicker Pk**		26
Billy Goat | **River N**		16
Bistronomic | **Gold Coast**		23
Z Blackbird | **W Loop**		27
Blokes/Birds | **Lakeview**		18
Boka | **Lincoln Pk**		26
NEW Bombay Spice | **River N**		21
Bristol | **Bucktown**		25
Carmine's | **Gold Coast**		21
Carnivale | **W Loop**		22
Chicago Chop | **River N**		24
Chicago Cut | **River N**		26
Z Davanti | **Little Italy/University Vill**		27
Deca | **Streeterville**		22
NEW Deuce's/Diamond | **Wrigleyville**		-
Epic Restaurant | **River N**		-
NEW Estate Ultra Bar | **River W**		-
Fifty/50 | **Wicker Pk**		19
Fred's | **Gold Coast**		20
NEW Frog n Snail | **Lakeview**		-
Gage | **Loop**		24
Z Gene/Georgetti | **River N**		25
Z Gibsons | **multi.**		26
Gilt Bar | **River N**		26
Z Girl/The Goat | **W Loop**		27
Graham Elliot | **River N**		25
Z Green Zebra | **Noble Sq**		28
GT Fish/Oyster | **River N**		26
Harry Caray's | **multi.**		23
Hearty | **Lakeview**		23
Z Henri | **Loop**		27
Hubbard Inn | **River N**		21
Hub 51 | **River N**		21

Z Hugo's | **multi.**		25
Il Mulino | **Gold Coast**		25
Japonais | **River N**		24
Z Joe's Sea/Steak | **River N**		27
Keefer's | **River N**		25
Z Kuma's | **Avondale**		27
NEW Lao Hunan | **Chinatown**		28
Le Colonial | **Gold Coast**		23
Lobby | **River N**		24
Z Longman/Eagle | **Logan Sq**		27
Luxbar | **Gold Coast**		19
Manny's | **S Loop**		24
Mastro's Steak | **River N**		26
Maude's Liquor | **W Loop**		25
Mercadito | **River N**		22
Mercat | **S Loop**		26
NEW Michael Jordan's | **Streeterville**		23
Z Mirai Sushi | **Wicker Pk**		27
Miramar | **Highwood**		17
Z MK | **Near North**		28
Z Naha | **River N**		27
NEW Nellcôte | **W Loop**		-
Z Next | **W Loop**		29
N9ne Steak | **Loop**		22
Z NEW NoMI Kitchen | **Gold Coast**		26
NEW Ogden | **W Loop**		-
NEW Old Town Pour Hse. | **Old Town**		-
Old Town Social | **Old Town**		24
Osteria/Pizzeria Via Stato | **River N**		23
Owen/Engine | **Logan Sq**		23
Paris Club | **River N**		21
NEW Perennial Virant | **Lincoln Pk**		26
Z Piccolo Sogno | **Near W**		26
Prosecco | **River N**		24
Province | **W Loop**		25
Z Publican | **W Loop**		26
Public House | **River N**		19
Z NEW Pump Room | **Gold Coast**		21
Z Purple Pig | **River N**		26
Quartino | **River N**		22
NEW Quay | **Streeterville**		19
NEW Roka Akor | **River N**		24
Rosebud | **multi.**		22
Rosebud Prime/Steak | **Streeterville**		24
NEW Scofflaw | **Logan Sq**		-
Scoozi! | **River N**		21
Z Sixteen | **River N**		25
NEW Slurping Turtle | **River N**		22
NEW Standard Grill | **Westmont**		-
NEW Storefront Co. | **Wicker Pk**		-

Sunda	**River N**	24
Sushisamba Rio	**River N**	22
NEW Tavernita	**River N**	-
Tavern/Rush	**Gold Coast**	21
Terzo Piano	**Loop**	22
Three Aces		24
Little Italy/University Vill	
NEW III Forks	**Loop**	22
NEW Tokyo 21	**Old Town**	-
NEW Union Sushi + BBQ	**River N**	22
Urbanbelly	**Logan Sq**	25
NEW Urban Union		-
Little Italy/University Vill	

POWER SCENES

Z Alinea	**Lincoln Pk**	29
NEW Allium	**Gold Coast**	-
Z Aviary	**W Loop**	27
Benny's Chop	**River N**	26
Z Blackbird	**W Loop**	27
Z Capital Grille	**Streeterville**	26
Z Charlie Trotter's	**Lincoln Pk**	28
Chicago Chop	**River N**	24
Chicago Cut	**River N**	26
Coco Pazzo	**River N**	25
Custom House	**Printer's Row**	26
David Burke Prime	**River N**	25
Epic Restaurant	**River N**	-
Z Everest	**Loop**	27
Fred's	**Gold Coast**	20
Z Gene/Georgetti	**River N**	25
Z Gibsons	**multi.**	26
Z Girl/The Goat	**W Loop**	27
GT Fish/Oyster	**River N**	26
Z Hugo's	**multi.**	25
Il Mulino	**Gold Coast**	25
Z Joe's Sea/Steak	**River N**	27
Keefer's	**River N**	25
Z Les Nomades	**Streeterville**	28
Z L2O	**Lincoln Pk**	25
Mastro's Steak	**River N**	26
Z MK	**Near North**	28
Z Morton's	**multi.**	26
Z Naha	**River N**	27
NEW Nellcôte	**W Loop**	-
Z Next	**W Loop**	29
Z NEW NoMI Kitchen		26
Gold Coast	
Z NEW Pump Room	**Gold Coast**	21
Z Ria	**Gold Coast**	27
RL	**Gold Coast**	24
Rosebud		22
Little Italy/University Vill	
Rosebud Prime/Steak	**multi.**	24
Z Sixteen	**River N**	25
NEW Slurping Turtle	**River N**	22

Smith/Wollensky	**River N**	23
Z Spiaggia	**Gold Coast**	26
NEW III Forks	**Loop**	22
Z Topolobampo	**River N**	28
Z Tru	**Streeterville**	28

PRIVATE ROOMS

(Restaurants charge less at
off times; call for capacity)

Z Alinea	**Lincoln Pk**	29
Athena	**Greektown**	21
Carnivale	**W Loop**	22
Catch 35	**multi.**	24
Z Charlie Trotter's	**Lincoln Pk**	28
Chicago Chop	**River N**	24
Club Lucky	**Bucktown**	22
Edwardo's Pizza	**multi.**	20
Z Everest	**Loop**	27
Z Francesca's	**multi.**	22
Z Frontera Grill	**River N**	27
Gabriel's	**Highwood**	25
Z Gene/Georgetti	**River N**	25
Z Gibsons	**multi.**	26
Gioco	**S Loop**	22
Goose Island	**multi.**	17
Greek Islands	**multi.**	22
Z Joe's Sea/Steak	**River N**	27
Kamehachi	**Northbrook**	22
Keefer's	**River N**	25
Lockwood	**Loop**	22
L. Woods Tap	**Lincolnwood**	20
Mercat	**S Loop**	26
Mesón Sabika	**Naperville**	25
Z MK	**Near North**	28
Z Naha	**River N**	27
N9ne Steak	**Loop**	22
Z NEW NoMI Kitchen		26
Gold Coast	
Park Grill	**Loop**	19
Pasteur	**Edgewater**	-
Pensiero	**Evanston**	21
Pete Miller	**multi.**	22
Rock Bottom	**multi.**	19
Rosebud	**multi.**	22
Russian Tea	**Loop**	22
Ruth's Chris	**multi.**	26
Scoozi!	**River N**	21
Sepia	**W Loop**	26
Z Shanghai Terrace	**River N**	27
Z Shaw's Crab	**multi.**	25
Z Spiaggia	**Gold Coast**	26
Sushisamba Rio	**River N**	22
Z Tallgrass	**Lockport**	27
312 Chicago	**Loop**	21
Z Topolobampo	**River N**	28
Trattoria Roma	**Old Town**	23

Vivo | **W Loop**	23
Z Wildfire | **multi.**	24

PRIX FIXE MENUS

(Call for prices and times)

Z Alinea | **Lincoln Pk**	29
Z Arun's | **NW Side**	27
Bank Lane | **Lake Forest**	22
Z Bonsoirée | **Logan Sq**	27
Z Charlie Trotter's | **Lincoln Pk**	28
Z Courtright's | **Willow Spgs**	28
NEW EL Ideas | **Pilsen**	29
Z Everest | **Loop**	27
NEW Goosefoot | **Lincoln Sq**	-
Z Green Zebra | **Noble Sq**	28
Z Les Nomades | **Streeterville**	28
Z L2O | **Lincoln Pk**	25
Z MK | **Near North**	28
Z Moto | **W Loop**	27
Z Next | **W Loop**	29
Z North Pond | **Lincoln Pk**	26
Oceanique | **Evanston**	25
Z Ria | **Gold Coast**	27
Roy's | **River N**	25
Z Schwa | **Wicker Pk**	28
Z Sixteen | **River N**	25
Z Spiaggia | **Gold Coast**	26
Z Tallgrass | **Lockport**	27
Z Topolobampo | **River N**	28
Z Tru | **Streeterville**	28

QUICK BITES

Aloha Eats | **Lincoln Pk**	19
Al's Beef | **multi.**	23
Art of Pizza | **Lakeview**	23
Artopolis | **Greektown**	21
NEW BadHappy Poutine | **River N**	-
Bagel | **multi.**	20
NEW Baker & Nosh | **Uptown**	-
Bakin' & Eggs | **Lakeview**	21
Ba Le Sandwich | **multi.**	23
NEW Banh Mi & Co. | **Lakeview**	-
Bar Louie | **multi.**	17
NEW Barrio | **Lakeview**	-
Belly Shack | **Humboldt Pk**	25
Berghoff | **O'Hare Area**	20
Big & Little's | **River N**	25
Big Bowl | **multi.**	20
Big Star | **Wicker Pk**	26
Bijan's | **River N**	19
Billy Goat | **multi.**	16
Bin | **River N**	22
Bin | **Wicker Pk**	20
Birchwood | **Wicker Pk**	24
Birrieria Zaragoza | **SW Side**	-
NEW Bongiorno's | **River N**	-

Bourgeois Pig | **Lincoln Pk**	21
Burger Bar | **Lincoln Pk**	23
NEW Burger Joint | **River N**	-
NEW Burger Point | **S Loop**	-
NEW Butcher/The Burger | **Lincoln Pk**	26
Byron's Hot Dog | **multi.**	21
Café Selmarie | **Lincoln Sq**	22
Cemitas Puebla | **Humboldt Pk**	24
Chicago Bagel | **Lincoln Pk**	25
Chicago Pizza | **Lincoln Pk**	25
NEW City Farms Mkt. | **Lakeview**	-
City Provisions | **Ravenswood**	25
Convito | **Wilmette**	20
Counter | **Lincoln Pk**	20
Crisp | **Lakeview**	24
Deca | **Streeterville**	22
Del Seoul | **Lakeview**	24
Depot/Diner | **Far W**	25
Dimo's Pizza | **Lakeview**	23
Z Edzo's | **Evanston**	27
Eleven City | **S Loop**	19
Epic Burger | **multi.**	19
Epic Restaurant | **River N**	-
NEW E wok Café | **NW Side**	-
Fat Willy's | **Logan Sq**	20
NEW Felice's Pizza | **Rogers Pk**	-
Five Guys | **multi.**	20
Z Fontano's Subs | **multi.**	28
Foodlife/Foodease | **Streeterville**	19
Fox & Obel | **Near North**	20
Frankie's Scaloppine | **Gold Coast**	19
Franks 'N' Dawgs | **Lincoln Pk**	26
Freshii | **multi.**	18
Gene & Jude's | **O'Hare Area**	24
Gold Coast | **multi.**	17
NEW Gratto Pizza | **Wicker Pk**	-
NEW Gyro-Ména | **Lakeview**	-
Hannah's Bretzel | **multi.**	23
Honey 1 BBQ | **Bucktown**	21
Jerry's | **Wicker Pk**	21
NEW Jimbo's Top Gun | **Wrigleyville**	-
Julius Meinl | **multi.**	21
Labriola Bakery | **Oak Brook**	25
La Lagartija | **W Loop**	-
Lillie's Q | **Bucktown**	22
Manny's | **multi.**	24
M Burger | **multi.**	17
NEW Melt Sandwich | **Bucktown**	-
Mr. Beef | **River N**	24
Mundial | **Pilsen**	26
NEW Native Foods | **multi.**	23
90 Miles | **Logan Sq**	23
Noodles by Yagihashi | **Loop**	23

Noon-O-Kabab	**Albany Pk**	24
Old Jerusalem	**Old Town**	20
Olive Mediterranean	**Old Town**	-
Pegasus	**SW Side**	21
Penny's	**multi.**	21
Pierrot Gourmet	**River N**	24
Piggery	**Lakeview**	19
Pompei Pizza	**multi.**	19
Pork Shoppe	**Avondale**	19
Potbelly Sandwich	**multi.**	18
Pret A Manger	**Loop**	19
Quartino	**River N**	22
Rootstock	**Humboldt Pk**	24
Roti	**River W**	22
Russell's BBQ	**Elmwood Pk**	19
NEW Sacco Bruno	**Bucktown**	-
NEW Soulwich	**Evanston**	-
Southern Mac	**Location Varies**	18
State/Lake	**Loop**	17
Stir Crazy	**multi.**	20
Superdawg	**NW Side**	21
Taco Joint	**Lincoln Pk**	24
Taqueria El Ojo/Agua	**Bucktown**	-
Tasting Room	**W Loop**	16
Tempo	**Gold Coast**	20
Tom & Eddie's	**multi.**	17
Top Notch	**Far S Side**	26
NEW Topper's Pizza	**Greektown**	-
NEW Township	**Logan Sq**	-
Uncle Bub's	**Westmont**	24
Uncommon Ground	**Lakeview**	23
Urbanbelly	**Logan Sq**	25
NEW Vapiano	**Lincoln Pk**	17
Webster's Wine Bar	**Lincoln Pk**	19
NEW Westminster Hot Dog	**Loop**	18
Wiener's Circle	**Lincoln Pk**	19
Zaleski/Horvath	**Kenwood**	23
NEW Zebra's	**Bridgeport**	-

QUIET CONVERSATION

Akai Hana	**Wilmette**	20
Aria	**Loop**	24
Z Arun's	**NW Side**	27
A Tavola	**Ukrainian Vill**	26
NEW Autre Monde	**Berwyn**	25
Bank Lane	**Lake Forest**	22
Barrington Country	**Barrington**	25
Basil Leaf	**Lincoln Pk**	20
Benny's Chop	**River N**	26
Bistro Bordeaux	**Evanston**	24
Café/Architectes	**Gold Coast**	24
Café Selmarie	**Lincoln Sq**	22
Café Spiaggia	**Gold Coast**	25
Cape Cod	**Streeterville**	22
Chalkboard	**Lakeview**	21
Z Charlie Trotter's	**Lincoln Pk**	28
Chef's Station	**Evanston**	25
Chicago Prime Steak	**Schaumburg**	-
Cité	**Streeterville**	19
NEW City Farms Mkt.	**Lakeview**	-
D & J Bistro	**Lake Zurich**	25
NEW Eggy's	**Streeterville**	-
Elate	**River N**	23
Erwin	**Lakeview**	23
Z Everest	**Loop**	27
NEW Filini	**Loop**	24
NEW French Quarter	**Lombard**	-
Gaetano's	**Forest Pk**	28
Gaylord Indian	**multi.**	22
NEW Goosefoot	**Lincoln Sq**	-
Z Henri	**Loop**	27
NEW Hota	**Evanston**	-
NEW Hutong	**Oak Pk**	-
Inovasi	**Lake Bluff**	26
Itto Sushi	**Lincoln Pk**	24
Jilly's	**Evanston**	21
Julius Meinl	**multi.**	21
Klay Oven	**multi.**	19
La Crêperie	**Lakeview**	21
La Gondola	**Lakeview**	20
La Petite Folie	**Hyde Pk**	26
Lawry's	**River N**	26
Z Les Nomades	**Streeterville**	28
Z Le Titi/Paris	**Arlington Hts**	27
Le Vichyssois	**Lakemoor**	26
Lovells	**Lake Forest**	22
Z L2O	**Lincoln Pk**	25
Merlo	**multi.**	24
NEW Moderno	**Highland Pk**	-
NEW My Mother's Kitchen	**Elmwood Pk**	-
NEW Nieto's	**Highland Pk**	-
Z North Pond	**Lincoln Pk**	26
Oceanique	**Evanston**	25
Pensiero	**Evanston**	21
Pierrot Gourmet	**River N**	24
Quince	**Evanston**	25
Rhapsody	**Loop**	21
RL	**Gold Coast**	24
Russian Tea	**Loop**	22
NEW Seven Ocean	**Oak Pk**	-
1776	**Crystal Lake**	26
Z Shanghai Terrace	**River N**	27
Signature Room	**Streeterville**	17
South Gate	**Lake Forest**	18
NEW Southport & Irving	**North Ctr/St. Ben's**	-
South Water	**Loop**	15
Z Spiaggia	**Gold Coast**	26

NEW Standard Grill | **Westmont**	-_
Table Fifty-two | **Gold Coast**	25
Z Tallgrass | **Lockport**	27
Tasting Room | **W Loop**	16
Terzo Piano | **Loop**	22
Z Tru | **Streeterville**	28
NEW Vera | **W Loop**	24
Village | **Loop**	22
Vinci | **Lincoln Pk**	22
Vivere | **Loop**	24
Zealous | **River N**	24

RAW BARS

NEW Argent | **River N**	-_
Balsan | **Gold Coast**	24
Benny's Chop | **River N**	26
Bob Chinn's | **Wheeling**	24
Brazzaz | **River N**	21
C-House | **Streeterville**	21
Davis St. Fish | **Evanston**	20
Deca | **Streeterville**	22
Frontier | **Noble Sq**	23
GT Fish/Oyster | **River N**	26
Half Shell | **Lakeview**	24
Z Henri | **Loop**	27
Niu | **Streeterville**	23
N9ne Steak | **Loop**	22
NEW Quay | **Streeterville**	19
Riva | **Streeterville**	20
Z Shaw's Crab | **multi.**	25
Signature Room | **Streeterville**	17
NEW Tavernita | **River N**	-_
Tin Fish | **Tinley Park**	25
NEW Urban Union | **Little Italy/University Vill**	-_

ROMANTIC PLACES

Abigail's | **Highland Pk**	25
NEW Ada St. | **Bucktown**	-_
Ai Sushi | **River N**	22
Alhambra | **W Loop**	18
NEW Amoremia | **Old Irving Pk**	-_
Angelina | **Lakeview**	24
NEW Anna's Asian | **W Loop**	-_
Z Arami | **W Town**	27
A Tavola | **Ukrainian Vill**	26
NEW Autre Monde | **Berwyn**	25
Balsan | **Gold Coast**	24
NEW Barrelhouse Flat | **Lincoln Pk**	-_
Barrington Country | **Barrington**	25
NEW Bar Toma | **Gold Coast**	17
Z Bedford | **Wicker Pk**	17
NEW Benjamin | **Highland Pk**	16
Bistro Bordeaux | **Evanston**	24
Bistro Campagne | **Lincoln Sq**	25

Bistrot Margot | **Old Town**	22
NEW Bistro Voltaire | **Near North**	23
Boka | **Lincoln Pk**	26
NEW Bombay Spice | **River N**	21
Browntrout | **North Ctr/St. Ben's**	24
Café Absinthe | **Bucktown**	23
Cafe Laguardia | **Bucktown**	22
NEW Caravan | **Uptown**	-_
Chez Joël | **Little Italy/University Vill**	26
Cité | **Streeterville**	19
Coco Pazzo | **River N**	25
Z Courtright's | **Willow Spgs**	28
D & J Bistro | **Lake Zurich**	25
DiSotto | **Streeterville**	25
NEW Eduardo's Enoteca | **Gold Coast**	-_
Elate | **River N**	23
Epic Restaurant | **River N**	-_
NEW Estate Ultra Bar | **River W**	-_
Z Everest | **Loop**	27
NEW Filini | **Loop**	24
Gaetano's | **Forest Pk**	28
Gaylord Indian | **Gold Coast**	22
Geja's | **Lincoln Pk**	22
Gilt Bar | **River N**	26
Gioco | **S Loop**	22
Gyu-Kaku | **Streeterville**	23
Z Henri | **Loop**	27
NEW Hota | **Evanston**	-_
Il Mulino | **Gold Coast**	25
Japonais | **River N**	24
Jin Ju | **Andersonville**	22
Kiki's | **Near North**	25
NEW Lady Gregory's | **Andersonville**	19
Lao | **Chinatown**	24
Le Colonial | **Gold Coast**	23
Leopold | **Noble Sq**	23
Z Les Nomades | **Streeterville**	28
Z L2O | **Lincoln Pk**	25
Macello | **W Loop**	-_
Maijean | **Clarendon Hills**	26
Marigold | **Uptown**	23
Maude's Liquor | **W Loop**	25
Merlo | **multi.**	24
Z Mirai Sushi | **Wicker Pk**	27
Z MK | **Near North**	28
Mon Ami Gabi | **multi.**	24
NEW Morso | **Lincoln Pk**	-_
Nacional 27 | **River N**	22
Z Naha | **River N**	27
NEW Nellcôte | **W Loop**	-_
Z Next | **W Loop**	29
Niche | **Geneva**	27

ZNEW NoMI Kitchen | **Gold Coast** 26

Z North Pond | **Lincoln Pk** 26

Oceanique | **Evanston** 25

NEW Old Town Pour Hse. | **Old Town** ⁻

Pane Caldo | **Gold Coast** 23

Paris Club | **River N** 21

Pasteur | **Edgewater** ⁻

NEW Patron's Hacienda | **River N** ⁻

Z Pelago | **Streeterville** 26

Pensiero | **Evanston** 21

NEW Perennial Virant | **Lincoln Pk** 26

Z Piccolo Sogno | **Near W** 26

Prasino | **La Grange** 23

NEW Premise | **Andersonville** ⁻

Prosecco | **River N** 24

ZNEW Pump Room | **Gold Coast** 21

Z Purple Pig | **River N** 26

NEW Quay | **Streeterville** 19

Quince | **Evanston** 25

Rhapsody | **Loop** 21

Z Ria | **Gold Coast** 27

Z Riccardo | **Lincoln Pk** 28

NEW Ripasso | **Bucktown** ⁻

RL | **Gold Coast** 24

NEW Roka Akor | **River N** 24

Rose Angelis | **Lincoln Pk** 26

NEW RPM Italian | **River N** ⁻

Sable | **River N** 24

Sepia | **W Loop** 26

Z Shanghai Terrace | **River N** 27

Signature Room | **Streeterville** 17

Z Sixteen | **River N** 25

Sola | **Lakeview** 24

Z Sprout | **Lincoln Pk** 28

Stained Glass | **Evanston** 25

Sunda | **River N** 24

Table Fifty-two | **Gold Coast** 25

Z Tallgrass | **Lockport** 27

Tasting Room | **W Loop** 16

NEW Taverna 750 | **Wrigleyville** 25

Taxim | **Wicker Pk** 26

NEW Telegraph Wine Bar | **Logan Sq** 23

NEW Todoroki Hibachi | **Evanston** ⁻

Z Tru | **Streeterville** 28

Turquoise | **Roscoe Vill** 25

NEW 25 Degrees | **River N** 22

NEW Union Sushi + BBQ | **River N** 22

Vermilion | **River N** 23

Z Vie | **W Springs** 29

Vincent | **Andersonville** 21

Vinci | **Lincoln Pk** 22

Vivo | **W Loop** 23

Webster's Wine Bar | **Lincoln Pk** 19

Wildfish | **Arlington Hts** 20

Zak's Place | **Hinsdale** 22

Zealous | **River N** 24

Zocalo | **River N** 22

SENIOR APPEAL

Andies | **Lakeview** 21

Ann Sather | **multi.** 22

Ashkenaz Deli | **Gold Coast** 19

A Tavola | **Ukrainian Vill** 26

Bacchanalia | **SW Side** 24

Bagel | **multi.** 20

Barrington Country | **Barrington** 25

Berghoff | **Loop** 20

Bistro Bordeaux | **Evanston** 24

Bob Chinn's | **Wheeling** 24

Boston Blackie's | **multi.** 17

Bruna's | **SW Side** 24

Calo Ristorante | **Andersonville** 22

Cape Cod | **Streeterville** 22

Carson's | **multi.** 22

Z Courtright's | **Willow Spgs** 28

Dave's Italian | **Evanston** 18

Davis St. Fish | **Evanston** 20

Del Rio | **Highwood** 21

Don Juan's | **Edison Pk** 19

Edelweiss | **Norridge** 22

Egg Harbor | **multi.** 22

EJ's Pl. | **Skokie** 22

Francesco's | **Northbrook** 23

Froggy's | **Highwood** 25

Gale St. Inn | **Jefferson Pk** 22

Hackney's | **multi.** 19

Jilly's | **Evanston** 21

Kiki's | **Near North** 25

La Gondola | **Lakeview** 20

La Petite Folie | **Hyde Pk** 26

Lawry's | **River N** 26

Z Les Nomades | **Streeterville** 28

Z Le Titi/Paris | **Arlington Hts** 27

Le Vichyssois | **Lakemoor** 26

Lou Mitchell's | **Loop** 24

Lovells | **Lake Forest** 22

L. Woods Tap | **Lincolnwood** 20

Margie's Candies | **multi.** 23

Melting Pot | **multi.** 19

Miller's Pub | **Loop** 18

Myron/Phil Steak | **Lincolnwood** 20

Next Door | **Northbrook** 21

Nick's Fish | **Rosemont** 25

NEW Nieto's | **Highland Pk** ⁻

Oak Tree Bakery | **Gold Coast** 16

Original/Walker Pancake | **multi.** 24

Parthenon | **Greektown**	21
Pegasus | **Greektown**	21
Rosebud | **Loop**	22
Russell's BBQ | **Elmwood Pk**	19
Russian Tea | **Loop**	22
Sabatino's | **Old Irving Pk**	25
1776 | **Crystal Lake**	26
South Gate | **Lake Forest**	18
☑ Tallgrass | **Lockport**	27
Tre Kronor | **Albany Pk**	25
Tufano's Tap | **Little Italy/University Vill**	24
Village | **Loop**	22
White Fence | **Romeoville**	24

SINGLES SCENES

Adobo | **Old Town**	21
NEW Balena | **Lincoln Pk**	-
Bar Louie | **multi.**	17
NEW Barrelhouse Flat | **Lincoln Pk**	-
Café Iberico | **River N**	22
Carnivale | **W Loop**	22
Clubhouse | **Oak Brook**	23
NEW Deuce's/Diamond | **Wrigleyville**	-
Ditka's | **Gold Coast**	22
NEW Estate Ultra Bar | **River W**	-
☑ Gibsons | **multi.**	26
Gilt Bar | **River N**	26
Hubbard Inn | **River N**	21
Hub 51 | **River N**	21
☑ Hugo's | **multi.**	25
Japonais | **River N**	24
NEW Lady Gregory's | **Andersonville**	19
NEW Linkin House | **Lincoln Pk**	-
Luxbar | **Gold Coast**	19
Mercadito | **River N**	22
N9ne Steak | **Loop**	22
NEW Ogden | **W Loop**	-
Old Town Social | **Old Town**	24
Paris Club | **River N**	21
P.J. Clarke's | **Gold Coast**	18
Public House | **River N**	19
Rock Bottom | **multi.**	19
Rockit | **River N**	19
NEW RPM Italian | **River N**	-
Scoozi! | **River N**	21
Stanley's | **Lincoln Pk**	19
Sullivan's Steak | **multi.**	24
Sunda | **River N**	24
Sushisamba Rio | **River N**	22
NEW Tavernita | **River N**	-
Tavern/Rush | **Gold Coast**	21
Zaleski/Horvath | **Kenwood**	23

SLEEPERS
(Good food, but little known)

Bien Trucha | **Geneva**	29
Bruna's | **SW Side**	24
Café Absinthe | **Bucktown**	23
City Provisions | **Ravenswood**	25
Depot/Diner | **Far W**	25
Dining Room/Kendall | **Near W**	23
DiSotto | **Streeterville**	25
Frontier | **Noble Sq**	23
Gaetano's | **Forest Pk**	28
Grafton Pub & Grill | **Lincoln Sq**	23
Karma | **Mundelein**	23
Koda | **Far S Side**	23
Kuni's | **Evanston**	26
Le Vichyssois | **Lakemoor**	26
Mago | **multi.**	25
Maijean | **Clarendon Hills**	26
Mundial | **Pilsen**	26
Nabuki | **Hinsdale**	26
Niche | **Geneva**	27
Noodles by Yagihashi | **Loop**	23
Over Easy | **Ravenswood**	27
Phò Xe Tång | **Uptown**	26
Ras Dashen | **Edgewater**	27
Rosal's | **Little Italy/University Vill**	29
Rosewood | **Rosemont**	26
Silver Seafood | **Uptown**	27
Sushi Naniwa | **River N**	23
Swordfish | **Batavia**	27
Tanoshii | **Andersonville**	28
Three Aces | **Little Italy/University Vill**	24
Top Notch | **Far S Side**	26
Toro Sushi | **Lincoln Pk**	28
Viaggio | **Near W**	26
Zaleski/Horvath | **multi.**	23

SPECIAL OCCASIONS

☑ Alinea | **Lincoln Pk**	29
☑ Arun's | **NW Side**	27
☑ Aviary | **W Loop**	27
Benny's Chop | **River N**	26
☑ Blackbird | **W Loop**	27
☑ Bonsoirée | **Logan Sq**	27
Brazzaz | **River N**	21
☑ Charlie Trotter's | **Lincoln Pk**	28
☑ Courtright's | **Willow Spgs**	28
Dan McGee | **Frankfort**	-
NEW EL Ideas | **Pilsen**	29
Epic Restaurant | **River N**	-
☑ Everest | **Loop**	27
☑ Gibsons | **multi.**	26
NEW Goosefoot | **Lincoln Sq**	-
☑ Henri | **Loop**	27

Ing	**W Loop**	23
Lawry's	**River N**	26
Lovells	**Lake Forest**	22
Z L2O	**Lincoln Pk**	25
Mastro's Steak	**River N**	26
Z Michael	**Winnetka**	27
NEW Michael Jordan's	**Streeterville**	23
Z Morton's	**multi.**	26
Z Moto	**W Loop**	27
Z Next	**W Loop**	29
Niche	**Geneva**	27
Z NEW NoMI Kitchen	**Gold Coast**	26
Palm	**Loop**	24
Z NEW Pump Room	**Gold Coast**	21
NEW Quay	**Streeterville**	19
Quince	**Evanston**	25
Z Ria	**Gold Coast**	27
Roy's	**River N**	25
Z Schwa	**Wicker Pk**	28
Z Shaw's Crab	**multi.**	25
Z Sixteen	**River N**	25
Z Spiaggia	**Gold Coast**	26
Z Takashi	**Bucktown**	28
Z Topolobampo	**River N**	28
Tramonto's Steak/Sea	**Wheeling**	21
Z Tru	**Streeterville**	28
Z Vie	**W Springs**	29
Zak's Place	**Hinsdale**	22
Zealous	**River N**	24

TEEN APPEAL

Al's Beef	**multi.**	23
Ann Sather	**multi.**	22
Art of Pizza	**Lakeview**	23
Aurelio's Pizza	**multi.**	23
Bacino's	**multi.**	22
Ba Le Sandwich	**multi.**	23
Bandera	**Streeterville**	23
Big Bowl	**multi.**	20
Bob Chinn's	**Wheeling**	24
Boston Blackie's	**multi.**	17
Burger Bar	**Lincoln Pk**	23
Byron's Hot Dog	**multi.**	21
Calo Ristorante	**Andersonville**	22
Cheesecake Factory	**multi.**	20
Chicago Pizza	**Lincoln Pk**	25
Counter	**Lincoln Pk**	20
Dimo's Pizza	**Lakeview**	23
DMK Burger Bar	**Lakeview**	21
Edwardo's Pizza	**multi.**	20
Z Edzo's	**Evanston**	27
Egg Harbor	**multi.**	22
Eggsperience	**multi.**	19
El Jardin	**Lakeview**	18

Epic Burger	**multi.**	19
Five Guys	**Rogers Pk**	20
Flat Top	**multi.**	19
Gene & Jude's	**O'Hare Area**	24
Giordano's	**multi.**	22
Gold Coast	**multi.**	17
Grand Lux	**River N**	21
Hannah's Bretzel	**Loop**	23
Hard Rock	**River N**	14
Harry Caray's	**multi.**	23
Heaven/Seven	**multi.**	21
Home Run Inn	**multi.**	25
Z Hot Doug's	**Avondale**	26
Joy Yee	**multi.**	21
Z Lou Malnati's	**multi.**	25
LuLu's	**Evanston**	22
L. Woods Tap	**Lincolnwood**	20
Margie's Candies	**multi.**	23
Medici/57th	**Hyde Pk**	19
Melting Pot	**multi.**	19
Nookies	**multi.**	21
Original Gino's	**multi.**	21
Original/Walker Pancake	**multi.**	24
Penny's	**multi.**	21
Pizzeria Uno/Due	**River N**	23
Pompei Pizza	**multi.**	19
Potbelly Sandwich	**multi.**	18
R.J. Grunts	**Lincoln Pk**	20
Robinson's Ribs	**multi.**	20
Russell's BBQ	**Elmwood Pk**	19
Smashburger	**Batavia**	19
Stanley's	**Lincoln Pk**	19
Stir Crazy	**Northbrook**	20
Superdawg	**NW Side**	21
Tempo	**Gold Coast**	20
Toast	**multi.**	23
Uncle Julio's	**Old Town**	19
Wiener's Circle	**Lincoln Pk**	19
Wishbone	**multi.**	20

TRENDY

NEW Acadia	**S Loop**	–
NEW Ada St.	**Bucktown**	–
NEW Anna's Asian	**W Loop**	–
NEW Anthem	**Ukrainian Vill**	–
Z Arami	**W Town**	27
NEW Argent	**River N**	–
NEW Au Cheval	**W Loop**	–
Z Avec	**W Loop**	28
NEW BadHappy Poutine	**River N**	–
NEW Balena	**Lincoln Pk**	–
NEW Barrelhouse Flat	**Lincoln Pk**	–
Z Bedford	**Wicker Pk**	17
Belly Shack	**Humboldt Pk**	25
Big Star	**Wicker Pk**	26

☑ Blackbird	**W Loop**	27
Boka	**Lincoln Pk**	26
NEW Bombay Spice	**River N**	21
☑ Bonsoirée	**Logan Sq**	27
Bristol	**Bucktown**	25
Carnivale	**W Loop**	22
Chizakaya	**Lakeview**	24
NEW Deuce's/Diamond	**Wrigleyville**	–
DMK Burger Bar	**multi.**	21
Epic Restaurant	**River N**	–
NEW Estate Ultra Bar	**River W**	–
NEW Farmhouse	**Near North**	22
NEW Filini	**Loop**	24
NEW Flight 1551	**Old Town**	–
Fred's	**Gold Coast**	20
NEW Frog n Snail	**Lakeview**	–
☑ Frontera Grill	**River N**	27
Frontier	**Noble Sq**	23
Gage	**Loop**	24
Gemini	**Lincoln Pk**	22
Gilt Bar	**River N**	26
Gioco	**S Loop**	22
☑ Girl/The Goat	**W Loop**	27
Graham Elliot	**River N**	25
NEW Grange Hall	**W Loop**	–
☑ Great Lake	**Andersonville**	27
GT Fish/Oyster	**River N**	26
Gyu-Kaku	**Streeterville**	23
Hot Chocolate	**Bucktown**	24
Hub 51	**River N**	21
Japonais	**River N**	24
Lao	**Chinatown**	24
Leopold	**Noble Sq**	23
☑ Longman/Eagle	**Logan Sq**	27
NEW Masa Azul	**Logan Sq**	–
Maude's Liquor	**W Loop**	25
Mercadito	**River N**	22
Mercat	**S Loop**	26
☑ Mirai Sushi	**Wicker Pk**	27
☑ MK	**Near North**	28
NEW Morso	**Lincoln Pk**	–
NEW Nellcôte	**W Loop**	–
☑ Nightwood	**Pilsen**	27
NEW Ogden	**W Loop**	–
Old Town Social	**Old Town**	24
Paris Club	**River N**	21
NEW Perennial Virant	**Lincoln Pk**	26
Prosecco	**River N**	24
Province	**W Loop**	25
☑ Publican	**W Loop**	26
☑ NEW Pump Room	**Gold Coast**	21
☑ Purple Pig	**River N**	26
Quartino	**River N**	22
NEW Quay	**Streeterville**	19

Revolution Brewing	**Logan Sq**	23
NEW Roka Akor	**River N**	24
NEW Roots Pizza	**W Town**	23
Rootstock	**Humboldt Pk**	24
NEW RPM Italian	**River N**	–
NEW Rustic Hse.	**Lincoln Pk**	22
☑ Ruxbin	**Noble Sq**	28
Sable	**River N**	24
☑ Schwa	**Wicker Pk**	28
NEW Scofflaw	**Logan Sq**	–
Sepia	**W Loop**	26
NEW Slurping Turtle	**River N**	22
Sola	**Lakeview**	24
Southern Mac	**Location Varies**	18
Southern	**Wicker Pk**	21
☑ Sprout	**Lincoln Pk**	28
State/Lake	**Loop**	17
NEW Storefront Co.	**Wicker Pk**	–
Sunda	**River N**	24
Sushisamba Rio	**River N**	22
NEW Tavernita	**River N**	–
Taxim	**Wicker Pk**	26
NEW Telegraph Wine Bar	**Logan Sq**	23
NEW Tozi	**Wicker Pk**	–
NEW 25 Degrees	**River N**	22
NEW 2 Sparrows	**Lincoln Pk**	20
NEW Union Sushi + BBQ	**River N**	22
Urbanbelly	**Logan Sq**	25
NEW Urban Union	**Little Italy/University Vill**	–
NEW Vera	**W Loop**	24
NEW Yusho	**Avondale**	–

VIEWS

Athena	**Greektown**	21
Balsan	**Gold Coast**	24
Bridge Bar Chicago	**River N**	24
NEW Bridge House	**River N**	18
Chicago Cut	**River N**	26
Chief O'Neill's	**NW Side**	17
Cité	**Streeterville**	19
☑ Courtright's	**Willow Spgs**	28
Deca	**Streeterville**	22
Dining Room/Kendall	**Near W**	23
Epic Restaurant	**River N**	–
☑ Everest	**Loop**	27
Fred's	**Gold Coast**	20
Frontera Fresco/Tortas	**Loop**	24
Fulton's	**River N**	19
Gage	**Loop**	24
Harry Caray's Tavern	**River N**	19
Lobby	**River N**	24
Mercat	**S Loop**	26
☑ NEW NoMI Kitchen	**Gold Coast**	26

☑ North Pond	**Lincoln Pk**	26
Opa! Estiatorio	**Vernon Hills**	23
Paris Club	**River N**	21
Park Grill	**Loop**	19
NEW Quay	**Streeterville**	19
Riva	**Streeterville**	20
☑ Shanghai Terrace	**River N**	27
Signature Room	**Streeterville**	17
☑ Sixteen	**River N**	25
Smith/Wollensky	**River N**	23
☑ Spiaggia	**Gold Coast**	26
Tasting Room	**W Loop**	16
Tavern/Rush	**Gold Coast**	21
Terzo Piano	**Loop**	22
NEW III Forks	**Loop**	22
Zed 451	**River N**	23

WINE BARS

NEW Autre Monde	**Berwyn**	25
☑ Avec	**W Loop**	28
☑ Bedford	**Wicker Pk**	17
Bin	**River N**	22
Bin	**Wicker Pk**	20
NEW Bombay Spice	**River N**	21
NEW Bread & Wine	**Old Irving Pk**	-
Broadway Cellars	**Edgewater**	24
Chicago's Pizza	**Ravenswood**	16
Cooper's Hawk	**multi.**	21
NEW Cyrano's	**River N**	-
☑ Davanti	**Little Italy/University Vill**	27
Devon Seafood	**River N**	21
DiSotto	**Streeterville**	25
Fleming's	**Lincolnshire**	24
Flight	**Glenview**	23
Jake Melnick's	**Gold Coast**	19
Joe's Crab Shack	**Schaumburg**	20
Mago	**multi.**	25
Quartino	**River N**	22
Rhapsody	**Loop**	21
Rootstock	**Humboldt Pk**	24
South Water	**Loop**	15
Stained Glass	**Evanston**	25
Tasting Room	**W Loop**	16
NEW Telegraph Wine Bar	**Logan Sq**	23
3rd Coast Cafe	**Gold Coast**	19
NEW Urban Union	**Little Italy/University Vill**	-
NEW Vera	**W Loop**	24
Webster's Wine Bar	**Lincoln Pk**	19
Yu's Mandarin	**Schaumburg**	23

WINNING WINE LISTS

NEW Acadia	**S Loop**	-
NEW Ada St.	**Bucktown**	-
☑ Alinea	**Lincoln Pk**	29

☑ Arun's	**NW Side**	27
☑ Avec	**W Loop**	28
NEW Balena	**Lincoln Pk**	-
NEW Bar Toma	**Gold Coast**	17
Benny's Chop	**River N**	26
Bin	**River N**	22
Bin	**Wicker Pk**	20
Bistro Bordeaux	**Evanston**	24
Bistrot Margot	**Old Town**	22
☑ Blackbird	**W Loop**	27
Bluebird	**Bucktown**	23
Boka	**Lincoln Pk**	26
Broadway Cellars	**Edgewater**	24
Campagnola	**Evanston**	24
Chalkboard	**Lakeview**	21
☑ Charlie Trotter's	**Lincoln Pk**	28
Chicago Cut	**River N**	26
Coco Pazzo	**River N**	25
Cooper's Hawk	**multi.**	21
☑ Courtright's	**Willow Spgs**	28
Custom House	**Printer's Row**	26
David Burke Prime	**River N**	25
Del Rio	**Highwood**	21
Epic Restaurant	**River N**	-
☑ Everest	**Loop**	27
NEW Filini	**Loop**	24
Fleming's	**multi.**	24
NEW Flight 1551	**Old Town**	-
Florentine	**Loop**	22
Gabriel's	**Highwood**	25
Geja's	**Lincoln Pk**	22
☑ Gibsons	**multi.**	26
Graham Elliot	**River N**	25
☑ Green Zebra	**Noble Sq**	28
☑ Henri	**Loop**	27
☑ Hugo's	**multi.**	25
Il Mulino	**Gold Coast**	25
☑ Joe's Sea/Steak	**River N**	27
Keefer's	**River N**	25
Koda	**Far S Side**	23
La Sardine	**W Loop**	25
☑ Les Nomades	**Streeterville**	28
☑ Le Titi/Paris	**Arlington Hts**	27
Le Vichyssois	**Lakemoor**	26
Lockwood	**Loop**	22
☑ L2O	**Lincoln Pk**	25
Mercat	**S Loop**	26
☑ Michael	**Winnetka**	27
NEW Michael Jordan's	**Streeterville**	23
Miramar	**Highwood**	17
☑ MK	**Near North**	28
☑ Morton's	**multi.**	26
☑ Moto	**W Loop**	27
☑ Naha	**River N**	27

Restaurant	Location	Score
🅩 Next	**W Loop**	29
Niche	**Geneva**	27
N9ne Steak	**Loop**	22
🅩 NEW NoMI Kitchen	**Gold Coast**	26
🅩 North Pond	**Lincoln Pk**	26
Oceanique	**Evanston**	25
Pane Caldo	**Gold Coast**	23
🅩 Pelago	**Streeterville**	26
Pensiero	**Evanston**	21
NEW Perennial Virant	**Lincoln Pk**	26
🅩 Piccolo Sogno	**Near W**	26
Prosecco	**River N**	24
Province	**W Loop**	25
🅩 Publican	**W Loop**	26
🅩 Purple Pig	**River N**	26
Rhapsody	**Loop**	21
🅩 Ria	**Gold Coast**	27
Ruth's Chris	**multi.**	26
Salpicón	**Old Town**	25
Sepia	**W Loop**	26
1776	**Crystal Lake**	26
Signature Room	**Streeterville**	17
🅩 Sixteen	**River N**	25
Smith/Wollensky	**River N**	23
NEW Southport & Irving	**North Ctr/St. Ben's**	–
🅩 Spiaggia	**Gold Coast**	26
🅩 Sprout	**Lincoln Pk**	28
Stained Glass	**Evanston**	25
Sunda	**River N**	24
🅩 Takashi	**Bucktown**	28
🅩 Tallgrass	**Lockport**	27
Tasting Room	**W Loop**	16
NEW III Forks	**Loop**	22
Tocco	**Bucktown**	–
🅩 Topolobampo	**River N**	28
Tramonto's Steak/Sea	**Wheeling**	21
Trattoria No. 10	**Loop**	25
🅩 Tru	**Streeterville**	28
Union Pizza	**Evanston**	21
NEW Urban Union	**Little Italy/University Vill**	–
NEW Vera	**W Loop**	24
Vivere	**Loop**	24
Webster's Wine Bar	**Lincoln Pk**	19
West Town	**Noble Sq**	26
Zealous	**River N**	24

MILWAUKEE

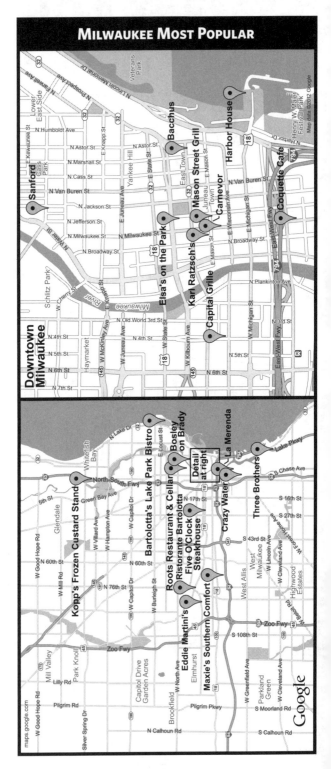

Top Ratings

MOST POPULAR

1. Sanford | *American*
2. Bartolotta's Lake Park | *French*
3. Eddie Martini's | *Seafood/Steak*
4. Harbor House | *Seafood*
5. Crazy Water | *Eclectic*
6. Rist. Bartolotta | *Italian*
7. Karl Ratzsch's | *German*
8. La Merenda | *Eclectic*
9. Coquette | *French*
10. Bacchus | *American*
11. Capital Grille | *Steak*
12. Kopp's Frozen Custard | *Dessert*
13. Three Brothers | *Serbian*
14. Elsa's on Park | *American*
15. Five O'Clock Steak | *Steak*
16. Bosley on Brady | *Seafood/Steak*
17. Carnevor | *Steak*
18. Mason St. Grill | *American*
19. Roots | *Californian*
20. Maxie's | *Cajun/Creole*

TOP FOOD

29 | Sanford | *American*
28 | Crazy Water | *Eclectic*
27 | Eddie Martini's | *Seafood/Steak*
Rist. Bartolotta | *Italian*
Bacchus | *American*
La Merenda | *Eclectic*
26 | Bosley on Brady | *Sea./Steak*
Roots* | *Californian*
Honeypie | *American*
Le Rêve* | *Dessert/French*

BY CUISINE

AMERICAN (NEW)
29 | Sanford
27 | Bacchus
25 | Hinterland Erie St.

AMERICAN (TRAD.)
26 | Honeypie
25 | Blue's Egg
Mason St. Grill

ECLECTIC
28 | Crazy Water
27 | La Merenda
25 | Blue's Egg

FRENCH
26 | Le Rêve
Bartolotta's Lake Park
25 | Pastiche

ITALIAN
27 | Rist. Bartolotta
25 | Mangia
23 | Il Mito Enoteca

STEAKHOUSES
27 | Eddie Martini's
26 | Bosley on Brady
Capital Grille

BY LOCATION

DOWNTOWN
27 | Bacchus
26 | Capital Grille
25 | Mason St. Grill

EAST SIDE
29 | Sanford
26 | Bosley on Brady
Bartolotta's Lake Park

---

* Indicates a tie with restaurant above; excludes places with low votes

OUTLYING AREAS

25 Mangia
24 Fleming's
Original Pancake

THIRD WARD

25 Hinterland Erie St.
24 Coquette
22 R. Braun's Graffito

WAUWATOSA

27 Eddie Martini's
Rist. Bartolotta
26 Le Rêve

TOP DECOR

28 Bacchus
Harbor House*
27 Umami Moto
Bartolotta's Lake Park
26 Sanford

25 Mason St. Grill
Capital Grille
24 Carnevor
Karl Ratzsch's
Elsa's on Park

TOP SERVICE

28 Sanford
Eddie Martini's
26 Capital Grille
Bacchus
Bartolotta's Lake Park

25 Pastiche
Rist. Bartolotta*
River Lane Inn
Mason St. Grill
24 Carnevor

BEST BUYS

In order of Bang for the Buck rating.

1. Kopp's Frozen Custard
2. Potbelly Sandwich Shop
3. Five Guys
4. Egg Harbor
5. Original Pancake

6. Blue's Egg
7. Honeypie
8. Comet Cafe
9. Water Street Brewery
10. Rock Bottom

Vote at zagat.com

MILWAUKEE RESTAURANT DIRECTORY

	FOOD	DECOR	SERVICE	COST

Z Bacchus ⓩ *American* — `27` `28` `26` `$71`

Downtown | Cudahy Tower | 925 E. Wells St. (Prospect Ave.) | 414-765-1166 | www.bacchusmke.com

Set in Cudahy Tower, this Downtown New American earns "high marks all around", from chef Adam Siegel's "top-notch" fare to the "beautiful surroundings" defined by "sophisticated decor" (it shares top Milwaukee honors), linear lines and windows facing Lake Michigan; add in "knowledgeable", "professional" servers and the "signature" "Bartolotta showmanship", and fans say it's one of the "best special-occasion places in town" – with "expensive" tabs to match.

Balzac Wine Bar *Eclectic* — ▽ `20` `22` `21` `$34`

East Side | 1716 N. Arlington Pl. (E. Brady St.) | 414-755-0099 | www.balzacwinebar.com

Fans fall for this East Side Eclectic thanks to "creative" small plates and "thoughtful, well-chosen" libations; dim lights and wine-lined walls make for a "cozy" setting, and with affordable tabs, it's a "solid choice."

Z Bartolotta's Lake Park Bistro *French* — `26` `27` `26` `$54`

East Side | Lake Park Pavilion | 3133 E. Newberry Blvd. (Lake Park Rd.) | 414-962-6300 | www.lakeparkbistro.com

A "top-of-the-list destination" say fans of this spendy East Side French, where a "beautiful setting" with "spectacular views of Lake Michigan" provides the backdrop for chef Adam Siegel's "excellent" "classic bistro fare"; "drool"-worthy wines, a "wonderfully helpful staff" and "romantic ambiance" also add "special-occasion" appeal.

Benihana *Japanese/Steak* — `21` `20` `23` `$37`

Downtown | 850 N. Plankinton Ave. (bet. Kilbourn Ave. & Wells St.) | 414-270-0890 | www.benihana.com

See review in Chicago Directory.

Blue's Egg *American* — `25` `16` `22` `$19`

West Side | 317 N. 76th St. (Blue Mound Rd.) | 414-299-3180 | www.bluesegg.com

"Traditional" yet "innovative" breakfast fare including "creative egg dishes" and a few globally accented plates are a "fabulous way to start a day" cheer West Siders of this daytime American in a "neighborhood shopping center"; "happily accommodating" servers work the art deco diner environs, and if a few sniff it's "spendy for the area", most say it's "quite a bargain" given what you get, just "arrive early" or be prepared for "long waits" on the weekend.

Z Bosley on Brady ⓩ *Seafood/Steak* — `26` `23` `24` `$43`

East Side | 815 E. Brady St. (bet. Cass & Marshall Sts.) | 414-727-7975 | www.bosleyonbrady.com

"Key West meets the Brew City" at this "delicious" East Side surf 'n' turfer where the "interesting" midpriced menu places an "emphasis on fresh seafood", making it a "rare Milwaukee treat"; the "Florida Keys theme" carries over to the decor with its "kitschy memorabilia", and "friendly" staffers contribute to the "upbeat environment", so it's an overall "wonderful" "escape."

	FOOD	DECOR	SERVICE	COST

NEW Braise ⊠ M *American*
- | - | - | E

Walker's Point | 1101 S. Second St. (Washington St.) |
414-212-8843 | www.braiselocalfood.com

Local ingredients are the focus of this Walker's Point New American putting out a daily changing menu of bar nibbles, small plates and somewhat pricey mains alongside regional brews and global wines; reclaimed materials feature heavily in the casual wood-accented space, and an open kitchen offers diners a glimpse of the action.

Brocach Irish Pub ● *Pub Food*
▽ 22 | 22 | 22 | $24

East Side | 1850 N. Water St. (bet. Humboldt Ave. & Van Buren St.) |
414-431-9009 | www.brocach.com

Gaelic specialties including "outstanding" bangers and mash "go down well with a Guinness" at this midpriced East Side pub that "makes you feel truly Irish"; a "friendly crowd" gathers in "cozy" confines to listen to live music on Sundays and play trivia on Wednesdays.

Buckley's *American*
▽ 25 | 23 | 22 | $34

Downtown | 801 N. Cass St. (Wells St.) | 414-277-1111 |
www.buckleysmilwaukee.com

"Quaint and cozy", this Downtown American cements its "nice neighborhood place" status with "delicious" dishes, "friendly" service and moderate prices; the casual space features an antique wooden bar from the 1870s that once stood in a New York City pub.

Cafe Corazón M *Mexican*
▽ 26 | 17 | 20 | $19

Riverwest | 3129 N. Bremen St. (Burleigh St.) | 414-810-3941 |
www.corazonmilwaukee.com

"Delicious, locally sourced" Mexican *comida* and "the best margarita for miles" earn admirers at this inexpensive Riverwest "sleeper", where crowds scramble for tables in the "tiny" space; diners noting the "charming", "friendly" vibe cheer owners who obviously "put a lot of love" into the place, ensuring it's a "neighborhood gem."

Café Manna ⊠ *Vegetarian*
- | - | - | M

Brookfield | Sendik's Towne Ctr. | 3815 N. Brookfield Rd.
(bet. San Fernando & Thomson Drs.) | 262-790-2340 |
www.cafemanna.com

"Even meat eaters will adore" this midpriced Brookfield vegetarian offering a "wide range" of dishes alongside organic wines and local beers; its eco-friendly focus can also be seen in the recycled building materials, from the metal light fixtures to the bamboo floors.

☑ Capital Grille *Steak*
26 | 25 | 26 | $65

Downtown | 310 W. Wisconsin Ave. (4th St.) | 414-223-0600 |
www.thecapitalgrille.com

See review in Chicago Directory.

Carnevor ⊠ *Steak*
24 | 24 | 24 | $69

Downtown | 724 N. Milwaukee St. (Mason St.) | 414-223-2200 |
www.carnevor.com

"Serious meat eaters" salivate over "large" chops and sides "to please any palate" at this Downtown steakhouse further enhanced

	FOOD	DECOR	SERVICE	COST

by "friendly, attentive" staffers; professionals and "beautiful people" fill the "dark", modern space, so it has all the makings for a "top" experience – just "bring your wallet", as it's accordingly "pricey."

Cempazuchi ◫ *Mexican*

17	15	17	$28

East Side | 1205 E. Brady St. (Franklin Pl.) | 414-291-5233 | www.cempazuchi.com

With "lots of unique dishes", including regional moles, this affordable East Sider on "trendy Brady Street" is "not your run-of-the-mill Mexican establishment"; a "fun crowd" mingles in the brightly colored space, so though it may be "better for happy hour than dinner", it's generally considered a "worthwhile stop."

Centro Café ▣ *Italian*

▽ 26	17	22	$33

Riverwest | 808 E. Center St. (bet. Bremen & Fratney Sts.) | 414-455-3751 | www.centrocaferiverwest.com

For a "New York vibe at Milwaukee prices", diners visit this "casual" Riverwest Italian known for "delish pasta" and other "standards", plus a "creative brunch"; the "intimate" (if "tight") environs with an open kitchen and banquettes crafted from church pews afford guests "the chance to talk over dinner", so many agree it's a "wonderful find."

Chancery Restaurant *Pub Food*

16	15	19	$21

Wauwatosa | 7613 W. State St. (Harwood Ave.) | 414-453-2300 | www.thechancery.com

A "reliable choice in a pinch", this Wauwatosa link of the local chain serves up "solid tavern fare" at a "good value for the money"; if detractors dub it a "bit of a yawn", it's "still the place to take a group", as the "mixed menu" ensures "everyone can find something to eat."

Cheesecake Factory *American*

20	20	20	$30

Glendale | Bayshore Mall | 5799 N. Bayshore Dr. (Towncenter Dr.) | 414-906-8550
Wauwatosa | 2350 N. Mayfair Rd. (bet. Burleigh St. & North Ave.) | 414-258-8512
www.thecheesecakefactory.com

See review in Chicago Directory.

Comet Cafe *American*

23	15	22	$23

East Side | 1947 N. Farwell Ave. (Irving Pl.) | 414-273-7677 | www.thecometcafe.com

"Exquisite bacon-wrapped meatloaf" and other similarly pork-enhanced dishes attract carnivores, while a number of meat-free alternatives keep vegheads happy at this "casual" East Side American; service gets high marks and tabs are affordable, so even if the decor lags a bit behind, it's an "easy" choice for a "casual" meal (as waits on the weekends attest).

▣ Coquette Cafe *French*

24	22	24	$37

Third Ward | 316 N. Milwaukee St. (St. Paul Ave.) | 414-291-2655 | www.coquettecafe.com

Those pining for "Paris in Milwaukee" say *oui* to this Third Ward French turning out "deliciously simple" fare plus some "imaginative"

		FOOD	DECOR	SERVICE	COST

preparations in "authentic bistro" surroundings; "understated", "first-rate" service and "value" tabs compensate for decor that some find "a bit faded", so most agree it's "definitely a place to return."

Crawdaddy's ☒ *Cajun/Creole* ▽ 18 | 17 | 20 | $33

Southwest Side | 6414 W. Greenfield Ave. (bet. 64th & 65th Sts.) | 414-778-2228 | www.crawdaddysrestaurant.com

"Start with a hurricane" and *laissez les bon temps rouler* advise buffs of this midpriced Southwest Sider, where more-than-competent staffers serve a "wonderful selection" of Cajun-Creole hits, from crawfish étouffée to jambalaya; meanwhile, critics who call the casual, eclectic vibe "chainlike" say they "never understood why everyone loves this place."

☑ Crazy Water *Eclectic* 28 | 18 | 24 | $42

Walker's Point | 839 S. 2nd St. (Walker St.) | 414-645-2606 | www.crazywaterrestaurant.com

With such "inventive", "high-quality" fare on offer, enthusiasts insist you could "just throw a dart at the menu and be happy" at this "charming" Walker's Point Eclectic, where "consistently great" service and moderate tabs contribute to a "relaxed, homey" atmosphere; despite "small", sometimes "noisy" digs, it's still "always crowded", so "call ahead."

Cubanitas ☒ *Cuban* 21 | 18 | 19 | $25

Downtown | 728 N. Milwaukee St. (bet. Mason St. & Wisconsin Ave.) | 414-225-1760 | www.getcubanitas.com

A "pleasant surprise" Downtown, this affordable Cuban delivers "authentic" eats, including "the best pork sandwich", via "friendly" servers in "warm, cozy" surroundings; sidewalk seating on a "fashionable street" and late-night weekend hours are other pluses, just beware – no-reservations can often mean "long lines."

Devon Seafood Grill *Seafood* 21 | 21 | 21 | $47

North Shore | Bayshore Town Ctr. | 5715 N. Bayshore Dr. (bet. N. Port Washington Rd. & N. Santa Monica Blvd.) | 414-967-9790 | www.devonseafood.com

See review in Chicago Directory.

Dream Dance Steak ☒Ⓜ *American/Steak* – | – | – | E

Downtown | Potawatomi Bingo Casino | 1721 W. Canal St. (W. Potawatomi Cir.) | 414-847-7883 | www.paysbig.com

"A dream" pronounce patrons of this over-21-only steakhouse set inside Downtown's Potawatomi Bingo Casino, where the "excellent" New American fare gets a boost from the 600-label wine list; "fine" service and a spacious wood-accented room decorated with Native American artwork complete the pricey picture.

☑ Eddie Martini's ☒ *Seafood/Steak* 27 | 24 | 28 | $67

Wauwatosa | 8612 W. Watertown Plank Rd. (86th St.) | 414-771-6680 | www.eddiemartinis.com

"High-quality white-glove" service "makes you feel like a king" at this Wauwatosa "classic" turning out "generous portions" of "to-die-for"

	FOOD	DECOR	SERVICE	COST

chops and "reliably excellent" seafood; the 1940s-style decor is a "real throwback to the days of the Rat Pack", giving it an "old-fashioned supper club feel", so though it's not cheap, devotees dub it the "epitome of what the steakhouse is supposed to be."

Edwardo's Natural Pizza *Pizza*

20	11	15	$19

West Side | 10845 W. Bluemound Rd. (Hwy. 100) | 414-771-7770 | www.edwardos.com
See review in Chicago Directory.

Egg Harbor Café *American*

22	17	21	$17

Lake Geneva | 827 Main St. (Broad St.) | 262-248-1207 | www.eggharborcafe.com
See review in Chicago Directory.

Elsa's on the Park ● *American*

24	24	21	$29

Downtown | 833 N. Jefferson St. (Wells St.) | 414-765-0615 | www.elsas.com
After more than 30 years, this "venerable" "favorite for a martini and burger" retains its "see-and-be-seen" status thanks to a "trendy" Downtown locale, "funky" space decorated with ever-changing artwork and "reasonably priced" American menu offered until 1 AM nightly; a "lively atmosphere" and solid service also keep it "packed" and "perfect" for a night out.

Envoy *American*

-	-	-	M

Downtown | Ambassador Hotel | 2308 W. Wisconsin Ave. (bet. 23rd & 24th Sts.) | 414-345-5015 | www.envoymilwaukee.com
"Retro" art deco surroundings provide the backdrop for "inventive" New American eats at this dining room situated inside Downtown's restored Ambassador Hotel; the "fabulous" Sunday brunch features small plates, and the adjacent Envoy Lounge tempts tipplers with cocktails from the original 1928 menu.

Five Guys *Burgers*

20	11	16	$11

East Side | 2907 N. Oakland Ave. (Locust St.) | 414-964-5303
Glendale | Bayshore Town Ctr. | 5800 N. Bayshore Dr. (Fountainview Dr.) | 414-962-3560
Delafield | Shoppes at Nagawaukee | 2900 Golf Rd. (Rte. 83) | 262-646-4897
Pewaukee | Pewaukee Commons | 1279 Capitol Dr. (Willow Grove Dr.) | 262-691-7566
www.fiveguys.com
See review in Chicago Directory.

Five O'Clock Steakhouse ⒮Ⓜ *Steak*

25	17	23	$54

Central City | 2416 W. State St. (24th St.) | 414-342-3553 | www.fiveoclocksteakhouse.com
The filet mignon "melts in your mouth like butter" and the other "classic" offerings don't disappoint at this circa-1948 Central City steakhouse where the "old-fashioned" experience includes ordering dinner at the bar before being seated; a "great staff" elevates the "blast-from-the-past" dining room featuring antique chandeliers and wood accents, so many put it "on the list for Milwaukee dining experiences."

	FOOD	DECOR	SERVICE	COST

Fleming's Prime Steakhouse & Wine Bar *Steak*

| 24 | 22 | 23 | $61 |

Brookfield | Brookfield Square Mall | 15665 W. Bluemound Rd. (Moorland Rd.) | 262-782-9463 | www.flemingssteakhouse.com
See review in Chicago Directory.

Ginza Sushi Bar *Japanese*

| - | - | - | E |

Wauwatosa | 2727 N. Mayfair Rd. (Center St.) | 414-771-3333 | www.ginzawauwatosa.com
"Hidden" inside a Wauwatosa strip mall, this Japanese lures sushi-lovers with "special rolls" and other "fresh offerings"; red walls and banquettes enliven the "hole-in-the-wall" digs, while affordable tabs add further appeal.

Harbor House *Seafood*

| 23 | 28 | 22 | $60 |

Downtown | 550 N. Harbor Dr. (Michigan St.) | 414-395-4900 | www.harborhousemke.com
Set in a "premier location" "looking out over Lake Michigan", this "trendy" Downtowner from the Bartolotta Restaurant Group offers "high-quality" seafood-focused fare in "warm surroundings" with "beautiful decor" (it shares top Milwaukee honors) and "large windows" that provide "spectacular views"; "attentive service" is another plus, just "bring your paycheck", as it's on the "pricey" side.

Harry's Bar & Grill ● *American*

| ▽ 18 | 19 | 19 | $34 |

North Shore | 3549 N. Oakland Ave. (bet. Edgewood Ave. & Menlo Blvd.) | 414-964-6800 | www.harrysbarandgrillmilwaukee.com
"Reasonably priced" American eats, including a "nice selection of burgers", make this North Shore haunt a "great place to meet up with friends"; it's "not fancy", but a recent remodel (which may not be reflected in the Decor score) added a heated outdoor patio, and there's also live music on Saturdays.

Heaven City 🅱Ⓜ *American*

| - | - | - | M |

Mukwonago | S91 W27850 National Ave./Hwy. ES (Edgewood Ave.) | 262-363-5191 | www.heavencity.com
Lovers of Wisconsin lore "step back in time" at this Mukwonago blend of the past and present, where the art deco decor smacks of Prohibition times (and infamous mobster Al Capone, who is said to have hidden out here); the midpriced menu is up-to-date New American, and the long-established Tapas Tuesday features live flamenco music.

Hinterland Erie Street Gastropub 🅱 *American*

| 25 | 23 | 24 | $64 |

Third Ward | 222 E. Erie St. (Water St.) | 414-727-9300 | www.hinterlandbeer.com
"Imaginative", "seasonal" plates (including housemade charcuterie) are "prepared with flavor and flair" at this Third Ward New American that's "much higher-end" than its name suggests; "excellent" service and "beautiful" wood-accented surroundings that "make you want to stay and linger" help compensate for pricey (some say "overpriced") tabs.

	FOOD	DECOR	SERVICE	COST

☑ Honeypie *American* | 26 | 17 | 22 | $21 |

Bay View | 2643 S. Kinnickinnic Ave. (Potter Ave.) | 414-489-7437 |
www.honeypiecafe.com

A "good spot to fill up" enthuse admirers of this affordable Bay View American where the "creative" comfort food is "better than mama could do" and the sweet offerings include pie that's "in the name for good reason"; solid service and "comfortable" "diner"-like digs further make it "well worth a stop."

Il Mito Enoteca Ⓜ *Italian* | 23 | 20 | 23 | $39 |

Wauwatosa | 6913 W. North Ave. (69th St.) | 414-443-1414 |
www.ilmito.com

Chef-owner Michael Feker's "light, Mediterranean-based fare" will "transport you to Italy" proclaim pasta-eating pundits of this "upscale" Wauwatosa Italian with "fair prices" and strong service; wine tastings and hands-on cooking classes make it all the more "popular."

Immigrant Restaurant Ⓢ Ⓜ *American* | ▽ 25 | 27 | 27 | $117 |

Kohler | American Club | 419 Highland Dr. (School St.) | 920-457-8888 |
www.destinationkohler.com

"Fabulous" servers "anticipate every need" while ferrying "delicious", "beautifully presented" New American dishes and wine from an "excellent selection" at this "old-school fine-dining" destination in Kohler's American Club; six dining rooms styled after the home countries of Wisconsin settlers make for a "romantic setting", so "special-occasion" celebrators deem "big price tags well worth it"; P.S. jackets required.

NEW Industri Café *American* | – | – | – | M |

Walker's Point | 524 S. 2nd St. (bet. Bruce & West Virginia Sts.) |
414-224-7777 | www.industricafe.com

The moderately priced American eats (including "finger food at its finest") at this Walker's Point cafe are perfect for people who "love Wisconsin and those who support it", thanks to the liberal use of local ingredients; situated in a former machine shop, it fuses an industrial look with a "chill and comfortable atmosphere."

Jackson Grill Ⓢ Ⓜ *American* | ▽ 28 | 18 | 26 | $52 |

South Side | 3736 W. Mitchell St. (38th St.) | 414-384-7384 |
www.thejacksongrill.com

"Sumptuous steaks" and other "outstanding" fare come as somewhat of a surprise at this "unassuming" South Side American where the "tavernlike atmosphere" belies the "quality" offerings; "friendly" service scores high marks too, and though the "old-fashioned" "supper club setting" can make you "feel like the Rat Pack still lives", spendy tabs can quickly summon reality.

Jake's Ⓢ *Steak* | ▽ 24 | 21 | 23 | $57 |

Pewaukee | 21445 W. Gumina Rd. (Capitol Dr.) | 262-781-7995 |
www.jakes-restaurant.com

Expect reams of red meat and "no better onion rings on the planet" at this "classic" Pewaukee steakhouse, which also offers casual bites in its intimate lounge; "top-notch" service, a lush garden patio and a working fireplace help give the converted century-old barn a "comfortable homestyle feeling."

Karl Ratzsch's ⌧ *German* | 23 | 24 | 24 | $40 |

Downtown | 320 E. Mason St. (bet. B'way & Milwaukee St.) | 414-276-2720 | www.karlratzsch.com

"Over-the-top authentic" Bavarian decor lends an "old-world feel" to this "time-honored" Downtown German (established in 1904) offering a "reasonably priced" menu of "sturdy", "traditional" must-haves including "thin, well-seasoned" Wiener schnitzel and "to-die-for" apple pancakes; what's more, staffers exude an "elegant grace gleaned from years of refinement", so admirers ask "how can you say anything bad" about it?

Kilawat Restaurant *American* | 22 | 24 | 22 | $46 |

Downtown | InterContinental Milwaukee Hotel | 139 E. Kilbourn Ave. (Water St.) | 414-291-4793 | www.kilawatcuisine.com

This New American may be located inside a hotel (the InterContinental Milwaukee), but with "unique", "solid" preparations and a chic orange-and-lime-hued dining room complete with "views of Downtown", it sure "doesn't feel that way"; its proximity to several performing arts venues makes it a "good spot before a show", while "attentive" service and moderate tabs help earn it devotees at any time of day.

King & I *Thai* | ▽ 18 | 18 | 18 | $29 |

Downtown | 830 N. Old World Third St. (bet. Kilbourn Ave. & Wells St.) | 414-276-4181 | www.kingandirestaurant.com

"Get adventurous" suggest surveyors of this solid Downtown Thai where the "spicy scale runs from careful to native" levels; "fine" service complements a spacious dining room accented with statues and artwork, and though tabs are already reasonable, bean counters note the weekday lunch buffet is even "cheaper."

The Knick ◑ *Eclectic* | 23 | 22 | 21 | $33 |

Downtown | Knickerbocker Hotel | 1028 E. Juneau Ave. (Waverly Pl.) | 414-272-0011 | www.theknickrestaurant.com

Fans find "something for everyone" at this "value" Eclectic in Downtown's Knickerbocker Hotel turning out "consistent, delicious" fare, from "juicy burgers" to "robust salads" to "flavorful" fish; recently remodeled with modern upholstery and funky sculptured-glass lighting, it's a "pleasureable" "hangout", especially when the "sunny" staff and "divine" patio are figured in.

Kopp's Frozen Custard Stand *Dessert* | 24 | 13 | 17 | $9 |

Glendale | 5373 N. Port Washington Rd. (bet. Lexington Blvd. & Richter Pl.) | 414-961-2006 | www.kopps.com

"Custard is king" – and "beyond sublime" – at this "classic" Glendale stand also vending "big, tasty" burgers and other "worth-a-trip" eats; service is generally "fast", so though there's "not much in the way of inside seating", it's still an "inexpensive" "place for a quick bite" and a "real treat" on "humid, sticky days."

	FOOD	DECOR	SERVICE	COST

☑ La Merenda ⬛ *Eclectic*　27 | 18 | 23 | $38

Walker's Point | 125 E. National Ave. (1st St.) | 414-389-0125 |
www.lamerenda125.com

Prepare for an "eating adventure" at this "top-notch" yet midpriced
Walker's Point Eclectic where "groups share plates, try different
things" and "linger" over the "diverse menu" of "outstanding", "inventive" tapas-style dishes; the colorful, casual space is often filled
with the "fervent buzz of chatting", and "friendly" staffers contribute to the festive vibe, so be sure to reserve "well in advance" as it
can otherwise be "impossible to get into."

☑ Le Rêve Patisserie & Café ⬛ *Dessert/French*　26 | 22 | 22 | $36

Wauwatosa | 7610 Harwood Ave. (Menomonee River Pkwy.) |
414-778-3333 | www.lerevecafe.com

"Traditional and novel" dishes full of "excellent, genuine French flavors" are worth "canceling your flight to Paris" effuse enthusiasts of
this midpriced Wauwatosa cafe where the "beautiful" baked goods
("oh, the bread") also win raves; set in a "historic bank building", it
has a "charming" vibe further elevated by "consistent" service, leading many to visit "every chance" they get.

Maggiano's Little Italy *Italian*　22 | 20 | 21 | $33

Wauwatosa | Mayfair Mall | 2500 N. Mayfair Rd. (North Ave.) |
414-978-1000 | www.maggianos.com

See review in Chicago Directory.

Mangia ⬛Ⓜ *Italian*　25 | 19 | 22 | $45

Kenosha | 5717 Sheridan Rd. (bet. 57th & 58th Sts.) | 262-652-4285 |
www.kenoshamangia.com

"Excellent pastas" and "delicious" pizzas from a wood-burning oven
lure diners "off the beaten path" to this rustic Kenosha Italian co-owned by Tony Mantuano (Chicago's Spiaggia); "reasonable prices"
and solid service take the edge off somewhat "aging" surroundings,
so most agree it's "worth the detour."

Mason Street Grill *American*　25 | 25 | 25 | $57

Downtown | Pfister Hotel | 424 E. Wisconsin Ave. (Jefferson St.) |
414-298-3131 | www.masonstreetgrill.com

"They can do it all" rave fans of this American in Downtown's historic Pfister Hotel, where "well-flavored" steaks, "to-die-for" seafood and other quality offerings are set down by "helpful" staffers in
upscale digs with a "nice atmosphere"; if a few cite "expensive" tabs
and leave "underwhelmed", more say it "continues to satisfy", especially since it's "the place to seen and be seen in Milwaukee."

Maxie's Southern Comfort *Cajun/Creole*　25 | 20 | 22 | $32

West Side | 6732 W. Fairview Ave. (68th St.) | 414-292-3969 |
www.maxies.com

"The cornbread itself is worth the trip" insist fans of this "boisterous" West Side Cajun-Creole turning out "authentic", "top-notch"
cooking "honoring the South"; the bi-level space is glitzed up with

chandeliers and dark-red walls and service gets solid marks, so it wins "kudos" all around, even if it "can be quite noisy."

Meritage ☒ *Eclectic*   21 | 17 | 22 | $41

West Side | 5921 W. Vliet St. (60th St.) | 414-479-0620 | www.meritage.us
"Farm-to-table in a legitimate sense" swear surveyors of this moderate West Side Eclectic where chef-owner Jan Kelly transforms "local ingredients" into "interesting" plates featuring a "good balance of flavors"; a staff that "attends to you very well" helps hush those who find the contemporary bistro surrounds "not much to look at."

Milwaukee Chophouse *Steak*   22 | 21 | 22 | $51

Downtown | Hilton Milwaukee | 633 N. Fifth St. (bet. Michigan St. & Wisconsin Ave.) | 414-226-2467 | www.chophouse411.com
"If you want to get dressed up and have a good steak", proponents point to this Downtown chophouse in the Hilton Milwaukee, where the standards are "solid" and the staff "tries hard and mostly gets it right"; the warm, upscale atmosphere adds "business-dinner" appeal, and there's also a 30-seat private dining room.

Mimma's Cafe *Italian*   ▽ 23 | 20 | 22 | $46

East Side | 1307 E. Brady St. (Arlington Pl.) | 414-271-7337 | www.mimmas.com
Matriarch Mimma Megna helms this midpriced East Side Italian, sending out "the most delicious" Sicilian fare offered alongside an extensive wine list; service earns solid marks, and a gold-and-cream-colored dining room with marble columns adds to the "high-end" appeal.

Mitchell's Fish Market *Seafood*   ▽ 19 | 19 | 23 | $46

Brookfield | 275 N. Moorland Rd. (W. Bluemound Rd.) | 262-789-2426 | www.mitchellsfishmarket.com
"Solid, consistent" seafood from an ever-changing menu draws diners to this pricey chain link in the Brookfield Square Mall; it "stands out" thanks to "casual, friendly" servers and a custom-made "cutting room" where guests can watch chefs break down today's catch.

Mo's: A Place for Steaks ☒ *Steak*   23 | 24 | 24 | $59

Downtown | 720 N. Plankinton Ave. (Wisconsin Ave.) | 414-272-0720 | www.mosrestaurants.com
"Make sure this is on your list" advise acolytes of this Downtown steakhouse where "wonderful" chops, "friendly" service and "warm", wood-accented stylings make it "Chicago good"; just be advised its "fantastic" location "right in the midst of it all" "explains the prices."

Mr. B's: A Bartolotta Steakhouse *Steak*   23 | 23 | 23 | $55

Brookfield | 18380 W. Capitol Dr. (bet. Brookfield Rd. & Mountain Dr.) | 262-790-7005 | www.mrbssteakhouse.com
"Quality" chops and "equally compelling" seafood bring diners to this Brookfield steakhouse from the Bartolotta Restaurant Group (Bacchus, Lake Park Bistro, Ristorante Bartolotta), where generally "top-notch" servers tend to guests in upscale-casual digs with green-checkered tablecloths and an "excellent" outdoor patio;

though it's not cheap and a few find it "disappointing at times", it remains a "favorite" to others insisting "you can't go wrong" here.

North Star American Bistro *American* | 23 | 20 | 24 | $35 |

Shorewood | Cornerstone Bldg. | 4518 N. Oakland Ave.
(Kensington Blvd.) | 414-964-4663
Brookfield | 19115 W. Capitol Dr. (Brookfield Rd.) | 262-754-1515
www.northstarbistro.com

Devotees dub these midpriced sibs "reliable" for their solid American fare (pizza, burgers, bourbon-glazed salmon) and "consistently excellent" service; the recently relocated Shorewood locale is smaller, with a curvy bar, while the larger Brookfield outpost features bistro-style decor, and both have outdoor seating.

NSB Bar and Grill Ⓢ *American* | - | - | - | M |
(fka North Shore Bistro)

North Shore | River Point Vill. | 8649 N. Port Washington Rd.
(Brown Deer Rd.) | 414-351-6100 | www.nsbbarandgrill.com

An upscale-casual setting with warm colors and cozy banquettes provides the backdrop for solid New American cooking at this North Shore "meeting place"; moderate prices and a flora-framed patio further entice locals who "go several times a month."

The Original Pancake House *American* | 24 | 14 | 20 | $17 |

East Side | 2621 N. Downer Ave. (Belleview Pl.) | 414-431-5055
Brookfield | 16460 W. Bluemound Rd. (Dechant Rd.) | 262-797-0800
www.walkerbros.net

See review in Chicago Directory.

Palms Bistro & Bar Ⓜ *American* | - | - | - | M |

Third Ward | 221 N. Broadway (bet. Buffalo & Chicago Sts.) |
414-298-3000 | www.palmsbistrobar.com

For "creative, well-seasoned" fare, diners find this moderate Third Ward New American a "reliable" pick; set inside a late-19th-century Cream City brick building, it features bistro-style surrounds decorated with artwork, while sidewalk seating provides "good people-watching" appeal.

Parkside 23 ⓈFC *American* | - | - | - | M |
(aka PS23)

Brookfield | 2300 Pilgrim Square Dr. (North Ave.) | 262-784-7275 |
www.parkside23.com

Sustainable, local ingredients – including some grown on its own farm – star on the "innovative" menu at this "reasonably priced" Brookfield New American; "inventive" cocktails, a "beautiful patio" and Tuesday night blues music further the appeal.

Pasta Tree *Italian* | ▽ 22 | 20 | 20 | $29 |

East Side | 1503 N. Farwell Ave. (Curtis Pl.) | 414-276-8867 |
www.pastatreerestaurant.com

Loyalists laud this East Side Italian for "consistently good" pastas and plentiful "specialty" sauces served in a "cozy" space with tin ceilings and antique chandeliers; generally "friendly" service and a secluded garden patio also work in its favor, so though there are "cheaper options in town", fans say "few" similar spots are better.

Pastiche 🗷 *French*   25 | 22 | 25 | $41

Bay View | 3001 S. Kinnickinnic Ave. (Rusk Ave.) | 414-482-1446 |
www.pastichebistro.com

Chef-owner Michael Engel's "fabulous, authentic" French cuisine has guests "involuntarily moaning in delight" at this midpriced Bay View bistro; "attentive, friendly" staffers and a "cozy" setting decorated with black-and-white photos give it a "homey feel", while a second-floor wine shop adds further appeal.

P.F. Chang's China Bistro   *Chinese*   20 | 20 | 20 | $31

Wauwatosa | Mayfair Mall | 2500 N. Mayfair Rd. (North Ave.) |
414-607-1029 | www.pfchangs.com

See review in Chicago Directory.

Polonez 🅼 *Polish*   - | - | - | I

South Side | 4016 S. Packard Ave. (Tesch St.) | 414-482-0080 |
www.polonezrestaurant.com

"Classic old-world offerings" like pierogi and *czarnina* (duck-blood soup) are "done well" at this inexpensive South Side Polish; imported specialty beers contribute to an authentic feel in the mural-enhanced space, and separate kids' and gluten-free menus broaden the appeal.

Potbelly Sandwich Shop   *Sandwiches*   18 | 13 | 17 | $11

Downtown | 135 W. Wisconsin Ave. (Plankinton Ave.) | 414-226-0014
Brookfield | 17800 W. Bluemound Rd. (bet. Brookfield & Calhoun Rds.) |
262-796-9845
www.potbelly.com

See review in Chicago Directory.

🗷 Ristorante Bartolotta   *Italian*   27 | 24 | 25 | $52

Wauwatosa | 7616 W. State St. (Harwood Ave.) | 414-771-7910 |
www.bartolottaristorante.com

"Imagination and flair" elevate the "top-notch" Italian cuisine at this "charming" Wauwatosa "gem" where longtime chef Juan Urbieta's "inventive" seasonal menus change often; slightly "pricey" tabs don't deter fans who maintain that its "no-pretensions" (if "noisy") atmosphere and "friendly, knowledgeable" staff make it a "perennial favorite."

River Lane Inn 🗷 *Seafood*   26 | 21 | 25 | $45

North Shore | 4313 W. River Ln. (43rd St.) | 414-354-1995 |
www.theriverlaneinn.com

"Who would have expected excellent seafood in the middle of Wisconsin?" opine "pleasantly surprised" diners at this North Shore "institution" where "quality never wavers" and prices are moderate; regardless of "rustic" decor that may "need a face-lift", most "thoroughly enjoy" the experience, since "friendly staffers who seem to really care about their customers" make each visit feel "like coming home."

	FOOD	DECOR	SERVICE	COST

Rock Bottom Brewery *American*
19 | 18 | 19 | $23

Downtown | 740 N. Plankinton Ave. (bet. Wells St. & Wisconsin Ave.) | 414-276-3030 | www.rockbottom.com
See review in Chicago Directory.

☒ Roots Restaurant & Cellar *Californian*
26 | 23 | 22 | $53

Brewers Hill | 1818 N. Hubbard St. (Vine St.) | 414-374-8480 | www.rootsmilwaukee.com
Guided by a "lovely philosophy about fresh, local, seasonal food", this "top" Californian attracts "foodies and vegetarians" alike with "creative cooking" that transforms sustainable, "premium ingredients" (often from the on-site garden) into "something unexpected"; it's somewhat costly, but service gets few complaints and "awesome views" from the "surprisingly cozy" Brewers Hill building (complete with a dual-level patio and pub-style cellar) flavor the "fun vibe."

NEW Rumpus Room ❶ *American*
▽ 25 | 25 | 25 | $38

Downtown | 1030 N. Water St. (State St.) | 414-292-0100 | www.rumpusroommke.com
With its "smart menu" of midpriced gastropub fare – think beer cheese soup, Scotch eggs, fish 'n' chips – and equally solid service, this Downtown American is a "great addition to the Bartolotta stable"; a "sophisticated bar" pours spirits and craft beers, while tin ceilings and antique light fixtures give the dining room warm appeal.

Ryan Braun's Graffito *Italian*
22 | 22 | 21 | $40

Third Ward | 102 N. Water St. (Erie St.) | 414-727-2888 | www.ryanbraungraffito.com
"Handmade is the hallmark" of this midpriced Third Ward Italian honoring Brewers baseball player Ryan Braun, where the cooking is "solid" and the bright, whimsical graffiti murals decorating the space help buck the stereotypical sports-bar formula – as does the picturesque patio overlooking the Milwaukee River.

Sabor *Brazilian*
- | - | - | E

Downtown | 777 N. Water St. (bet. Mason & Wells Sts.) | 414-431-3106 | www.saborbrazil.net
Arrive "very, very hungry" to this all-you-can-eat Brazilian steakhouse Downtown where gaucho servers deliver "seemingly endless" amounts of skewered meats and the "marvelous" salad bar includes "unique, flavorful" options; on Tuesday–Saturday nights, the lounge operates as Beta, a small plates–focused "gem."

Sake Tumi *Asian*
▽ 22 | 19 | 23 | $43

Downtown | 714 N. Milwaukee St. (bet. Mason St. & Wisconsin Ave.) | 414-224-7253 | www.sake-milwaukee.com
Korean and Japanese specialties feature heavily on the "inventive Asian-fusion" menu at this midpriced storefront on tony Milwaukee Street, where sashimi and sushi are offered alongside bulgogi and bibimbop, plus a number of izakaya-style small plates; service gets high marks, and the "hip, urban atmosphere" also adds appeal.

Sala da Pranzo 🗷 Ⓜ *Italian*

| | - | - | - | M |

East Side | 2613 E. Hampshire Ave. (Downer Ave.) | 414-964-2611 | www.sala-dapranzo.com

Hand-tossed pizza and other "authentic" Italian standards like pasta and saltimbocca draw diners to this midpriced East Sider close to the University of Wisconsin–Milwaukee; the "homey", trattoria environs are decorated with colorful artwork, and there's also sidewalk seating.

🛛 Sanford 🗷 *American*

| | 29 | 26 | 28 | $82 |

East Side | 1547 N. Jackson St. (Pleasant St.) | 414-276-9608 | www.sanfordrestaurant.com

"Simply exquisite" rave regulars of this East Side New American, where the "unsurpassed creativity" of co-owner and chef Sanford D'Amato results in "innovative", "consistently delicious" cuisine that makes it the "gold standard in Milwaukee" and earns it top Food and Most Popular honors too; staffers (rated No. 1 for Service) are "superb" "without being pretentious" and the storefront setting is "elegant", so pricey tabs are considered a "bargain", especially since a similar experience "would cost double in Chicago."

Sebastian's 🗷 *American*

| | - | - | - | M |

Caledonia | 6025 Douglas Ave. (5 Mile Rd. & Hwy. 32) | 262-681-5465 | www.sebastiansfinefood.com

"In-the-know" diners seek out this "surprising" New American in a "middle-of-nowhere" Caledonia locale for "consistently good" fare highlighting "interesting preparations"; with "accommodating" staffers, a "lovely" atmosphere and "reasonable prices", fans and groupies consider it a true "gem."

Singha Thai *Thai*

| | - | - | - | I |

West Side | 2237 S. 108th St. (Lincoln Ave.) | 414-541-1234 | www.singhathaimilwaukee.com

The "large selection" goes "way beyond" the basics at this "solid" West Side Thai; set in a strip mall, its no-frills storefront space is good for a casual meal.

Smyth *American*

| | ∇ 26 | 24 | 22 | $53 |

Walker's Point | Iron Horse Hotel | 500 W. Florida St. (6th St.) | 414-831-4615 | www.theironhorsehotel.com

"High hopes" are realized at this "solid performer" in the Walker's Point Iron Horse Hotel, where "wonderful" New American fare is served in "stylish" digs featuring old heart-pine posts and leather banquettes; somewhat costly tabs don't deter fans, who say it "always comes through."

Tess Ⓜ *Eclectic*

| | ∇ 25 | 23 | 25 | $50 |

East Side | 2499 N. Bartlett Ave. (Bradford Ave.) | 414-964-8377

"Imaginative", "delicious" fare, "excellent" service and "cozy", "comfortable" confines including a standout patio beckon diners to this East Side Eclectic; it's not cheap, but devotees dub prices "reasonable" given the "uniformly good" quality.

Third Ward Caffe ⓜ *Italian*

| - | - | - | M |

Third Ward | 225 E. St. Paul Ave. (bet. B'way & Water St.) |
414-224-0895 | www.thirdwardcaffe.com

"Like being in Italy" cheer *amici* of this Third Ward longtimer turning out "delicious" Northern Italian dishes enhanced with vegetables and herbs from the owners' farm; set in a converted warehouse on the historic Commission Row, it has an "intimate, romantic" feel, and there's also sidewalk seating facing the Milwaukee Public Market.

Three Brothers ⓜ⊐ *Serbian*

| 23 | 17 | 21 | $30 |

Bay View | 2414 S. St. Clair St. (Russell Ave.) | 414-481-7530

It's "like eating at grandma's" say fans of the "mouthwatering" "Serbian delights" and "old-world charm" at this cash-only Bay View "institution" that's "a little hard to find" "if you don't have a GPS device"; set in a historic former Schlitz tavern, it has "good local color" and a "time-warp" vibe – that plus "friendly" staffers further make it "a must."

Triskele's ⓢⓜ *American*

| - | - | - | M |

Walker's Point | 1801 S. Third St. (Maple St.) | 414-837-5950 |
www.triskelesrestaurant.com

An "off-the-beaten-path find", this Walker's Point New American appeals with a somewhat "small but interesting menu" of "well-prepared" dishes; "warm, cozy" surroundings, moderate tabs and nightly dining deals also work in its favor.

Umami Moto *Asian*

| 24 | 27 | 22 | $43 |

Downtown | 718 N. Milwaukee St. (bet. Mason St. & Wisconsin Ave.) |
414-727-9333 | www.umamimoto.com

"Sleek" and "chic", this "tony" Downtown Asian draws a "see-and-be-seen" crowd with its modern stylings and "elegant" menu featuring "inventive yet classic sushi and sashimi"; it can get "loud at times", service can range from solid to "indifferent" and tabs don't come cheap, but even so, most leave ready to go "back again and again."

Ward's House of Prime ●ⓢ *Steak*

| - | - | - | E |

Downtown | 540 E. Mason St. (bet. Jackson & Jefferson Sts.) |
414-223-0135 | www.wardshouseofprime.com

This Downtown meating place offers all that steak-lovers crave (including the "best prime rib") and rounds out the pricey menu with seafood, flatbreads, pastas and more; dark wood and leather chairs give it an upscale, masculine feel, befitting the suits who congregate here; P.S. valet parking alleviates the limited street parking situation, and a more casual bar menu is served until 1 AM.

Wasabi Sake Lounge *Japanese*

| - | - | - | M |

Brookfield | 15455 W. Bluemound Rd. (bet. Fairway Dr. & Moorland Rd.) |
262-780-0011 | www.wasabisakelounge.com

Sushi-lovers deem this midpriced Japanese in a Brookfield strip mall a "gem" for its "inventive rolls" and other "quality" offerings bolstered by many varieties of sake plus wine, beer and cocktails; a "friendly" staff works the dimly lit, upscale-casual surrounds, and weekly happy-hour deals add further appeal.

Water Buffalo *Eclectic* ▽ 18 | 21 | 17 | $30

Third Ward | 249 N. Water St. (Buffalo St.) | 414-431-1133 | www.swigmilwaukee.com/wb

"Pull up your boat" to this Third Ward riverside restaurant where "people-watching abounds" on the waterfront patio and members of the "be-seen scene" enjoy an Eclectic menu of sandwiches, salads and an array of ales; some say food could "use a little more oomph" and service scores are middling, but the real reason to go is for the "excellent ambiance."

Water Street Brewery *American* 17 | 19 | 20 | $23

Downtown | 1101 N. Water St. (Highland St.) | 414-272-1195 | www.waterstreetbrewery.com

"Awesome beer" is the star at this circa-1962 Downtown American, home of the city's first brewpub; the fare draws mixed opinions ("upscale" vs. "mediocre and plain"), but most appreciate the "exceptional" staff that helps infuse the place with "plenty of vitality."

Zarletti ☒ *Italian* 24 | 22 | 22 | $48

Downtown | 741 N. Milwaukee St. (Mason St.) | 414-225-0000 | www.zarletti.net

"Out-of-this-world" ragu and other "well-prepared, creative" dishes are offered alongside a "decent"-sized wine list including many by the glass at this midpriced Downtown Italian; service and the modern, minimalist space also get high marks, though it's on the "tiny" side, making "reservations a good idea."

MILWAUKEE INDEXES

Cuisines

Includes names, locations and Food ratings.

AMERICAN

☑ Bacchus | **Downtown**	27
Blue's Egg | **W Side**	25
NEW Braise | **Walker's Point**	-
Buckley's | **Downtown**	25
Cheesecake Factory | **multi.**	20
Comet Cafe | **E Side**	23
Dream Dance | **Downtown**	-
Egg Harbor | **Lake Geneva**	22
Elsa's/Park | **Downtown**	24
Envoy | **Downtown**	-
Harry's B&G | **N Shore**	18
Heaven City | **Mukwonago**	-
Hinterland | **Third Ward**	25
☑ Honeypie | **Bay View**	26
Immigrant | **Kohler**	25
NEW Industri Café | **Walker's Point**	-
Jackson Grill | **S Side**	28
Kilawat | **Downtown**	22
Kopp's | **Glendale**	24
Mason St. Grill | **Downtown**	25
North Star | **multi.**	23
NSB B&G | **N Shore**	-
Palms Bistro | **Third Ward**	-
Parkside 23 | **Brookfield**	-
Rock Bottom | **Downtown**	19
NEW Rumpus Room | **Downtown**	25
☑ Sanford | **E Side**	29
Sebastian's | **Caledonia**	-
Smyth | **Walker's Point**	26
Original/Walker Pancake | **multi.**	24
Triskele's | **Walker's Point**	-
Water Street | **Downtown**	17

ASIAN

Umami Moto | **Downtown**	24

BRAZILIAN

Sabor | **Downtown**	-

BURGERS

Elsa's/Park | **Downtown**	24
Five Guys | **multi.**	20

CAJUN

Crawdaddy's | **SW Side**	18
Maxie's | **W Side**	25

CALIFORNIAN

☑ Roots | **Brewers Hill**	26

CHINESE

P.F. Chang's | **Wauwatosa**	20

COFFEEHOUSES

Egg Harbor | **Lake Geneva**	22

CREOLE

Crawdaddy's | **SW Side**	18
Maxie's | **W Side**	25

CUBAN

Cubanitas | **Downtown**	21

DESSERT

☑ Honeypie | **Bay View**	26
Kopp's | **Glendale**	24
☑ Le Rêve | **Wauwatosa**	26

DINER

Original/Walker Pancake | **multi.**	24

ECLECTIC

Balzac Wine Bar | **E Side**	20
Blue's Egg | **W Side**	25
Brocach Irish Pub | **E Side**	22
☑ Crazy Water | **Walker's Point**	28
Knick | **Downtown**	23
☑ La Merenda | **Walker's Point**	27
Meritage | **W Side**	21
Tess | **E Side**	25
Water Buffalo | **Third Ward**	18

FRENCH

☑ Le Rêve | **Wauwatosa**	26

FRENCH (BISTRO)

☑ Bartolotta's | **E Side**	26
☑ Coquette | **Third Ward**	24
Pastiche | **Bay View**	25

GASTROPUB

Hinterland | **Amer.** | **Third Ward**	25

GERMAN

Karl Ratzsch's | **Downtown**	23

ITALIAN

(N=Northern)

Centro Café | **Riverwest**	26
Edwardo's Pizza | **W Side**	20
Il Mito | **Wauwatosa**	23
Maggiano's | **Wauwatosa**	22
Mangia | **Kenosha**	25
Mimma's Cafe | **E Side**	23
Pasta Tree | N | **E Side**	22
☑ Rist. Bartolotta | **Wauwatosa**	27
R. Braun's Graffito | **Third Ward**	22
Sala/Pranzo | **E Side**	-
Third Ward | N | **Third Ward**	-
Zarletti | N | **Downtown**	24

JAPANESE

(* sushi specialist)

Benihana | **Downtown**	21
Ginza Sushi | **Wauwatosa**	-
Sake Tumi* | **Downtown**	22
Wasabi Sake* | **Brookfield**	-

KOREAN

(* barbecue specialist)

Sake Tumi* | **Downtown**	22

MEXICAN

Cafe Corazón | **Riverwest**	26
Cempazuchi | **E Side**	17

PIZZA

Edwardo's Pizza | **W Side**	20

POLISH

Polonez | **S Side**	-

PUB FOOD

Chancery | **Wauwatosa**	16

SANDWICHES

Potbelly Sandwich | **multi.**	18

SEAFOOD

☑ Bosley/Brady | **E Side**	26
Devon Seafood | **N Shore**	21
☑ Eddie Martini's | **Wauwatosa**	27
Harbor House | **Downtown**	23
Mitchell's Fish Mkt. | **Brookfield**	19
River Ln. Inn | **N Shore**	26

SERBIAN

Three Bros. | **Bay View**	23

SMALL PLATES

NEW Braise | **Amer.** | **Walker's Point**	-
NEW Industri Café | **Amer.** | **Walker's Point**	-

SOUTHERN

Maxie's | **W Side**	25

STEAKHOUSES

Benihana | **Downtown**	21
☑ Bosley/Brady | **E Side**	26
☑ Capital Grille | **Downtown**	26
Carnevor | **Downtown**	24
Dream Dance | **Downtown**	-
☑ Eddie Martini's | **Wauwatosa**	27
Five O'Clock | **Central City**	25
Fleming's | **Brookfield**	24
Jackson Grill | **S Side**	28
Jake's | **Pewaukee**	24
Milwaukee Chop | **Downtown**	22
Mo's: Steak | **Downtown**	23
Mr. B's: Steak | **Brookfield**	23
Ward's House | **Downtown**	-

THAI

King & I | **Downtown**	18
Singha Thai | **W Side**	-

VEGETARIAN

Café Manna | **Brookfield**	-

Locations

Includes names, cuisines and Food ratings.

Milwaukee Metro Area

BAY VIEW

Ⓩ Honeypie | *Amer.* — 26
Pastiche | *French* — 25
Three Bros. | *Serbian* — 23

BREWERS HILL

Ⓩ Roots | *Cal.* — 26

CENTRAL CITY

Five O'Clock | *Steak* — 25

DOWNTOWN

Ⓩ Bacchus | *Amer.* — 27
Benihana | *Japanese/Steak* — 21
Buckley's | *Amer.* — 25
Ⓩ Capital Grille | *Steak* — 26
Carnevor | *Steak* — 24
Cubanitas | *Cuban* — 21
Dream Dance | *Amer./Steak* — -
Elsa's/Park | *Amer.* — 24
Envoy | *Amer.* — -
Harbor House | *Seafood* — 23
Karl Ratzsch's | *German* — 23
Kilawat | *Amer.* — 22
King & I | *Thai* — 18
Knick | *Eclectic* — 23
Mason St. Grill | *Amer.* — 25
Milwaukee Chop | *Steak* — 22
Mo's: Steak | *Steak* — 23
Potbelly Sandwich | *Sandwiches* — 18
Rock Bottom | *Amer.* — 19
NEW Rumpus Room | *Amer.* — 25
Sabor | *Brazilian* — -
Sake Tumi | *Asian* — 22
Umami Moto | *Asian* — 24
Ward's House | *Steak* — -
Water Street | *Amer.* — 17
Zarletti | *Italian* — 24

EAST SIDE

Balzac Wine Bar | *Eclectic* — 20
Ⓩ Bartolotta's | *French* — 26
Ⓩ Bosley/Brady | *Seafood/Steak* — 26
Brocach Irish Pub | *Pub* — 22
Cempazuchi | *Mex.* — 17
Comet Cafe | *Amer.* — 23
Five Guys | *Burgers* — 20
Mimma's Cafe | *Italian* — 23
Pasta Tree | *Italian* — 22
Sala/Pranzo | *Italian* — -

Ⓩ Sanford | *Amer.* — 29
Tess | *Eclectic* — 25
Original/Walker Pancake | *Amer.* — 24

GLENDALE

Cheesecake Factory | *Amer.* — 20
Five Guys | *Burgers* — 20
Kopp's | *Dessert* — 24

NORTH SHORE

Devon Seafood | *Seafood* — 21
Harry's B&G | *Amer.* — 18
NSB B&G | *Amer.* — -
River Ln. Inn | *Seafood* — 26

RIVERWEST

Cafe Corazón | *Mex.* — 26
Centro Café | *Italian* — 26

SHOREWOOD

North Star | *Amer.* — 23

SOUTH SIDE

Jackson Grill | *Amer.* — 28
Polonez | *Polish* — -

SOUTHWEST SIDE

Crawdaddy's | *Cajun/Creole* — 18

THIRD WARD

Ⓩ Coquette | *French* — 24
Hinterland | *Amer.* — 25
Palms Bistro | *Amer.* — -
R. Braun's Graffito | *Italian* — 22
Third Ward | *Italian* — -
Water Buffalo | *Eclectic* — 18

WALKER'S POINT

NEW Braise | *Amer.* — -
Ⓩ Crazy Water | *Eclectic* — 28
NEW Industri Café | *Amer.* — -
Ⓩ La Merenda | *Eclectic* — 27
Smyth | *Amer.* — 26
Triskele's | *Amer.* — -

WAUWATOSA

Chancery | *Pub* — 16
Cheesecake Factory | *Amer.* — 20
Ⓩ Eddie Martini's | *Seafood/Steak* — 27
Ginza Sushi | *Japanese* — -
Il Mito | *Italian* — 23
Ⓩ Le Rêve | *Dessert/French* — 26
Maggiano's | *Italian* — 22
P.F. Chang's | *Chinese* — 20
Ⓩ Rist. Bartolotta | *Italian* — 27

WEST SIDE

Blue's Egg | *Amer.*	25
Edwardo's Pizza | *Pizza*	20
Maxie's | *Cajun/Creole*	25
Meritage | *Eclectic*	21
Singha Thai | *Thai*	-

Outlying Areas

BROOKFIELD

Café Manna | *Veg.*	-
Fleming's | *Steak*	24
Mitchell's Fish Mkt. | *Seafood*	19
Mr. B's: Steak | *Steak*	23
North Star | *Amer.*	23
Parkside 23 | *Amer.*	-
Potbelly Sandwich | *Sandwiches*	18
Original/Walker Pancake | *Amer.*	24
Wasabi Sake | *Japanese*	-

CALEDONIA

Sebastian's | *Amer.*	-

DELAFIELD

Five Guys | *Burgers*	20

KENOSHA

Mangia | *Italian*	25

KOHLER

Immigrant | *Amer.*	25

LAKE GENEVA

Egg Harbor | *Amer.*	22

MUKWONAGO

Heaven City | *Amer.*	-

PEWAUKEE

Five Guys | *Burgers*	20
Jake's | *Steak*	24

LOCATIONS

Special Features

Listings cover the best in each category and include names, locations and Food ratings. Multi-location restaurants' features may vary by branch.

BRUNCH

☑ Bartolotta's	E Side	26
Cafe Corazón	Riverwest	26
Comet Cafe	E Side	23
☑ Honeypie	Bay View	26
NEW Industri Café	Walker's Point	–
Kilawat	Downtown	22
Knick	Downtown	23
Polonez	S Side	–
☑ Roots	Brewers Hill	26
NEW Rumpus Room	Downtown	25

BUFFET

(Check availability)

Harbor House	Downtown	23
King & I	Downtown	18
Polonez	S Side	–

BUSINESS DINING

☑ Bacchus	Downtown	27
☑ Bartolotta's	E Side	26
Benihana	Downtown	21
☑ Capital Grille	Downtown	26
Carnevor	Downtown	24
☑ Coquette	Third Ward	24
☑ Eddie Martini's	Wauwatosa	27
Envoy	Downtown	–
Fleming's	Brookfield	24
Harbor House	Downtown	23
Jake's	Pewaukee	24
Karl Ratzsch's	Downtown	23
Kilawat	Downtown	22
Knick	Downtown	23
Mason St. Grill	Downtown	25
Milwaukee Chop	Downtown	22
Mo's: Steak	Downtown	23
Mr. B's: Steak	Brookfield	23
North Star	Brookfield	23
NSB B&G	N Shore	–
Parkside 23	Brookfield	–
☑ Rist. Bartolotta	Wauwatosa	27
River Ln. Inn	N Shore	26
☑ Roots	Brewers Hill	26
Smyth	Walker's Point	26
Umami Moto	Downtown	24
Ward's House	Downtown	–

CELEBRITY CHEFS

Sandy D'Amato	
☑ Sanford	E Side	29
Mike Engel	
Pastiche	Bay View	25
Michael Feker	
Il Mito	Wauwatosa	23
Jimmy Jackson	
Jackson Grill	S Side	28
JoLinda Klopp	
Triskele's	Walker's Point	–
Adam Lucks	
Comet Cafe	E Side	23
☑ Honeypie	Bay View	26
Peggy Magister	
☑ Crazy Water	Walker's Point	28
Mimma Megna	
Mimma's Cafe	E Side	23
Joe Muench	
Blue's Egg	W Side	25
Maxie's	W Side	25
Mark Weber	
Mason St. Grill	Downtown	25

CHILD-FRIENDLY

(Alternatives to the usual fast-food places; * children's menu available)

Benihana*	Downtown	21
Cempazuchi	E Side	17
Edwardo's Pizza*	W Side	20
Five Guys*	multi.	20
Karl Ratzsch's*	Downtown	23
Knick	Downtown	23
Maggiano's*	Wauwatosa	22
Mangia*	Kenosha	25
Palms Bistro	Third Ward	–
Pasta Tree	E Side	22
P.F. Chang's	Wauwatosa	20
Rock Bottom*	Downtown	19
Tess	E Side	25
Third Ward*	Third Ward	–

DINING ALONE

(Other than hotels and places with counter service)

☑ Bartolotta's	E Side	26
Cempazuchi	E Side	17
☑ Coquette	Third Ward	24
Cubanitas	Downtown	21
NSB B&G	N Shore	–
Rock Bottom	Downtown	19
Singha Thai	W Side	–

ENTERTAINMENT

(Call for days and times
of performances)

Immigrant | piano | **Kohler** 25
Karl Ratzsch's | piano | **Downtown** 23
NSB B&G | jazz | **N Shore** -

FIREPLACES

Heaven City | **Mukwonago** -
Jake's | **Pewaukee** 24
Palms Bistro | **Third Ward** -
Pasta Tree | **E Side** 22
Sebastian's | **Caledonia** -

HISTORIC PLACES

(Year opened; * building)

1875 | Third Ward* | **Third Ward** -
1890 | Elsa's/Park* | **Downtown** 24
1890 | Three Bros.* | **Bay View** 23
1893 | Mason St. Grill* | **Downtown** 25
1900 | Rist. Bartolotta* | 27
  Wauwatosa
1900 | River Ln. Inn* | **N Shore** 26
1904 | Karl Ratzsch's | **Downtown** 23
1907 | Heaven City* | **Mukwonago** -
1914 | Coquette* | **Third Ward** 24
1918 | Immigrant* | **Kohler** 25
1927 | Envoy* | **Downtown** -
1948 | Five O'Clock | **Central City** 25

HOTEL DINING

Ambassador Hotel
  Envoy | **Downtown** -
Hilton Milwaukee
  Milwaukee Chop | **Downtown** 22
InterContinental Hotel
  Kilawat | **Downtown** 22
Iron Horse Hotel
  Smyth | **Walker's Point** 26
Knickerbocker Hotel
  Knick | **Downtown** 23

LATE DINING

(Weekday closing hour)

Brocach Irish Pub | 2 AM | **E Side** 22
Elsa's/Park | 1 AM | **Downtown** 24
Harry's B&G | 12 AM | **N Shore** 18
Knick | 12 AM | **Downtown** 23
NEW Rumpus Room | varies | 25
  Downtown
Ward's House | 1 AM | **Downtown** -

MEET FOR A DRINK

(Most top hotels and the
following standouts)

🔒 Bacchus | **Downtown** 27
🔒 Bartolotta's | **E Side** 26
🔒 Bosley/Brady | **E Side** 26

Buckley's | **Downtown** 25
🔒 Capital Grille | **Downtown** 26
Carnevor | **Downtown** 24
Cempazuchi | **E Side** 17
Comet Cafe | **E Side** 23
🔒 Coquette | **Third Ward** 24
Crawdaddy's | **SW Side** 18
🔒 Crazy Water | **Walker's Point** 28
Cubanitas | **Downtown** 21
🔒 Eddie Martini's | **Wauwatosa** 27
Elsa's/Park | **Downtown** 24
Envoy | **Downtown** -
Harbor House | **Downtown** 23
🔒 Honeypie | **Bay View** 26
Il Mito | **Wauwatosa** 23
Jackson Grill | **S Side** 28
Knick | **Downtown** 23
Mason St. Grill | **Downtown** 25
Maxie's | **W Side** 25
Mo's: Steak | **Downtown** 23
North Star | **multi.** 23
NSB B&G | **N Shore** -
Palms Bistro | **Third Ward** -
Parkside 23 | **Brookfield** -
Pastiche | **Bay View** 25
R. Braun's Graffito | 22
  Third Ward
Sake Tumi | **Downtown** 22
Smyth | **Walker's Point** 26
Tess | **E Side** 25
Triskele's | **Walker's Point** -
Umami Moto | **Downtown** 24
Ward's House | **Downtown** -
Zarletti | **Downtown** 24

NEWCOMERS

Braise | **Walker's Point** -
Industri Café | **Walker's Point** -
Rumpus Room | **Downtown** 25

OUTDOOR DINING

Edwardo's Pizza | **W Side** 20
Knick | **Downtown** 23
Maggiano's | **Wauwatosa** 22
Mangia | **Kenosha** 25
NSB B&G | **N Shore** -
Palms Bistro | **Third Ward** -
Pasta Tree | **E Side** 22
P.F. Chang's | **Wauwatosa** 20
Potbelly Sandwich | **multi.** 18
🔒 Rist. Bartolotta | **Wauwatosa** 27
River Ln. Inn | **N Shore** 26
Rock Bottom | **Downtown** 19
🔒 Roots | **Brewers Hill** 26
Tess | **E Side** 25
Third Ward | **Third Ward** -

PEOPLE-WATCHING

Ⓩ Bacchus | **Downtown** 27
🆕 Braise | **Walker's Point** -
Buckley's | **Downtown** 25
Carnevor | **Downtown** 24
Centro Café | **Riverwest** 26
Comet Cafe | **E Side** 23
Ⓩ Coquette | **Third Ward** 24
Cubanitas | **Downtown** 21
Ⓩ Eddie Martini's | **Wauwatosa** 27
Elsa's/Park | **Downtown** 24
Envoy | **Downtown** -
Harbor House | **Downtown** 23
Ⓩ Honeypie | **Bay View** 26
Kilawat | **Downtown** 22
Knick | **Downtown** 23
Ⓩ Le Rêve | **Wauwatosa** 26
Mason St. Grill | **Downtown** 25
Maxie's | **W Side** 25
Mimma's Cafe | **E Side** 23
Mo's: Steak | **Downtown** 23
NSB B&G | **N Shore** -
Palms Bistro | **Third Ward** -
Parkside 23 | **Brookfield** -
Pasta Tree | **E Side** 22
Ⓩ Rist. Bartolotta | **Wauwatosa** 27
River Ln. Inn | **N Shore** 26
Rock Bottom | **Downtown** 19
🆕 Rumpus Room | **Downtown** 25
R. Braun's Graffito | **Third Ward** 22
Sake Tumi | **Downtown** 22
Ⓩ Sanford | **E Side** 29
Smyth | **Walker's Point** 26
Three Bros. | **Bay View** 23
Umami Moto | **Downtown** 24
Ward's House | **Downtown** -

POWER SCENES

Ⓩ Bacchus | **Downtown** 27
Ⓩ Bartolotta's | **E Side** 26
Carnevor | **Downtown** 24
Ⓩ Eddie Martini's | **Wauwatosa** 27
Envoy | **Downtown** -
Harbor House | **Downtown** 23
Mason St. Grill | **Downtown** 25
Mo's: Steak | **Downtown** 23
Mr. B's: Steak | **Brookfield** 23
North Star | **Brookfield** 23
Ward's House | **Downtown** -

PRIVATE ROOMS

(Restaurants charge less at off times; call for capacity)
Ⓩ Coquette | **Third Ward** 24
Ⓩ Eddie Martini's | **Wauwatosa** 27
Edwardo's Pizza | **W Side** 20

Heaven City | **Mukwonago** -
Immigrant | **Kohler** 25
Maggiano's | **Wauwatosa** 22
Mangia | **Kenosha** 25
Mimma's Cafe | **E Side** 23
Mr. B's: Steak | **Brookfield** 23
Polonez | **S Side** -
River Ln. Inn | **N Shore** 26
Rock Bottom | **Downtown** 19
Sebastian's | **Caledonia** -

PRIX FIXE MENUS

(Call for prices and times)
Ⓩ Bartolotta's | **E Side** 26
Immigrant | **Kohler** 25
Ⓩ Sanford | **E Side** 29

QUICK BITES

Blue's Egg | **W Side** 25
Comet Cafe | **E Side** 23
Cubanitas | **Downtown** 21
Edwardo's Pizza | **W Side** 20
Elsa's/Park | **Downtown** 24
Five Guys | **multi.** 20
Ⓩ Honeypie | **Bay View** 26
Knick | **Downtown** 23
Ⓩ Le Rêve | **Wauwatosa** 26
Maxie's | **W Side** 25

QUIET CONVERSATION

Dream Dance | **Downtown** -
Ⓩ Eddie Martini's | **Wauwatosa** 27
Envoy | **Downtown** -
Jake's | **Pewaukee** 24
Karl Ratzsch's | **Downtown** 23
Kilawat | **Downtown** 22
Milwaukee Chop | **Downtown** 22
North Star | **Brookfield** 23
Polonez | **S Side** -
Ⓩ Sanford | **E Side** 29
Third Ward | **Third Ward** -

RAW BARS

Benihana | **Downtown** 21
Harbor House | **Downtown** 23
Maxie's | **W Side** 25
Milwaukee Chop | **Downtown** 22
Mitchell's Fish Mkt. | **Brookfield** 19

ROMANTIC PLACES

Ⓩ Bartolotta's | **E Side** 26
Centro Café | **Riverwest** 26
Ⓩ Crazy Water | **Walker's Point** 28
Heaven City | **Mukwonago** -
Il Mito | **Wauwatosa** 23
Immigrant | **Kohler** 25
Mimma's Cafe | **E Side** 23
Pasta Tree | **E Side** 22

Pastiche	**Bay View**	25
Third Ward	**Third Ward**	-
Three Bros.	**Bay View**	23
Zarletti	**Downtown**	24

SENIOR APPEAL

Blue's Egg	**W Side**	25
Buckley's	**Downtown**	25
Egg Harbor	**Lake Geneva**	22
Envoy	**Downtown**	-
Immigrant	**Kohler**	25
Jake's	**Pewaukee**	24
Karl Ratzsch's	**Downtown**	23
North Star	**multi.**	23
Pastiche	**Bay View**	25
Polonez	**S Side**	-
Three Bros.	**Bay View**	23

SINGLES SCENES

Carnevor	**Downtown**	24
Comet Cafe	**E Side**	23
Crawdaddy's	**SW Side**	18
Cubanitas	**Downtown**	21
Elsa's/Park	**Downtown**	24
Knick	**Downtown**	23
Mo's: Steak	**Downtown**	23
Palms Bistro	**Third Ward**	-
Rock Bottom	**Downtown**	19
R. Braun's Graffito	**Third Ward**	22
Sake Tumi	**Downtown**	22
Umami Moto	**Downtown**	24

SPECIAL OCCASIONS

☒ Bacchus	**Downtown**	27
☒ Bartolotta's	**E Side**	26
Carnevor	**Downtown**	24
☒ Crazy Water	**Walker's Point**	28
Dream Dance	**Downtown**	-
☒ Eddie Martini's	**Wauwatosa**	27
Envoy	**Downtown**	-
Five O'Clock	**Central City**	25
Harbor House	**Downtown**	23
Heaven City	**Mukwonago**	-
Il Mito	**Wauwatosa**	23
Immigrant	**Kohler**	25
Jake's	**Pewaukee**	24
Karl Ratzsch's	**Downtown**	23
Kilawat	**Downtown**	22
Mangia	**Kenosha**	25
Mason St. Grill	**Downtown**	25
Milwaukee Chop	**Downtown**	22
Mimma's Cafe	**E Side**	23
Mo's: Steak	**Downtown**	23
Mr. B's: Steak	**Brookfield**	23
Pasta Tree	**E Side**	22

Pastiche	**Bay View**	25
☒ Rist. Bartolotta	**Wauwatosa**	27
☒ Sanford	**E Side**	29
Sebastian's	**Caledonia**	-
Smyth	**Walker's Point**	26
Third Ward	**Third Ward**	-
Three Bros.	**Bay View**	23
Umami Moto	**Downtown**	24

TRENDY

☒ Bacchus	**Downtown**	27
☒ Bartolotta's	**E Side**	26
NEW Braise	**Walker's Point**	-
Carnevor	**Downtown**	24
Cempazuchi	**E Side**	17
Comet Cafe	**E Side**	23
Cubanitas	**Downtown**	21
Elsa's/Park	**Downtown**	24
☒ Honeypie	**Bay View**	26
NEW Industri Café	**Walker's Point**	-
Mo's: Steak	**Downtown**	23
Palms Bistro	**Third Ward**	-
☒ Rist. Bartolotta	**Wauwatosa**	27
NEW Rumpus Room	**Downtown**	25
R. Braun's Graffito	**Third Ward**	22
Sake Tumi	**Downtown**	22
☒ Sanford	**E Side**	29
Umami Moto	**Downtown**	24
Zarletti	**Downtown**	24

VIEWS

☒ Bacchus	**Downtown**	27
☒ Bartolotta's	**E Side**	26
Harbor House	**Downtown**	23
☒ Roots	**Brewers Hill**	26
R. Braun's Graffito	**Third Ward**	22
Water Buffalo	**Third Ward**	18

WINNING WINE LISTS

☒ Bacchus	**Downtown**	27
☒ Bartolotta's	**E Side**	26
Carnevor	**Downtown**	24
☒ Coquette	**Third Ward**	24
Dream Dance	**Downtown**	-
Fleming's	**Brookfield**	24
Harbor House	**Downtown**	23
Mangia	**Kenosha**	25
Mason St. Grill	**Downtown**	25
Milwaukee Chop	**Downtown**	22
Pastiche	**Bay View**	25
☒ Rist. Bartolotta	**Wauwatosa**	27
☒ Sanford	**E Side**	29
Smyth	**Walker's Point**	26
Ward's House	**Downtown**	-

Wine Vintage Chart

This chart is based on a 30-point scale. The ratings (by U. of South Carolina law professor **Howard Stravitz**) reflect vintage quality and the wine's readiness to drink. A dash means the wine is past its peak or too young to rate. Loire ratings are for dry whites.

Whites	95	96	97	98	99	00	01	02	03	04	05	06	07	08	09	10
France:																
Alsace	24	23	23	25	23	25	26	22	21	22	23	21	26	26	23	26
Burgundy	27	26	22	21	24	24	23	27	23	26	26	25	26	25	25	-
Loire Valley	-	-	-	-	-	-	-	25	20	22	27	23	24	24	24	25
Champagne	26	27	24	25	25	25	21	26	21	-	-	-	-	-	-	-
Sauternes	21	23	25	23	24	24	29	24	26	21	26	25	27	24	27	-
California:																
Chardonnay	-	-	-	-	22	21	24	25	22	26	29	24	27	23	27	-
Sauvignon Blanc	-	-	-	-	-	-	-	-	-	25	24	27	25	24	25	-
Austria:																
Grüner V./Riesl.	22	-	25	22	26	22	23	25	25	24	23	26	25	24	25	-
Germany:	22	26	22	25	24	-	29	25	26	27	28	26	26	26	26	-

Reds	95	96	97	98	99	00	01	02	03	04	05	06	07	08	09
France:															
Bordeaux	25	25	24	25	24	29	26	24	26	25	28	24	24	25	27
Burgundy	26	27	25	24	27	22	23	25	25	23	28	24	24	25	27
Rhône	26	22	23	27	26	27	26	-	26	25	27	25	26	23	27
Beaujolais	-	-	-	-	-	-	-	-	-	-	27	25	24	23	28
California:															
Cab./Merlot	27	24	28	23	25	-	27	26	25	24	26	24	27	26	25
Pinot Noir	-	-	-	-	-	-	26	25	24	25	26	24	27	24	26
Zinfandel	-	-	-	-	-	-	25	24	26	24	23	21	26	23	25
Oregon:															
Pinot Noir	-	-	-	-	-	-	-	26	24	25	24	25	24	27	24
Italy:															
Tuscany	25	24	29	24	27	24	27	-	24	27	25	26	25	24	-
Piedmont	21	27	26	25	26	28	27	-	24	27	26	26	27	26	-
Spain:															
Rioja	26	24	25	22	25	24	28	-	23	27	26	24	24	25	26
Ribera del Duero/ Priorat	25	26	24	25	25	24	27	-	24	27	26	24	25	27	-
Australia:															
Shiraz/Cab.	23	25	24	26	24	24	26	26	25	25	26	21	23	26	24
Chile:	-	-	-	-	24	22	25	23	24	24	27	25	24	26	24
Argentina:															
Malbec	-	-	-	-	-	-	-	-	25	26	27	26	26	25	-

ZAGAT
Chicago Map

Google

W Kinzie St

Chicago River

W Wacker Dr

Kennedy Expy

N Columbus

E Wacker Dr

N Michigan Ave

N Wacker Dr

W Randolph St

S Wacker Dr

W Washington St

The Loop

W Madison St

S Halsted St

90

94

Millennium
Park

S Columbus Dr

Map data ©2012 Google

Most Popular Restaurants

Map coordinates follow each name. For places with more than two locations, only flagship or central locations are plotted. Sections A-H show the city of Chicago (see adjacent map); sections I-P show nearby suburbs (see reverse).

1 Alinea (C-2)

2 Frontera Grill (E-4)

3 Girl & The Goat (F-2)

4 Gibsons † (D-4)

5 Charlie Trotter's (B-2)

6 Joe's Sea/Steak (E-4)

7 Topolobampo (E-4)

8 Lou Malnati's † (E-4)

9 Next (F-2)

10 Blackbird (F-3)

11 Tru (E-5)

12 Avec (F-3)

13 Wildfire † (E-4)

14 Spiaggia (D-5)

15 Shaw's Crab (E-4, L-2)

16 Purple Pig (E-5)

17 Gene & Georgetti (E-3)

18 Capital Grille (E-5)

19 Morton's Steak † (D-4)

20 Publican (F-2)

21 Les Nomades (E-5)

22 Everest (G-4)

23 Hot Doug's (N-6)

24 Xoco (E-4)

25 Francesca's † (H-1)

26 MK (D-3)

27 Hugo's Frog/Fish † (D-4)

28 Smoque BBQ (M-6)

29 Piccolo Sogno (E-2)

30 Naha (E-4)

31 Giordano's † (G-4)

32 Chicago Cut Steak (F-4)

33 Bob Chinn's Crab (K-4)

34 Coco Pazzo (E-3)

35 Maggiano's † (E-4)

36 Al's Beef † (G-3)

37 Portillo's Hot Dogs* (E-4)

38 Takashi (N-6)

39 Lawry's Prime Rib (E-4)

40 Longman & Eagle* (N-6)

41 L2O* (A-3)

42 Quartino (E-4)

43 Mercat a la Planxa (G-5)

44 North Pond (A-3)

45 Ruth's Chris † (E-4)

46 Le Colonial (D-4)

47 Big Star (N-6)

48 Bistro Campagne* (M-6)

49 Chicago Chop* (E-4)

50 Heaven on Seven (F-4)

51 Vie* (O-4)

52 Cooper's Hawk (P-1)

53 GT Fish & Oyster* (E-4)

54 Mon Ami Gabi* (O-3)

*Indicates tie with above   † Indicates multiple branches